Difficult Life in a Refugee Camp

Although refugee camps are established to accommodate, protect, and assist those fleeing from violent conflict and persecution, life often remains difficult there. Building on empirical research with refugees in a Ugandan camp, Ulrike Krause offers nuanced insights into violence, humanitarian protection, gender relations, and coping of refugees who mainly escaped the conflicts in the Democratic Republic of the Congo. This book explores how risks of gender-based violence against women, in particular, but also against men, persist despite and partly due to their settlement in the camp and the system established there. It reflects on modes and shortcomings of humanitarian protection, changes in gender relations, as well as strategies that the women and men use to cope with insecurities, everyday struggles, and structural problems occurring across different levels and temporalities.

ULRIKE KRAUSE is Junior Professor of Forced Migration and Refugee Studies at the Institute for Migration Research and Intercultural Studies (IMIS) and the Institute for Social Sciences, Osnabrück University, Germany, and affiliated Research Associate at the Refugee Studies Centre, University of Oxford. She is co-editor of the volume *Gender, Violence, Refugees* (2017), and co-founder and co-editor of the *German Journal of Forced Migration and Refugee Studies*. Her research focuses on the conflict-displacement nexus, refugee protection, gender, gender-based violence, resilience, and agency; with a regional concentration on Sub-Saharan Africa as well as global developments.

Difficult Life in a Refugee Camp

Gender, Violence, and Coping in Uganda

ULRIKE KRAUSE
Osnabrück University

CAMBRIDGE
UNIVERSITY PRESS

CAMBRIDGE
UNIVERSITY PRESS

Shaftesbury Road, Cambridge CB2 8EA, United Kingdom

One Liberty Plaza, 20th Floor, New York, NY 10006, USA

477 Williamstown Road, Port Melbourne, VIC 3207, Australia

314–321, 3rd Floor, Plot 3, Splendor Forum, Jasola District Centre, New Delhi – 110025, India

103 Penang Road, #05–06/07, Visioncrest Commercial, Singapore 238467

Cambridge University Press is part of Cambridge University Press & Assessment, a department of the University of Cambridge.

We share the University's mission to contribute to society through the pursuit of education, learning and research at the highest international levels of excellence.

www.cambridge.org
Information on this title: www.cambridge.org/9781108821605

DOI: 10.1017/9781108909013

First published 2021
First paperback edition 2023

A catalogue record for this publication is available from the British Library

ISBN   978-1-108-83008-9   Hardback
ISBN   978-1-108-82160-5   Paperback

Contents

Figures and Images

Figures

Images

Acknowledgments

Does research ever come to an end? This book is supposed to mark the final piece in the jigsaw of the project 'Gender Relations in Confined Spaces' that I carried out under the lead of Professor Susanne Buckley-Zistel at the Center for Conflict Studies, Marburg University, Germany. The research was made possible by the generous funding of the German Foundation for Peace Research, for which I am very thankful. The project started in 2013 and with it my work in Marburg. Although its lifespan and funding came to an end in 2016, here I am four years, two other research projects, and three university postings later, still unable to entirely let go of it. Carrying out this research has influenced me in many ways. I was able to continue my work with refugees and return to Uganda, where I had lived, worked, and conducted parts of my doctoral research three years prior; I was able to meet, speak with, and, most of all, listen to many women and men in Uganda's refugee camp Kyaka II who shared their often very personal experiences of war, violence, and life in encampment; and I was able to learn about the hardships and cruelties they had faced but also the strengths they continued to possess not only to endure but to move on from their manifold challenges and create better lives.

The narratives that the women and men trustfully shared in Kyaka II stood at the heart of this work throughout, and I am endlessly thankful for each and every person who took the time and had sufficient faith in this study to speak with me and my research team. With this book, I hope I can do justice to their stories and reveal the various difficulties they encountered—but also the strategies they devised and used to cope, to contest imposed restrictions, and to improve livelihoods. My gratitude also goes to the aid workers in Kyaka II who took part in the research, reflected on the humanitarian system in the camp critically, and gave insights into their own experiences and hardships. Herewith I would also like to thank the Office of the Prime Minister, Government of Uganda, for granting research permission, as well as the Danish Refugee Council for helping in gaining access to the camp and providing initial contacts.

The research in Kyaka II would have scarcely been possible if it were not for the team that I collaborated with: Christine Nimusiima, Atuhaire Pearl Karuhanga, and the refugees as peer-researchers— who I sadly cannot address individually by name due to confidentiality and security reasons. They greatly supported our data collection, and I am extremely grateful for our inspiring discussions, constructive cooperation, and personal connections formed. Sadly, I was unable to continue the collaboration through to data analysis, an aspect that I have promoted and hope to continue promoting with great vigor in future research.

Over the course of the past few years, many people have played important roles in supporting me to bring this research forward in one way or another. First and foremost, Susanne Buckley-Zistel deserves my sincerest gratitude; over many hours she discussed the research with me, provided instrumental feedback, supported my ideas and endeavors, and gave invaluable guidance. Susanne was first a mentor and has since become a dear friend. Workwise and personally, Timothy Williams has been my trusted 'ally' with whom I have discussed extensively much of the work presented—but also life both in and beyond academia. The team at the Center for Conflict Studies, Marburg University, were a great source of inspiration and critical reflection for me, including discussions with Melanie Hartmann, Mariam Salehi, Thorsten Bonacker, Anne Menzel, Werner Distler, Judith von Heusinger, Joana Amaral, Christian Braun, Kristine Avram, Dominik Pfeiffer, Philipp Schultheiss, Tareq Sydiq, and others during different stages of the projects.

In 2017, supported by the German Academic Exchange Service, I was fortunate to be granted a visiting fellowship at the Refugee Studies Centre, University of Oxford, where I am still an affiliated research associate. While in Oxford, I benefited from discussing my research with colleagues, including Alexander Betts, Gil Loescher, Naohiko Omata, Chloe Lewis, Roger Zetter, Carrie Perkins, Cathryn Costello, Matthew Gibney, Tom Scott-Smith, Jeff Crisp, Georgia Cole, Dawn Chatty, Natascha Zaun, Evan Easton-Calabria, and others. I wish to thank all colleagues very much and especially Gil, whose passing in April 2020 still saddens me greatly; I recall our conversations, and his inspiring feedback, with great fondness.

The revisions and finalization of the book took place at a time when I had been appointed Junior Professor of Forced Migration and Refugee Studies at the Institute for Migration Research and Intercultural Studies (IMIS) and the Institute for Social Sciences, Osnabrück University, Germany. This being the first professorship focusing solely on Forced Migration and Refugee Studies in German academia, I was honored to continue the research as well as address some of the final aspects of this manuscript with colleagues. In addition to my team, Hannah Schmidt, Nadine Segadlo, and Inga Zimmermann, I also wish to thank Jochen Oltmer, Helen Schwenken, Andreas Pott, Christoph Rass, Frank Wolff, Jannis Panagiotidis, Hamza Safouane, Anna-Lisa Müller, Ulrich Schneckener, Andrea Hartmann Firnkorn, and Simone Pika for our discussions.

Moreover, the open exchange with many colleagues all over the world as well as in Germany—including the German Network for Forced Migration Studies (Netzwerk Fluchtforschung e.V.)—has been inspirational for me, my work, and thus also this book, particularly Elena Fiddian-Qasmiyeh, Simon Turner, Rose Jaji, Tamirace Fakhoury, Karin Scherschel, Christiane Fröhlich, Cordula von Denkowski, Joel Glasman, Hanno Brankamp, Philipp Schulz, Marcus Engler, Nora Markard, Natalie Welfens, Franzisca Zanker, and Janna Wessels.

With this book's realization, I would like to express my sincere appreciation to the reviewers and especially Reviewer One for their invaluable comments and critical perspectives that have helped to make the contents better. I hope I have done justice to the highly inspiring feedback provided. Moreover, my student assistants in Marburg and in Osnabrück were of great help, for which I would like to thank each of them in chronological order: Elisabeth Schmidt, Dorothee Fees, Vanessa Köster, Lucia Heisterkamp, Sarah Spasiano, and Aniela Jesse. For his invaluable editing, critical view, and 'final touch' to the manuscript, I am especially grateful to James Powell. Moreover, the cooperation with and guidance of Cambridge University Press, namely, of Daniel (Dan) Brown, Maria Marsh, and Atifa Jiwa, have been instrumental for completing the final necessary steps. Of course, despite all the exchange and support, any errors appearing in the book are mine alone. The perspectives I articulate do not necessarily represent those of the funding institution, the universities, or any other relevant organization.

Finally, my family and friends deserve not only my greatest appreciation but also a big apology. This project has been very important to me and I have spent much time pursuing it. I apologize to my loved ones for not being available more, and at the same time thank them for their understanding, support, encouragement, and various welcome distractions. I would like to thank my family for their emotional support and continuous backing. The same goes to my dear friends Susanne Hassel, Bianka Kurz, Antje Holinski, Julia Schwarz, Gareth Burge, and Andy Gooch for welcome interruptions, sometimes keeping me sane, and for being there for me—no matter where we each are in the world. Most of all, I wish to honor the invaluable time I had with my four-legged best friend, Lala. As a puppy the size of my hand, she simply walked into the compound where I was living in Uganda in 2009. Over the following decade, she was by my side throughout; not during the data collection in Kyaka II, but most certainly along the way regarding analyzing data, generating findings, discussing research, sometimes at presentations, and when putting together publications—including the first draft of the book in front of you now.

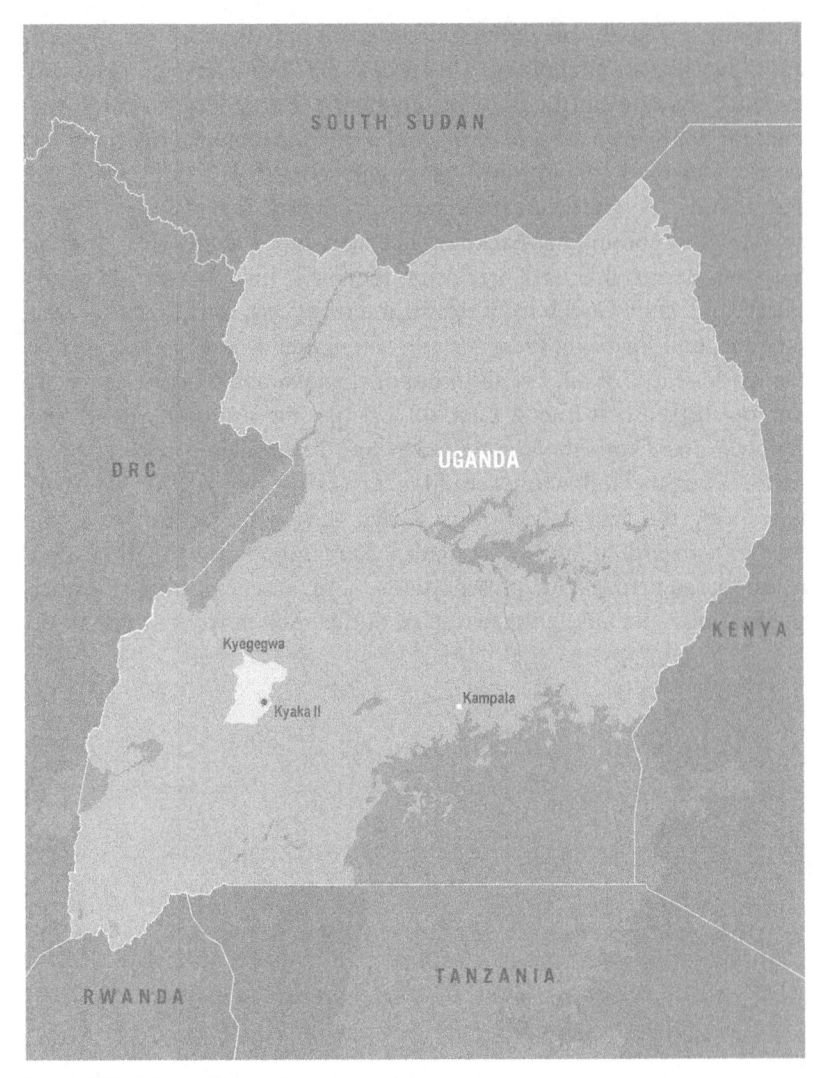

Image 0.1 Map of Uganda
Source: Map created by REACH Initiative, October 24, 2018.[1]

[1] For access, see https://www.reachresourcecentre.info/country/uganda/cycle/1252/p/8/#cycle-1252.

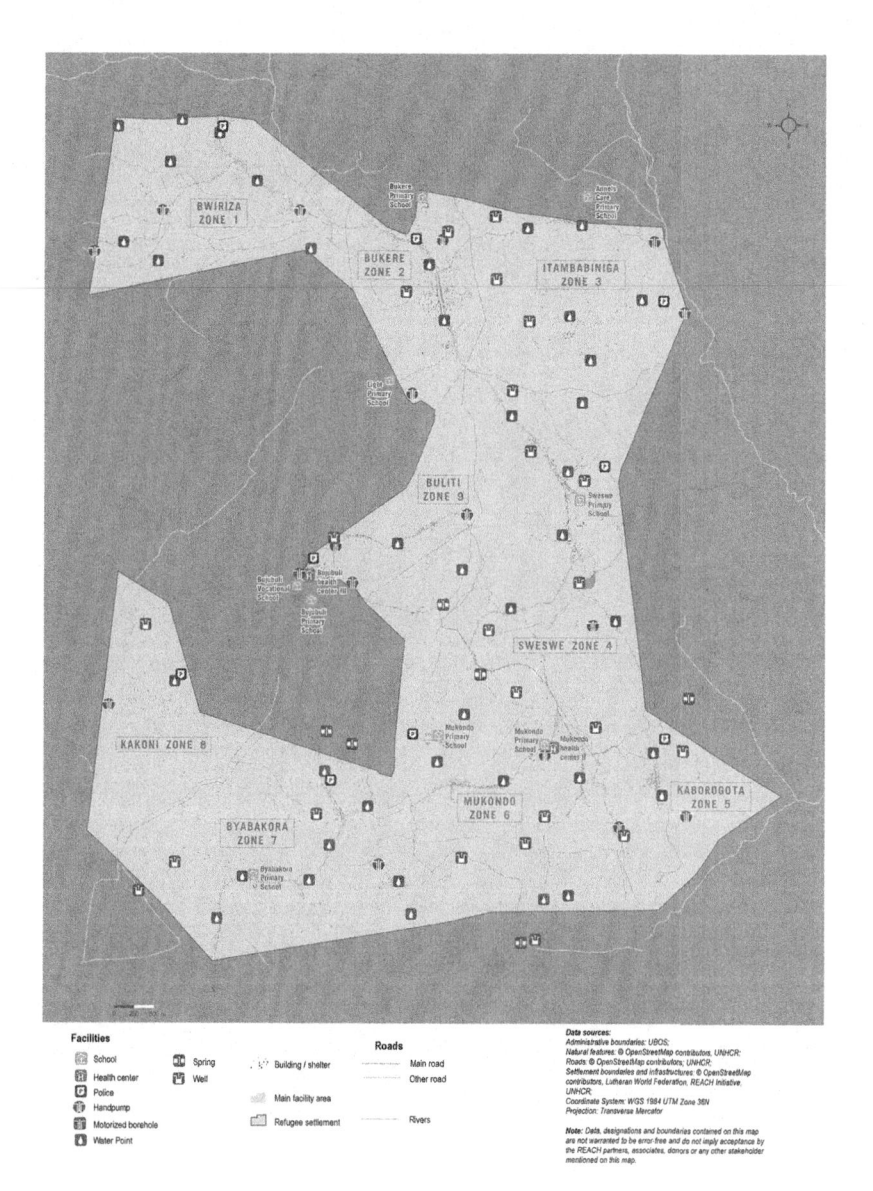

Image 0.2 Facilities map of Kyaka II settlement, Kyegegwa District, Uganda
Source: Map created by REACH Initiative, October 24, 2018.[2]

[2] For access, see https://www.reachresourcecentre.info/country/uganda/cycle/1252/p/8/#cycle-1252.

1 | Introduction

"Being beaten like a drum"—with this comparison, a number of women and men[1] who had escaped the conflict in the Democratic Republic of the Congo (DR Congo) and now lived in Uganda's refugee camp Kyaka II would describe the violence to which women especially but also others are exposed in the camp. For my research into gender, violence, humanitarianism, and refugees' encampment, this phrase would become a synonym for the gender-based violence in this camp in Uganda as it signifies so succinctly the intensity of the risks refugees feared and experienced there; risks that made their lives difficult.

How is it possible though that violence like this occurs in such sites of humanitarian protection? After all, camps like Kyaka II constitute purposefully established places for refugee accommodation, protection, and assistance, as well as for government control over refugees until one of the three durable solutions[2] is found. As in most camps, humanitarian and government agencies run them, provide access to aid and services, and retain decision-making functions (see Turner 2010; Agier 2011; McConnachie 2014; Krause 2018b). The paradox arising from accounts of gender-based violence in camps like Kyaka II rests in the contradiction not only of these sites serving as humanitarian shelters but also of forced migration per se. Refugees have fled insecurities in countries of origin in search of finding safety, security, and livelihoods in another region or country but instead continue to face challenges there. Most of the inhabitants of Kyaka II had escaped a broad spectrum of violence due to the conflicts in the Kivu regions of DR Congo—tensions that have lasted more than 30 years now and that are known for the intensity of sexual violence (see Autesserre

---

[1] The cited empirical data was collected during research in Uganda's refugee camp Kyaka II; see discussion 2 with female refugees, March 12, 2014, Base Camp; discussion with male refugees, March 13, 2014, Base Camp.

[2] These are voluntary repatriation to the country of origin, resettlement to a safe third country, or local integration in a country of asylum.

2010; Eriksson Baaz and Stern 2013a). Most refugees I spoke with had been in Uganda—and in fact encamped—for more than a decade when our paths crossed; two men were even in camps since the 1960s. Despite their access to aid in the camp, they remained in difficult positions due to risks, restrictions, uncertainties—and not least due to gender-based violence.

Gender, Violence, Displacement, Protection, and Coping

Dilemmas associated with gender-based violence are limited neither to contemporary times nor regionally to this one refugee camp in Uganda. Yet that gender-based violence is no longer a trivialized but now a widely discussed phenomenon is not least the achievement of earlier work by feminist scholars and activists. In the 1980s and 1990s, scholars slowly yet increasingly adopted feminist perspectives, attended to encounters of displaced women especially, and shed light on the gender-specific threats that triggered their decisions to flee countries of origin, as well as complicated their lives in ones of asylum (see, e.g., Indra 1987; Greatbatch 1989; Ljungdell 1989; Ferris 1990; Friedman 1992). A growing body of research continues to illustrate risks of gender-based violence in refugee situations all over the world, focusing especially on women (for literature reviews, see Buckley-Zistel et al. 2014; Vu et al. 2014; Araujo et al. 2019). Drawing on and seeking to contribute to these debates, this book examines the conditions in Kyaka II, and with it the risks of gender-based violence there—yet not limited to women.

Of course, the research debates over the past decades were accompanied by reflections on what 'gender' actually means. In the past, gender was mainly explained as concerning related social roles and differentiated from biological sex. The separation of gender and sex was soon criticized, among other places, in doing gender approaches (West and Zimmerman 1987), as the distinction of the biological from the social fails to recognize that the broad conception of what is even perceived as 'biological' directly depends on what is socially constructed as such. In line with this, Indra emphasized already two decades ago that gender constitutes "a key relational dimension of human activity and thought" (1999a: 2). Ensuing approaches assume correspondingly that gender includes social, cultural, political, biological, and other components of various groups, ones that can dynamically change over time and across contexts (see, e.g., Harrison 2006; Villa 2019). In this book, gender is thus not understood as a static condition but as the interaction of various physical and social factors in a broad sense. This includes the fundamental relevance of social notions and constellations and the production of power relations, along with socially ascribed yet individually perceived, performed, and contested positioning. As a socio-structural dimension, gender does not simply occur in a vacuum—be it a refugee camp or other setting—but is socially constructed, relational, changeable and variable, context-dependent, as well as influenced by and influential for experiences of individuals and groups.

Feminist research and activism has furthermore disclosed the 'gendered nature' of violence within as well as beyond times of displacement. Respective debates about violence related to gender, and more specifically against women, have demonstrated varying tendencies and focus areas regarding different types of violence over the past few decades, including sexual abuse, wife battering or beating, and discrimination. These debates have contributed to extensive reflection on and better understandings of gender-specific causes and effects of violence not only in public spaces but also in private ones. Such attacks and threats have in common that they are inherently intertwined with individuals' gender and the respective ascriptions, which is thus not limited to women; nevertheless, research shows that women are often affected (for recent comprehensive volumes, see Brown and Walklate 2012; Lombard 2018; Shepherd 2019). The gendered character of violence is, consequently, at the core of this book. For its exploration in Kyaka II, the focus is on 'gender-based violence' broadly understood as harmful acts of force committed against a person on the grounds of gender and gender-related attributions. This resonates with current international approaches (IASC 2015: 5). As a general framework, Galtung's (2010, 2004, 1990, 1969) concept of violence is used, which distinguishes between direct, structural, and cultural types thereof. The book's theoretical underpinnings are complemented by a gender-sensitive conceptualization following Confortini (2006), as discussed in Chapter 2.

By examining and making public the life conditions that many women experience in displacement, feminist studies and activism have also increased awareness among political and humanitarian actors. This has brought about changes in the way international refugee law is interpreted and humanitarian protection realized (Edwards 2010; Martin 2017). With a focus on protection and assistance, political and humanitarian agencies—most notably, the United Nations High Commissioner for Refugees (UNHCR)—initially considered gender-related aspects insufficiently but have moved toward delivering specific measures for women. UNHCR's Executive Committee stressed in its first conclusion on *Refugee Women and International Protection* of 1985 the need for the particular protection of women due to their "vulnerable situation which frequently exposes them to physical violence, sexual abuse, and discrimination" (UNHCR ExCom 1985: para. d). This was followed by further conclusions and recommendations (UNHCR ExCom 1988, 1989, 1990, 2006). In 1990, UNHCR published the *Policy on Refugee Women* as well as its guidelines in the following year, which were revised in 2008 (UNHCR 1990, 1991, 2008a). Additional policies and strategies were issued, and they set global standards for improving protection and assistance for women and reducing the risks of gender-based violence (see, e.g., UNHCR 1997a, 2001c, 2001b, 2003b, 2011b). In recent years, UNHCR increasingly also considers the roles of men, seeking their protection and involvement in actions against gender-based violence (see UNHCR and RLP 2012). Notwithstanding these developments, the findings from Kyaka II as well as the above-noted studies exemplify that risks especially for women in camps remain prevalent worldwide, and therefore constitute a great and ongoing challenge for those uprooted.

However, although gender-based violence without doubt constitutes a grave and horrific issue for many women in refugee situations, singular focus on them alone is not sufficient to understand its occurrence; doing so might even have unintended negative consequences (see Davies and True 2015; Ozcurumez et al. 2020). Only addressing women's suffering of such violence risks portraying them as inherently helpless and passive victims, politically innocent, and devoid of agency. Binary categorizations of female 'vulnerability' and masculine 'forcefulness,' of the "victim-women and perpetrator-men" (Krause 2017c: 80, my translation), may be produced, somewhat rendering women's vulnerabilities 'normal' and them 'ordinary victims.' Such bias carries the danger of ignoring how women can also be among those perpetrating violence—an issue thus far insufficiently addressed in Forced Migration and Refugee Studies but increasingly noted in other fields such as Peace and Conflict Studies (see Moser and Clark 2001; Coulter

2008; MacKenzie 2012). Moreover, this bias threatens neglect of the fact that risks and needs also exist for those who do not fit neatly within these categorizations, men especially (Jaji 2009a; Kabachnik et al. 2013; Schulz 2018a; Turner 2019). Yet, men are also exposed to gender-specific forms of violence in refugee situations and beyond (Henry et al. 2013: 9–20; Dolan 2014, 2017; Janmyr 2017; Chynoweth 2017). I investigate these critical nuances by means of gender-sensitive perspectives and drawing on but also going beyond current research debates.

Moreover, honing in on this violence per se could entail paying little attention to the other difficulties regularly faced within refugee camps, which is not my intention. Limited access to their rights, uncertainties of various kinds, insufficient livelihoods and services, structural restrictions, and top-down decision-making by humanitarian and political actors are just some of the many significant issues that often complicate the lives of those inhabiting such sites—and these affect the women and men in gender-specific ways. Due to camp conditions and disruptions of social structures as a result of flight, studies note that women have to take on additional responsibilities in camps, which can be overwhelming or empowering for them (Martin 2004: 15; Freedman 2015a: 34ff) —or it may only be portrayed as 'empowering,' as Fiddian-Qasmiyeh (2014a) critically discusses in her book on Sahrawi women. Moreover, men might experience a loss of their leading social status due to the limitations encountered in camps (Turner 1999; Lukunka 2011). Contributing to these debates, a key aspect of this book lies in its exploring of how humanitarian structures are realized in the camp, how the women and men perceive these, as well as how gender relations change. It will be shown that neither of the issues and their effects can actually be seen as separate cases because they are inherently connected.

Yet a focus on violence and difficulties in camps can produce a victimizing notion of refugees. Despite—as well as due to—the problems faced, the 'camp population' do not passively submit to the conditions at hand, merely give in and obey imposed regulations and restrictions, or just wait for aid to be handed to them. In stark contrast, they practice agency. Research increasingly reflects how refugees cope with issues through individual and collective strategies, and engage socially, economically, politically, and culturally in camps. They build lives and homes, create livelihoods, resist limitations, make their voices heard, and stand up to violence and other forms of wrongdoing (see Horst 2006; Jansen 2011; Oka 2014; Doná 2015; Erdener 2017)— something the practices of refugees in Kyaka II[3] also represent. By not only reflecting on the various issues that refugees face while living in the camp but also placing emphasis on addressing the practices that they employ to deal with, overcome, reject, and navigate the difficult camp landscape, the book runs counter to the victimizing notion of refugees, shedding light, instead, on their agency and coping strategies.

I therefore seek to take a broad perspective on refugees' lives in encampment throughout this book, in order to explore the effects of and practices in refugee camps. Based on a large body of original empirical insights gathered through an in-depth, micro-level case study of Kyaka II conducted in Uganda in 2014, the book provides nuanced accounts regarding four main interrelated subject areas, each addressed in its own respective chapter: the forms, scopes, and conditions of gender-based violence; the structures of humanitarian aid, and their influence on the women and men concerned as well as on the prevalence of violence; changing gender roles and relations among the women and men; and the strategies to cope with risks and challenging conditions in the camp. For the analyses hereof, I employ critical and gender-sensitive perspectives as well as draw on and seek to contribute to international debates within Forced Migration and Refugee Studies —particularly its gender literature.

Whereas the book's main interest lies in women's views, experiences, and practices within the camp, I believe that they cannot be gauged and depicted without taking into account those of the other people around them—as these are influential too. Following Indra's (1999a: 2) early emphasis on gender as a relational dimension, this study therefore goes beyond singular focus on women to also continuously consider the intertwined positioning of women and men, girls and boys, and aid workers. An unfortunate lacuna is the perspectives of LGBTIQ+ people. At the time of research, the 'anti-homosexuality bill' had just been enacted in Uganda—criminalizing same-sex relations. Its impact was far-reaching, with wide-ranging political debates and media coverage—as well as public violence—ensuing (Nyanzi and Karamagi 2015; Zomorodi 2016). Although Kyaka II is situated in a remote

---

[3] See also the important research by Clark-Kazak (2010a, 2010b, 2011, 2014) carried out with youth in Kyaka II.

region, political debates and subsequent tensions were also visible in the camp. After careful assessment of local conditions, I decided to refrain from proactively trying to work with LGBTIQ+ people—and in fact also potential male victims of violence, as they are often labeled 'homosexual'—to ensure the safety of research participants. Their security was more important than any data that might have been collected.

In this book, emphasis is placed on giving as much room as possible to the 'voices' of the women and men who took part in the research. To this end, I present many quotes by those involved to analyze and discuss their perspectives, experiences, worries, and hopes, and essentially their strength, despite as well as due to their vulnerabilities. This chosen wording of these people having 'strength' and 'vulnerabilities' is not meant to be in any way patronizing; researching and writing about sensitive subjects such as gender-based violence and humanitarian situations without victimizing those affected or trivializing and normalizing acts of brutality is a delicate balancing act, one that I strive to achieve throughout and address in more detail below.

Refugees in Uganda

Since independence from British rule in 1962, the Republic of Uganda has been known to host a relatively large number of refugees—with the figure growing further in recent years. Located in sub-Saharan Africa and specifically the Great Lakes Region, an area that experienced enduring violent conflicts in the course of the second half of the twentieth century, many people have sought refuge in Uganda. However, displacement has also occurred within the country, not least due to the war between the Government of Uganda and the Lord's Resistance Army occurring from the mid-1980s onward and lasting for more than twenty years. It would contribute to more than 1.6 million people being internally displaced in northern Uganda (see Dolan 2009).

Refugees in Uganda have mainly come from neighboring countries such as DR Congo, South Sudan, Burundi, and Rwanda, but also from Ethiopia, Somalia, Eritrea, and other states. According to UNHCR statistics, the refugee population there ranged between 190,000 and 260,000 individuals from the mid-1990s until 2005 and decreased to a figure of 135,000 by 2010. Since 2012, the refugee population has grown once more. At the time of research in 2014, more than 380,000 refugees were in the country (for demographic statistics until 2018, see UNHCR 2020d). The renewal of violent conflicts in South Sudan and DR Congo would lead to an increase in the number of refugees to nearly 1.4 million by early 2020 (UNHCR 2020c). In addition to newly arriving refugees, many in Uganda find themselves in protracted situations,[4] which is also illustrated by the ongoing existence of refugee camps. Some of these were established in the 1980s; Nakivale in western Uganda, indeed, was already set up in the 1950s (Krause 2013: 146–147; Betts et al. 2017b: 109).

Uganda's approach to refugee protection is often considered to be 'progressive' (e.g., Akello 2009; Krause 2013: 147; Vemuru et al. 2016; Betts et al. 2017b: 10). On the one hand, the new Refugee Act was introduced in 2006 and entered into force in 2009, which replaced the prior so-called Control of Alien Refugees Act, Cap. 64 of 1960 (Uganda 2006, 1960). While the latter was criticized for its complex restrictions, including on refugees' freedom of movement (see Kaiser 2005: 354), the new act incorporates a number of revisions. For example, Article 29 presents refugees' rights to own property, engage in agriculture, industry, handicrafts and commerce, establish commercial and industrial companies (according to domestic law), practice a profession according to qualification, and access employment opportunities. The 2006 Refugee Act also notes the right to freedom of movement in its Article 30—which, however, is simultaneously limited in its Article 44. The latter states that refugees have to live in designated places—meaning 'settlements'—and may only leave them with official permission to do so.

On the other hand, refugee protection and assistance in Uganda are not limited to traditional humanitarian relief but rather linked with development cooperation. To this end, policies including the Self-Reliance Strategy (SRS), Development Assistance for Refugee Hosting Areas (DAR), and the recent Refugee and Host Population Empowerment (ReHOPE) scheme have been put in place, aiming to connect rather short-term humanitarian refugee aid with longer-term development initiatives. This approach strives to integrate services delivered to refugees into national structures in order to avoid

---

[4] For the official definition of protracted refugee situations, see UNHCR ExCom (2009); see also Chapter 3 in this book.

overlaps, provide nationals with access to these services, and to maintain the structures in question long-term—even after refugees repatriate. Moreover, these policies target the promotion of refugees' empowerment, self-reliance, and more recently resilience, so that they are able to live relatively independent from aid structures—which is mainly sought to be achieved by means of agriculture (see Kaiser 2000, 2005, 2006; Krause 2013, 2016a). For the realization of these aims, the aforementioned 'settlements'—and, more specifically, 'local rural refugee settlements'—are used.

These 'settlements' are located in the northwestern, western, and southwestern regions of Uganda bordering South Sudan, DR Congo, Rwanda, and Tanzania. They operate under the overall supervision of the Office of the Prime Minister (OPM), Government of Uganda, and of UNHCR, while measures of protection and support are implemented by different aid agencies—mainly NGOs. Due to the development orientation of refugee aid, Ugandans who live in the areas of and near such 'settlements' are granted access to some of the related services. Moreover, with its strategic focus on self-reliance, refugees are assigned land for accommodation as well as for agriculture by OPM.

Despite these features, the labeling of such sites as 'refugee settlements' is critical, and thus requires close scrutiny. Approaching the subject semantically, the term 'settlement' signifies a place "where people establish a community" per the Oxford English Dictionary (Stevenson 2010: 476). 'Refugee settlements' would, accordingly, denote a location where refugees are free and able to live among their communities. This is, however, not the case, as refugees of diverse nationalities and backgrounds are not free to dwell there but are rather bound by Ugandan law and governed by humanitarian agencies. Although 'settlements' in Uganda consist of 'village-like setups,' these structures are still planned, artificially established, and earmarked by humanitarian and government agencies specifically as refugee camps. They subsequently present features of setup, structure, and services typical of the refugee camp phenomenon worldwide (see, e.g., Inhetveen 2010; Agier 2011; Turner 2010, 2016a; McConnachie 2014; Krause 2018b).

The problematic and ambivalent nature of these sites' labeling in Uganda is further evident when looking at UNHCR's global trends reports, in which designations for them vary fairly wildly. Whereas the sites were categorized as 'camps/centres' in the reports of 2003, 2004,

2005,2006, and 2009,[5] this changed to 'settlements' in those of 2010 and 2011—then returning to the camp categorization in the one of 2012, by denoting these sites as 'planned/managed camps.' A contradictory modification occurred in the report of 2013 in which most of the sites were suddenly categorized as 'individual accommodations.' This was maintained in subsequent reports up until 2017. The one of 2018 then designated most of the sites 'self-settled camps.'[6] Simultaneously with these changes in nomenclature, other UNHCR documents continued to categorize the sites as 'settlements'[7]—or even identified them as 'camps.'[8]

Renaming these locations 'individual accommodations,' 'self-settled camps,' and ultimately 'settlements' idealizes them, while also masking the fact that they are humanitarian sites of new or protracted encampment. Also obscured by such terminology is—again—the reality that refugees in Uganda are legally obliged to stay there, rather than that happening out of individual choice. In lieu of reproducing 'humanitarian speak' by using 'settlements,' I hence employ the term 'camp' throughout this book.

Kyaka II

In keeping with the above-outlined characteristics of a camp, Kyaka II constitutes a confined space purposely set up for refugee accommodation, protection, and assistance. This site is successor to the previous camp Kyaka, which was established at the end of 1967. Along with 7 other such sites (4 of these 8 camps are still in use as of 2020),[9] Kyaka served to provide assistance to about 68,500 refugees from Rwanda. Then as well as now, these camps maintain an agricultural

---

[5] Details are not accessible for the 2007 and 2008 global trends reports (UNHCR 2009b, 2008b).

[6] See the following global trends reports and their respective annexes (UNHCR 2004b: table 11; 2005b: table 11; 2006: table 12; 2007b: table 11; 2010: annex 15; 2011a: annex 15; 2012: annex 15; 2013a: annex 15; 2014c: annex 15; 2015b: annex 16; 2016a: annex 16; 2017b: annex 15; 2018c: annex 16; 2019a: annex 15 and 16).

[7] See as examples (UNHCR 2013b: 1–3; 2014d, 2015a, 2016b, 2017d, 2018b).

[8] See, among other sources, the map created by UNHCR (2015d).

[9] These include "Oruchinga, Nakivale, Kahunge, Kinyara, Rwamwanja, Kyangwali, Kyaka and Ibuga" (UNHCR 1969: para. 150). Of these, Oruchinga, Nakivale, Rwamwanja, and Kyangwali are still operational in 2020.

focus so that refugees are "practically self-supporting in terms of food"—as UNHCR (1969: para. 150–151) notes. Within a year of Kyaka's founding, UNHCR reported that the "Rwandese refugees became self-supporting as far as their food production was concerned, many reaching a standard of living comparable to that of the local population. In Kyaka and Nakivale, cattle-breeding has proved a source of income for the refugees. In Kyaka, the cultivation of crops has been expanded" (1970: para. 155).

As a result of unrest witnessed in 1984 in central, western, and southwestern Uganda, Rwandese refugees who had self-settled in the region were relocated to already established camps. Furthermore, the new Kyaka II was created "for some 17,000 refugees and 22,000 head of cattle" (UNHCR 1985: para. 151). Due to ongoing tensions, Kyaka II was not fully used—eventually reopening and expanding from 1994 onward as many refugees from DR Congo (then Zaire) and later also Rwanda began to seek refuge in Uganda (UNHCR 1994: 3, 7). In the early and middle years of the first decade of the new century, ongoing violence in DR Congo contributed to more people fleeing— and many were settled in Kyaka II (UNHCR 2003a, 2005a). After large-scale repatriation measures sent refugees back to Rwanda in 2008, Kyaka was eventually closed and the remaining refugee population relocated to Kyaka II (Danish Refugee Council 2018: 2).

The latter is in Kyegegwa District, a remote, rural region located relatively centrally in Uganda. The nearest towns are Mubende and Kyenjojo, approximately 83 km and 73 km away, respectively. One instantly gets a sense of how remote Kyaka II is when leaving the asphalt highway on the way there, turning onto a dirt track marked by its red, sandy soil—then having to drive through a rural, sparsely populated region to reach Kyaka II. Yet the beginning of the camp is not immediately noticeable. There are no borders, boundaries, or fences marking it. There are also no gates, guards, or signposts signifying where the camp either starts or ends. In the Base Camp, however, a number of signposts from humanitarian agencies exist, which directly identify the center of the site. Kyaka II therefore blends into its rural surroundings; it is, regardless, still distinct and purposefully established for refugees' settlement as well as humanitarian protection and assistance.

Covering an area of more than 80 km², the camp was planned to have the capacity to house an estimated 17,000 refugees. Yet the population size in Kyaka II had increased to 22,680 refugees and asylum seekers by the time of my research in 2014. It grew even further in the following years due to renewed violence in DR Congo; by 2018, the population had almost doubled to 44,988, and as of early 2020 it had even reached 121,106 (UNHCR 2014f, 2018b, 2020a). The majority of those living in Kyaka II originate from DR Congo, while smaller groups are from Rwanda, Burundi, and South Sudan. When I conducted the research there, most Congolese were said to belong to the Banyabwisha, Alur, Munyanga, and Hema ethnic groups originating from the eastern Kivu regions of their country of origin.

As with the other camps in Uganda, Kyaka II is administered by OPM and UNHCR, while mainly NGOs deliver aid and services. Such measures are realized in different sectors such as health and nutrition, education, food, water, sanitation and hygiene, and community services. Kyaka II is structured into nine zones and further divided into twenty-six clusters set up as villages (UNHCR 2014f), with refugees living side-by-side with Ugandan nationals. Refugees receive two plots of land to be used for accommodation and agriculture, so as to become self-reliant and thus live relatively independent from aid relief. The zones and clusters are spread across the entire area in question, with the Base Camp located relatively centrally. In that Base Camp, one can find the offices of aid agencies, a police station, the clinic Bujubuli Health Centre, a local market, as well as safe houses. The latter are tents in which the 'most vulnerable' or recently threatened persons can find immediate (albeit short-term) accommodation and protection.

Although camps like Kyaka II generally serve as humanitarian sites for refugees' accommodation, protection, and support, during my time there the women and men spoken with frequently stressed facing manifold problems. They referred to limited livelihoods, prevailing violence, unsatisfactory living conditions, diverse restrictions, and what I term in this book 'multidimensional uncertainties.' These issues occurred despite the humanitarian programs for protection and assistance. Among the many critical statements made about conditions in Kyaka II, one elderly woman from DR Congo who had lost her husband and son during the conflict there said: "You can spend even three months without even eating meat. Getting washing soap, just soap is hard. Everything is hard here."[10] Another woman voiced

---

[10] Female refugee, dialogue, March 18, 2014, Base Camp.

concerns about how to provide for her children. During the war in DR Congo, she witnessed rebels kidnap her husband—a terrible memory others also shared. After waiting for his return for some time, she eventually decided to flee with their three children when the security situation worsened. In Kyaka II, she explained, they have little food, no clothes for the children, and no money to take them to school, so she has to work a lot.[11] One man who witnessed rebels capture his father, beat and rape his mother, and abduct his wife and two children during the conflict in DR Congo explained: "Here in Kyaka II, we are living a miserable life. [...] We have no jobs that we may earn a living with, only poor nutrition, no proper medication, and the water in Kyaka II is dirty, not pure water."[12]

Such criticism of 'camp life' echoes the various daily adversities highlighted by many of the other women and men spoken with. These articulated difficulties stand in stark contrast to the aforementioned notion of Uganda's refugee policies being 'progressive.' Given the development orientation within the country's refugee aid, refugees are encouraged to engage in agricultural activities so as to become self-reliant. However, the opportunities offered did not adequately improve life circumstances. Harvests were rarely of sufficient quantity to sustain daily lives,[13] while reduced humanitarian rations further complicated refugees' livelihoods and indeed survival.[14] Together, these challenges resulted in a situation whereby refugees had to live 'from hand to mouth'—constituting circumstances that other scholars have similarly criticized in the context of refugee populations elsewhere (see Hansen 1979: 370; Crisp 2000: 19; Jaji 2009b: 153; Omata 2017: 18).

Moreover, in spite of refugees' rights to freedom of movement (Article 30) and work (Article 29) as stipulated in Uganda's current Refugee Act, those spoken with considered themselves to be confronted with limited employment opportunities due to the remote location of Kyaka II—where mainly aid agencies operate. Some refugees worked for Ugandans as agricultural laborers, established their own businesses, or received short-term employment with aid agencies; none of these options, however, constituted sustainable or secure sources of income that can be relied on. Contrary to Uganda's policy

---

[11] Female refugee, dialogue, February 25, 2014, Base Camp.
[12] Male refugee, dialogue, March 18, 2014, Base Camp.
[13] Male refugee, dialogue, March 5, 2014, Kaborogota Zone.
[14] Female aid worker, interview, April 2, 2014.

of refugees having the right to freedom of movement, those in Kyaka II were required to seek permission from OPM prior to leaving the camp.[15] This led one Congolese man to criticize how "your movements are very limited, because you do not have travel documents to go anywhere any time you please; you have to report your movements, and are not free."[16]

While humanitarian services such as medical aid and primary education are supposed to be free of charge for refugees (and partly for Ugandans too), time and again research participants stated that they had to pay for these services. This complicated their lives and well-being.[17] Besides this, the basic educational infrastructure on-site revealed difficulties: at the time of research, there were more than 22,000 refugees living in Kyaka II—approximately 10,600 of whom were girls and boys aged between 5 and 17 years (UNHCR 2020b). Yet only six primary schools and one secondary school existed in the camp, and the educational infrastructure was criticized by informants too. Among other people, one man from Rwanda lamented: "UNHCR does not think refugees need secondary education. [...] Our children have a right to a good education, and more especially university education."[18]

Furthermore, refugees spoke of corruption and limited support from agencies as well as security actors such as the police. One man criticized having to pay a bribe for "a piece of land to dig"[19] (meaning farming). Others explained that when a violent attack was reported, the police commonly asked for transport costs to be covered as well as for money to even take up the case. Some refugees were unable to pay such fees, and as a result cases were often not registered with or handled by the police. However, police reports were necessary for victims to access related medical care.[20] This leads to the critical question of the intensity of violence in the camp. In addition to theft and physical abuse, refugees spoke about a high level of gender-based

---

[15] Male refugee, dialogue, March 27, 2014, Base Camp; aid worker, interview, February 4, 2014.

[16] Male refugee, dialogue, March 28, 2014, Base Camp.

[17] Discussion with religious leaders, March 19, 2014, Base Camp.

[18] Discussion with male refugees, March 13, 2014, Base Camp.

[19] Male refugee, dialogue, March 18, 2014, Base Camp.

[20] Female refugee, dialogue, March 17, 2014, Bujubuli; discussion with religious leaders, March 19, 2014, Base Camp.

violence in Kyaka II—thus forming the central axis of this book. Given this, issues of insufficient medical care and psychosocial support are particularly problematic for victims hereof—as pointed out by informants in Kyaka II themselves.[21] These ultimately formed just some of the multitude of issues those living in Kyaka II were confronted with, as will be scrutinized more closely in due course.

Notes on the Research with Refugees in Kyaka II

The case study as well as empirical material used in this book are based on the research project 'Gender Relations in Confined Spaces. Conditions, Scope and Forms of Sexual Violence against Women in Conflict-related Refugee Camps,' led by Professor Susanne Buckley-Zistel at the Center for Conflict Studies, Marburg University, Germany, and funded by the German Foundation for Peace Research.[22] I conducted the research within the project using Kyaka II as a single case study, so as to undertake an in-depth, micro-level analysis of which forms of gender-based violence occur against women in the camp, how often, and why. Yet the information shared by research participants not only reflected issues of gender-based violence but furthermore shed light on various other critical subjects—including camp governance, gender relations, and coping strategies.

Carrying out research on a highly sensitive subject such as gender-based violence with potentially traumatized individuals in a humanitarian context like the refugee camp gives rise to a number of methodological and ethical questions, and requires a suitable research design.

Empirical Research

Prior to this project, I had already worked, lived, and conducted research in Uganda over a period of three years from 2008 until 2011. At that time, I was employed by different humanitarian and development agencies—among other things, working in the fields of

---

[21] Female refugee, dialogue, March 18, 2014, Base Camp; female refugee, dialogue, March 27, 2014, Base Camp; male refugee, dialogue, March 18, 2014, Base Camp.

[22] The project was carried out from 2013 until 2016. For its final report, see Krause (2019a).

refugee assistance and human rights—and pursuing doctoral research into development-oriented refugee assistance. I was, therefore, very familiar with the situation in Uganda, and could draw on well-established contacts. Empirical data collection in Kyaka II took place during a three-month stay there from February to April 2014, together with two Ugandan women and twelve refugees as peer-researchers.

The refugees, whom I sadly cannot address in this book by their actual names for confidentiality and security reasons, mainly supported the surveys we carried out. I am exceptionally grateful for their support, and our collaboration. The process of us working together was extremely fruitful, provided platforms for various insightful discussions, and helped me gain a deeper understanding of issues. I will discuss the vital involvement of these individuals further below. The research conducted was also assisted by Christine Nimusiima, who has an academic background in Clinical Psychology, and Atuhaire Pearl Karuhanga, whose background is in Political Science with a focus on gender; I am also extremely grateful for the cooperation with both. Given their fields of expertise, working with them was highly valuable. Christine contributed to the project through her expertise in counseling traumatized victims of violence, including children who had experienced gender-based forms thereof, and Pearl through her knowledge of gender relations. Moreover, in addition to research permission from OPM, the Danish Refugee Council greatly helped in gaining access to the camp. As a key humanitarian actor in Kyaka II, the Danish Refugee Council provided contacts in the beginning as well as assisted logistically, for which I am very thankful.

Most of all, I am extraordinarily appreciative of each and every person who took the time and had sufficient trust in this study to speak with myself and the research team. The research was based on a mixed-methods approach, using both qualitative and quantitative methods. In detail, these included participant observation, ero-epic dialogues, focus group discussions, journal writing and surveys with refugees, as well as structured and semi-structured expert interviews with staff of humanitarian and government agencies. More weight was put on qualitative methods, but taking a mixed-methods approach facilitated the collection of relevant comprehensive data and helped balance the respective advantages and disadvantages of qualitative and quantitative methods. The triangulation of different methods served to validate the results and to generate additional insights. Most of all, the methods were chosen so as to proceed carefully and to consider ethics in light of the highly sensitive topic of gender-based violence.

More concretely, refugees took part through sixty-five ero-epic dialogues (shortened in the book to 'dialogues') as an unstructured ethnographic form of interview following Girtler (2001: 147–154). These were carried out in surroundings comfortable for the participants, and involved forty-two women and twenty-three men, fifty-eight originated from DR Congo, four from Burundi, two from Rwanda and one from South Sudan. In seven focus group discussions (shortened in the book to 'discussions'), thirty-five participants took part, consisting of sixteen women and nineteen men; twenty-nine came from DR Congo and six from Rwanda. Moreover, thirty-seven adolescents (eighteen were female, nineteen male) were engaged through journal writing with open-ended questions as a youth-friendly method for gathering empirical data. The participants ranged from fifteen to nineteen year olds; thirty-four originated from DR Congo, two from Rwanda, and one from Tanzania. Random sampling via informal information channels was used for the dialogues, journal writings, and some of the discussions, while purposive sampling was employed for other discussions with people of a specific social status—such as community leaders.

To complement the qualitative data, two surveys were conducted. One was on general questions about gender-based violence, with 351 refugees surveyed. It included broad questions to gain insight into, for example, who respondents perceived to be most affected by gender-based violence, where such risks would mainly occur, and how often. The second survey focused on the overall conditions and aid structures in Kyaka II, with 400 refugees interviewed. It also included broad questions about each participant's perceptions, among other things, regarding life conditions in Kyaka II, the aid provided, and their assumptions about gender relations and responsibilities. Of the overall 751 survey participants in both surveys, 53 percent were women and 47 percent men, with an average age of 36.1 years old. Some 675 originated from DR Congo, 45 from Rwanda, 21 from Burundi, 1 from South Sudan, and with 9 individuals not disclosing their nationality. The surveys comprised anonymous, written, multiple-choice questionnaires with randomly selected participants.

For the data collection with employees of aid agencies and other institutions operating in Kyaka II, structured and semi-structured interviews were used to gain insights into what kind of aid projects was implemented, how and why, as well as the way gender was considered. Overall, twenty-eight Ugandan employees took part in the research; an equal number of women and men were involved. They were systematically selected through purposive sampling based on their field of expertise, and time previously spent working in it. Additional materials included the analyses of reports and medical statistics.

Data collection primarily took place in English, which most refugees who took part spoke well—not least because of the long periods of time many had spent in Kyaka II and partly other places in Uganda, where English is the official language. At times, they used words in French, Swahili, or local languages, which either they explained to me or that Christine and Pearl knew and simultaneously translated. In only rare cases, Christine carried out dialogues with refugees in languages other than English that she then translated. The quotes included in this book have been lightly edited, but only for any necessary grammatical corrections. Other larger changes for clarity are indicated.

The analysis differed for the qualitative and quantitative data. In brief, I assessed the data gathered in dialogues, journal writings, discussions, and interviews through qualitative data analysis following Kuckartz (2014) and using the software MAXQDA. In a multistage procedure, I developed a comprehensive coding scheme; data was analyzed and coded first deductively from the existing literature, the project concept, and the guiding research questions, and then indicatively from the data itself. Another round of analysis was carried out and summaries prepared. This analysis aimed to capture, extract, structure, and assess overarching issues posited by respondents. The survey data was assessed through a simple descriptive analysis using the software SPSS. The initial analysis was prepared by Vanessa Köster, student assistant for the project in Marburg, which I then revised, completed, and finalized. The descriptive analysis served to illustrate distributions of responses and general tendencies among respondents.

Based on this empirical data, I have previously published a number of articles—among other topics, on gender-based violence during conflict, forced migration, and encampment mainly with regard to women (Krause 2015a, 2017a; on literature discussions see Buckley-Zistel et al. 2014; Krause 2016c, 2018a, forthcoming), the impact of humanitarian practices on refugees, violence, gender roles and relations (Krause 2015b, 2016e, 2016f, 2020, 2021a), as well as on refugees' coping strategies (Krause 2016d; Krause and Schmidt 2018; Krause and Gato 2019). These publications partly form the foundations of this book, but none of the chapters replicates an article already published. Most were in German in fact, and so with this book I seek to discuss the research findings in English—and thus make them available to a broader audience, including the refugees of course. Another key aspect in my work is research ethics, which I consider not only in my teaching and writings but also obviously during empirical research in Uganda itself (e.g., Krause 2016b, 2017b; Krause and Williams 2020; Krause and von Denkowski 2020). There, I continually reevaluated the research design, methods, and questions together with the research team, and if necessary made adjustments to ensure the most sensitive approach was taken. However, ethical reflections went beyond reevaluations of methods and procedures.

Ethical Considerations

In every research design with human participants, ethical standards are crucial—especially when research is taking place with potentially traumatized persons in conflict-related or humanitarian settings. This is not only because these contexts can be dangerous for participants and scholars, but because researchers can cause harm to participants in the process of data collection (see, e.g., Krause 2017b; Block et al. 2013; Hugman et al. 2011; Mackenzie et al. 2007). Scholars have, over the past few years, increasingly discussed ethical research in the context of Forced Migration and Refugee Studies.[23] I drew on these discussions when planning and conducting the research in Kyaka II, so as to prevent harm and proceed as carefully as possible. At the time of

---

[23] A number of contributions to thought on research ethics have come out over the past few years (for an overview, see Krause 2017b). Among others, edited volumes are available on ethics in Forced Migration and Refugee Studies by Block et al. (2013) on *Values and Vulnerabilities. The Ethics of Research with Refugees and Asylum Seekers* and by Temple and Moran (2011) on *Doing Research with Refugees: Issues and Guidelines*. In addition, in 2007, the *Journal of Refugee Studies* published a special issue on *Methodologies of Refugee Research* (see Voutira and Doná 2007) and the *Refugee Survey Quarterly* on *Researching Refugees: Lessons, Challenges and Ways Forward* (see Bakewell 2007).

research, ethical reviews were not required in either Germany or in Uganda.[24] Ethical standards were nonetheless key. The *Ethical Guidelines for Good Research Practices* published by the University of Oxford's Refugee Studies Centre (2007) served as the guiding framework, and empirical work in Uganda started with training of research assistants on the project aims, questions, and data-collection methods—along with ethical reflections. This was to ensure the safety of all participants and respect of their rights, the requirement to do no harm, the need for confidentiality of all information shared, as well as other ethical standards.

Moreover, before traveling to Uganda and while in Kyaka II, do-no-harm analyses were conducted to prevent any possible unintended consequences arising from data collection (see Krause 2017b). In connection with these analyses, questions about informed consent and building trust with participants during data collection were paramount. All those participating in the research did so voluntarily, and based on informed consent. While participants signing standardized forms to signify the latter has become a common tool in empirical research in many disciplines, including the Social Sciences, these forms are still "no guarantee that research takes place in an ethical and moral way" (de Laine 2000: 8). Such forms are rather fairly limited in their applicability and usability with people in refugee situations, and can, indeed, create fear among them (Ellis et al. 2007: 467; Mackenzie et al. 2007: 301–306).

To take into consideration contexts, conditions, and the characteristics of participants, Mackenzie et al. (2007: 306–312) propose using a relational approach when seeking voluntary and informed participation instead of individual, standardized consent forms. A similar approach was adopted in Uganda. The research team discussed with all participants their rights, the general project orientation, as well as the data analysis and usage both at the beginning of and during our interactions. We furthermore asked if we could give detailed project descriptions only at the end of our meetings in order to avoid affecting their responses to questions, which all participants agreed to. This laid the foundations for addressing the expectations, hopes, and wishes

---

[24] Uganda's policy later changed, and for a subsequent research project on refugee-led community-based organizations (see Krause 2019b; Krause and Schmidt 2019), we underwent an ethical review.

that individuals may have associated with their participation in the research (e.g., improving their living conditions or security) and for speaking about possibilities from and limitations to the project. In the course of our interactions, we thus continuously kept space to reflect on any questions, expectations, and positions that respondents might have had to ensure their informed and voluntary involvement. The relational approach taken also served to protect their identity—in line with that, quotes from them in this book are anonymized for their safety. In interviews with humanitarian staff, we used written consent forms to secure formal authorization.

Considering that the main subjects of interest were gender-based violence and life in the camp, building trust with informants was key. It may be rightfully asked whether some questions might be *too* personal or *too* intimate to even raise. For her research in Burundi, Malkki stresses the importance of "willingness to leave some stones unturned, to listen to what my informants deemed important, and to demonstrate my trustworthiness by not prying where I was not wanted" (1995a: 51). This principle similarly applied in our work in Uganda. To build trust and refrain from posing questions too intimate in nature, ero-epic dialogues were used with women and men. These dialogues ensured flexibility and sufficient time to elaborate on subject matters raised, and they provided significant room for participants to address the subjects they found important, which sometimes went beyond the scope of the research. Moreover, the dialogues facilitated responsiveness to particular dynamics within the conversation, and helped to point to topics carefully. Depending on how dialogues went and how well we knew participants, sensitive issues could be addressed or even personal questions asked. Yet, questions were usually formulated in the third person and remained rather general; we thus did not approach participants with direct ones about their past or their experiences, but brought forward general questions about why they think certain developments would arise. The approach helped to foster trustful interactions and relations, and provided the basis for participants explaining as much as they wanted to and felt comfortable with. In addition, while we focused on sensitive processes to prevent possible re-traumatization, several participants noted that these dialogues were a way for them to talk—a chance to tell *their* stories. Thus, similar to other studies (see Sieber 2008; Dyregrov et al. 2000), research participation appeared to be beneficial for them as well, which was further shown by the fact that a number of people approached us and offered their participation.

Another crucial ethical component in Forced Migration and Refugee Studies is the question of refugees' involvement in research. Based on the criticism of research *about refugees*, scholars have instead called for research *with refugees* (see, e.g., Harrell-Bond and Voutira 2007; Temple and Moran 2011). The scope of refugees' engagement may vary from interviewed subjects to involved participants in data collection, or individuals consulted in the framing and designing of the research (see Doná 2007; Krause 2017b). In line with that, I placed emphasis on engaging refugees as interviewed participants with sufficient space for them to voice their own issues and topics of interest. Moreover, as noted above, twelve refugees were also involved in the data collection, through surveys. I selected those who supported conducting the surveys sensitively and sought to prevent cultural, social, or political biases on my part. They were an equal number of women and men from DR Congo as well as one person who was from South Sudan; they either had or were enrolled in university degrees, and expressed interest in research. We started our collaboration with a week of training. In this, we discussed the data collection and research ethics as well as the overall project, its objectives, and approaches. Our reflections were highly fruitful and constructive; they resulted in a joint process of adapting the concept, through which these individuals directly impacted on the project and data collection. In light of that, it is unfortunate that I was unable to also carry out the data analysis with them—an aspect I increasingly pursue in current and future research.

Writing

Concerning this book as well as my other publications on gender-based violence, a key ethical question was and remains how to work with and present empirical findings from the research in Uganda. In other words, how can I produce and communicate knowledge based on the data obtained? As a matter of fact, I discovered a high prevalence of different forms of gender-based violence mainly against Congolese women in Kyaka II, and learned about human tragedies, hardships, and sufferings that I could not have imagined—and would not have imagined possible—before this project, and this even though I had been researching and working with displaced people in Uganda for several years prior to it. Some of the personal accounts of violence shared depicted a devastating level of cruelty, atrocity, and balefulness hard to put in attenuating words or abstract academic language.

Of course, emotions play a role in research (see Darling 2014; Thomson et al. 2013) and my prior experiences helped me to contextualize the narratives and maintain an analytical perspective. Working with Pearl and especially Christine was also crucial. After long days of data collection, hearing stories about terrible brutality, we sat together, reflected on the stories, and discussed what they meant for the research.[25] More importantly, sharing stories can be an emotional, exhausting, or even painful process for the women and men speaking. As noted, many approached us wanting to share *their* stories. We still constantly considered possible side effects, and sought to prevent negative ones by proceeding carefully. When they shared accounts of violence, we provided information about psychosocial counseling offered by aid agencies in Kyaka II—which, however, all of them knew about and rarely wanted to use, for reasons that will be discussed in due course.

I am well aware that the way in which I present the women's and men's stories may convey certain images of them and produce specific knowledge. For instance, the way I spoke just now of 'tragedies,' 'a devastating level of cruelty,' and 'terrible brutality' narrows the focus to vulnerabilities. These exist, but the mere emphasizing of them risks literally framing and highlighting them to a degree of almost spectacular intensity—such that those behind the stories may become sexualized invisible bodies or mere objects of suffering (see also Gray et al. 2020; Mertens 2019; Mookherjee 2015; Baxi 2014). Contrary to the focus solely on misery and pain, acute academic abstraction may overgeneralize the personal stories of violence as well as of coping—which can become lost in academic translation.

Going to either of these extremes is not the intention of this book. Instead, I pursue an approach similar to the one discussed by Mertens (2019) who raises ethical and methodological questions concerning her research on sexual violence in DR Congo. She finds that colonial imaginaries containing racial and sexual hierarchies can be generated,

---

[25] Of course, working with the twelve refugees in the context of the survey was extremely constructive as well, and we also sat together to talk. However, I refrained from discussing the sorrows others shared with them.

and harmful framings of victims produced. As a result, she suggests 'undoing' research on sexual violence "in a way that still allows room for Congolese people to tell their story outside of the rape experience" (Mertens 2019: 681). Similar to her proposal regarding suitable methods as well as her methodological reflections, I chose and employed the above-noted methods for data collection so as to approach the research sensitively—thereby considering possible risks and opportunities, adhering to ethical standards, and ensuring enough room for participants to share insights they found relevant, also beyond violence. What is presented reflects not only gender-based violence against women but also perspectives on such violence against men and perpetrated by women, the effects of humanitarian structures, changing gender relations, and various practices of coping.

Acknowledging this complexity is key in avoiding the portrayal of the people who shared their stories as passive and inherently vulnerable, or alternatively 'normalizing' the cruelties suffered through academic abstraction. Of course, as a scholar I have to have—and seek to keep—an analytical perspective on subject matters, but I do not want to lose grip of these women's and men's personal views. Thus, their individual narratives are at the heart of the book. I aim to present their knowledge; how they described and subsequently made sense of their various experiences (see also Gray et al. 2020; Skjelsbæk 2006). In addition to partly summarizing some of their backgrounds and experiences, I use an extensive number of direct quotes. In doing so, I strive to shed light on the experiences as well as coping of women and men who have fled violent conflicts and lived in Kyaka II for years now. It would be presumptuous of me to think of my work, this book, as a 'voice for refugees'; rather, I aim to reproduce their own various voices and thoughts through turning to such direct quotes.

Holding on to and using the term 'victim' in this book may appear contradictory, with the expression 'survivor' perhaps seen as better highlighting these people's strength and persistence (Kelly 2013: 159ff; Nissim-Sabat 2009; Skjelsbæk 2006; Kelly et al. 1996). Yet those who participated in the research primarily spoke of themselves or other having become victims; by maintaining their own chosen language, I hope to present their insights as faithfully as possible. Moreover, I also continue to use the term 'refugee' in the book. Most of the research participants had been recognized as refugees in Uganda, but I do not address the term as the legal status and politicized bureaucratic classification defined in the 1951 Convention relating to the Status of Refugees and its 1967 Protocol as well as Uganda's Refugee Act. A purely legalistic and bureaucratic approach risks essentializing the human effects and experiences that people undergo as refugees. Instead, I see 'refugee' as a relational analytical category and place a focus on exploring the narratives and testimonies of refugees themselves with the aim to understand, portray, and reflect which experiences shape their lives, how they perceive and make sense of them, and how they cope. Exactly this situation of being a refugee is unique, as these people fled sites of danger and sought safety in Uganda where they would endure encampment for many years. Distancing myself from a legalistic approach and moving toward inquiries into the individual and collective encounters and strategies of these people is thus key.

Finally, worth mentioning is the fact that in the course of the book I will refer time and again to data 'I' collected and insights the women and men in Kyaka II shared with 'me.' With these references, I do not intend to disregard the important work contributed by Christine and Pearl as well as by the refugees as peer-researchers. I would much rather write inclusively about a 'we' and 'us' throughout the book; unfortunately, this would be confusing for the reader if not clarified regularly. Moreover, despite the teamwork during data collection, I was unable to involve the team in the data analysis and generate findings together with them, as noted earlier.

Outline of the Book

With the objective here being to explore the risks of gender-based violence in the camp, how humanitarian aid and structures affect the women and men as well as the violence experienced, how gender relations change, as well as how those affected cope with risks and 'realities' during encampment, the book does not present—nor is it guided by—one overriding key argument. Instead, in each chapter a number of contentions are put forward, which link up with the book's core objectives, while the different chapters are all interconnected.

Chapter 2 focuses on the forms, scopes, and conditions of gender-based violence that particularly women are confronted with in Kyaka II. Yet, even though women were said to be the main group of victims, violence was not limited to them. Men also suffered gender-based violence, and women perpetrated it on occasion. Moreover, during dialogues and discussions, women as well as men continuously referred to the risks that they faced during the war in their countries of origin, mainly DR Congo, and during flight to Uganda. This laid the foundation for a closer look at how gender-based violence is connected during conflict, flight, and encampment. The chapter therefore argues, on the one hand, that women and men in Kyaka II were confronted with sexual and domestic abuse, structural and cultural violence, and militarized dangers to varying degrees and in gender-specific ways. On the other hand, such violence in camps like Kyaka II cannot be seen as an isolated phenomenon; rather, it is connected to gender-based forms during conflict and flight too—thereby representing a continuum of violence. I conclude the chapter by stressing the need to go beyond research focused on refugee camps per se, so as to understand violence better and consider the nexus between conflict and displacement.

Such perils prompt the question of why gender-based violence is prevalent during encampment even despite humanitarian agencies implementing a host of measures to protect and assist refugees. Chapter 3 attends to this question. It first sheds light on humanitarian measures and structures, on decision-making regulations, and on self-reliance strategies in Kyaka II with respective effects on 'camp residents.' I argue that humanitarian structures are imposed on the refugees; not only do they provide access to services, they also give rise to certain limitations. In the process, refugees are generally reduced to 'protection objects' afforded limited space for participation themselves. The second part of the chapter then explores how humanitarian agencies strive to tackle gender-based violence. I study how local aid is linked to global policies and norms, thus drawing on debates about norm localization, and discuss the preventive and responsive measures implemented in Kyaka II. I argue that humanitarian projects primarily define women as vulnerable victims, and therefore treat them as 'vulnerable protection objects,' which gives rise to critical impact on women and men. Moreover, although humanitarian aid serves the protection and assistance of refugees, I show in the chapter's third part how it can actually contribute to the ongoing violence too. The chapter closes by reflecting on whether such criticism of humanitarian structures contributing to violence is reasonable considering the various challenges that these agencies face.

Chapter 4 turns its attention to the gender roles and relations of the people living in Kyaka II—along with how respective changes therein are linked with gender-based violence. By drawing on and broadening Hearn's (2004, 2012, 2015) theory of the hegemony of men, I look at how women, men, youth, as well as aid workers perceived but also challenged gender roles and relations through their social practices. To understand life conditions, I argue that it is necessary to take into consideration the time before encampment—and thus gender roles and relations prior to flight too. Although women, men, youth, and aid workers mutually believed that men constitute the hegemonic actor to whom women and youth should submit, which appears to be similar to the gender hierarchies upheld before flight too, shifts in perceptions did also occur. Some women saw themselves in various different roles, especially when they depicted these not directly linked to gender relations; teenager girls and boys found their peers to be equal, but expressed patriarchal perceptions about adults. These shifts contributed to the renegotiating of gender relations, and different patterns hereof were found to be practiced in Kyaka II. Through the nature of humanitarian support offered, aid workers were influential too; I argue that they assigned roles, but at the same time hindered men and women in fulfilling them. Moreover, with their power, aid workers figuratively became part of the gender systems on-site.

But, how did those living in Kyaka II cope with the insecurities and restrictions faced there? This is the key question tackled by Chapter 5, which illustrates how women and also men dealt with violence as well as other hardships. By linking the coping strategies with Lister's (2004) agency theory, I discuss how women and men in Kyaka II "got by," "got out," "got organized," and "got back at" in dealing with the camp conditions; their strategies essentially reveal how these people practiced agency. In the first part, I argue that flight from violence during conflict constitutes a conscious decision rather than a passive reflex, and thus a concrete coping strategy. In Kyaka II, inhabitants handled the prevalent violence by means of diverse individual and collective practices, including silence, through which they strove to prevent and reduce the levels of risk. Yet their coping was not limited to overcoming these risks; as I portray in the second part of the chapter, they employed various economic, social, and political practices to improve their lives and livelihoods. This meant consciously using or going beyond humanitarian regulations, creating some form of normalcy, and claiming their rights. Hope for and belief in a better future is revealed not only to have been a coping strategy but also a driver for dealing with other difficulties. This also included belief in witchcraft, as a way of making sense of certain difficult developments.

The book closes with a brief sixth chapter summarizing main findings as well as reflecting on how gender-based violence, humanitarian structures, gender relations, and coping strategies represent inherently intertwined subject matters that cannot be discussed separately. In addition, I reflect on the role of time and space—running as a core theme throughout the book, albeit one not directly theorized. I then finish by identifying areas requiring close further research going forward.

2 | Gender-Based Violence in the Camp and Beyond

On my first day in Kyaka II, I met a woman who had escaped DR Congo eight years ago due to the conflict there. She said her family had had a good life at home, but the violence destroyed it. She fled together with her three children, and later told me that her husband was murdered by rebels. The loss triggered her decision to seek safety in Uganda—safety for her children and herself. When we started speaking about the conditions in Uganda and their life in Kyaka II, she quickly mentioned gender-based violence here as well. I asked her why she thinks such violence occurs in Kyaka II. At first she laughed for a moment, shrugged her shoulders, and then shook her head for a long while. She said that she could not understand it either "because there is no war in Kyaka II." Then she explained that the social and economic hardships in the camp caused frustration, which she thought contributed to the prevalence of gender-based violence against women. She spoke with intensity about the experiences of violence. She recalled memories as if they had happened yesterday; she vividly delved into memories of her husband and their life prior to the conflict but also flinched when speaking about the cruelties she had witnessed during conflict, flight, and encampment.[1]

During my research in Uganda, our paths would cross over and over again. To me, her story would become paradigmatic for the experiences of violence but also for the strength in coping among the women and men I was able to speak with in Kyaka II. Such experiences were therefore not limited to her; many others also shared stories about the threats and attacks, as well as the overall difficult life conditions, encountered both prior to and within the camp.

That refugees and women particularly are exposed to insecurities in exile is not an unheard-of phenomenon. Women's risks have received increasing academic attention since the 1980s, when feminist scholars

---

[1] Female refugee, dialogue, February 18, 2014, Base Camp.

started to address conditions in refugee situations. In addition to criticism of the male-dominated approaches in international refugee law and protection that marginalized women (e.g., Indra 1987; Greatbatch 1989; Johnsson 1989; Cipriani 1993), early feminist studies brought to light issues of violence against women of different age groups such as rape and domestic abuse (e.g., de Neef and de Ruiter 1984; Ferris 1990; Friedman 1992). Recent research continues to reveal the hardships and risks of gender-based violence in refugee situations (for literature reviews, see Buckley-Zistel et al. 2014; Vu et al. 2014; Araujo et al. 2019), and the findings presented in this chapter are in line with this deepening notion of a high level of insecurity being faced by women, especially, during encampment.

However, research on gender-based violence tends to focus on women as victims and men as perpetrators (see Ozcurumez et al. 2020). This prompts the question of whether this binary of 'victim-women' and 'perpetrator-men' reflects actual local conditions in camps. Are only women affected, or do they also perpetrate violence? What about men suffering such violence? In what forms and scope does gender-based violence occur, against whom, and why? And, how is violence in the camp linked to the respective risks faced during both conflict and flight? These questions are central to this chapter, and guide its analysis. While my research in Uganda's Kyaka II supports the tendency toward it being women and girls who are mainly affected by gender-based violence, it nevertheless indicates risks for men and boys as well—alongside violence being perpetrated by women on occasion too.

As noted in Chapter 1, gender-based violence is understood in this book as harmful acts of force committed against another person due to their gender and gender-related attributions. Gender-based violence is not limited merely to physical attacks such as rape but can occur in various forms. In order to avoid restricting the analysis to predefined forms of gender-based violence, thus instead seeking to maintain a broader perspective and to explore the knowledge and experiences shared by the women and men in Kyaka II, I draw on Galtung's understanding of violence. He develops a three-dimensional model—a so-called triangle of violence—and distinguishes between direct, structural, and cultural types (Galtung 2010, 2004, 1990, 1969; Galtung and Höivik 1971). Direct violence takes physical and personal forms, which can range from verbally abusing to wounding or murdering people. The second type of violence is inherently entangled in the structures surrounding and influencing people, and covers unequal power relations, unjust opportunities, and other disadvantages anchored in those structures. Cultural violence, similarly, is embedded in the 'culture' or cultural sphere, such as in religious or ideological practices, which can be marginalizing or otherwise oppressive and restrictive. While direct violence is visible, structural and cultural violence remain invisible; the latter types can nonetheless contribute to or leverage the former, while direct violence can, in turn, intensify both structural and cultural violence.

As with any attempt to define and categorize complex social phenomena, the Galtungian concept can of course be criticized, modified, and extended (e.g., Coady 2007; Dilts et al. 2012; Winter 2012). The latter mode of extending—or rather complementing—his concept of violence is what I pursue in this work with regard to gender and gender-based violence. To this end, I draw on the approach offered by Confortini (2006) to enrich Galtung's understanding and employ a gendered conceptualization of direct physical, structural, and cultural violence. In lieu of assuming violence simply occurs, such an approach enables us to explore the varying degrees and forms of violence against a person due to the recognized role of gender and its respective ascriptions. This addresses violence as a socially constructed phenomenon embedded in the respective contexts and power relations for which gender is key; gender shapes and structures social life and order. It is thus not only about 'gendering' the Galtungian types of violence regarding, for example, physical violence occurring with rape, structural violence with discrimination, and cultural violence with harmful customs. It is about, moreover, how violence is entangled with surrounding social and power relations; as Confortini notes, how it presents "a complicated process through which social relations of power are built, legitimized, reproduced, and naturalized" (2006: 356). While some types of violence appear visible and others invisible, in this chapter—and partly also the following ones—I outline how the mere idea of in/visibility is socially influenced and carries meanings. Such an approach facilitates a social-constructivist analysis of gender-specific experiences and practices of violence with regard to meanings, triggers, and effects.

At its core, this chapter depicts the scope, forms, and conditions of gender-based violence first briefly during conflict and flight, then particularly during encampment. While the main interest lies in women's perspectives, the chapter addresses how women as well as men of different age groups experience and commit gender-based violence. In the final section, I link findings about violence during conflict, flight, and encampment and outline the continuum of gender-based violence. As I attend to the conditions of those who have fled war and sought safety in Uganda, where they live in a refugee camp, I draw on and seek to contribute to discourses about gender-based violence in Peace and Conflict Studies as well as Forced Migration and Refugee Studies. Important research has been published about forced migration due to violent conflicts and thus conflict-induced displacements (see Zolberg et al. 1989; Lischer 2005, 2007; Salehyan 2007; Lubkemann 2008a; Adhikari 2013; Salehyan 2014; Hovil 2016; Bank et al. 2017; Bohnet et al. 2018; Krause 2018a). Yet debates in these two fields of research have rarely been connected systematically. Contributing to overcoming this separation and linking the two together is therefore an underlying interest in this chapter.

Finally, I would like to briefly revert to the ethical reflections put forward in Chapter 1. Many refugees I spoke with in Kyaka II were personally affected by gender-based violence, either by being assaulted or by seeing family members, friends, or strangers suffer attacks. Each and every one of the experiences recounted is terrible in its own right, but such an incident is by no means the only factor that influences or defines these individuals. Despite this chapter's focus on gender-based violence, I do not intend to portray those affected as vulnerable, helpless, passive bodies.

Gender-Based Violence during Conflict and Flight

This chapter began with reference to a woman I met on my first day of research in Uganda. She had escaped the conflict in DR Congo with her children to seek safety in Uganda, where conditions remained dire. Her vivid memories of the atrocities, alongside the ongoing insecure situation faced, indicate that leaving violence in conflicts behind does not necessarily mean that it has come to an end.[2] Many other people that I met in Kyaka II also shared stories of having experienced violence both prior to and during encampment. The more they spoke of their

---

[2] Female refugee, dialogue, February 18, 2014, Base Camp.

experiences, the more I realized how much these influence them and how gender-based violence cannot thus be seen as limited to the camp alone—which is what I had originally planned to focus exclusively on.

The following section sheds light on the risks encountered during the phases of conflict and flight. The conflict in the Kivu regions of DR Congo, which most of the people in Kyaka II had fled, is so complex that entire books could be and indeed have been written about it (see Turner 2007; Autesserre 2010; Maedl 2010; Eriksson Baaz and Stern 2013a; Freedman 2015b; Berwouts 2017). Naturally, I have to set my focus and so will center on risks. Moreover, with my research carried out in and concentrating on a refugee camp, I draw on the memories shared by the refugees in Kyaka II in addition to other empirical studies on the scope of the violence witnessed during the conflicts in DR Congo.

"Burning down houses, stealing and raping": Violence during Conflict

The vast majority of refugees in Kyaka II had escaped the war in North Kivu and South Kivu, parts of DR Congo's eastern region. The conflict situation here is complex and protracted and certainly not limited to contemporary times alone. Already shortly after the country's independence from Belgium in 1960, tensions arose over power-sharing and land issues (Autesserre 2008). Since the 1990s, three conflicts have occurred—each leading to a level of violence of devastating intensity. The first between the military and the Banyamulenge began in 1996, and lasted for about a year. Yet related violence continued in the second conflict of 1998 already—only eventually coming to an end in 2003, when a transitional government took power. However, the violence persisted and contributed to a reoccurrence of the conflict between government forces and the rebel group Mouvement du 23 Mars (M23) in 2012 (Breytenbach et al. 1999; Reyntjens 2009; Doevenspeck 2016). While many had fled the conflicts years ago and stayed in exile, tensions increased again at the end of 2017—contributing to wide-scale violence and displacement (Human Rights Watch 2017; UNHCR 2017a, 2018e).

In addition to theft, looting, murder, and displacement, the conflicts in the Kivu regions are known for the particularly high prevalence of gender-based violence and specifically of sexual violence within it

(Pratt and Werchick 2004; Eriksson Baaz and Stern 2009; Meger 2010; Krause 2017a).[3] Sexual violence occurs mainly in the forms of rape, gang rape, sexual slavery, defilement, and genital mutilation, primarily against women (see OHCHR 2011). Other forms of gender-based violence include abduction and subsequent forced recruitment into military or rebel structures of men as warriors and of women as 'bush wives.' Although legal steps toward obtaining justice for the victims have been initiated in recent years, impunity continues to persist for many perpetrators (see MONUSCO and OHCHR 2016; Human Rights Watch 2018; OHCHR 2019).

The extent of the conflict-related violence witnessed in North Kivu and South Kivu was severe, for women and girls as well as for men and boys. Among the various accounts, one woman said most of her family —including her husband and parents—had been murdered during the war. She was raped, and said, "I almost died afterward," but was able to then flee to Uganda with her three children.[4] Another woman whose husband had been abducted by rebels explained the situation when the violence intensified. She remembered that rebels "were burning down houses and they were stealing animals and sometimes they would attack them in the houses. In the houses, they would tie up the men to the wall and then they would rape the women."[5]

The scenario the woman described was similar to that experienced by others too. One man explained, "I have experienced two wars in Congo that make me hate it"; he would eventually flee to Uganda with his sisters and mother. During the war, rebels abducted his father, wife, and children and attacked his mother. They came "during the night and beat up my mum, raped her, broke her leg, and infected her with HIV."[6] Also attacked in her home, one woman recalled, "men came to my house [...], they hit the door with a big stone, it fell in, and they came in. They put me on gunpoint and I gave them the money. Some were stealing, others were raping me. My children were hiding."[7] The next day, she decided to flee with her children.

---

[3] Based on archival research, Mertens (2016) reveals similar sexual cruelty during colonial times. For critical reflections on discourses of resources and rape, see also Laudati and Mertens (2019).

[4] Female refugee, dialogue, March 26, 2014, Bukere Zone.

[5] Female refugee, dialogue, February 25, 2014, Base Camp.

[6] Male refugee, dialogue, March 18, 2014, Base Camp.

[7] Female refugee, dialogue, March 5, 2014, Kaborogota Zone.

Many in Kyaka II shared stories indicating a high level of visibility of violence, not only against family members who were present but also against others in the community—with it appearing intentional. Although neither women nor men in Kyaka II mentioned incidences of sexual violence against men and boys, research depicts these risks existing as well (Dolan 2014; Johnson et al. 2010; Sivakumaran 2007). Among others, Christian et al. (2011: 234) note that sexual violence against men during the conflict in DR Congo could occur in the presence of family members—further adding to the humiliation of victims.

The continuous references made to sexual violence as well as kidnapping and abduction show how prevalent such abuse was. One young man in Kyaka II had survived the ordeal of abduction; he explained that rebels came to his village, killed his father, mother, and little sisters before kidnapping him. At night, he was able to flee; eventually he reunited with his aunt in Kyaka II.[8] Another man fled because he recalled "there was fighting and shooting all over. I was staying with my parents, and was the eldest of my siblings." He said that he fled alone without his family out of fear of violence and being abducted, as "the rebels were enlisting young boys of my age into the army."[9] Although a number of studies have acknowledged the risk of forced recruitment, it is not always recognized as a form of gender-based violence against men (Eriksson Baaz and Stern 2013a: 35; Carpenter 2006: 91ff). During the conflict in DR Congo, it has affected many; it can also occur in refugee camps, however (see Janmyr 2017). Abducted women and girls in DR Congo are forcibly integrated mainly for domestic support and the "smooth running" of the structures (Maedl 2010: 55), but this is often connected with rape and sexual slavery (on research in Sierra Leone, see Coulter 2011).

Gender-based violence in DR Congo also took place somewhat detached from the conflict, as seen in the case of domestic abuse and intimate partner violence (see also Mulumeoderhwa 2020; Tlapek 2015; Kohli et al. 2015; Babalola et al. 2014). The intensity and scope of the violence was generally perceived to vary and as depending on the different ethnic customs and gender systems of the people involved

---

[8] Male refugee, dialogue, April 4, 2014, Base Camp.
[9] Male refugee, dialogue, March 28, 2014, Base Camp.

(see also Chapter 4).[10]Among other people, one man in Kyaka II reflected on how men who used violence against wives in the camp would also have done so in the past before flight.[11] Another indicated that the scope of violence against wives had reduced in the camp, highlighting: "In Congo, the men would beat their wives so much."[12] On the contrary, one woman felt that this form of abuse was more prevalent in the camp than it was in DR Congo.[13] Such insights prompt the question of how to identify practices brought with people as related to those that were adopted after flight. Since refugee situations often last for many years or even decades, such identification is scarcely possible. However, it is important to note that the continued use of violence is a strong indication that the phenomenon is not limited to either of the two sites: to homes in countries of origin or camps in those of asylum.

While violence less connected to the conflict occurred between intimate partners, family members, and other acquaintances mainly in the private sphere, conflict-related forms were primarily perpetrated by members of armed groups and the Congolese armed forces or the police—that largely in public, but also in private spaces too (Maedl 2010: 44; Pacéré 2007; Pratt and Werchick 2004: 9). The people in Kyaka II were rarely able to identify to which group perpetrators belonged, describing them as "uniformed men"[14] or "rebels and trained soldiers,"[15] or referring to their ethnic groups or "tribes."[16] While the data collected in Uganda does not allow for statistical overviews, Johnson et al. (2010: 557) found a wider range of attackers existing based on their study of 998 households in DR Congo: some 58.9 percent of reported conflict-related sexual violence against women was perpetrated by men and 41.1 percent by women; meanwhile, 91.4 percent of such cases against men were committed by men and 10 percent by women. Moreover, while no one spoken with in Kyaka II talked of women as soldiers or perpetrators of violence during

---

[10] Discussion with local leaders, March 20, 2014, Base Camp; discussion with male refugees, March 19, 2014, Base Camp.
[11] Male refugee, dialogue, March 5, 2014, Kaborogota Zone.
[12] Male refugee, dialogue, March 5, 2014, Base Camp.
[13] Discussion 1 with female refugee, March 12, 2014, Base Camp.
[14] Female refugee, dialogue, March 5, 2014, Kaborogota Zone.
[15] Male refugee, dialogue, March 18, 2014, Base Camp.
[16] Female refugee, dialogue, March 27, 2014, Base Camp.

the war, Eriksson Baaz and Stern (2013b) discuss their roles in the widespread violence.

"People were raped, I saw them": Violence during Flight

Standing in contrast to violence during conflict being a well-researched field that during the phase of flight has received relatively little academic attention even though it constitutes a crucial part of conflict-induced displacement. Due to the influx of numbers of people seeking asylum in Europe between 2015 and 2017, the routes, means, and dangers of forced migration toward Europe are now being increasingly explored by scholars (see Squire et al. 2017; Crawley et al. 2016; Freedman 2016a While some studies on other world regions have mentioned the risks faced during flight (see Krause forthcoming), the phenomenon remains under-researched within sub-Saharan Africa—and specifically from DR Congo to Uganda.

The stories that the people in Kyaka II shared about their flight reveal that they escaped the conflicts due to its violence. They experienced, witnessed, or feared attacks, lost members of their families or communities through killings or abductions, and thus left in order to find safety and security elsewhere. While this may appear to suggest flight being a mere reaction to the conflict-related violence for survival, I will discuss these people's flight as a conscious decision in Chapter 5. Yet not only their desire to leave the direct and indirect violence during conflict behind but also their hope for safety in Uganda were both overshadowed by ongoing issues, not least the risk of gender-based violence.

Flight journeys to Uganda were described as long, difficult, and arduous due to a lack of food, water, shelter, and security. Such flight often took from several days up to a number of months. One man explained that his journey lasted the latter. He used to be a teacher in a village in DR Congo. Because rebels repeatedly attacked schools in seeking to recruit children, he and other teachers initiated a discussion with parents to "look for a way to stop the rebels from taking children from school to recruit them into their movement." The other teachers selected him as the leader of the group. When the violence came closer to the village "the rebels decided to look for us and kill us, it is what made me flee because I was the first person to get targeted by the rebels because I was the leader of the group." Although he was able to take cover, during his flight he heard and witnessed violence time and again. Being only able to move slowly and oftentimes at night to avoid attacks, it took him nine months to reach Uganda.[17]

The man quoted earlier regarding his flight out of fear of abduction said that he escaped the war alone, mainly moving at night over the course of several days. He traveled from "Goma to Rutshuru, a place near the Ugandan border"—there he found other people who had also escaped the war, joining up with them. However, he stressed "the same people who attacked Goma were there in Rutshuru. The same rebels were still rounding up young boys for enlisting. So I had to run away." He eventually crossed the border to Uganda, and took buses to Kisoro and then to Kampala, the capital.[18] Later he moved to the camp Kyaka II.

While both of these men remembered their constant fear of attack during flight, others were also confronted with violence. One woman recalled her terrible experiences. After her father was murdered during the war, she fled DR Congo together with her mother, sisters, and niece. When they reached the border with Uganda, Congolese armed men stopped them. These individuals, whom she called "soldiers," attacked them. They killed her sisters in front of them as punishment for fleeing. She explained their murder in an intensely brutal way, as "cutting with a panga into several pieces; then we ran away and arrived in Uganda, just the three of us": her, her mother, and her orphaned niece. After reaching western Uganda, a UNHCR vehicle brought them to Kyaka II.[19]

Issues at border or checkpoints with armed groups were also mentioned by several other research participants in Kyaka II; the risks were pointedly outlined by one male informant. He had fled the conflict with his wife and children as well as "other people" from their village in DR Congo, noting that they encountered rebels at the border. He recalled that they "took our properties like clothes and bags, among other things, and also were beating my wife because she was quarreling with them."[20] Such risks are not limited to flight from DR Congo to Uganda; Schon (2016) reflects how Syrian and Somali refugees encountered violence by armed groups at checkpoints, which fostered

[17] Male refugee, dialogue, March 27, 2014, Base Camp.
[18] Male refugee, dialogue, March 28, 2014, Base Camp.
[19] Female refugee, dialogue, March 18, 2014, Sweswe Zone.
[20] Male refugee, dialogue, March 27, 2014, Base Camp.

high levels of fear and uncertainty among those fleeing. Squire et al. (2017: 66) and Crawley et al. (2016: 33) furthermore stress heightened risks of violence including kidnapping, against people en route to European countries.

Not least due to risks such as these, many in Kyaka II shared memories of hiding during their journeys. However, this did not always ensure their safety—and especially women who had fled without husbands or fathers were confronted with risks. The woman quoted above on seeing rebels burning down houses took the journey to Uganda with her children and other people fleeing the war, but without her husband who had been abducted. The community did not provide protection for her. She was raped twice by different men during her flight. Although she could not identify them, she stressed they were "refugees"—and thus individuals also escaping DR Congo.[21] Another woman who was raped during the conflict underlined that during her flight "people were raped, and I saw them";[22] again, this reveals the high level of visibility of the violence. Experiences like these were widely addressed by refugees in Kyaka II, and show that despite wanting to flee violence these people continued to be exposed to insecurity during flight.

The narratives shared reveal that in addition to the risks of being murdered or robbed, women and men faced varying degrees of gender-based threats during flight too. While men and boys were confronted with risks of abduction and forced recruitment into armed groups, women and girls were exposed to sexual violence including rape and gang rape. Although neither women nor men reflected on sexual violence against men or boys, two aid workers in Kyaka II mentioned such risks during flight while noting that they are rarely reported in Uganda due to the fear of stigmatization.[23] During flight, these different forms of violence were discussed as being mainly committed in public spaces by members of armed groups but, as indicated, also by other refugees. With lives shattered by the conflict, it could be assumed that those who flee tend to support and potentially protect each other where possible; while often the case, it certainly is not always so however. Violence from combatants and those also en route increases

[21] Female refugee, dialogue, February 25, 2014, Base Camp.
[22] Female refugee, dialogue, March 5, 2014, Kaborogota Zone.
[23] Female aid worker, interview, April 10, 2014; male aid worker, interview, April 10, 2014.

risks, particularly for people who travel alone and in small groups. Such attacks were linked with theft, especially as survival needs such as food, water, and shelter were scarcely able to be satisfied during flight.

Extent of Gender-Based Violence in Kyaka II

Having reached Uganda and been settled in Kyaka II, most—if not all —of these women and men probably hoped for safety, security, and stability. However, as signified by the statement from a member of the Refugee Welfare Council that "violence is very common everywhere," the risks of gender-based violence remained prevalent in Kyaka II— being mainly directed toward women and perpetrated by men.[24] However, far beyond a clear binary, women were also found to commit and men to experience violence. The following section portrays the general scope, victim–perpetrator structures, as well as locations of gender-based violence in Kyaka II, and then addresses the risks for women and men of different age groups specifically.

Scope of Violence

Tracing the exact scope of gender-based violence in refugee camps such as Kyaka II is often complicated, thus making recording and identifying possible changes—any increases or decreases—in occurrence equally challenging. Nonetheless, some studies and reports do provide overviews. For example, with a focus on Kenya, Agier notes in an early article: "Rapes occur commonly in and around the camps at a rate which exceeded 10 a month during the first semester (six months) of 2000 according to the records of meetings of the camp police, a number generally acknowledged to be well below reality" (2002: 327). Also concerning refugees in Kenya, Care International (2011) would state that cases of gender-based violence in the Dadaab refugee camps quadrupled between 2010 and 2011. Regarding the civil war in Liberia, the German NGO Medica Mondiale estimates that during flight two out of three women and girls were confronted with sexual violence, often mass rape; in camps in Liberia, Guinea, and Sierra Leone, meanwhile, girls especially faced sexual exploitation (Lindorfer 2009: 4). Moreover, Freedman stresses that gender-based

---

[24] Discussion with Refugee Welfare Council leaders, March 19, 2014, Base Camp.

violence constitutes a "hidden aspect" (2016b: 21) in the increased refugee movements toward European countries occurring in 2015. She notes that "[m]any of the women interviewed had also experienced violence from various sources during their journeys to the EU" (2016b: 22).

In Kyaka II, gender-based violence did not appear to be such a hidden aspect; instead, it seemed visible, widespread, and omnipresent. Without having raised direct questions about such violence at the beginning of our dialogues or discussions with refugees in Kyaka II, many of interlocutors brought up this and related issues on their own initiative. Also, humanitarian workers appeared to be well aware of these problems, addressing them in our interviews.

To understand the scope of gender-based violence in Kyaka II, I was granted access to records of cases of violence as collected and handled by the police, health services, and psychosocial focal points in Kyaka II combined. According to these records, 178 cases of gender-based violence were reported in Kyaka II in 2013. These included 37 cases of sexual assault and rape, 120 of physical assault and denial of resources,[25] 20 of psychological and emotional abuse, and one case of forced marriage (also Krause 2017a). With a view to the aforementioned widespread forms of gender-based violence as well as a population size of more than 20,000 refugees in Kyaka II at the time of research (UNHCR 2014f), this caseload appears relatively unlikely to be accurate. Moreover, women and men as well as humanitarian staff noted that victims often refrain from reporting attacks due to fear of stigmatization and social exclusion, fear of further violence by perpetrators, or because they are unable to pay reporting fees to the police.[26] Besides, a number of research participants explained that they prefer to handle cases of violence and dispute at the community level.[27]

In order to develop an overview of the scope of the violence independent of the humanitarian agencies and government data given in

---

[25] Physical assault was explained as mainly referring to domestic violence, while denial of resources concerned gender-based discrimination and the rejection of resources within intimate partnerships or inside households.

[26] See female refugee, dialogue, March 17, 2014, Bujubuli; discussion with religious leaders, March 19, 2014, Base Camp; female aid worker, interview, April 22, 2014; female aid worker, interview, April 10, 2014.

[27] For further analysis, see Chapter 5; female refugee, dialogue, March 27, 2014, Base Camp.

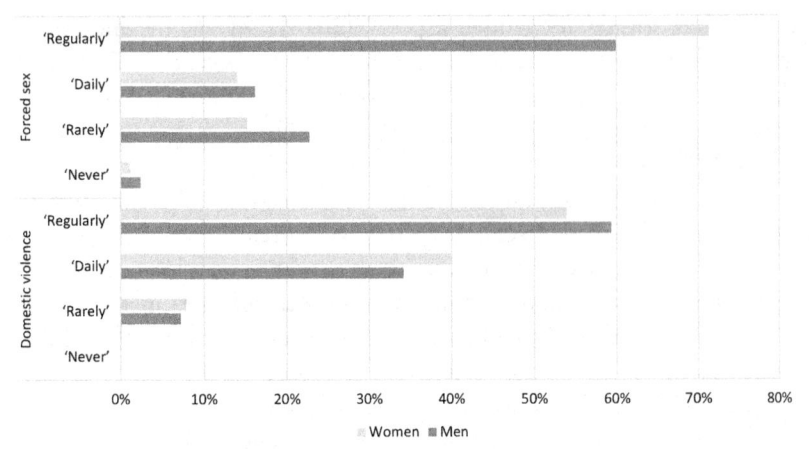

Figure 2.1 Perceptions of scope of forced sex and domestic violence in Kyaka II

official reports, a survey was conducted with 351 women and men resident in Kyaka II. It included questions about how often participants believe sexual as well as domestic violence to occur in the camp. Such perceptions—in lieu of their actual experiences of violence—were asked about in order to ensure ethical and sensitive research procedures. It is assumed that participants' beliefs and thus responses are influenced and guided in their perceptions by their own lived experiences.

Contrary to official statistics indicating a relatively small number of cases, Figure 2.1 illustrates that most survey participants believed that these forms of violence were prevalent in Kyaka II. The majority of the participating women and men recognized forced sex as well as domestic violence as widespread, occurring 'regularly.' Besides, almost 40 percent of the participating women and 34 percent of the men believed that domestic violence took place on a daily basis, whereas about 16 percent of the men and 14 percent of the women assumed forced sex to occur 'daily.' About every sixth woman and almost every fifth man believed forced sex takes place 'rarely,' but less than one in ten of the women and men assumed that domestic violence happens 'rarely.' It is important to note that none said that domestic violence 'never' takes place. Figure 2.1 furthermore reveals the different perceptions of women and men. On the one hand, more women than men believed that forced sex occurred 'regularly' and that domestic violence took place 'daily.' On the other hand, more men than women believe that forced sex only occurred 'rarely.' These different perceptions are likely to have been influenced by experiences of violence.

Victims and Perpetrators

Findings based on the survey carried out in Kyaka II further shed light on the nexus of victims and perpetrators in the camp's gender-based violence. Participants were asked who they believed the main victims or perpetrators to be. The responses of all revealed a significant leaning toward women and girls being seen as the main group of victims, and men the main one of perpetrators.

Among participants, several gave not only their initial response to our questions but a second and thus additional one—which the research team did not inquire after. Instead, a number of individuals came forward and provided these follow-up answers independently. Because they obviously wanted to or felt the need to share further insights, I believe it is important to not only analyze preliminary answers[28] but to take all responses into account. By and large, almost every sixth survey participant wanted to give a second response about who they believed the main group of perpetrators to be. In contrast, far fewer participants (only 11 out of 351) wanted to offer a second response on who they thought the main victim groups to be—indicating positions of relatively certainty hereon.

When considering both the first and the second responses about victim–perpetrator structures by gender, the overarching tendency toward male refugees being assumed to mainly commit violence and female refugees being seen as especially vulnerable to it remained. In detail, 77.9 percent of the women and 81.7 percent of the men believed that these acts are primarily committed by male refugees, while 5 percent of the women and 1.8 percent of the men believed they were mainly perpetrated by female refugees. Moreover, 92.2 percent of the women and 87 percent of the men believed that the main group of victims were female refugees (including both women and girls), while

---

[28] In previous publications, I exclusively explored the first responses without examining gender-related distributions therein (see Krause 2015b, 2015a, 2017a), which this book now expands on.

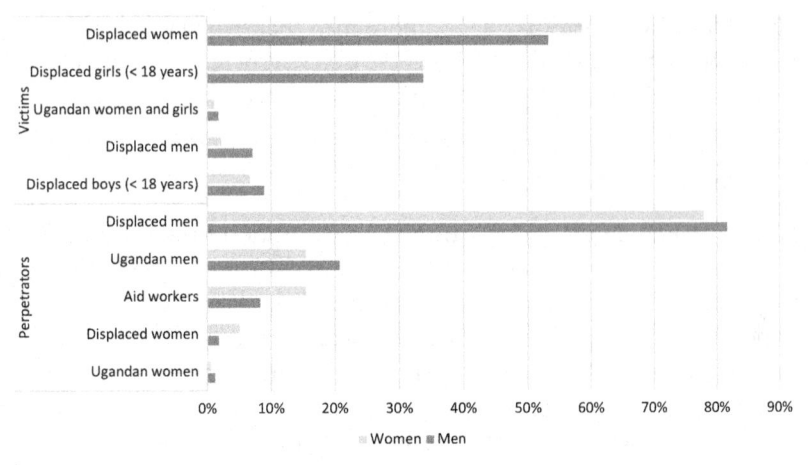

Figure 2.2 Perceptions about victims and perpetrators of gender-based violence in Kyaka II

8.8 percent of the women and 16 percent of the men assumed it was male refugees (including both men and boys).[29]

Many of the second responses revolved around aid workers, and it is thus particularly the scope for these individuals—who are supposed to be committed to refugees' protection—being potential perpetrators that increases therewith. Overall 8.3 percent of the men and 15.5 percent of the women participating believed humanitarian staff to be among the main perpetrator group. This is illustrated in Figure 2.2. The quantitative data echoes the earlier-mentioned strong inclination to see female victims and male perpetrators in gender-based violence. However, it is important to note that a clear dichotomy cannot be drawn—with victim–perpetrator structures turning out to be more diverse. The survey findings show that both men and women can fall victim to and be perpetrators of gender-based violence, contradicting the prevailing strict binary of male perpetrators and female victims. How women commit violence and what risks men face are explored in the section that follows. In line with this complexity in the victim–perpetrator structures, relations between victims and perpetrators are diffuse and include marital or intimate partners, acquaintances such as

---

[29] Note that Ugandan men and boys were not noted to be potential victims. This does not mean they do not ever experience such violence, but with the surveys' focus on refugees, no further inquiry was pursued.

neighbors or teachers, and strangers who appear to have assaulted their victims randomly.

Locations of Violence

The locations where the different forms of gender-based violence occur are diverse. They include domestic spheres, neighborhoods, meeting points such as markets or water boreholes, familiar but also remote areas like forests, fields, and schools, as well as random sites such as public roads. With multiple answers possible, the survey findings show that most believed that gender-based violence mainly took place at home—which is in line with the prevalence of domestic abuse. Almost six out of ten participants considered gender-based violence to occur when working in the fields publicly, and about half of all participants assumed it did so when collecting firewood in remote regions, while at schools, or at health facilities. About four out of ten participants believed such violence to occur at boreholes when fetching water. Although there was only limited variation in the responses of participating women and men, differences nonetheless did exist therein as illustrated in Figure 2.3. More women than men thought that gender-based violence takes place at home and at markets, whereas more men than women assumed violence to occur at schools (affecting children), at health facilities, and at bars in the evening/at night. As indicated

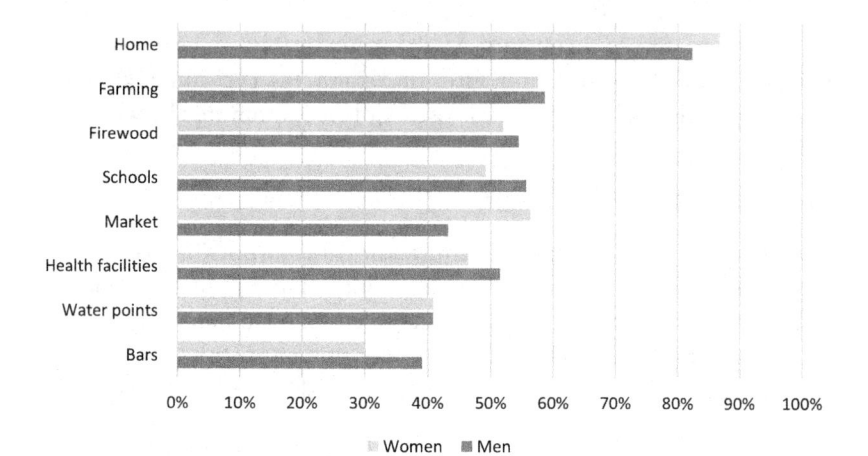

Figure 2.3 Perceptions of sites of gender-based violence in Kyaka II

earlier, such variation is likely to be the result of diverse personal experiences of violence. These sites encompass both public and private spaces, and reveal the omnipresence of gender-based violence within the confines of Kyaka II likely to occur during daytime and nighttime. But were there safe places within the refugee camp? Although humanitarian agency-run protection areas with safe houses were established in the Base Camp of Kyaka II at the time of research, where victims received short-term shelter in cases of direct threat, these tents can only provide safety for a certain number of people or households at a time and they merely served as temporary interim solutions until those cases are settled. These safe houses were without any doubt important, but their range and effectiveness remained limited. Besides, since by no means all cases were reported, an unknown (high) number of victims continued to live without access to such protection.

Women as Victims—and Perpetrators—of Gender-Based Violence in Kyaka II

"Women face a lot of problems in society and they are violated."[30] This statement by a Congolese woman in Kyaka II echoes the above-discussed survey findings as well as the information shared by many women, men, and aid workers who took part in the research; they identified women and girls as the main victims of gender-based violence. Interlocutors mostly spoke of sexual abuse and harassment, domestic and intimate partner violence, denial of resources, as well as early and forced marriages as the main forms of gender-based violence against women and girls in Kyaka II. Yet, although less frequently, interlocutors also addressed violence committed by women.

"I was raped, defiled many times": Sexual Violence

That refugee camps may not constitute the 'safe harbors' hoped for or anticipated by refugees as well as humanitarian and political agencies is illustrated most concretely by the statement of a woman in Kyaka II: "I was raped, defiled many times."[31] Yet this insecurity can also be seen in studies shedding light on the diverse risks faced by refugees in

[30] Female refugee, dialogue, February 26, 2014, Sweswe Zone.
[31] Discussion 2 with female refugees, March 12, 2014, Base Camp.

other camps—including different forms of sexual violence (see, e.g., Iyakaremye and Mukagatare 2016; Patel et al. 2012; Keygnaert et al. 2012; Fiddian-Qasmiyeh 2010b; Abdi 2006; Farmer 2006; Beswick 2001). Among others, through her ethnographic research in Algerian refugee camps, Fiddian-Qasmiyeh (2014a: 248ff; 2010b) highlights that violence against women occurs in both public and private spheres. Abdi reveals how Somali women suffer rape not only during conflict in their country of origin but also in Kenya's Dadaab refugee camps. She illustrates how women who have often undergone female circumcision are opened up with "weapons such as knives, cans and other sharp instruments [. . .] thus inflicting excruciating physical and mental pain" (Abdi 2006: 238).

The research in Uganda's Kyaka II resonates with these tendencies in such circumstances and finds that sexual violence there was widespread. Primarily occurring in the forms of rape, attempts at rape, and sexual harassment in diverse locations, varying groups of victims were affected but they were mainly female. Several women spoke about attempts at or acts of rape by strangers during their daily work in the fields, when fetching water, or collecting firewood. Others reflected on the risks of sexual violence at home, as committed by acquaintances including husbands and neighbors. Yet others mentioned prostitution, commercial sex, and sex for favors.

Sexual Abuse of Adults and Minors

Among the many accounts of sexual violence given by interlocutors, one Congolese woman recalled an attack that she had experienced in Kyaka II while out searching for firewood. Two men approached her; although she tried to run away and call for help, she explained how they were stronger than her, taking her captive and raping her. She did not report the case because they threatened to kill her if she went to the police.[32] One elderly Congolese woman recounted a similar incident. She had visited the market, and, on her way back home, she was attacked by men who sexually abused her. She said she had fainted due to fear, and only woke up the next day when she found herself laying in the bush besides the road.[33] One young Congolese woman explained that she got her first baby from being raped. She was

---

[32] Female refugee, dialogue, March 13, 2014, Bujubuli.
[33] Female refugee, dialogue, March 18, 2014, Base Camp.

attacked by a stranger when she went to the well to fetch water, suffering injuries as a consequence; she said she did not receive any help afterward.[34]

In addition to such narratives of sexual violence perpetrated by strangers, women spoke about marital rape by their husbands. One noted that sometimes when she comes home from working in the fields her husband forces her to have sex although she is tired and expresses her discomfort.[35] Her story echoes the experiences of sexual violence in partnerships that a number of women in Kyaka II would point out. They relayed that they are "beaten and forced to have sex [at home],"[36] and that their husbands expected sex with their wives regardless of whether or not they themselves wanted to sleep with them.[37] The forceful nature of the act was highlighted by all women who spoke about being sexually abused by their husbands, but a number understood it as a part of their marital responsibility to satisfy their partner. While this perception connects with gender roles and relations, which I will discuss in Chapter 4, the extent of sexual violence between intimate partners is strongly linked with the other forms of domestic abuse addressed below.

During one particular discussion with women, an individual who had fled Rwanda due to violence spoke of her continued experiences of sexual abuse. "I was raped, defiled many times and now have three children, two are out of being defiled," she said. Contrary to many others affected by sexual violence, this woman emphasized that she had reported all cases hereof to the authorities but never received any help. She criticized how:

I feel that we as Rwandese are not taken as good care of as other refugees from other countries. [...] As I reported all this to UNHCR [...] UNHCR would tell us to go back to Rwanda; yet for me, since I came [here] at an early age, I do not even know where home or my family is and more so, Rwanda is not yet stable and we fear for our lives.

Since she was hardly able to satisfy her children's needs, she found herself in the position in which she felt she was "forced to stay with a man." She said she did not love him, but remained with him "just

---

[34] Female refugee, dialogue, April 12, 2014, Bujubuli.
[35] Female refugee, dialogue, March 12, 2014, Bukere Zone.
[36] Female refugee, dialogue, March 11, 2014, Bukere Zone.
[37] Female refugee, dialogue, March 18, 2014, Sweswe Zone.

because I needed support for my children and protection, since I feared to be raped again." However the man started to force her to have sex with him as well, before eventually leaving her. Her hopes of feeling safe and protected were therefore not realized; instead, she said, she remained in a state of fear and confusion.[38]

In another group discussion, women revealed a number of accounts of the horrific sexual violence that they had experienced. One explained that her adult daughter was raped in Kyaka II and became pregnant. She said that her daughter at first did not want to report the case out of fear of stigmatization and suffering further attack. Yet she later decided to move forward with contacting the police. The bitter memories were very present in the woman's narrative, particularly when she spoke of how the baby girl was born and how her daughter struggled emotionally as she was unable to get justice because of the perpetrator having since left Kyaka II.[39] A similar story was shared by a woman who was a single parent of twelve children. One of her daughters was also raped and became pregnant. The woman explained the sorrows of the daughter who suffered from nightmares about the rape and had a difficult time connecting to the baby, both while she was pregnant as well as after giving birth.[40]

Such accounts of violence against adolescents reveal how sexual abuse and harassment is not limited to adults. Girls—and, as I discuss later in this chapter, also boys—faced danger on their way to school largely from unknown persons, while at school from teachers, as well as at home from family members. An adolescent who fled DR Congo when he was six years old said that in Kyaka II "[s]ome parents are found mistreating children [...] whereby some girls and boys are even raped by their stepfathers, [or are] overworked and underfed by their stepmothers or stepfathers."[41] Both girls and boys not only face physical violence mainly from their fathers, but girls are especially also confronted with the ordeal of "[f]orced sex with fathers in families."[42]

[38] Discussion 2 with female refugees, March 12, 2014, Base Camp.
[39] Discussion 1 with female refugees, March 12, 2014, Base Camp.
[40] Discussion 2 with female refugees, March 12, 2014, Base Camp.
[41] Male adolescent, 18 years old, journal writing, March 5, 2014, Bujubuli Secondary School.
[42] Male adolescent, 17 years old, journal writing, April 3, 2014, Bujubuli Secondary School.

Another adolescent who lost her parents during the war in DR Congo and who had lived in Kyaka II for seven years with her uncle, stressed that the rape of girls occurs there "day and night in thick forests on their way to fetch water."[43] Yet another adolescent stressed "girls [are] facing a challenge of sexual harassment, be [it] at school, in the villages, or other areas. Sometimes they are raped, young girls are defiled, whereas they are supposed to be dignified and respected in the community they live in."[44] Such stories were shared widely by adolescents who took part in journal writing. A 17-year-old markedly commented that violence against girls is "very common" in Kyaka II. "In fact, girls' rights are being violated by their parents, neighbors, and relatives. Some girls [...] are raped by neighbors and even defiled, which results in them acquiring sexually transmitted diseases and unwanted pregnancies, and dropping out of school among others." She went on to explain that sexual violence occurs among other reasons due to their "provocative dressing" within the community. "This tempts boys and men to rape them. So many people especially men have resorted to drug abuse, which leads them to do immoral things at night in dark corners to those girls who move alone at night."[45] This switching of blame to the victims was relatively widespread, and could also be noted in the signposts (photos hereof are given in Chapter 3) carrying messages, among other things, calling for girls' abstinence to prevent sexual violence instead of making statements directed at potential perpetrators.

During a discussion with men, participants also noted that the livelihood limitations in the camp not only make refugees' overall lives difficult but also prevent some parents from paying school fees. Informants complained that, at times, "big men" come to the camp and "try to seduce our young girls." These men are said to be refugees as well as Ugandans, and lure girls in with gifts and various promises—especially ones of financial assistance with school fees, but also of marriage prospects.[46] However, threats of sexual violence even

---

[43] Female adolescent, 15 years old, journal writing, March 5, 2014, Bujubuli Secondary School.
[44] Female adolescent, 17 years old, journal writing, March 5, 2014, Bujubuli Secondary School.
[45] Female adolescent, 17 years old, journal writing, April 3, 2014, Bujubuli Secondary School.
[46] Discussion with male refugees, March 13, 2014, Base Camp.

occurred in supposedly protected spheres such as the school, and a number of adolescents referred to these risks. Among them, an adolescent pointed out that "at school most of the girls have been harassed by male teachers, through them demanding sex—and when they refuse, they are made to fail and of course that affects their education."[47] Another adolescent similarly stated: "In schools, girls are harassed sexually by some male teachers and boys. This takes the form of rape, defilement, and other harassment. Corporal punishment of boys and girls in schools also presents another form of violence against students."[48]

These issues are known by authority figures in Kyaka II; a female teacher also acknowledged such risks for girls. She explained that sometimes "teachers approach them for sex in order to award them more marks and get other privileges."[49] Moreover, an adolescent critically reflected on the extent of the violence and the role of aid agencies in it. He stressed that, no matter who the perpetrators are, aid agencies are "neglecting their work and don't follow up with those such cases, which is also a big violence against girls."[50]

Prostitution, Commercial Sex, and Sex for Favors

As a particular form of sexual violence, some in Kyaka II referred to the occurrence there of (forced) prostitution. Although this phenomenon was noted less frequently by research participants, the prostitution of adult and especially adolescent women was explained to occur as a consequence of the poverty and hopelessness in the camp. Forced prostitution was seen as arising due to coercion, by way of external pressure from fathers or partners. A notable aspect of the empirical data from Uganda is that it was mostly adolescents who expressed their fear of having to engage in prostitution, which they mainly spoke of in relation to access to education.[51] Among other individuals, one 17-year-old noted, "[v]iolence against girls in Kyaka is very common,"

---

[47] Female adolescent, 16 years old, journal writing, March 5, 2014, Bujubuli Secondary School.

[48] Female adolescent, 17 years old, journal writing, April 3, 2014, Bujubuli Secondary School.

[49] Female teacher, interview, March 25, 2014, Base Camp.

[50] Male adolescent, 17 years old, journal writing, March 5, 2014, Bujubuli Secondary School.

[51] Female refugee, dialogue, April 11, 2014, Bukere Zone; female adolescent 1, 16 years old, journal writing, March 5, 2014, Bujubuli Secondary School; male

and explained further that risks of violence and poverty can lead to school dropouts and "[t]his makes them desperate and hate their lives, hence resorting to prostitution."[52]

While such risks existing for adults and minors in refugee situations may have been overlooked in the past, awareness of them has generally grown in the past few years (see Ferris 2007; Williams et al. 2018). Aid workers in Kyaka II also spoke of sex for favors, 'commercial,' or 'survival' sex. One of them stated that "[c]ommercial sex is often carried out in the night, usually in bars and lodges" in Kyaka II and "Byabakora Zone has been found to be having the biggest and most expensive sex workers, followed by Bukere and then Sweswe." She added that it is "common to find married and unmarried women practicing commercial sex work as a source of earning [as they] do not know any other means to survive."[53] Other aid workers stressed how "women also practice adultery to solve their financial needs,"[54] and noted:

There is sex for favors when girls and women are forced to exchange sex for food or a better life, commercial sex [as] transactional sex when women, girls, and at times young men exchange sex for money, and survival sex where women and girls are forced to enter into sexual relations in order to be supported and to take care of their large families.[55]

Although sex for favors, commercial sex, and survival sex are not always directly imposed by another person, they nevertheless constitute forms of abuse and exploitation. In lieu of voluntarily engaging in sexual activities, the restricted and difficult livelihood conditions in Kyaka II rather compelled some people to undertake such work (see also Chapter 4). They therefore feel forced into it. Despite making several attempts during my research in Kyaka II to find out the scope of such risks in general as well as the extent to which aid workers are involved in these particular forms of sexual violence, it was unfortunately not possible to do so. No woman in Kyaka II dared to speak

---

refugee, dialogue, March 18, 2014, Bukere Zone; male adolescent, 15 years old, journal writing, April 4, 2014, Bujubuli Secondary School.

[52] Female adolescent, 17 years old, journal writing, April 3, 2014, Bujubuli Secondary School.

[53] Female aid worker, interview, May 11, 2014.

[54] Male aid worker, interview, April 14, 2014.

[55] Female aid worker, interview, April 10, 2014.

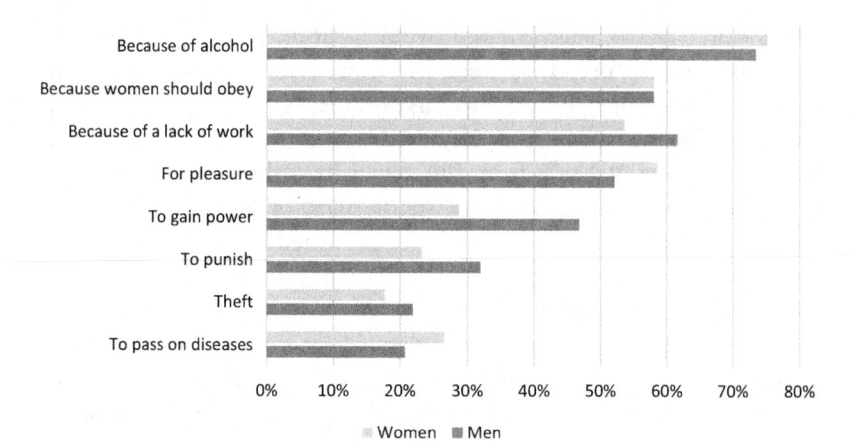

Figure 2.4 Perceptions of reasons for forced sex in Kyaka II

about her involvement in sex work, and aid workers mainly referred to some cases of colleagues' wrongdoing (see also Chapter 3).

Conditions of Sexual Violence

But why is sexual violence committed in Kyaka II? In addition to the role of limited livelihoods, an elderly man from DR Congo remarked: "It is better to force a woman to have sex because they do not want to give us men when we ask for it. They have to do it!"[56] A younger woman, however, stated that some men believed "they will be healed from HIV/Aids sleeping with them, which is why the men rape and defile young girls."[57] What these statements indicate is that the reasons for sexual violence are diverse, and cannot be subsumed to a couple of concrete factors alone.

For further insight into the conditions of sexual violence, the above-mentioned survey included a question on why participants believe forced sex occurs in Kyaka II. Of course, this covers only one form of sexual violence but it still sheds light on leanings regardless. The survey findings reveal several perceived reasons for the occurrence of this violence. While multiple answers were possible, Figure 2.4 illustrates a clear tendency in the answers that participants gave. Most responded that forced sex occurs 'because of alcohol,' while many

[56] Male refugee, dialogue, March 14, 2014, Base Camp.
[57] Female refugee, dialogue, February 27, 2014, Base Camp.

others said it takes place because 'women should obey,' 'of a lack of work,' or 'for pleasure.' Less often, participants noted that it occurs 'to gain power,' 'to punish,' and 'to pass on diseases'; a few referred to theft and taking away property. Additional individual responses included reasons of being from different tribes, the effects of war or stress, because leaders 'don't care,' poor rules, or 'too much love for sex.' These additional responses are not presented in the graph as each was stated by one participant only. The graph illustrates that the responses of women and men overlap, with a focus on alcohol, women's obedience, and theft. Yet more men than women thought that the lack of work, gaining power, and punishment contributed to forced sex, whereas more women than men believed it was due to pleasure or to pass on diseases. How these different positions are associated with humanitarian aid in Kyaka II and its occupants' understandings of gender roles and relations is discussed in subsequent chapters.

"Beaten like a drum": Domestic and Intimate Partner Violence

Domestic violence was also prevalent in Kyaka II, but it contrasts with the idea of 'home'—as symbolizing a site of "nurture, stability, reliability, and authenticity" (De Alwis 2004: 215). Studies about the home and home-making practices in refugee situations show the importance for displaced people of finding and establishing private zones of safety, comfort, well-being, and belonging while in exile (see Omata 2016; Čapo 2015; Brun 2015a; Brun and Fábos 2015). Distinguishing between a cultural-spiritual, a relational, and a practical home, Omata (2016) explores what meanings Liberian refugees in Buduburam refugee camp, Ghana, ascribe to their homes. These, thus, not only signify symbolic sites of safety and belonging, but the physical domestic spheres and houses also materialize these meanings. Omata portrays how their understandings hereof influence their decisions to remain in exile or to repatriate to their country of origin. In contrast to such protective private spaces of the home, the people in Kyaka II noted that domestic violence was widespread—with it mainly occurring between intimate partners.

Physical Abuse in Domestic Spheres
The high level of violence is revealed through the quote that I mentioned in opening this book, with it comparing physical abuse

in domestic spheres to being 'beaten like a drum.' Among such comparisons made, one woman spoke about how her husband married
another woman and then started beating her "like a drum."[58] This was
similarly noted in an interview with security personnel who underlined
that "[d]omestic violence begins at home" and some "men get other
women from outside" or "two wives," using physical force against
them and "not providing necessities to her children."[59] Many other
women in Kyaka II criticized how domestic violence was very commonplace, and how some men would "just beat the woman without
any explanation,"[60] some would do so when women "did something
wrong,"[61] and that some men would "never consider women to be
people"—with them being "beaten and forced to have sex in their own
homes."[62]

Domestic abuse was often framed as 'wife beating' by participants in
dialogues and discussions, and this appeared to be the most prevalent
form of gender-based violence in Kyaka II. In most cases, it was
described as men using physical force against women, mainly wives,
by hitting them. The likelihood and level of violence occurring would
increase when men had been drinking. In a discussion, women shared
various experiences.[63] One story they recalled and explained widely
was the then-recent case of a woman in Kyaka II who separated from
her husband due to the intensity of sexual abuse and domestic violence
she had to endure. They said that the woman was "beaten every
night," something widely known in the community where she lived.
When she decided to leave her husband, he moved back to DR Congo;
shortly thereafter, however, the woman was attacked. At night, a
group of men came to her home, broke down the door, and raped
the woman. Later, they killed her. The discussion participants accused
the husband of having planned the attack and having sent these men to
rape her, to prove that the wife was a prostitute.

Moreover, in another discussion, a 23-year-old woman who had fled
Rwanda with her sister after their parents were killed spoke of enduring domestic violence. In Uganda, she sought safety and got married

---

[58] Discussion 2 with female refugees, March 12, 2014, Base Camp.
[59] Security personnel, interview, February 26, 2014.
[60] Discussion 1 with female refugees, March 12, 2014, Base Camp.
[61] Female refugee, dialogue, March 18, 2014, Base Camp.
[62] Female refugee, dialogue, March 11, 2014, Bukere Zone.
[63] Discussion 1 with female refugees, March 12, 2014, Base Camp.

while living in Kyaka II. Yet she lamented: "The biggest problem here is that you can marry a man, thinking he is going to help you but later he marries another woman and then you are chased out of the house and left to be homeless. My husband would beat me every day like a drum."[64] Due to such issues, women emphasized in one discussion that victims of domestic violence often feared separating from their husbands. Although they wished to go far away to have some peace of mind and safe spaces for them and their children, they were afraid their husband would come after them or would send people to hurt them. Staying alone somewhere would therefore put them at risk, and safe shelters with protection systems were rare. They eventually reasoned that these dangers can force women to stay with the violent husbands, or to quickly find new partners "just to feel protected from the other men" but "who beat them as well."[65]

The issue of safe places and protection systems not only links up to the vital symbol of home as a private, safe, and protective space but also to the way refugee protection is realized and camps are run. In Kyaka II, so-called safe houses were set up in the form of tents pitched in the Base Camp for especially vulnerable people exposed to direct threats. In spite of these options to receive shelter, there were only few of these tents; furthermore, I saw a small number of them occupied during my research in Kyaka II. These safe houses merely provided an interim solution—one that may only last for a short period of time. And because of their location in the Base Camp, the safe houses as well as their inhabitants were visible to people passing through.

However, domestic violence was not limited to adults but also took place against minors. Among the accounts of adolescents, a 17-year-old who had escaped the war in DR Congo and arrived in Kyaka II in 2006 stated: "Some parents give corporal punishment to their children, for example they burn them, beat them heavily, and sometimes deny them their right to education, right to eat, right to play among others."[66] In addition to physical violence in the form of beatings,[67] such abuse also occurs in less overt ways. Girls and boys are generally

---

[64] Discussion 2 with female refugees, March 12, 2014, Base Camp.
[65] Discussion 1 with female refugees, March 12, 2014, Base Camp.
[66] Female adolescent, 17 years old, journal writing, March 5, 2014, Bujubuli Secondary School.
[67] Male adolescent, 18 years old, journal writing, March 5, 2014, Bujubuli Secondary School.

responsible for specific household tasks, such as girls for cleaning, washing clothes, cooking, and fetching water, while boys are to help cultivate fields. However, an adolescent rued, "[m]ost girls are over-worked in that they are given heavy jobs especially [at] home."[68]

This corresponds with other empirical studies about refugee camps documenting the scope and complexity of domestic violence against women, perpetrated as an act of control and power (Wachter et al. 2018; Horn 2010; Carlson 2005). Some have suggested that violence against women increases when humanitarian actors deliver specific support to women or promote their empowerment (Grabska 2011; Szczepaniková 2005; Horn 2010; Buscher 2009, 2017)—a correlation that will receive closer attention in the course of this book. Furthermore, Horn (2010) uses a nested ecological approach to domestic violence and illustrates how the individual, family, socio-economic, and cultural levels, as well as their interaction, all contribute to the likelihood of domestic violence occurring in Kenya's Kakuma refugee camp.

Conditions of Domestic Violence

But why was domestic violence so widespread in Kyaka II? The empir-ical findings reveal a similar yet also differentiated perspective on the complex aspects contributing to the high prevalence of such violence in the camp. As a part of the previously mentioned survey, the question was raised why participants believe domestic violence occurs in Kyaka II. Figure 2.5 outlines the responses received. While multiple answers were possible, most noted that they believed domestic violence to be committed due to 'drugs and alcohol.' Many alternatively said it was because of 'a lack of work or boredom,' 'women should obey,' 'to punish,' 'to take away women's property,' 'for pleasure,' and to increase their own power or women had gained too much power. The graph shows that the responses of participating women and men widely overlapped concerning most of the conditions. However, more women than men believed that domestic violence occurred due to pleasure whereas more men than women considered it to take place because women should obey and because men were striving to gain power. This requires an overview of Kyaka II's setting. With the camp

---

[68] Male adolescent, 19 years old, journal writing, April 3, 2014, Bujubuli Secondary School.

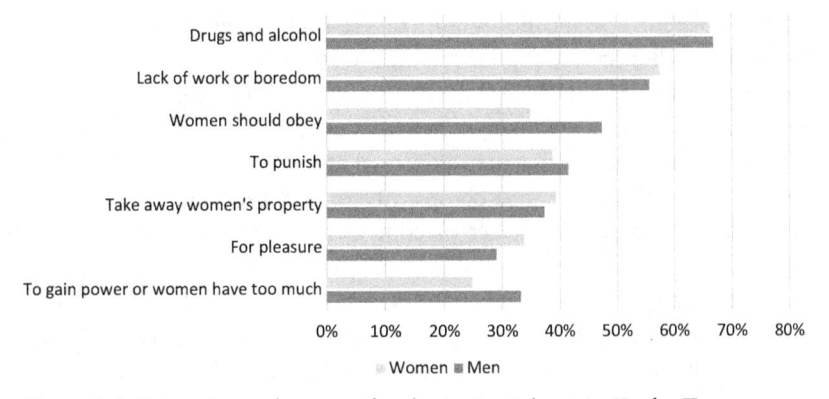

Figure 2.5 Perceptions of reasons for domestic violence in Kyaka II

being in a rural, remote region, with the next big city about an hour's drive away, opportunities in the camp are limited. Moreover, humanitarian agencies regulate camp life through the aid measures undertaken. The reasons participants noted for the prevalence of domestic violence link up to this sparse setting. Insufficient opportunities for employment are likely related to the setup and the location of the camp, drug and alcohol consumption to the restrictive conditions onsite, and women's assumed disobedience with the aid structures that often focus on them as especially vulnerable and thus in need of prioritized aid.

"Married at a tender age": Forms of Structural and Cultural Violence

In addition to the above-discussed forms of largely direct and physical violence, structural and cultural types also occurred in Kyaka II—mainly in the guise of the denial of resources or the early/forced marriage of minors, respectively. None of these forms of direct, structural, and cultural violence stand alone, but occur in interrelated ways and thus are interdependent with one another. Drawing on a gendered understanding of the Galtungian concept of violence, the denial of resources as well as early/forced marriage constitute specific forms of gender-based discrimination and thus structural and partly cultural violence. These can, however, lead to or be connected with physical risks too. Such forms of gender-based violence were found to mainly affect women and girls.

Early and Forced Marriage

For many children, refugee situations mean a long confrontation with challenges, being trapped in camp settings, dependent on humanitarian agencies and structures, and faced with an uncertain future (see Ensor and Gozdziak 2016; Hart 2014; FMR 2002). At times separated from their families or exposed to insufficient protection and assistance, such circumstances can leave them in limbo and with poor conditions to grow up in. Considering the obstacles and hardships on-site, Harrell-Bond (2000) raises the fundamental question of whether refugee camps are even good for children and stresses the lack of protection and assistance—including basic services—in them. In contrast to growing up with stabile support structures and spaces to play and be children, studies stress the dangers of trauma and possible posttraumatic stress disorder (PTSD) and other disorders (see Vossoughi et al. 2018)—which may remain insufficiently treated in aid programs. Many children, therefore, find themselves in situations "characterized by feelings of loss, deprivation and hardship so intense that they shape to a large extent the ways boys and girls come to think about and try to make sense of their lives" (Mann 2012: 458).

During journal writing in Kyaka II, about half of the participating male and female adolescents highlighted that girls are confronted with risks of early and forced marriage. One individual noted that "most girls here in Kyaka have been denied their right of getting married at the correct age, and even they are made to marry by old men."[69] Another linked early and forced marriage with sexual abuse and the rejection of education, emphasizing in his journal writing:

First of all, there is forced marriage for girls. Some parents have deliberately given off their young girls for marriage, with old men denying them education. There is also a sex-based violence that is incest, for real, thus it has happened several times that some people are involving their young close relatives in love affairs who are mainly girls and give them no chance to refuse.[70]

A great difference among girls and boys was noted in this respect, as a "girl can be forced by her parents to get married when she is still [too]

---

[69] Female adolescent, 16 years old, journal writing, March 5, 2014, Bujubuli Secondary School.

[70] Male adolescent, 16 years old, journal writing, March 5, 2014, Bujubuli Secondary School.

young to get married. The boy cannot be forced in marriage when he does not want to."[71] Reasons for early and forced marriage are not only found in cultural traditions and customs among certain refugees, who believe that girls should be married at a young age. One woman from Rwanda underlined that refugees from her country received less humanitarian support, which complicated the situation of how to take care of their children and ensure that their needs are met. As a result, she said: "At times we are forced to send our girl children early for marriage to Congolese men or Ugandan men so that they can have a sense of belonging and be accepted."[72] This not only indicates the deep interconnection with questions of ethnicity but especially also touches on the link between the various shortcomings in the camp and forced and early marriage. Since the girls' families or caretakers received financial bride prices for giving the daughters away, forced and early marriage was also economically motivated or driven by income deficiencies.[73]

The difficult and oftentimes poor living conditions, alongside the various limitations to earning sufficient income in the camp, can be seen as decisive factors behind some parents arranging marriages for their daughters. Other studies also refer to the economic incentives contributing to parents' and caretakers' decisions to have their daughters married early. With a focus on Syrian girls in Lebanon, Bartels et al. (2018) show that about 40 percent of their 1,346 research participants spoke of child marriage. Despite the similar economic, social, and security issues noted, the study also saw different perspectives raised by female and also male participants—with women mainly referring to concerns of protection, security, or education, whereas men primarily speaking of financial insecurity or sexual exploitation. In another study about child marriage among Syrian refugees in Lebanon, Mourtada et al. (2017) stress that these practices were common already prior to the conflict in Syria. In Lebanon, additional issues contributed to the prevalence of child marriage, including insecurity, insufficient education, and economic instability.

---

[71] Male adolescent, 17 years old, journal writing, March 26, 2014, Bujubuli Secondary School.

[72] Discussion 2 with female refugees, March 12, 2014, Base Camp.

[73] Female adolescent, 17 years old, journal writing, March 5, 2014, Bujubuli Secondary School.

Such safety and social problems as well as insecure economic conditions were also found in Uganda's Kyaka II. One adolescent there precisely pointed out that "[t]here is forced marriage for girls where parents want to get money to care for the family, and then force young girls to get married without them wishing to."[74] Another similarly stressed that "[p]arents are going bankrupt, and decide to give the daughter to a married man." She further highlighted that the risks of physical violence affected female child brides particularly, as their husbands often beat them.[75] These economic issues undoubtedly contribute to early and forced marriage being relatively common practices in Kyaka II.

Denial of Resources

The second form of violence addressed here, denial of resources, describes the rejection of access to specific resources by intimate partners or family members. An aid worker explained the denial of resources as including "denying shelter to a person, denial of right to economic benefits, denial of support, school fees to the children, etc. The women are always denied these things by their spouse or even their family relatives and in-laws."[76] Two examples were frequently brought up by refugees in Kyaka II: the denial of access to agricultural and monetary resources by intimate partners as well as the denial of access to education for girls, both carrying complex consequences.

On the one hand, people in Kyaka II often referred to the tensions arising due to the denial of harvest yields—and to subsequently increasing levels of domestic violence. Women and men explained that husbands would frequently sell the crop and spend the money on alcohol without sharing the profits or food with their wives and families. When women asked for their share, men would use physical force against them—especially when drunk.[77] Such perspectives were not only shared by refugees, but also by humanitarian and governmental agency staff too—who spoke in conversation of the close

---

[74] Female adolescent, 17 years old, journal writing, March 5, 2014, Bujubuli Secondary School.

[75] Female adolescent, 15 years old, journal writing, March 5, 2014, Bujubuli Secondary School.

[76] Female aid worker, interview, May 20, 2014.

[77] Discussions 1 and 2 with female refugees, March 12, 2014, Base Camp; discussion with Refugee Welfare Council leaders, March 19, 2014, Base Camp.

connection between harvests and domestic abuse. An interview with security personnel underscored these threats. In addition to noting that domestic violence is very common in Kyaka II, she stressed: "The men, they are beating their wives. This mostly in the days of harvesting seasons. They get food at home, so the man decides to take all the food or all the money after selling their harvests [...]."[78]

On the other hand, although primary education is supposed to be free and accessible for girls and boys alike in Kyaka II, girls often lack access to primary and/or secondary education. While one adolescent stated "I am afraid of not proceeding with my studies,"[79] another explained:

Some parents refuse to pay school fees for girls because they believe it is a waste of money to educate the girl child. They give us a lot of work at home like fetching water, washing clothes, and cooking. This does not allow us to have time to read our books. [...] They undermine us girls because our parents believe we are useless in the families. Some parents believe that taking a girl to boarding school is going to waste their money on school fees. As a result, the girl is not given enough requirements such as books and pads. That is why they undermine us as girls.[80]

The fear and risk of girls having to drop out of school was widespread, and occurred even though humanitarian agencies undertook campaigns to promote girls staying in school. High dropout rates among girls were either caused by caretakers being unable to pay school fees or due to cultural beliefs about traditional gender roles. Such notions include the one that it is women who are responsible for looking after domestic spheres, which is why girls would not need an education.

These hardships, dangers, and fears are influenced by the experiences and impacts of conflict, forced migration, and life in refugee camps; they are also affected by and rooted in social and family structures however. In Kyaka II, insecurity, restrictive living conditions, lack of livelihoods and employment, as well as fractured family structures created intense challenges for adults and children alike. Children feared that families may separate and break apart, removing

---

[78] Security personnel, interview, February 26, 2014.
[79] Female adolescent, 18 years old, journal writing, March 5, 2014, Bujubuli Secondary School.
[80] Female adolescent, 16 years old, journal writing, April 3, 2014, Bujubuli Secondary School.

sources of stability and safety in the home.[81] One adolescent explained his fears as follows:

When I arrived here in Kyaka II life was not altogether good. After a few years, my father died, that was in 2004. Then life became worse, although refugees were given some help by providing us with everything we wanted besides money. But now, I don't know whether I will continue with my studies because my mum is getting old, she is jobless and poor, and she is unable to afford the school fees. I'm really studying now because of God's mercy, otherwise my life is really in danger. What a miserable life this is![82]

This quote is indicative of the earlier-mentioned "feelings of loss, deprivation and hardship" (Mann 2012: 458) that refugees must live with, and provides insight particularly into the challenges and fears of an adolescent who had lived in Kyaka II for more than a decade. These fears go beyond physical violence, and also include structural limitations in the context of protracted refugee situations. Worries about access to education, the family's livelihood, or even things as fundamental as food reveal how the camp structures within which many refugees have to live contribute to the exacerbation of these issues. They are rooted in diverse life conditions including, among other things, a lack of basic services, restrictive living conditions, and insufficient livelihood opportunities. The general living conditions in the camp are framed by these limitations, and by the remote and isolated geographic location. Due to the latter, adults lack access to employment and thus can only insufficiently support their families.

"Some women beat their husbands": Women as Perpetrators

Without any doubt, it is an achievement from feminist scholars and activists that gender-based violence against women in conflict, post-conflict, and refugee situations is no longer trivialized as being the mere result of men's "sexual urge" (critical Seifert 1996: 35). With research revolving around women in the past, they were seen as the prime victims of violence. Concerning humanitarian crises, Hilhorst et al. point out: "Women are deemed homogenously more vulnerable than

---

[81] Female adolescent, 16 years old, journal writing, March 5, 2014, Bujubuli Secondary School.

[82] Male adolescent, 18 years old, journal writing, March 5, 2014, Bujubuli Secondary School.

men, and are more associated with victimhood" (2018: 56). This has resulted in the neglect of gender-based violence suffered by men and that committed by women. Yet scholars in Peace and Conflict Studies increasingly reflect women as perpetrators in conflict and post-conflict situations. In an early volume on the subject edited by Moser und Clark (2001), the different roles of women as victims, perpetrators, and actors in armed conflict and political violence—alongside the possible dangers of men being victims—are explored. Further studies have focused on female soldiers, women committing violence during the Rwandan genocide, or on sexual violence during the conflict in DR Congo (see Sjoberg and Gentry 2008; Coulter 2008; Johnson et al. 2010; MacKenzie 2012; Brown 2014).

This perspective on women as perpetrators of gender-based violence has remained largely ignored in Forced Migration and Refugee Studies. In her research on women's roles in the rebel group Democratic Forces for the Liberation of Rwanda active in eastern DR Congo, Hedlund (2018) understands some of the study participants as refugees and thus draws linkages to forced migration. Yet she essentially explores the rebel group and how women fear threats of as well as participate in violence. To the best of my knowledge, there has been no study regarding women in refugee camps committing violence, indicating a key gap in the literature. The need for further analysis is supported by findings from a growing body of research on female offenders in Peace and Conflict Studies; they may not be immediately applicable to the conditions in refugee camps though. While such studies often explore the intertwined roles of women as soldiers, 'bush wives,' and victims in (post-)conflict regions, overall conditions in refugee camps differ. Despite possible rebel activities, camps are highly regulated settings governed by political and humanitarian agencies.

A clear demarcation between women as victims, actors, and perpetrators in times of (post-)conflict and displacement is rarely possible, as they—as people in general do—hold and fulfill several roles simultaneously. For the scholarship, though, it is important to capture and reflect on the variety of roles upheld to better understand local social structures and their effects. This ultimately means to not only view women as victims, possibly idealizing their vulnerabilities, but to address their roles as actors too—which could include as perpetrators of violence.

Although most women, men, girl, boys, and aid workers in Kyaka II believed that women represented the main group of victims of gender-based violence, the survey as well as qualitative data from dialogues and discussions also specified violence perpetrated by women. In the above-discussed survey, the number of participants who identified female refugees as perpetrators is significantly lower than the majority view—with most believing violence to be mainly enacted by male refugees. The data nevertheless indicates the existence of women as perpetrators. A gendered breakdown of the figures further illustrates that a high number of both participating men and women referred to men as perpetrators, yet female participants identified women as perpetrators three times more often than male participants did (see Figure 2.2). These numbers are certainly very low; however, they suggest that if women did commit violence, they mainly did so against other women.

Insights gathered through dialogues and discussions further reflected the forms of violence committed by women. The following section about violence against men will address accounts of violence by women against men. Among others, male adolescents described their painful experiences herewith. They explained how a woman harassed them, and how female teachers sexually abused boys in school.[83] Other men shed light on stories about neighbors and friends who were confronted with domestic violence from their wives.[84] Moreover, an employee of a humanitarian agency noted: "Many times, women take advantage of men's sexual weakness and entice them in."[85]

The people who took part in my research in Kyaka II seldom discussed gender-based violence against men as well as that perpetrated by women to a similar level of detail and openness as that committed by men against women. That such hesitation arose does not mean the risks hereof did not exist, but instead that they represented a social taboo—as revealed in the continuously brief references participants made to assault by women. A crucial observation in this context is that many who spoke of violence by women stressed that these are few or rare cases, and that the abuse of women is much more prevalent. The following examples show the close similarities in their argumentation:

---

[83] Male adolescent, 15 years old, journal writing, April 4, 2014, Bujubuli Secondary School; male adolescent, 15 years old, journal writing, April 3, 2014, Bujubuli Secondary School.
[84] See male refugee, dialogue, March 5, 2014, Base Camp.
[85] Female aid worker, interview, May 11, 2014.

"There are some women here who beat their husbands, but they are few."[86]

"Congolese women beat their husband because they drink [but there was] one case in which a husband beat the wife to death."[87]

"Ugandan women do not beat their husbands. They are very peaceful. But Congolese women beat their husbands especially when they are drunk, but husbands beat wives more often."[88]

Relatedly, security personnel explained: "I witnessed one fight when they were co-wives. But men, they fight when they are in bars."[89] According to interviews and dialogues, violence perpetrated by women against 'co-wives' was due to disputes over rank and resources. "Polygamous homes are often violent with co-wives fighting, failing to balance the services to all," as noted by a young man from Rwanda. He then explained: "On my side I do not recommend polygamy because it causes a lot of violence in the community."[90] An aid worker noted similarly:

[I]n most cases we have had SGBV [i.e. sexual and gender-based violence] cases from polygamous families. Most polygamous men do not treat their wives equally, for example you find a man taking saucepans and other things from the old wife to the young wife which often triggers quarrels between the two. Some young women will often confront the old one, for example to pick a fight such that the old woman is hated by her husband.[91]

However, violence was not limited to co-wives but also directed toward children or strangers. It appeared to still be linked to the dynamics of marital relations; as one aid worker articulated, "[it is about] women beating co-wives or even a woman in an extramarital affair with the husband. In some cases, a certain wife beats the wife of another man; maybe, she heard rumor-mongering or saw the man with another woman and tells his wife."[92] One woman also spoke about how rumors contribute to women's violence against other women at more length:

---

[86] Female refugee, dialogue, March 5, 2014, Kaborogota Zone.
[87] Female refugee, dialogue, March 18, 2014, Sweswe Zone.
[88] Female refugee, dialogue, March 23, 2014, Base Camp.
[89] Security personnel, interview, February 26, 2014.
[90] Male refugee, dialogue, March 18, 2014, Base Camp.
[91] Male aid worker, interview, March 18, 2014.
[92] Male aid worker, interview, March 25, 2014.

Here in Kyaka II, one day while I was up doing my business, my neighbor called me and said come I give you some milk. I said I don't take milk. The following day, the wife to that man came to my home and asked me to go to her home and then took me to her house. She asked me why I was talking to her husband when she doesn't talk to me. She had a metal [stick] and she used it to hit my hand. I reported the case to the police but the perpetrator has not been given any punishment. The police asked me why I went to attack someone else at their house, even though I didn't attack her. Nothing has been done except for the treatment of my hand. The woman beat my arm with a heavy-metal object. The arm is all wrapped around with a bandage. Also my children are being beaten for nothing. That woman now sends other women, her friends to insult me, to verbally abuse me. They tell me I am a prostitute, that I take other people's husbands because me, I have no husband. Everyone knows that I don't sleep around, but I get accused and I feel scared all the time, scared of people.[93]

This woman further emphasized her helpless situation in Kyaka II, being unable to afford school fees for her children and having insufficient food: "I don't have any relatives here, I am just alone." While I reflect on the relevance of social support systems in Chapter 5 about coping, this narrative exemplifies how women are not only victims but can also be perpetrators of violence. Her explanation of being assaulted because she spoke with the woman's husband was similarly mentioned during discussions with other women too. They stressed that women tend to be suspicious of single women trying to "snatch their husbands."[94]

Reasons for resorting to violence can of course differ from case to case, but these narratives suggest that women mainly committed violence due to personal motives in the private sphere. This is supported by other studies, going beyond the focus on forced migration, that note the level of violence in domestic spheres perpetrated by women (see Carney et al. 2007). Yet, existing works on gender-based violence in refugee situations center on male offenders and neglect female ones. While structural issues of limited livelihoods and job opportunities as well as the influences of drugs and alcohol were stated to contribute to the likelihood of physical violence being enacted by men against women, similar conditions appear to apply to violence being unleashed by women against their husbands or intimate partners. Particularly in

[93] Female refugee, dialogue, March 26, 2014, Bukere Zone.
[94] Discussion 1 with female refugees, March 12, 2014, Base Camp.

domestic spheres, beating men seems to be linked to women's frustrations arising from a lack of resources—at times, also when drunk.

A key reason for violence being perpetrated by women against other women appears to be the perceived 'need' to defend one's own social and family circle. Violence against co-wives in polygamous relationships was intertwined with questions of power and hierarchy within families. This relates to, but sheds different light on, gender-based violence constituting a performative practice inherently entangled with gender identities and social power orders (see Confortini 2006: 356). Women physically 'defending' their position in family hierarchies against other, mostly 'newer,' wives or keeping women away from 'their' husbands points to motives of maintaining power and retaining access to resources.

Although most research participants in Kyaka II spoke of the high prevalence of gender-based violence against women, the preceding narratives reveal the existence of abuse enacted by women too—and thus the need for further research on the subject in Forced Migration and Refugee Studies. Despite the preliminary findings presented here, little is still known about how often, why, and in what forms women in refugee situations commit violence. These questions require exploration from various disciplinary perspectives, ranging from the Social Sciences to Psychology.

Gender-Based Violence against Men in Kyaka II

When I spoke with a man in his mid-thirties about life in Kyaka II and the risks of gender-based violence, he stressed the commonplaceness of domestic abuse against women but also noted the dangers men are confronted with. Our dialogue lasted about an hour, and after a short break between the stories, he shared details about violence between married couples as well as his own experiences of fights occurring between his parents, with his father frequently hitting his mother. Moreover, he stressed: "Men here fear!"[95] With this brief yet very powerful statement, he emphasized what was rarely ever addressed publicly: violence against men in Kyaka II.

In comparison with the vast number of narratives about violence against women in Kyaka II, such stories of gender-specific violence

---

[95] Male refugee, dialogue, March 5, 2014, Base Camp.

against men were shared significantly less often—and especially less openly. As explained below, the hesitation to speak freely was not only because of the tense political situation due to the anti-homosexuality bill enacted in Uganda at the time of research (see Chapter 1) but also because gender-based violence against men was then still viewed as taboo. Research in Forced Migration and Refugee Studies has in the past paid fairly little attention to the issues, hardships, and specifically to the gender-based violence faced by men; these were rarely recognized as gender-specific, and also in humanitarian projects, men in refugee situations are still mostly seen as perpetrators, troublemakers, or actors (see Olivius 2016). These tendencies risk neglecting and trivializing men's experiences of violence and forced migration as mere everyday and apparently normal issues.

Attention hereto has been slowly growing in recent years, however, with scholars addressing not only the difficult life conditions but also the forms of gender-based violence that men can experience, including sexual and domestic violence, and forced recruitment into conflict parties (see Turner 1999; Jaji 2009a; Henry et al. 2013; Kabachnik et al. 2013; Dolan 2014; Charsley and Wray 2015; McGinnis 2016; Chynoweth 2017; Janmyr 2017; Suerbaum 2018; Turner 2018, 2019). These risks occur on the basis of gender or gender-specific attributions, and are to be categorized as gender-based violence. In his research on Syrian refugees in Za'tari refugee camp in Jordan, Turner (2018), for example, depicts humanitarianism and masculinities. He analyzes how the increasing humanitarian tendency of engaging men and boys in debates and prevention activities regarding gender-based violence is realized in the camp. Focusing also on Syrian refugees, Chynoweth (2017) shed light on different forms of sexual violence against men and boys. The Women's Refugee Commission (2018) addresses the scope of sexual violence perpetrated against Rohingya men and boys in Bangladesh's Cox's Bazar in one of its reports, including accounts of both witnessing and experiencing sexual violence and physical assault.

Although the majority of research participants in Kyaka II discussed women as the main victim group, some also delicately spoke of gender-based violence against men—as did aid workers too. This is also reflected in the earlier-presented scope of gender-based violence, in which 16 percent of the participating men and 8.8 percent of the women were noted to believe that male refugees constitute the main group of victims of gender-based violence in Kyaka II (Figure 2.2). But which forms hereof were men and boys exposed to? The data reveals that men of different age groups were confronted with risks of militarized, sexual, and domestic violence, as well as structural and cultural forms in Kyaka II.

"They suffer silently": Sexual and Domestic Violence

Whereas adult men generally rarely spoke about sexual violence against men in Kyaka II, some participants nonetheless raised such issues on their own. Among them were two male adolescents who shared their personal experiences of sexual assault and harassment by both known and random women. One of them had experienced the killing of his parents during the conflict in DR Congo and been living with caretakers in Kyaka II for five years. He said that he was harassed by a woman in public. She approached him, and "asked me that we become friends and then have sex."[96] The other adolescent spoke about sexual harassment and abuse by female teachers, explaining that "[t]eachers also tend to use young students, especially female teachers using boys for sexual activities in school."[97] Neither of the two adolescents explained these situations in more depth, which indicates that the memories of their experiences still affected them deeply.

Few other studies also shed light on the issue of sexual violence against refugee men in the East African country. Nagai et al. (2008) reveal in an earlier survey with Sudanese refugees in Uganda and non-refugees in Sudan the high prevalence of sexual violence against men and women, both in refugee situations in Uganda and in a conflict-affected state in Sudan (see the table in Nagai et al. 2008: 258). Moreover, Dolan (2014, 2017) reflects on these risks for Congolese and South Sudanese refugee men. Based on research with Congolese refugees in Rwamwanja refugee settlement in western Uganda, he notes that out of 447 male refugees 38.5 percent had experienced sexual violence in their lifetime and 13.4 percent during the past year —and hence while already in the camp (Dolan 2014: 2). In a study with newly arriving South Sudanese refugees in northern Uganda, Dolan (2017: 27–31) finds a lower scope of sexual violence against

---

[96] Male adolescent, 15 years old, journal writing, April 4, 2014, Bujubuli Secondary School.

[97] Male adolescent, 15 years old, journal writing, April 3, 2014, Bujubuli Secondary School.

men compared to women but nonetheless diverse forms of gender-based violence that do also affect the former. In reaction to these risks for men as well as insufficient assistance being offered, the Refugee Law Project in Uganda—in which Dolan is the director—provides counseling and legal advice, and also supports clients to form self-help groups. Such support led to the founding of the Men of Hope Association in Kampala in 2012 (see Chapter 5 about coping strategies).

In Kyaka II, research participants also detailed the risks of domestic and intimate partner violence against men; again, only hesitantly though. In a discussion, local leaders emphasized that some men suffered violence when wives were drunk: "Alcohol is one of the causes [for violence]. Some women who also have money can beat their husbands."[98] Another man in his late twenties recalled memories of growing up in Kyaka II. He spoke of many incidences of violence at home, and noted: "My mother, she suffered. In fact, we all suffered." By that, he not only referred to himself and his siblings witnessing the violence against his mother but that they were also affected. "My father would come home and beat my mother and then he would also beat us children. You know when a man is beating your mother and then you the children, you come in to defend your mother. That's what used to happen."[99] The violence that he and his siblings were exposed to differentiated between boys and girls. Beatings of the boys were said to be more intense, and last longer.

The person I quoted earlier about men living in "fear" in Kyaka II recalled a then-recent incident he had observed. In his neighborhood, a woman turned violent against her husband:

My neighbor, his wife used to beat him. He was living three houses away from here. The man was being tortured; the wife was controlling everything and even beating him. She would even slap him in public. Because of the law in Uganda, the man wouldn't hit back. You know men, even if the law exists, they are always embarrassed to report. How will it be perceived by the public that a man was beaten by a woman? Personally, I wouldn't report to the police or the resettlement offices.[100]

---

[98] Discussion with local leaders, March 19, 2014, Base Camp.
[99] Male refugee, dialogue, March 5, 2014, Base Camp.
[100] Male refugee, dialogue, March 5, 2014, Base Camp.

In a similar way, other men cautiously mentioned such experiences of 'neighbors' or 'friends' too—but few directly addressed their own experiences of violence in domestic spheres. This reflects how violence against men still represents an almost 'unmentionable subject,' a taboo. This resonates with the findings of El-Bushra et al. about displacement in northern Uganda who find "openness about male survivors of sexual violence during the conflict seems to be increasing, [but] sexual violence after the conflict or within a community remains a taboo subject" (2013: 22). Such silence in a humanitarian setting like Kyaka II—especially when sitting in contrast to the widely discussed gender-based violence against women—is problematic. It hinders effective assistance and protection for *all* victims, reproduces (even unintentional) patriarchal gender systems of powerful men and vulnerable women, and essentially affirms that gender-based violence against men remains an issue off-limits.

The silence is expressive in itself; although such physical violence is highly visible, the silence makes it somewhat invisible. But just because few people (dared to) directly address these risks does not mean that they do not exist. Instead, Wokorach reflects the "loud silence" of male victims and survivors and highlights the lack of support (2020). Moreover, in his research about male sexual-violence survivors in transitional justice processes in northern Uganda, Schulz explains such silence as a form of "continuous and systematic, externally imposed silencing [...] by various layers of neglect by society, his surroundings, his community and official institutions" (2018b: 594). This appears to apply similarly to the situation in Kyaka II. Although publically available overviews by UNHCR partly mention cases of gender-based violence against men (e.g., UNHCR 2014b), some aid workers neglected or appeared to downplay the extent and effects of gender-based violence against men, and only few even acknowledged its existence in Kyaka II. One aid worker merely stated, "[m]en are not raped"[101]; another said: "I can't say that men are raped, because on average we have received 1 percent of such cases; this was a 14-year-old boy who was sodomized after he was kidnapped to Kampala."[102] Others did recognize the risks to varying degrees, noting that men "are also raped

---

[101] Male aid worker, interview, April 14, 2014.
[102] Female aid worker, interview, May 20, 2014.

by fellow men"[103] and that "[m]en may not really experience physical violence, but will experience psychological violence and informal torture. For example, when their wives deny them sex or food. Their wives beat them in psychological ways."[104]

Despite these differing statements, some aid workers explained the lack of reporting as being because it is "difficult for men to speak out openly if they are raped or sexually abused because it will count negatively against them, being referred to as impotent men, hopeless, etc."[105] Another noted: "Men who are violated sexually are there, but most men hide these cases and never report them because of cultural values. They never report it because a man in their culture is not supposed to be beaten by a woman or looked down on by a woman."[106] In line with that, it was emphasized that "men are afraid to report abuse because they are shy, they suffer silently; at times, they are not heard."[107]

Research participants confirmed this and men's fear of stigmatization[108] but also addressed a lack of institutional assistance. A young woman from DR Congo articulated that "men also are being violated, and when they report it they are not helped because everyone knows it is mainly women who are always beaten."[109] Correspondingly, a middle-aged man from Burundi shared a story about a man in his neighborhood who suffered violence at the hands of his wife and others, but who was left without assistance—supporting the idea of imposed silencing.

The wife used to beat the husband, until he separated from her. Even then, she organized and set people to come and beat the husband; this made him suffer from kidney dysfunction. When the man was requesting help at the health center because the woman was still against him, he did not receive protection because he was the man and supposed to control his wife.[110]

[103] Female aid worker, interview, May 11, 2014.
[104] Male aid worker, interview, March 14, 2014.
[105] Male aid worker, interview, April 10, 2014.
[106] Male aid worker, interview, March 18, 2014.
[107] Male aid worker, interview, April 4, 2014.
[108] Male refugee, dialogue, March 5, 2014, Base Camp; female refugee, dialogue, March 18, 2014, Sweswe Zone; male refugee, dialogue, February 28, 2014, Base Camp.
[109] Female refugee, dialogue, March 18, 2014, Base Camp.
[110] Male refugee, dialogue, February 28, 2014, Bukere Zone.

"A man has no power": Cultural and Structural Violence

In addition to direct physical violence, the latter quote also hints at the other forms hereof that exist—ones that are less visible, or perhaps even entirely invisible to the naked eye: that is, structural and cultural violence. These forms were inherently intertwined with humanitarian aid programs and power structures, as well as cultural beliefs regarding gender roles and relations in Kyaka II. Although I will address both humanitarian aid and gender relations in more detail in the chapters that follow, their effects as forms of gender-based violence against men require reflection on here already.

On the one hand, humanitarian agencies have over the past few years placed increasing focus on offering aid to women as vulnerable victims and "an uncontroversial object of humanitarian concern," as Turner (2019: 595) frames it. Women are granted access to specific aid programs, among other things for their empowerment, and are at times given prioritized treatment. This also applied to aid in Kyaka II; whereas this focus on women has served their better protection, it has also affected men. On the grounds of their sex and gender, men have not been given equal or similar access to aid and opportunities, regardless of their background, experiences, and status—for instance, as single parents. This represents discrimination, and thus indicates the structural violence rooted in such aid programs.

The story above exemplifies this impact: the man had experienced violence committed by his wife and sought "help at the health center," but "he did not receive protection because he was the man."[111] In a similar vein, one local leader stressed in a discussion "only women get more help, not us men. Men do not learn about new things." With regard to protection activities by humanitarian agencies, another criticized that "sometimes SGBV programs violate men," whereas another stated, on the contrary, that "SGBV [programs] helps us to treat a woman like a human being."[112]

On the other hand, many women and men as well as most aid workers who participated in the research expressed that they adhere to patriarchal gender relations. In these, men were generally believed to be the decision-makers and providers while women (and children)

[111] Male refugee, dialogue, February 28, 2014, Bukere Zone.
[112] Discussion with local leaders, March 20, 2014, Base Camp.

were supposed to simply obey.[113] These gender relations were often substantiated by cultural and religious ideas and customs. However, the local conditions in Kyaka II complicated their realization; limited livelihoods, a lack of job opportunities, imposed humanitarian regulations, as well as aid at times prioritizing women made it difficult for men to fulfill the gender roles of providing for and protecting their families. Yet exactly these roles were largely expected of them by women and aid workers, which constitutes a form of cultural violence leaving some men in challenging positions.

Among the various accounts and perspectives shared by men and women, one man pointed out that the Bible would reinforce men's dominant positions and wives should adopt and submit to the husbands' culture for safety.[114] Others worried women would not pay men respect if they were unable to care for families.[115] While reflecting on conditions in the camp in a discussion, local leaders also pointed to the grave livelihood limitations affecting gender relations. One said that men mostly keep the money gained from selling crops but the wife at times "steals" it to "keep it in her home," stressing: "That's violence to men."[116]

In contrast to the hesitant way in which direct physical forms of gender-based violence such as sexual and domestic abuse were discussed, men in Kyaka II widely criticized these structural and cultural forms hereof. Interestingly, they were often addressed as intertwined phenomena—being perceived as unjust treatment and unfair conditions for men. One man explained that women received "favors" from aid agencies in Kyaka II, and therefore had "more power than men"—which differentiated the site from DR Congo, where men had dominant roles.[117] In a discussion, a religious leader furthermore noted, "a man has no power, has no property, and therefore this has caused problems and separation in the family because some women have taken over. For example, some women want to get food cards to put themselves and their children first, and the man is left out."[118]

---

[113] Variation in gender roles and relations existed, but this represents the overarching view; see Chapter 4.
[114] Discussion with male refugees, March 13, 2014, Base Camp.
[115] Discussion with male refugees, March 13, 2014, Base Camp.
[116] Discussion with local leaders, March 20, 2014, Base Camp.
[117] Male refugee, dialogue, March 17, 2014, Sweswe Zone.
[118] Discussion with refugee religious leaders, March 19, 2014, Base Camp.

That men often perceive displacement and humanitarian aid and especially gender programs as discriminative is also addressed in other studies (see Turner 1999; Lwambo 2013).

Being vulnerable to violence does not correspond with or even seem appropriate to the strength and dominance that men—as well as women, youth, and aid workers—ascribe to men and masculinity in Kyaka II and beyond. Yet men's ascribed gender roles as well as their treatment in aid programs represent issues of cultural and structural violence. This, in turn, contributes to the silence and the silencing of male victims of sexual and domestic violence. That this silence was not limited to individual choices in speaking out about abuse or not but rather occurred due also to structural constraints in the refugee-aid system within the camp was illustrated by men's vocal criticism of their own lack of assistance (see also Chapter 3).

"Establishing that thing of the jungle": Militarized Violence

Militarized violence, and with it forced recruitment into armed groups, as forms of gender-based violence against men and boys can also occur in refugee situations (see, e.g., Carpenter 2006; Muggah 2006b; McConnachie 2014; Jansen 2011; Lischer 2005; Salehyan 2007). Muggah (2006a), Janmyr (2017), as well as Haer and Hecker (2018) address respective issues in refugee and internally displaced person (IDP) camps in northern and western Uganda, suggesting the prevalence of these risks. During my research in Kyaka II, the subject was rarely discussed by interlocutors; yet the few accounts that were shared are insightful, and reveal militarized violence and its accompanying recruitment dangers.

Among these accounts, one man posited that "rebels and trained soldiers" from DR Congo were living in Kyaka II, whom he identified as members of M23. He said that they were living "together with civilians" (as a descriptive term for nonmilitarized displaced persons), and argued that they should instead stay "in a separate place"—also because they "steal food from people's gardens." He furthermore expressed worries: "The M23 people fight among themselves and other refugees every time. These still have [the] mentality of staying as rebels. They are not supposed to live with fellow refugees."[119] Insights offered

---

[119] Male refugee, dialogue, March 18, 2014, Base Camp.

by a local authority figure and an aid worker supported this. In addition to local theft and violence, the latter mentioned the consumption of marijuana as an issue; "the main perpetrators are child soldiers, M23, though this is not really confirmed," she said.[120]

The local authority figure, meanwhile, also noted the presence of "ex-combatants" in Kyaka II, and almost dismissively said: "They have a right to seek asylum like every other person as long as they come in a civilian manner."[121] Yet a person's form of involvement in a given war is relevant to their refugee status. The 1951 Refugee Convention states in its Article 1F(a) that provisions do not apply to a person who "has committed a crime against peace, a war crime, or a crime against humanity, as defined in the international instruments drawn up to make provision in respect of such crimes." This is effective in Uganda, as it signed the Convention; its domestic 2006 Refugee Act contains similar restrictions in its Article 5a too. Whether and how Ugandan authorities investigate such crimes remains unclear; the authority figure merely stated: "We start right away by telling them 'Yes, you are in a foreign land. In foreign lands, there are foreign laws [and] you must abide by them!'" Whereas he said some would comply, he also gave examples of "boys" who "had their command" and maintained military customs and hierarchies. He remarked of M23: "That's just a drop in ocean; there are very many groups, very many individuals [. . .] in the settlement." He even noted that "we had majors, people of high rank" in Kyaka II, and acknowledged: "There is still a gap in [the] rehabilitation of the ex-soldiers. It's a general gap in the whole country."

Effects of these individuals' presence were diverse; he assumed "such a character" can cause fear as "the community could feel they are coming to spy" or be "welcome" as "[t]he community feels that this person should pay for his having caused them to leave their homes. They want revenge." While vigilante justice is critical, he argued: "To us, all of them are refugees." However, he also pointed to gender-based violence against women and men, and narrated how some "still feel they are strong and can get a girl by force and rape. They think they still have those laws." Besides, he mentioned there are "[t]hose who have not been fully trained and those who are still growing up" and for

---

[120] Female aid worker, interview, March 26, 2014.
[121] Local authority figure, interview, March 19, 2014, Base Camp.

them "military activity, peer group influence, alcohol, and marijuana" are influential factors. While he recognized that some "are silent, they know why they have come," implying their search for safety, others would "tend to show that 'we are still carrying some strength,' they want to come here and establish that thing of the jungle." For that, they were "silencing other individuals who are around. Of course that affects those who have been here for a long time."

Exactly this tendency of 'silencing' others in Kyaka II may be the reason why rebel activities were so rarely discussed by research participants; however, his words about some seeking to 'establish that thing of the jungle' are meaningful and indicate militarization and the recruitment of (boy) soldiers. This was further confirmed by four religious leaders in a discussion. In a similar vein to the local authority figure remarking that militarized activities were targeted at men and especially boys, the religious leaders stated that it was "only boys."[122] One man explained:

The combatants being in the same place with civilians is a threat to the community. Some have been given refugee status, and some are still seeking asylum. They are a threat to the community. Some of them used to live in detention centers, and when they were destroyed they fled. When they moved here and settled, they formed a slum within Kyaka II. They are the ones who mainly rape, steal, and do drugs like marijuana. They are very many, and they roam around the villages claiming they are looking for jobs. They know when to steal, when to rape, because they were trained in doing all this.

Another commented: "Those rebels who were recruited are very unruly. They cannot be convinced or even counseled." He added that "[i]n some cases, they are given special treatment" by aid agencies, for example, in the prompt provision of food cards. Other participants supported this, and one criticized how it was "very unfair" that the combatants received aid. He also warned "other young people can imitate them, and this can cause danger to society," and noted that the recruitment of boys was "not voluntarily but it comes automatically. And in most cases we are not aware." After a short pause, one of the participants went on to add:

There is some rumor circulating that they are trying to form new rebel movements to go back to DR Congo and fight because of the frustrations

---

[122] Discussion with refugee religious leaders, March 19, 2014, Base Camp.

in the refugee camp. These are mainly brought about by the reductions in food from about 50 percent to 30 percent, which is not really enough for them so they are tired of life. You know people here are very frustrated, and if something similar happens, I think they will join.

This statement about a possible rebel movement being set up in the camp relates to academic debates about 'refugee warriors,' who are noted to form or engage in groups to go against the regime in the country of origin—as already addressed by Zolberg et al. (1986, 1989) over three decades ago. Since then, scholars have explored several cases all over the world (e.g., Perera 2013; McConnachie 2012; Leenders 2009; Adelman 1998). Jansen (2011: 81–122), for example, reflects a rebelization in Kenya's Kakuma refugee camp along with the causes and humanitarian responses. Milner (2005) discusses militarization and deficient demobilization in Guinean camps.

With regard to underage persons, a dual perspective on militarized violence and forced recruitment needs to be taken: the recruitment of boys into armed groups along with possible pressure to commit violence means that they are both potential perpetrators and victims.[123] As in many refugee camps, the living conditions in Kyaka II were shaped by uncertainty, difficulties, and limitations. Boys may have felt pressure to join such peer groups without knowing what would come; they may have looked for social alliances and a group spirit after experiences of war and displacement, and they may then have had to perform acts of violence to maintain their membership and roles in the group (for other cases, see Lee 2009; Achvarina and Reich 2006). Besides these boys' possible search for, or feelings of, belonging, fear could well have also affected them. This is illustrated by a statement of the local authority figure about an "M23 boy" in a leading position: "When these M23 boys came, they had their command. There was a young boy, when he would come the rest would stand and salute. They would not sit before he sits. He was around 14 years old."[124] In addition to the risk of violence committed by rebels, the authority figure indicated 'peer pressure'; the religious leaders, meanwhile, indicated an involuntary yet almost 'automatic'—and at times unnoticed—recruitment process. It is thus not only that, as the authority figure

---

[123] For a general discussion, see Honwana (2011); Denov (2010); Wessells (2006); Rosen (2005). For academic debates about this dual perspective, see Happold (2008); Derluyn et al. (2015).

[124] Local authority figure, interview, March 19, 2014, Base Camp.

stated, rehabilitation projects are lacking; protection projects to prevent recruitment in the first place are also found wanting.

Linking Violence in the Camp with Conflict and Flight

Especially feminist analyses in Peace and Conflict Studies have shown that the end of war does not represent an end of conflict-related violence in post-conflict situations (see Turshen et al. 2001; Giles and Hyndman 2004; Suhrke and Berdal 2012). Research in Forced Migration and Refugee Studies has shed light on the diverse forms of gender-based violence in refugee situations, especially in camps (see Martin and Tirman 2009; Buckley-Zistel et al. 2014). Moreover, scholars have discussed the impact of war on refugees, their decisions to flee as well as the concept of conflict-induced displacement (see Lischer 2005, 2007; Loescher and Milner 2005; Lubkemann 2008a; Adhikari 2013; Hovil 2016; Bank et al. 2017; Bohnet et al. 2018).

Despite such important research, and despite Agier noting that "camps [are] in the heart of wars" (2002: 319), cases explored in the two aforementioned fields of research remain fairly separate from each other, and violent conflicts are often reduced to a cause of flight.[125] However, the case of Kyaka II reveals paradigmatically how such refugee camps can actually embody specific post-conflict sites, ones where risks prevail. Moreover, as a result of the often insufficient linkage, only few scholars have explored how gender-based violence persists through conflict, flight, and encampment. The empirical insights from the women and men in Kyaka II suggest the existence of a continuum of gender-based violence.[126] Among the scholars who have addressed such a continuum, Ferris (1990) describes how women face different forms of violence during conflict, flight, and protected encampment. Cockburn (2004) discusses how diverse incidents of violence are connected across the 'uneasy' peace, conflict, and post-conflict settings, and stresses the power imbalance between women and

---

[125] Moreover, refugee situations have rarely been conceptualized or theorized as distinct post-conflict settings. For exceptions, see, among others, the research by Lubkemann (2008a) on social transformation, Milner (2005, 2011) on militarization and peacebuilding, and Jansen (2011) on refugee camps as warscape.

[126] Previous analyses on the continuum of gender-based violence primarily against women were published (see Krause 2017a, 2015a), which this part now expands on.

men. Alden (2010) analyzes the prevalence of gender-based violence against women in post-conflict reconstruction, while Abdi (2006) highlights particular dangers of sexual violence faced by women during war in Somali and encampment in Kenya.

In addition, Freedman not only reveals a continuum of violence against women in the context of persecution and asylum (2015a: 45–68) but she also sees the war-related violence within DR Congo as "a wider continuum of gendered violence which exist in the country" (2015b: 77–79). Nagai et al. (2008) take a psychological perspective in analyzing gender-based violence in the different phases of conflict, flight, and encampment. Moreover, El-Bushra et al. (2013) focus on ongoing violence against IDPs in Uganda due to the war and its aftermath. Complementing these studies, the research in Kyaka II reveals how and why gender-based violence in the case of refugees from DR Congo continues across conflict, flight, and encampment.

The scopes, forms, and conditions of gender-based violence experienced by both women and men reveal linkages from conflict zones to camps of eventual refuge. For that, it is crucial to look at the characteristics of the phenomenon—meaning the structures and relations binding together victims and perpetrators, the types and conditions of attacks, and the spaces in which violence occurs. *During conflict in DR Congo*, different forms of gender-based violence were committed mainly by members of armed groups. Among the main forms hereof, they perpetrated sexual violence primarily against unacquainted women but also men, as well as abducted and forcefully recruited men but also women. The violence took place primarily in public spaces and seemingly private ones—yet by entering homes and assaulting people so as to spread fear, these formerly private spaces turned public. In addition, domestic violence occurred between intimate partners but appeared fairly disconnected to the conflict per se. *During flight*, forms of sexual violence were committed by members of armed groups and partly by fleeing individuals—mostly against unacquainted women in public spaces, to cause fear, and in the course of theft. Men were primarily confronted with threats of forced recruitment into armed groups and it is likely that they also faced risks of sexual abuse. *In the refugee camp*, diverse forms of gender-based violence were perpetrated mainly by displaced men but also women, Ugandan nationals, and aid workers primarily against both unacquainted and acquainted displaced women but also men, and that in public and private spaces alike. Women were mainly affected by sexual and domestic violence, the denial of resources, as well as early/forced marriage, while men were exposed to structural and cultural violence, partly sexual and domestic forms as well as militarized ones.

In sum, a prevalent linearity exists herein—and with it, a continuum of gender-based violence across conflict, flight, and encampment. This continuum affects both women and men as potential victims and reveals patterns of diffusion; violence during conflict was mostly committed by unknown members of armed groups, but in the camp, it was also perpetrated by other refugees, by nationals, or even by aid workers. The violence thus increasingly seeps from public into private spaces too. In lieu of exploring forms of gender-based violence in each phase in isolation, conflict, flight, and encampment are revealed to be connected dynamically through social, political, and economic factors forming part of the surrounding contexts. The empirical findings from Uganda point to three key factors contributing to the violence in each of these phases: insufficient or ineffective law enforcement, traumatic events and their consequences, as well as gendered power structures.

Law Enforcement

Each of the phases of conflict, flight, and encampment is characterized by a lack—or at least the insufficient scope—of governance, legal regulations and protection, as well as law enforcement, along with impunity for perpetrators,—which increases the risk of prevalent and prolonged violence. While crimes during conflict are carried out on a broad scale and largely by members of conflict parties against their enemies and against civilians (Meger 2010: 126; see also Eriksson Baaz and Stern 2013a; Pratt and Werchick 2004), as evidenced above people that flee can also enact violence during flight. In these first two phases, authorities in DR Congo are generally unable to enforce the law and protect civilians due to conflict-related disruptions—or they are even involved in the violence themselves. Although Uganda's authorities and domestic laws as a country of asylum are supposed to protect refugees, and despite most of the latter being part of the refugee-aid system practiced in camps, the case of Kyaka II reveals gaps and insufficient legal structures exist there too.

Considering the scope of gender-based violence in the conflict in DR Congo and in Uganda's Kyaka II, insufficient law enforcement certainly poses a major problem. Whereas a local leader stated that "human rights and the Ugandan Constitution" would not allow violence against women and provide protection,[127] many others voiced opposing perspectives. In addition to criticizing the prevalent violence, those in Kyaka II explicitly stressed that there is "no strict law enforcement" in the camp[128] and reasoned that women cannot do anything against violence as "the law is not effective in Kyaka II."[129] In a similar vein, one woman explained that prior to the conflict in DR Congo, "if someone violates you, they arrest them and at the end of it all, they charge the offender a lot of money. But here, a person is arrested, after a few day days, three or four, the person is released without being charged anything."[130] An aid worker shared another unfavorable story, saying that she came across a case of a "man who had raped the woman back in DR Congo" and the latter then met him again in Kyaka II. The woman "got very scared and she reported the man because she was being traumatized." The aid worker assumed "he wasn't around to do the same thing, but then it is just because she was traumatized. The man was transferred to another settlement."[131] Thus, instead of legal investigation, the man appears to have been simply relocated.

Such perspectives were also shared by others, and they exist in stark contrast to the reports of humanitarian agencies about providing legal assistance, attending court cases, and visiting prisoners. This perceived lack of justice indicates that those affected had insufficient access to legal structures in Kyaka II. Other studies have explored and criticized deficient legal practices in refugee camps (see Lomo 2000; Crisp 2000; Holzer 2013), which I consider influential for the continued use of violence due to the impunity it grants perpetrators. This also applies to during conflict (Meger 2010: 127–128) and most probably flight too. Moreover, the general lack of reporting of cases has indirect effects on the perpetuation of violence. Victims in Kyaka II noted among other things their fear of increased violence if they reported cases, as they were likely not adequately protected from retribution due to

---

[127] Discussion with local leaders, March 20, 2014, Base Camp.
[128] Female refugee, dialogue, March 18, 2014, Base Camp.
[129] Discussion with male refugees, March 13, 2014, Base Camp.
[130] Female refugee, dialogue, March 18, 2014, Base Camp.
[131] Female aid worker, interview, March 26, 2014.

insufficient law enforcement;[132] yet legal steps cannot be taken if cases remain unknown.

Trauma and Traumatization

The impact of traumatic violent events that women and men are exposed to during conflict, flight, and encampment constitute possible causes of psychological disorders such as PTSD (see Vossoughi et al. 2018; Bogic et al. 2015; Johnson and Thompson 2008). Of course, being a political scientist without medical and psychology training, my view on the effects of trauma and traumatization is mainly influenced by the literature. From my understanding, the findings addressed in studies reveal the possibility that trauma is a contributing factor to the aforementioned continuum of violence. Psychology studies assume that about half of all victims of rape, war, and forced displacement suffer from PTSD (Flatten et al. 2013: 4). While this affects victims individually through, among other things, emotional withdrawal, insomnia, mental and emotional avoidance issues, and attachment disorders, increased irritability and aggressiveness are possible other symptoms too (Maercker 2009: 17–18; Flatten et al. 2013: 3–4). The latter may contribute to continued violence.

The narratives of the women and men in Kyaka II offer relevant insights here. As explained above, they spoke about having been confronted with different forms of gender-based violence during conflict, flight, and encampment. They further recounted suffering from nightmares about their violent experiences during conflict and flight, an inability to sleep, flashbacks during the day, increased alcohol consumption, continuous fear, and being easily irritated—all in line with the symptoms of PTSD. Just how intense the effects of experiences of violence can turn out to be is witnessable in the sharing of one young man. He fled the war in DR Congo, where his parents were murdered, and had been living in Kyaka II for seven years when we met:

I fear to be called an orphan. I fear to become poor in the community and in the future. I fear to be defeated in class because I am always the first. I fear to stay and live in the temporary house. I fear my fellows to give me a nickname. I fear to walk at night alone because the assassins may kill me. I fear anything against my religion. I fear the bad wishers to burn our house.

[132] Female refugee, dialogue, March 17, 2014, Bujubuli.

I fear my sister to be called a prostitute by my colleagues. I fear whether I will complete my studies. I fear how refugees are treated at school. I fear witchcraft. I fear to be caught in the wrong. I fear to be caught by disease. I also fear not to have a bright future in life.[133]

Such fears as well as flashbacks and an inability to sleep could suggest that those spoken with suffered from disorders caused by the traumatic events that they had experienced in the past. Additionally, perpetrators can be in the camp; in addition to the above story in relation to the lack of legal processes, an aid worker also stated: "In DR Congo, rape was not really a crime and when they fled, their perpetrators then also fled here following them and even raping them here in Uganda. Some were being raped in DR Congo and meet their perpetrators here. Actually some still marry those men that raped them back home."[134] Such meetings can put victims in very difficult situations, as they may bring back memories of wartime atrocities that they have been trying to cope with, and thus also prolong their suffering.

The complex impact of experiences of war and violence is also reflected in research from Psychology. One study on conflict-related violence in eastern DR Congo by Johnson et al. (2010: 559–560) found that of the 998 households surveyed, 50.1 percent of adult participants showed symptoms of PTSD and 40.5 percent of major depressive disorder. Another by Karunakara et al. (2004) underlines that experiencing and witnessing violence in refugee camps increases the likelihood of developing such disorders. Witnessing traumatic events is revealed to psychologically impact people more than experiencing violence, as it increases anxiety levels through the recognition of one's insecure situation.

Moreover, the sequence of victims' experiences and the risks of violence require consideration. Since people can encounter traumatic events during all of conflict, flight, and encampment, they may be exposed to extreme traumatization and transgenerational effects thereof. Scholars generally differentiate between additive trauma with multiple simultaneous incidents thereof, cumulative trauma with multiple independent but coincidental episodes, and sequential traumatization with several successively occurring experiences (Ermann 2005:

---

[133] Male adolescent, 15 years old, journal writing, March 5, 2014, Bujubuli Secondary School.
[134] Male aid worker, interview, March 18, 2014.

213; Figley 2012: 570). Cumulative exposure to traumatic events correlates with disorders arising; the more traumatic events that refugees are exposed to, the higher is the probability of disorders emerging (Maedl 2010: 65).

While psychology studies have referred to the likelihood of traumatization (especially PTSD) among those fleeing conflict (for research about refugees in Uganda see Karunakara et al. 2004; Ainamani et al. 2017; Ainamani et al. 2020), it is not only victims of violence who can suffer from it; perpetrators can too. While linear and exclusive explanations for the phenomenon may not be possible, such studies provide evidence for a correlation between aggressive behavior and symptoms of PTSD among current or former combatants. Regarding former child soldiers and violence in northern Uganda, Weierstall et al. conclude that "attraction to aggression when being exposed to the victim's struggling can lead to a substantial risk-reduction for developing PTSD" (2012: 1). Additionally, Hecker et al. (2015) explore the link between exposure to violence, trauma-related symptoms, and aggression among Congolese refugees in Uganda. The authors find a positive association between exposure to trauma and reactive aggression, but a negative one between appetitive aggression and PTSD. They state that "refugees who perceive witnessing violence and one's own aggressive behavior to be fascinating and arousing are more likely to integrate violence-related behavior, sensory input, cognitions, and emotions into the hunting network" (Hecker et al. 2015: 453).

Considering how widespread gender-based violence in the case of Congolese women and men during conflict, flight, and encampment was, it can be assumed that the identified continuum of gender-based violence correlates with the psychological effects of traumatization.

Gendered Power Structures

A third factor impacting on the continuum of gender-based violence is gendered power structures. Women and men generally experience conflict, flight, and life in refugee camps differently. To explain gender-based violence in conflict and refugee situations, scholars in Peace and Conflict Studies as well as Forced Migration and Refugee Studies have deconstructed prevailing assumptions and drawn on similar approaches. In the past, violence against women (during conflict especially) was trivialized; it was mainly seen as a part of the dichotomies of male perpetrators versus female victims and of gendered stereotypes of male strength, power, and independence in contrast to female peacefulness, docility, and innocence. In this context, sexual violence against women during conflict was explained as a "'regrettable side effect' of war" and perpetrated, as noted earlier, due to warriors' sexual urge (critical Seifert 1996: 36, 35). However, this reduces and legitimizes gender-based violence as being an inherent part of 'male nature' (Eriksson Baaz and Stern 2009: 498; Eifler and Seifert 1999: 13).

By deconstructing such assumptions, scholars have contributed to overcoming the banalization of gender-based violence against women in particular and later also men, and have developed an understanding of it as a politically and socially constructed act meant to weaken the other conflict party as well as civil society (see Turshen et al. 2000; Hirschauer 2014; Eriksson Baaz and Stern 2013a). In a similar vein, research in Forced Migration and Refugee Studies has revealed that violence against women in refugee camps is also context-specific. It is explained to occur in connection with the prevailing camp conditions of humanitarian power structures, men's loss of dominant roles, and exists also as a way to weaken women's roles (see Lukunka 2011; Grabska 2011; Krause 2015b). Important to note here is that researchers in both fields interpret gender-based violence as performative power practices, underlining therein the demonstration of (male) dominance.

But how does this relate to the continuum of gender-based violence? Similar to all social relations, gender ones are influenced by experiences and settings of coexistence. These change due to conflict and forced migration. Upon displacement, people find themselves in a new and unfamiliar environment—one that, in the case of a refugee camp, is regulated by hitherto-unknown actors. As a result of these changes, gender roles and relations have to be renegotiated. Forced migration, therefore, represents a gendered process. Both in Kyaka II and during their time in DR Congo pre-flight, men were discussed as the breadwinners and decision-makers, whereas women were said to be responsible for parenting and the household within a patriarchal social system. These structures reveal imbalances of power, yet ones with which the women and men spoken with were familiar. The conflict not only unleashed violence, but also disrupted entrenched social structures. In Kyaka II, women frequently took up new and/or additional responsibilities (which can be empowering but also overwhelming), while men appeared to lose erstwhile dominance. Moreover, humanitarian agencies took on influential functions. This translated into *unfamiliar* imbalances of power—ones perpetuating over the years in Kyaka II. In this struggle to reestablish social relations, orders, and hierarchies, gender-based violence seems to have become a tool of power and at times part of the renegotiation of gender relations—yet it was also part of gender systems prior to flight (see also Chapter 4).

In Conclusion: Beyond Isolated Cases of Violence in Camps

Refugee camps such as Uganda's Kyaka II are established to provide displaced people shelter and access to protection and assistance. Yet the various narratives of women and men that have been presented in this chapter reveal that these individuals continue to be confronted with risks, threats, and trauma long after having left the conflict setting, most prominently in the guise of gender-based violence.

The level thereof in Kyaka II is alarming. Women and men of different age groups were confronted with such dangers—ones not limited to certain spaces or moments in time within the camp. Whether when walking to school or at school, while farming or collecting firewood, or while at home, gender-based violence was widespread and omnipresent. Statements such as "violence is very common everywhere"[135] or women are "beaten like a drum"[136] epitomize the prevalence of gender-based violence against women and girls in Kyaka II, whereas those of "[m]en here fear!"[137] or "they suffer silently"[138] exemplify the hesitantly discussed risks hereof for men and boys too.

However, gender-based violence occurs not only in refugee camps. It has been shown how these risks in fact prevail across conflict, flight, and encampment, and thus constitute a continuum. In this regard, the academic debates about the nexus of conflict and displacement are significant (see, e.g., Zolberg et al. 1989; Loescher and Milner 2005; Lischer 2007; Adhikari 2013; Bohnet et al. 2018; Krause 2018a).

---

[135] Discussion with Refugee Welfare Council leaders, March 19, 2014, Base Camp.
[136] Discussion 2 with female refugees, March 12, 2014, Base Camp.
[137] Male refugee, dialogue, March 5, 2014, Base Camp.
[138] Male aid worker, interview, April 4, 2014.

While scholars in Peace and Conflict Studies have traditionally focused on conflict or post-conflict regions, those in Forced Migration and Refugee Studies have mainly addressed refugee situations. Beyond the latter's refugee and exile orientation or the former's conflict focus, conflict-induced displacement as a core concept can help us to systematically explore the life conditions of those affected, how they change, and how they may remain similar. Acknowledging the nexus of conflict and displacement, academic inquiry should neither treat exile as an isolated case nor conflict as a mere cause of displacement, but instead consider both prior conditions and conflict aftermaths.

Despite the growing body of literature on gender-based violence in conflict and refugee situations, several matters still require further research. The continuum of violence scrutinized in this chapter—including how and why risks persist, and, in turn, how they can best be prevented—should now receive close academic attention. Moreover, as detailed, women have rarely been seen as perpetrators and men as victims in Forced Migration and Refugee Studies; it therefore remains largely unknown how often and why women commit violence as well as how often and why men experience it. Finally, since diverse forms of gender-based violence were found to be widespread in Kyaka II, the question arises of how this is linked to the very aid structures in the camp put in place precisely to protect and assist refugees. Are such measures in fact sufficient for the protection of these people? Do they reduce or perhaps even contribute to the levels of violence witnessed? Deficient law enforcement has already been examined in this regard; the connections between camp conditions and gender-based violence will be explored further in Chapter 3.

3 | *Humanitarian Aid and the Camp Landscape*

The life of a refugee is like left and right. We don't have assurance of life. They [the aid and government agencies] think for us we are refugees, if we can leave this country maybe we could be better. We are refugees but cannot make decisions of our own. [...] It seems you don't have identity, you don't belong. You are just there, like just something. Anytime they take decisions on you.[1]

With these words, a woman who had fled the war in DR Congo would criticize the aid and government agencies and their treatment of refugees in Uganda's refugee camp Kyaka II. It made her feel to have no identity, to be dehumanized. She later added that the dependence on the agencies' decisions "is what is disturbing refugees most." Some other refugees also reflected on the importance of assistance and protection and, thus, their access to much needed resources—but in fact all refugees spoken with raised points of criticism. One woman, for example, said: "I can thank UNHCR, I have learned many things in the settlement." Yet she went on to explain that her treatment by aid workers at times felt "minimizing," and that she would only be awarded "a low job" with aid agencies despite her high level of education.[2] Many others echoed these and additional concerns, complaining about insufficient aid, corruption, poor treatment, and the overall difficult camp life. Some victims of gender-based violence, as addressed Chapter 2, even lamented the limited support received. One woman from Rwanda who had been sexually abused and "reported all this to UNHCR" said that she was left without assistance, and was only told to "go back to Rwanda."[3] As revealed in these words, those in Kyaka II often named UNHCR in their accounts; when speaking they actually referred to the whole aid

---

[1] Female refugee, dialogue, March 27, 2014, Base Camp.
[2] Female refugee, dialogue, March 27, 2014, Base Camp.
[3] Discussion 2 with female refugees, March 12, 2014, Base Camp.

system in the camp however, and used 'UNHCR' rather as an umbrella term for aid and government agencies.

Such critical narratives prompt a range of questions. What kind of protection and assistance are carried out in Kyaka II, and how? Do aid projects differ for women and men, and, if so, how? What are the effects of these differences for them? Against the backdrop of the prevalent gender-based violence recounted in Chapter 2, how do aid agencies seek to prevent and overcome such abuse? Do these agencies and their projects possibly link with or even contribute to the violence, and, if so, how exactly? These thorny issues form the core of this chapter and guide its analysis, allowing us to explore the overall structures, humanitarian power practices, and decision-making in Kyaka II as well as the scope and effects of aid delivery there.

Providing refugees shelter, protection, and assistance in camps like Kyaka II is not a new phenomenon, being common even before today's global refugee regime emerged with the establishment of the 1951 Refugee Convention and the founding of UNHCR (McConnachie 2016). During the First World War and the subsequent era of the Weimar Republic, camps were set up for control, ordered sheltering, and the provision of relief for refugees (Gatrell 2008; Oltmer 2017). Following the end of the Second World War, camps were widely used for displaced persons and refugees in numerous European countries, and, as Malkki points out, they became a "standardized, generalizable technology of power [...] in the management of mass displacement" (1995b: 498). This mode of control has persisted to this day. Since the 1960s, forced migration has primarily occurred in regions in the Global South, where many countries of asylum continue to use camps[4]—often over protracted periods of time (see Milner 2014; Kibreab 2007).

Although over the years different types of—or names for—camps have been distinguished in the humanitarian discourse, they have similar setups, structures, and services. Refugee camps generally comprise temporally and geographically limited spaces in countries of asylum, being purposefully created to shelter, assist, and protect refugees until, as mentioned in Chapter 1, one of the three durable solutions is found. The governments of asylum countries, and often

---

[4] It is generally up to the government of the country of asylum to decide whether refugees have to stay in camps while in their country.

UNHCR, administrate over the camps, while mainly NGOs deliver aid within them (see Inhetveen 2010; Turner 2010; Agier 2011; McConnachie 2014; Janmyr 2014b; Krause 2018b). Over time, the camps have turned into a key aspect of the humanitarian system, granting the governments and aid agencies access to the displaced as well as a certain degree of control over them. This point applies in locations all over the world.

The protracted use of many camps poses a significant issue (Milner 2014). Such sites largely serve the immediate and short-term supporting of refugees, but this usually remains an unfulfilled hope or even illusion because the durable solutions are rarely attainable shortly after these people's arrival in host countries and thus also their placing in camps. Kyaka II represents a case in point here: established first in the early 1980s and reopened in the 1990s, it is still in operation today. But this protraction is of global reach, affecting almost 78 percent of all refugees worldwide in 2018 (calculation based on UNHCR's statistics, UNHCR 2019a: 22–23). UNHCR's Executive Committee defines protracted situations as those where refugees live in exile for "5 years or more after their initial displacement, without immediate prospects for implementation of durable solutions" (UNHCR ExCom 2009: 3). UNHCR (2019a: 22) also often uses the margin of at least 25,000 refugees of the same nationality in the same situation. These long-running circumstances contradict the provisional structures and temporary services in camps, which are rarely created with planning for protracted stays in mind due to the aid logic behind it. Even if camps over time turn into city-like surroundings—"accidental cities" as Jansen (2011) frames them—government and humanitarian agencies stay in control. The typically short-term approach of the aid system positions camps as sites of transition, and refugee protection as transitory protection, but in reality, they find themselves in use for years or even decades. Indeed, I spoke with two men from DR Congo who have been living in Ugandan camps since 1965 and 1968 respectively, thereby demonstrating how protracted displacement becomes reality.

How camp structures and aid projects are operationalized in the case of Uganda's Kyaka II is addressed in the course of this chapter. The following part explores developments and humanitarian aid measures in the camp alongside investigating how hierarchies and the limited camp conditions affect those living there, arguing that refugees become 'protection objects.' The second part then centers on projects tackling gender-based violence, and their links with global refugee policies. It examines how humanitarian agencies strive to deliver protection against gender-based violence, and as part of that how they create, use, and reproduce the label of 'vulnerable women', making them 'vulnerable protection objects.' The third part revolves around the question of how aid projects and the camp architecture correlate with the prevalence of gender-based violence. It considers aid workers perpetrating violence, structural effects of aid, and risks resulting from the camp landscape. Before concluding, the fourth part reflects whether the broad critique on aid and the camp is reasonable in light of the challenges aid agencies face.

Humanitarian Landscape in Kyaka II: A Matter of Power and Restrictions?

When driving to Kyaka II, one may not immediately recognize where the camp starts and where it ends. The local village-like scheme is structured into zones and clusters connected with untarred field tracks and ends without a border fence. Kyaka II blends, then, into its natural surroundings.

Merging somewhat into the surrounding landscape is typical of many refugee camps in fact. Despite the confined sites and spatial definition of camps, their territories are not always enclosed with fences—with these locations often remaining indistinguishable from the 'outside.' Camps are mainly established with provisional aid structures in rural regions of countries of asylum, and at times close to national borders. The remote locations of camps contribute to physical, social, and economic separation from the outside world; they nevertheless offer humanitarian and government agencies the aforementioned control over the camp's inhabitants as well as direct access to them (Agier 2011; Turner 2016a; Jaji 2012). Turner stresses the contradictory nature of camps in not only signifying "a means of maintaining order and removing impurity in society, rendering refugees invisible" but also making "refugees become highly visible by being placed in the camps and becoming the objects of state of the art humanitarian programmes" (2016a: 144).

Aid Agencies, Structures, and Cooperation in Kyaka II

When driving to Kyaka II, one really only notices that one has reached the site when arriving at its Base Camp. A sea of signposts erected by humanitarian agencies and their partners marks the entrance to it, as

Image 3.1 Signposts of humanitarian organizations in the Base Camp of Kyaka II.
Source: Photo taken by Ulrike Krause on February 24, 2014.

revealed in the Image 3.1. After one passes by these, the offices of those agencies come into view—some in concrete buildings, others provisional containers. The Base Camp constitutes a crucial part of camp administration. At the time of research, the Base Camp held the offices of humanitarian and government agencies, the housing for aid workers and a guesthouse, the Bujubuli Health Centre, a police station, a market area, and the previously discussed safe houses. More or less surrounding the Base Camp were the village-like sections, the so-called clusters and zones, in which refugees lived side-by-side with Ugandan nationals. Although this spatial complexity to Kyaka II could appear to represent a 'normal' rural life for the 'camp population,' conditions were heavily regulated by the aid system. Issues were multiple, meanwhile. Kyaka II was not only large, leaving those living in the peripheral areas with a long way to travel in order to reach the Base Camp where all aid agencies were located; those in Kyaka II also criticized the confined nature of the camp even despite its vast size.

The humanitarian projects and related decision-making certainly contribute to the perceptions of confinement and control in the camp. Kyaka II was administered by OPM, Government of Uganda, and UNHCR, while NGOs provided aid. According to standard procedures, after arrival, registration, and status determination, refugees generally received ration cards, some nonfood items, access to humanitarian services, and land for agriculture. This applied to all individuals regardless of their gender. A wide variety of aid measures were implemented as part of protection and assistance across different sectors such as health; nutrition; education; food; water, sanitation, and hygiene (WASH); infrastructure and shelter; community service; and environmental management.

More concretely, OPM was at that time responsible for overall management, security, and land issues; and UNHCR for supervision, security, and protection. The Danish Refugee Council appeared to operate as the main implementation partner of UNHCR, covering a number of sectors: namely, child protection, legal assistance, livelihood, community services and development, psychosocial support, WASH, and logistics, alongside prevention, response, and psychosocial counseling for gender-based violence. Windle Trust International was involved in educational programs, Samaritan Purse in food distribution, while the Uganda Red Cross supported the reunification of families separated during conflict or flight. The work of these organizations was largely funded by UNHCR. In addition, Africa Humanitarian Action implemented US-funded health projects offering counseling for victims of gender-based violence; the Finnish Refugee Council carried out livelihood and adult education projects funded by that country's government.

Based on interviews and observations, the humanitarian and government agencies appeared to communicate regularly and align operations, thus providing cross- and multisectoral assistance. Yet through their projects, the agencies exercised power over the camp population, deciding about aid and target groups. Due to these power practices as well as 'containment politics,' the camp essentially served as a technology of control over the 'refugees.' As a biopolitical way of governing refugees, Jaji presents similar observations about the Kakuma and Dadaab refugee camps in Kenya. She notes the "rules, techniques and physical structures and arrangements underpinning the organization, administration and control of populations in particular settings"; as a result, "camps constitute a technology of power and control that compartmentalizes refugees and regulates their movement" (2012: 223, 225). In Kyaka II, this contributed to restrictions for the displaced; they also complained about insufficient aid and overall difficult conditions. One man pointed out that "life is hard" here due to the infrastructures, the lack of jobs and opportunities, and the restrictions on movement making him feel like he was living "in a prison of some sort."[5]

"Refugees depend on aid": Paradox of Self-Reliance Strategies and Refugees' Dependency

The way the aid was delivered in Kyaka II connects with the idea of 'the refugees' as 'needy' recipients and 'passive' beneficiaries hereof (see also Harrell-Bond 1999; Agier 2011: 214). Seemingly running contrary to this perception and such top-down humanitarian processes is the Government of Uganda having promoted refugees' self-reliance for years now. This would suggest a move away from the understanding of refugees merely as beneficiaries toward seeing them as actors instead. Self-reliance is promoted in all such camps in Uganda as part of linking short-term humanitarian refugee aid with sustainable development, as noted in Chapter 1.

Uganda's first such strategy of self-reliance was developed in the 1990s and included a variety of empowerment and livelihood measures: among others, fishery, animal husbandry, and small-business enterprises. The overall focus, however, was on the agricultural productivity of refugees, so as for them to live relatively independent of humanitarian aid (UNHCR and OPM 2004; Meyer 2006). In 2017, the Refugee and Host Population Empowerment (ReHoPE) strategy was finalized, which drew on the previous one. ReHoPE extends the approach to self-reliance and resilience support at the household, community, and system levels (Government of Uganda et al. 2017: 7, 10; Krause and Schmidt 2020). Uganda's strategies generally also seek to integrate humanitarian service structures (e.g., education or health) into the national social service schemes (UNHCR and OPM 2004: v; Government of Uganda et al. 2017: 10). This makes these services available to those refugees and Ugandans who live in the confines or vicinity of camps, supports the long-term use of these services even after repatriation, and contributes to local infrastructure development (Krause 2013, 2016a). Despite this sustainability ambition, the 'integration' of services—not of refugees—is what is paramount; the politically pursued durable solution in Uganda remains the repatriation of refugees rather than their local integration.

[5] Male refugee, dialogue, March 27, 2014, Base Camp.

The central feature of Uganda's refugee aid and self-reliance approach constitutes farming. To this end, individuals receive two plots of land for residence and agriculture upon their arrival in the camp in addition to essential nonfood items, but some informants complained that it had taken long until the authorities allocated land to them.[6] Whereas the self-reliance approach in Uganda is often said to be 'progressive' (see Betts et al. 2017b: 10; Krause 2013: 147) and the agricultural focus appears to be supportive of refugees and portrays them as actors capable of self-reliance, issues remain and complicate these people's lives. Recent studies have increasingly divulged the problems with self-reliance and resilience approaches,[7] while the situation in Kyaka II brings to light the shortcomings of a focus on farming.

That these self-reliance and resilience orientations are ultimately of limited impact was readily recognized by aid workers. They noted that "[r]efugees depend on aid a great deal"[8] or to "a greater extent,"[9] but that they "also do some business and practice farming to supplement aid from organizations."[10] Refugees had similar views, and one man in Kyaka II even lamented: "To get a piece of land you must bribe people responsible for land."[11] Another stressed that instead of education, the physical strength of refugees became key since farming was the only or at least the main source of income: "The conditions in the settlement have oriented them toward one career, which is digging. One cannot think about business. The stronger a person is, the more powerful they are. This is why education is undermined, since the ones digging achieve more than the educated in their community. [...] Farmers and cattle keepers are doing much better."[12]

Even where individuals did engage in farming, the land was criticized as rarely being of sufficient quantity. The amount allocated

---

[6] For example, male refugee, dialogue, March 18, 2014, Base Camp.
[7] On forced migration and refugees, see the related special issue of the *Journal of Refugee Studies* (Easton-Calabria and Skran 2020) and, for example, Krause and Schmidt (2020); Pasha (2020); Easton-Calabria and Omata (2018); Omata (2017); Ilcan and Rygiel (2015). Regarding resilience debates in other fields, see Lorenz and Dittmer (2016); Welsh (2014); Evans and Reid (2013); Chandler (2012).
[8] Female aid worker, interview, April 10, 2014.
[9] Female aid worker, interview, May 20, 2014.
[10] Male aid worker, interview, April 14, 2014.
[11] Male refugee, dialogue, March 18, 2014, Base Camp.
[12] Discussion with local leaders, March 20, 2014, Base Camp.

generally depends on the size of the receiving household. At the time of research, those of up to seven people were said to receive plots of 50 × 100 meters, while households of eight or more received plots of 100 × 100 meters.[13] Although refugees in Kyaka II appeared to receive more land than those in other camps in Uganda did (Krause 2013: 167), these benchmarks only present the 'ideal' plot sizes; other studies have argued that such quantities of land are too small for the required fallow seasons (Beaudou et al. 2003: 70). Besides, many refugees criticized the fact that they were unable to achieve full self-reliance and so continued to depend on humanitarian support. Among others, one man explained:

One cannot depend on this one acre for both food and money to buy other basics and to pay school fees. There is also a fear that as time goes on, the other refugees will come and then it will also be cut in half. Now that my son is married, he also has his acre of land but it is still not enough because he has his own children. My daughter has been married for around three months now but she is still on my card [for food distribution]. I also fear because they said that they are going to stop distributing food to us, and the land is little.[14]

Continuing to rely on aid despite the self-reliance approach practiced in Kyaka II indicates the wide-ranging problems faced. Whereas the self-reliance strategy appears to structurally engage refugees in active ways and to build on their capacities, it also serves to define what activities are deemed 'acceptable' in their self-reliance—corresponding to the habits of the neoliberal paradigm. Based on this strategy, humanitarian and government agencies transfer responsibilities and especially food self-sufficiency to refugees, and put them in charge of sustaining themselves. This means that it is no longer only about providing protection and assistance but also about support for refugees in their becoming independent; in other words, 'helping them to help themselves'—a concept that has been circulating and criticized in the development discourse since the early 1990s (Büschel 2014). As a basic principle, the politically intended self-reliance through agricultural productivity leads to a homogenization of all refugees as farmers regardless of their diverse occupational backgrounds, skills, and interests (Krause 2016d: 208). The focus on agriculture reduces the idea of a self-reliant lifestyle to economic output and the mere production of

[13] Local authority figure, interview, March 19, 2014, Base Camp.
[14] Male refugee, dialogue, March 5, 2014, Kaborogota Zone.

food, indispensable to life. It is thus about refugees' 'survivability' (see Krause and Schmidt 2020; Evans and Reid 2013: 91–93).

The pressing issue here is that the overall camp conditions remain difficult to navigate. So while humanitarian and government agencies create restrictions and dependencies through the aid system implemented on-site, they simultaneously also expect refugees to become self-reliant within these same limiting structures. Adhering to the neoliberal paradigm directs focus away from changing structural problems toward emphasizing instead the individual's responsibility to find solutions, and this through farming and economic performance. Alongside aid measures, the contributions of refugees themselves become key herein—but that while they remain regulated in a top-down fashion by humanitarian and government agencies as well as while they continued to rely on aid.

In this paradox of simultaneous self-reliance and dependency, the transfer of responsibilities risks shifting blame to the displaced if they do not or simply cannot fulfill expectations of self-reliant lives to the anticipated or imposed degree. This occurs even if refugees are not physically strong enough for farming, as pointed out by one conversation partner,[15] or if insufficient soil conditions for agriculture partly hamper possibilities (Kaiser 2006: 612; Krause 2013: 170–171; Beaudou et al. 2003). Such "forced farming" has a long history in aid strategies (Easton-Calabria 2015: 414), and criticisms were voiced by refugees in Kyaka II. They narrated how they 'have to' engage in agriculture to survive despite crop yields often being insufficient to support a whole family—which results in continued dependency on external food assistance.[16] One man emphasized, "if you do not dig, you may not really survive,"[17] while one woman reasoned that people tend to prefer to live in Kampala because "here [in Kyaka II], there are no jobs for people and the food delivery is not enough to feed on"[18] (see also Krause and Gato 2019). Due to reduced food rations, one adolescent expressed worries meanwhile of her "family dying from hunger" as her "mum is very old, [so] that she cannot dig for the

---

[15] Discussion with local leaders, March 20, 2014, Base Camp.
[16] Among others, male refugee, dialogue, March 18, 2014, Base Camp; male refugee, dialogue, March 28, 2014, Base Camp; female refugee, dialogue, March 27, 2014, Base Camp.
[17] Male refugee, dialogue, March 28, 2014, Base Camp.
[18] Female refugee, dialogue, March 11, 2014, Bukere Zone.

family."[19] Such concerns are further complicated when food deliveries are sometimes delayed due to a lack of funding.[20]

"Anytime they take decisions on you": Camp Hierarchies and Hierarchizations

In line with humanitarian projects and approaches, decision-making in Kyaka II was clearly also regulated—giving rise to top-down structures. OPM and UNHCR maintained the leadership positions to which other aid agencies as well as refugees were to adhere. However, these structures encompassed far greater complexity than one-dimensional decision-making could successfully rule over.

Each of the humanitarian and government agencies in Kyaka II maintained their organizational rules, institutional norms and values, and power relations among employees. The agencies also existed within an overarching hierarchy; under the supervision and administration of OPM and UNHCR, aid-implementing agencies collaborated to deliver cross- and multisectoral assistance. Hierarchies and responsibilities, thus, had to be continuously negotiated and clarified, and the various agencies appeared to meet regularly to do just that and thus harmonize operations.

Besides the hierarchies existing within and between the respective agencies, humanitarian regulations also affected refugees, the people living in Kyaka II. Humanitarian agencies not only practiced power over them in a broad sense through their assistance, but locally established and dynamically changing rules were also put in place by these organizations and government agencies. These rules were at times a very broad interpretation of Uganda's 2006 Refugee Act, or even went beyond it. For example, while the Act grants refugees the freedom of movement in its Article 30, it stresses in its Article 44 that refugees are to live in "designate[d] places or areas on public land [that are] to be transit centres or refugee settlements" and they may only leave and reside in other places after being "authorised" to do so. In Kyaka II, such permission was broadly interpreted by decision-makers: Refugees were meant to seek permission from the camp commandant, an OPM

---

[19] Female adolescent, 17 years old, journal writing, March 5, 2014, Bujubuli Secondary School.
[20] Female aid worker, interview, April 2, 2014.

official stationed there, even when they wanted to leave only for a short time in order to find temporary work. Since permission often took long to get and was at times declined, many people said that they would leave the camp without it.[21]

Another example of local restrictions at the time of research was the prohibition on using metal sheets for roofing on refugees' homes. They offered protection from the weather, and thus helped improve physical well-being in the home. OPM, however, was said to have forbidden the use of these metal sheets; in the event of a 'breach,' refugees had to pay a fine.[22] During a discussion, one man stated that "a refugee has a right to live happily. However, here in this settlement, you cannot build a house with iron sheets and again you are told to live temporarily. You have to give money to build a permanent house." Another man responded to his point, adding that "the officers know that it is allowed [by Ugandan law] and they just want to get money from the refugees."[23] These local regulations, thus, gravely affected the lives of those resident in Kyaka II.

Hierarchies and hierarchizations furthermore existed among the displaced themselves. In Kyaka II, the Refugee Welfare Councils (RWCs) constituted an important elected collective—one initiated and supported, by humanitarian agencies however. The RWCs followed the political model of local councils used in Uganda, with different levels representing different groups. RWC 3 stands for the camp and RWC 2 for groups of RWC 1, which, in turn, represents respective households. As Gottschalk writes, this "structure is by nature hierarchical: in many cases, before a refugee can bring his or her concerns to UNHCR [...], he or she must first consult the RWC 1 [or equivalent]" (2007: 37–38). The RWCs supported individuals in settling cases of conflict or dispute, but crucially also channeled information to humanitarian agencies—particularly in cases of gender-based violence. An aid worker explained that:

Reporting starts in the community at the Refugee Welfare Council, which refers or reports the case to police or health center depending on the urgency of it. The case is then referred for psychosocial support, and later on for

---

[21] Male refugee, dialogue, March 27, 2014, Base Camp; female aid worker, interview, April 2, 2014.

[22] Discussion with religious leaders, March 19, 2014, Base Camp.

[23] Discussion with religious leaders, March 19, 2014, Base Camp.

shelter or further assessment regarding physical, legal, and any other needs like durable solutions—usually resettlement in a third country.[24]

Humanitarian agencies, thus, interacted with and were involved in the daily running of these RWCs. As a result, these structures did not merely constitute a form of own political representation for and of the people alone. Rather, they were strongly intertwined with the camp's overarching humanitarian-agency authority.

Hierarchical structures among the displaced themselves further included self-organized forms of representation. Elders, clan, and religious leaders were key examples of such authority figures. They represented and guided different groups, as well as secured an important role in the life of Kyaka II's inhabitants. These leaders held informal gatherings at the community or village level, and also helped to settle disputes among refugees. They were not elected by the camp population; these representative structures already existed prior to flight to Uganda, and thus constituted previous social systems that had been maintained for social order in the camp.

Kyaka II's hierarchical apparatus, thus, encompassed organizational rules, administrative procedures, and institutionally developed norms and values that entailed the creation of both structural and formal hierarchies among the aid agencies and the camp's inhabitants further to the relatively informal structures found among the displaced themselves. Through this, the hierarchies in Kyaka II were in line with what Inhetveen identifies as "polyhierarchical structures" in refugee camps (Inhetveen 2010: 193–212, my translation). On the one hand, power structures evolve among and between the administration and the camp population. On the other hand, formal hierarchizations and informal hierarchies occur among the refugees themselves. The latter point about formal and informal representations among refugees is also discussed by Lecadet (2016) who identifies hybrid forms of politics in Agamé refugee camp in Benin.

Those living in Kyaka II also influenced the camp's local organization and regulation. Their own power structures illustrate how they autonomously established a political life within the camp. This representation process and ensuing political constellation emphasize that they shaped the camp environment and how they contributed to or

---

[24] Female aid worker, interview, May 11, 2014.

established order themselves. However, much authority remained with humanitarian and government agencies. Through their aid measures and decision-making procedures, Kyaka II essentially represented a sphere of power created and maintained by these agencies for the explicit purpose of ordering refugee lives.

With this apparatus, Kyaka II resembles the conditions that exist in refugee camps worldwide. Since camp and aid structures are based on globally produced norms, they share similarities. With the various actors, hierarchical processes, bureaucratic functions, and established practices of power involved, camps signify arenas in which humanitarian aid is transformed into everyday politics (Hilhorst and Jansen 2010). The asymmetrical power relations make clear that it is the agencies who ultimately decide who is to be supported and how, which shapes refugees' daily lives by defining the parameters within which they can act (see Turner 2010; Agier 2011; Jaji 2012).

Effects of Top-Down Power Structures: Refugees as 'Protection Objects'

But how do these power asymmetries affect the women and men resident in Kyaka II beyond hierarchizations? Although a number of global refugee policies emphasize that aid is supposed to be delivered through participatory approaches—a prime example of early policy is "people-oriented planning" (UNHCR 1992)—and although refugee aid in Kyaka II was said to focus on promoting self-reliance, the displaced were rather left in the position of being 'beneficiaries' and 'recipients' of humanitarian assistance. While some of the aid workers interviewed in Kyaka II emphatically stated that "assistance is never enough; needs always outweigh availability,"[25] others spoke of refugees in derogatory terms. They remarked that refugees lacked hygiene in the home,[26] or blamed them for 'abusing and misusing' aid—selling it and "asking for more."[27] One such informant highlighted the relevance of and need for strict hierarchies: "I think it is a top-down [structure], and I think it is better because the bottom-up approach can cause commotion. [...] It seems to me the refugees are short-

---

[25] Female aid worker, interview, April 10, 2014.
[26] Interview with aid worker, March 27, 2014.
[27] Female aid worker, interview, May 11, 2014.

sighted."[28] Yet another aid worker commented: "This [system of handouts] renders the refugees expectant, lazy; [with] no sense of ownership or sustenance of the development process."[29]

Not only expressing negative ascriptions in interviews, aid workers at times also acted harshly toward the refugees. During my research, I regularly saw people forced to wait for hours on end in front of aid-agency offices, so as to eventually voice their concerns. Those in Kyaka II criticized the behavior of humanitarian staff too. One man complained: "There is no hope for being a refugee in Uganda now. This is because the people who are supposed to help us are not really doing their work. For example, UNHCR is supposed to protect the refugees but I do not see them playing that role."[30] Other women and men explained that aid workers do not treat refugees "humanely," are "violent," or "harass" them.[31] As illustrated at the outset of this chapter, one woman pointed out that: "We are refugees but cannot make decisions of our own." This left her with a feeling of having no identity and belonging—of being dehumanized. "You are just there, like just something. Anytime they take decisions on you."[32]

This questionable treatment by some aid workers, alongside the restrictions and power structures that their agencies imposed on the camp's inhabitants, correspond ultimately with the limited involvement of the displaced themselves in humanitarian aid, policy and decision-making on-site. One man, thus, highlighted how in DR Congo people were able "to solve their own problems, but now conditions and relief organizations are the ones that solve their problems. You cannot do anything; you have to wait for someone to solve the problems on your behalf. Our decisions are actually limited."[33]

To gain a broader overview of whether informants felt they could participate in the aid system, we raised this question in the second survey conducted with 400 participants. A total of 70.5 percent of the participating women and 65.7 percent of the men said that aid agencies take all decisions, while 42.9 percent of the women and 30.4 percent of

[28] Male aid worker, interview, March 26, 2014, Base Camp.
[29] Male aid worker, interview, April 10, 2014.
[30] Male refugee, dialogue, March 28, 2014, Base Camp.
[31] Male refugee, dialogue, March 5, 2014, Kaborogota Zone; female refugee, dialogue, March 12, 2014, Base Camp.
[32] Female refugee, dialogue, March 27, 2014, Base Camp.
[33] Discussion with local leaders, March 20, 2014, Base Camp.

the men stated that they would indeed involve refugees in aid structures. Moreover, 70 percent of the participating men and 63.8 percent of the women in Kyaka II believed that women receive more aid than men do. Hence, on average, about two-thirds of survey participants perceived aid agencies as making all decisions, felt uninvolved in the aid system, and observed an imbalance toward more aid for women. These responses mirror the hierarchical structures found in Kyaka II. Due to the power arrangements there, refugees were engaged with mainly as aid beneficiaries, not as actors—via top-down processes, not on an equal footing. This, in turn, made them anonymous, and put them in the position of being mere 'protection objects'—with little to no regard for their individual traits, hopes, or stories.

This resonates with other studies that have also revealed refugees' limitations (but also their coping, contestation, and, thus, agency) within the humanitarian camp system (see, e.g., Harrell-Bond 1986; Turner 2010; Inhetveen 2010; Agier 2011; Jansen 2011; McConnachie 2014). Through their presentation as helpless protection objects in need of humanitarian support, refugees are rendered apolitical (Hyndman and Giles 2011: 362). The humanitarian camp system, thus, leads to the figure of "refugee-as-victim" (Turner 2010: 44) and a "social and political non-existence" (Agier 2002: 322). From a post-colonial viewpoint, refugee camps can furthermore be seen as "sites of neo-colonial power relations where refugees are counted, their movements monitored and mapped, their daily routines disciplined and routinized by the institutional machinery of refugee relief agencies" (Hyndman 1997: 17). Under hegemonic aid agencies, refugees are thus cast in subaltern positions within the humanitarian system of care.

Humanitarian Protection against Gender-Based Violence in Kyaka II

Of course, humanitarian agencies on-site were aware of the prevalence of gender-based violence in Kyaka II as well as of the various needs of women and men. One aid worker highlighted that: "In Kyaka, there are very many cases of SGBV but they differ in form; rape, domestic violence, sexual assault."[34] To provide protection against these risks, humanitarian agencies implemented a range of measures: among

---

[34] Female aid worker, interview, March 26, 2014.

others, informing women about their rights, putting in place short-term shelter (the previously mentioned safe houses), and developing reporting and assistance schemes for cases of attack. These measures and their effects inform the second section of this chapter.

Yet such projects were not unique to the humanitarian aid system in Kyaka II, being similarly realized in other camps elsewhere too.[35] The projects drew on and were influenced by guidelines and norms set out in global refugee policies for (women's) protection in refugee situations everywhere (see, e.g., UNHCR 2008a, 2011b). Interviews with aid workers revealed these influences, but at the same time also indicated that those global norms were in fact locally interpreted—and thus not realized 'automatically' in Kyaka II. This links with debates in International Relations as well as in interdisciplinary fields of Peace and Conflict, Humanitarian, and Development Studies about how global norms 'travel,' are localized, and come to shape procedures on the ground (see Bonacker et al. 2017). Research into norm localization depicts how local actors connect global norms with local social and normative orders, and subsequently adopt, debate, contest, erode, or even strengthen them (Acharya 2004; Sandholtz 2008; Zimmermann 2016; Deitelhoff and Zimmermann 2018). While local actors at times discursively frame these norms so as to increase the legitimacy of their work (Finnemore and Sikkink 1998; Heusinger 2017), strong deviations can nevertheless occur—being partly perceived as noncompliance therewith (Goodman and Jinks 2008).

Such norm localization processes, have rarely been addressed in forced migration and refugee studies, however.[36] My research with aid workers, who all came from Uganda, enables us not only to explore which projects countering gender-based violence were implemented in Kyaka II and how, or the effects hereof on the women and men living there; it offers us also the opportunity to scrutinize links to the norms outlined in the policies of the global refugee regime. To this end,

---

[35] Reviews of such projects regarding gender-based violence and their effectiveness in refugee settings are available; see Robbers and Morgan (2017); Wirtz et al. (2013); Asgary et al. (2013).

[36] Scholars in this field have mainly addressed norm dynamics on the international and state levels (Coen 2019; Fresia 2014; Schattle and McCann 2014; Betts 2014; Ahlborn 2011; Chiu 2009; Betts and Durieux 2007). Yet I have not found studies specifically on norm localization within refugee camps.

I mainly use here policy documents of UNHCR mandated for international refugee protection. The following first addresses the role of the 'vulnerability' categorization, and then explores reactive and preventative projects against the violence before attending to empowerment ones.

"Women are considered weak and vulnerable": Protection of Women and Vulnerability as a Key Category

After increasing criticism—especially from feminist scholars—about the insufficient protection and assistance offered to women in refugee situations, as noted in Chapter 1, the situation started to change in the late 1980s and early 1990s. Global policies were adopted that sought to ensure the protection of women and to counter gender-based violence (UNHCR ExCom 1985, 1988, 1989, 1990; UNHCR 1990, 1991, 2003b, 2008a, 2011b). UNHCR's *Handbook on the Protection of Women and Girls* would identify "[t]he protection of women and girls of concern [as] a core activity and an organizational priority for UNHCR" (UNHCR 2008a: 5). Yet some observers saw limitations; Edwards (2010: 32), for example, criticized the focus on sexual violence (rather than the social and structural aspects of gender-based violence) as well as the patronizing choice of language in UNHCR's handbook, such as how "women and girls of concern show great resilience, resourcefulness and courage in adapting to and surmounting these problems" (UNHCR 2008a: 11).

To tackle gender-based violence in refugee situations and improve protection mechanisms, a number of operational measures are proposed in UNHCR's handbook: for example, legal protection and advice, counseling, projects for ensuring physical safety, and ones for empowerment too (UNHCR 2008a: 42–44, 77, 108, 210–214 ; 2011b: 14–19). As I will show below, such projects were delivered in Kyaka II; they can generally be divided into preventative and responsive ones—thus, those carried out to reduce the scope of gender-based violence and those delivered to assist victims after attack. In tandem with other policies (UNHCR 2003b, 2011b), the handbook places emphasis on the protection of women and partly notes the importance of involving men. In recent years, policies have increasingly promoted the protection of men and LGBTIQ+ people affected by gender-based violence (UNHCR and RLP 2012; UNHCR 2011c, 2015c); it remains to be seen, however, whether and how local protection endeavors will go beyond women (and girls) as the main victim group.

Not least through these measures, gender and gender sensitivity have received greater attention and begun to inform a cross-cutting programmatic approach to refugee protection and assistance. Gender-sensitive policies are, therefore, meant to be applied across all sectors of refugee protection and assistance, being enacted to meet women's and men's needs, to reduce risks, and to promote gender equality. UNHCR stresses that: "Gender equality is thus first and foremost a human right" (2008a: 12). For the further integration of gender sensitivity into refugee aid, one key tool used is Age, Gender and Diversity Mainstreaming (AGDM), being promoted globally and taking an intersectional perspective. According to UNHCR, it is to

support the meaningful participation of girls, boys, women and men of all ages and backgrounds, who are of concern to the Office. AGDM operates to make their participation integral to the design, implementation, monitoring and evaluation of all UNHCR policies and operations so that these impact equitably on everyone of concern. Its overall goals are gender equality and the enjoyment by everyone of concern of their rights regardless of their age, sex, gender or background. (UNHCR 2008a: 34)

In Kyaka II, aid workers similarly highlighted how they aligned their work with such globally formulated projects and approaches. Corresponding with the global language of humanitarianism, one aid worker underlined that "project design starts with refugees, where there are joint assessments like AGDM, JAM [Joint Assessment Mission], KAP [Knowledge, Attitude, and Practice] surveys, etc. that direct activity designing."[37] Another said, similarly, that "AGDM, KAP survey, JAM, etc. [are done] every year."[38] Moreover, and also perfectly in line with global policies (see among others UNHCR 2008a: 34), one aid worker even stated that "programming follows and is informed by the AGDM design, which involves refugees and host populations."[39]

Such precise alignments of statements to global policies reveal how the aid workers constitute 'takers of global norms.' As such norm-takers, they have undergone learning processes about how global

[37] Female aid worker, interview, May 11, 2014.
[38] Female aid worker, interview, May 20, 2014.
[39] Female aid worker, interview, April 10, 2014.

norms function and reference them so as to legitimate their work (Acharya 2004; Schneiker 2017). That these alignments to global policy language do not mean an exact local implementation of globally outlined concepts but instead go hand-in-hand with reinterpretations, contestations, and adjustments (for other humanitarian and development cases, see Heusinger 2017; Groß 2015) therein is evident in how the notion of vulnerability is handled in Kyaka II.

Global and Local Approaches to Vulnerability

The humanitarian concept of vulnerability and related ones like 'at risk' have become a key part of the refugee aid system—as well as the ascribed refugee identity—over the past few years worldwide (see Turner 2010: 47; Agier 2011: 150–151; Clark-Kazak 2011: 69ff; Freedman 2019). The global vulnerability-screening tool holds that 'situations of vulnerability' vis-à-vis forcibly displaced people can change dynamically and affect different groups in specific ways (UNHCR and IDC 2016). Vulnerability assessments serve to identify the needs of particular groups in order for humanitarian and government actors to plan and implement protection and assistance projects based on global policies.

While the screening tool does not limit vulnerability to women, UNHCR's *Handbook for the Protection of Women and Girls*, of course, focuses specifically on this group—stating, among other things, the need to "address inequalities and support the empowerment and protection of discriminated groups, in particular women and girls at risk" (UNHCR 2008a: 34). Yet, the AGDM tool that aid workers in Kyaka II often referred to does not merely concentrate on women (of different age groups) but promotes the provision of humanitarian support based on various relevant categories too (see, e.g., UNHCR 2007a: 9).

Vulnerability played a crucial role in the humanitarian system in Kyaka II, being translated, interpreted, and thus localized by aid agencies there—which materialized in a variety of projects on-site. One aid worker in Kyaka II explained that it meant to "implement projects and activities driven toward filling the gaps [in protection] that make women and men vulnerable to gender-based violence."[40] Contrary to this informant's reference to 'women and men,' the local

---

[40] Female aid worker, interview, April 22, 2014.

application of the vulnerability concept deviated in fact from the one outlined in global policies, as aid agencies in Kyaka II concentrated exclusively on women. They used the category of 'vulnerable women' particularly to denote single-headed households home to children and single, widowed, and/or elderly women.[41] Correspondingly, one aid worker stressed, "women are considered weak and vulnerable"— which is also how she rationalized the occurrence of gender-based violence. She further explained: "Usually the vulnerable ones [are] single, widowed, elderly women."[42]

Centering vulnerability on women might appear plausible in light of the various difficulties, limitations, and risks they faced during encampment, as well as conflict and displacement. However, this approach had far-reaching implications for women—and for men too. Although the vulnerability concept aimed to serve women's needs and interests, ensure their protection against gender-based violence, and to integrate gender sensitivity into refugee assistance, in the final reckoning it was the aid agencies and ultimately their staff who defined what was locally understood as 'vulnerability' in humanitarian terms; they associated, as noted, this understanding solely with women and girls. Such a narrow interpretation bears the risk of neglecting the various possible vulnerabilities that different people see themselves. Those determined to be vulnerable were portrayed as helpless, and, as such, also gained material benefit from their status as a result of prioritized humanitarian protection and resources. While this was meant to help them, it at times had the reverse effect—increasing the risks as, for example, new, unfamiliar imbalances arose, others felt neglected or discriminated against, and frustration and, perhaps, violence consequently intensified.

Women as 'Vulnerable Protection Objects'

The focus on vulnerability—instead of different vulnerabilities—as an apparently clearly definable and separate humanitarian concept signifying insecurity and difficulties and requiring particular assistance is exemplified by the statements of the interviewed aid workers in Kyaka II. Among others, one noted that women need and indeed receive more

---

[41] Female aid worker, interview, May 11, 2014; female aid worker, interview, April 22, 2014.
[42] Female aid worker, interview, April 10, 2014.

humanitarian protection and support "due to their physical and social vulnerability and also because many of them are single mothers, survivors of rape and defilement, and many other circumstances that worsen their vulnerability and expose them to more SGBV."[43] Another contradictorily reasoned: "People receive equal support, but special consideration is put on women because of their vulnerability status and their low position in the social development arena. Keen interest is placed in literacy of women, economic activities of women, health of women, and their position—which makes them easily prone to suffering SGBV and its associated problems."[44]

Such insights indicate that vulnerability does not constitute a 'neutral' concept vis-à-vis aid effectiveness, but is rather one locally interpreted and framed. With aid workers' aim to provide women with more support due to their identified precarious position, the approach is not only used to identify and distinguish between refugees' local needs and provide assistance effectively but rather to 'heal' women and 'save' them from a core vulnerability as defined by humanitarian agencies. The latter notion leads to a meaning thereof that portrays women in Kyaka II as victims, as 'vulnerable protection objects'— which pathologizes women, and calls for therapeutic-like intervention on their behalf. Women are therefore 'vulnerabilized' as a humanitarian strategy.

Women generally appear to fulfil the criteria for vulnerability and the accompanying image of victims *par excellence* as the notion is fundamentally associated with stereotypical female ascriptions of innocence, peacefulness, and weakness, in contrast to (the apparently male) strength and violence—thereby ultimately continuing to frame the female as apolitical (Grabska 2011: 90). As a consequence, the vulnerability concept—or actually the 'vulnerabilization'—contributes to the victimization of women who seem inherently unable to act or protect themselves. As such victims, women are pushed into the passive and needy representation category of "womenandchildren"—making them individuals who remain dependent on their hegemonic counterparts, whether men or humanitarian agencies (Fiddian-Qasmiyeh 2014a: 4–7; 2014b: 398; in line with Enloe 2014: 1). This portrayal of women to some extent normalizes violence against them as part of a quasi-

---

[43] Female aid worker, interview, May 11, 2014.
[44] Male aid worker, interview, April 10, 2014.

ordinary status quo; yet, it also leads to the neglect of other risks and potential victims, especially men and boys—who are, even if at times indirectly, depicted as perpetrators (Olivius 2016; Krause 2016e).

Signposts, Conferences, and Other Measures against Gender-Based Violence

Aid agencies implemented different projects, mainly for women, to counter gender-based violence. Some of these were highly visible as soon as one entered Kyaka II: most notably, in the form of signposts carrying various messages. Aid agencies developed and installed the signposts throughout the camp to increase awareness of risks, reduce the scope of violence, and provide information about protection procedures. Examples of such signposts are further given in Images 3.2, 3.3, 3.4, and 3.5. Beyond that, aid agencies generally aimed to provide protection and build awareness among (potential) victims to respond to and prevent gender-based violence. This reveals two approaches being taken: a reactive one to assist victims and a proactive one to prevent attacks. Such activities are similarly outlined in global refugee policies (UNHCR 2008a: 42–44, 77, 108, 210–214; 2011b: 14–19).

Reactive Projects against Gender-Based Violence

Key projects reacting to gender-based violence included temporary protective shelter, medical support, and psychosocial counseling for victims thereof. Protective shelter—the previously discussed safe houses—took the form of tents established centrally in the Base Camp, which served to provide short-term accommodation for victims who were under immediate threat. They could stay there until disputes were resolved but the shelters were generally thought to be for short-term use. As follow-ups, aid agencies mentioned carrying out home visits after cases of physical assault, denial of resources, or abuse were reported in order to monitor the well-being of survivors and to ensure their safety in the home and in the community.

In various interviews, aid workers explained the importance of the medical support, psychosocial counseling, and referral system put in place for victim support. Medical treatment following attack was provided in Bujubuli Health Centre. During research in the camp, there were always a number of patients sitting on benches in front of the clinic, waiting to see medical staff. The aid workers of two

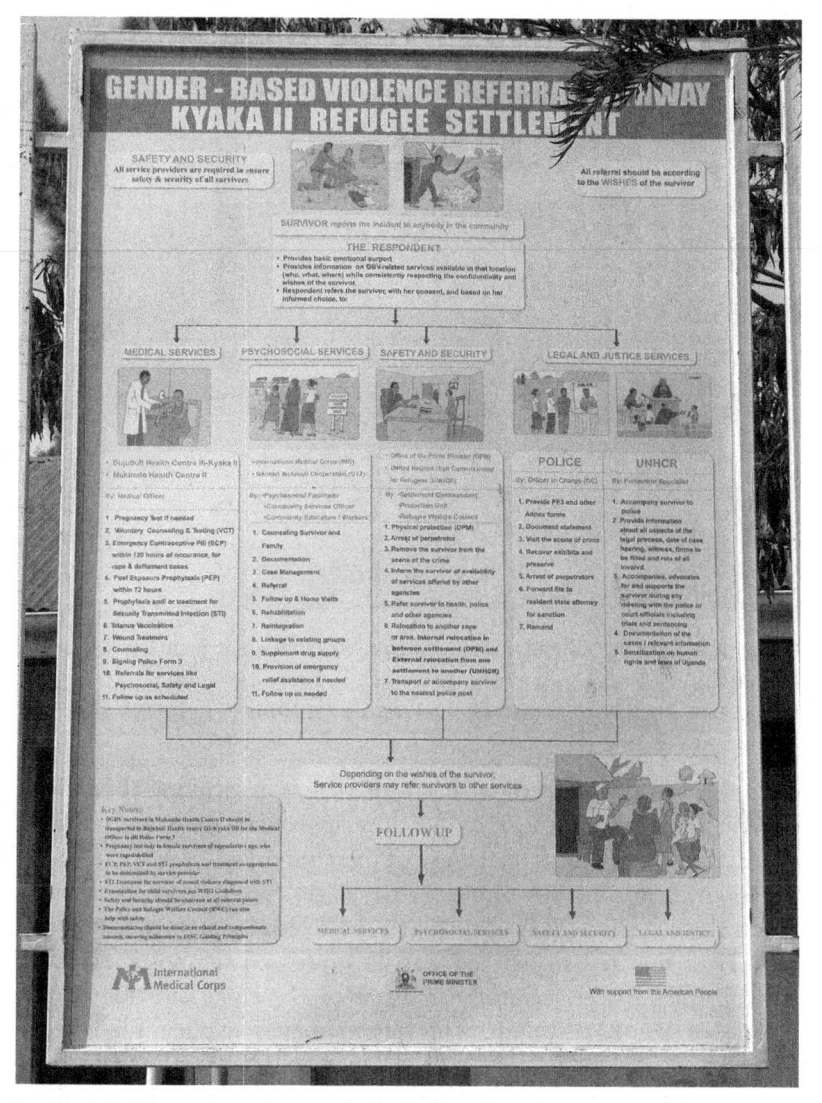

Image 3.2 Signpost on the reporting system of gender-based violence cases in Kyaka II.
Source: Photo taken by Ulrike Krause on February 24, 2014.

organizations also provided counseling to help victims of gender-based violence cope with their experiences. Such therapy sessions were held in offices located in provisional containers in the Base Camp and used by a number of employees. The containers, thus, did not

Image 3.3 Signpost calling for abstinence, in front of a primary school in Kyaka II.
Source: Photos taken by Ulrike Krause on February 25, 2014.

offer much—or in fact any—privacy for victims in speaking about their experiences and concerns. It is, therefore, understandable why refugees noted hardly wanting to make use of these services.[45]

Moreover, for victims of gender-based violence to even be able to access these services in the first place, the referral system was mandatory. How this system worked was illustrated on signposts installed, among other places, centrally in front of the clinic situated in the middle of the Base Camp. This photo makes explicit the system whereby victims of gender-based violence could report an attack to and seek subsequent help from the authorities in Kyaka II. The signpost essentially presented a 'step-by-step guide' to what victims should do and where they should go in such cases. This also included information on how they could access medical, psychosocial, protection, and legal services. Illustrated through a number of sketches, gendered figures in the sign are clear, with women being attacked by men. The

[45] Two aid workers, interview, February 24, 2014.

Image 3.4 Signpost calling for virginity, in front of a primary school in Kyaka II.
Source: Photos taken by Ulrike Krause on February 25, 2014.

sign, thus, does not allow for alternative interpretations of risks other than women as victims and men as perpetrators.

Although humanitarian services such as medical and psychosocial care were generally supposed to be free of charge, victims only had such access to medical treatment in the clinic if they complied with the referral system —and thus if they had reported the case to the police and subsequently received an official police report. Similarly, those affected only obtained free psychosocial counseling if they had been given a related referral from the clinic. This referral cycle complicated the lives of many victims—not to mention it contributing to the impunity of perpetrators too. Women and men in Kyaka II often noted that victims refrained from reporting cases of gender-based violence not only due to fear of stigmatization, social exclusion, and increased violence but also simply because they could not afford the fees the police demanded for compiling reports.[46]

---

[46] For example, female refugee, dialogue, March 17, 2014, Bujubuli; discussion with religious leaders, March 19, 2014, Base Camp.

Image 3.5 Signpost opposing sex, in front of a primary school in Kyaka II.
Source: Photos taken by Ulrike Krause on February 25, 2014.

Preventative Projects against Gender-Based Violence

Humanitarian projects to prevent violence ironically maintained the focus on (potential) victims as well, and placed particular emphasis on building awareness by informing them about the risks of gender-based violence—in lieu of addressing those who likely commit violence. Some of these preventative measures were also highly visible, such as the signposts illustrated here. At first sight, these short messages promoted sexual self-discipline among children—especially girls. Yet aid workers explained to me that they particularly also aimed to prevent gender-based violence and increase awareness about respective risks—again, especially among girls. This astounded me as none of the signs provided any information about possible actions that can be taken against the violence. So what do they mean? By directly addressing sexual self-discipline and indirectly serving to prevent the violence, these signs 'speak to' potential victims in a problematic way. The messages tell girls to abstain from sex and remain virgins but when girls—as well as others—experience gender-based violence, they do not 'willingly have sex' or 'give up their virginity.' In stark contrast, they are forced into it and become victims of attack. The signs thus become inadvertent modes of 'victim shaming'—as those suffering gender-based violence are presented as being responsible for their own loss of virginity and foregoing of abstinence. Although aid workers emphasized the underlying aim of targeting girls as victims, an alternative reading is possible: The signs could be understood as a tool to reduce gender-based violence by addressing potential perpetrators to practice sexual self-discipline. This would be disturbing, however, as sexual intercourse would virtually be equated with sexual violence—which would ultimately trivialize the latter.

In addition to such signs, information sessions concerning the prevention of such violence were carried out most prominently in primary schools as well as during a conference convened for women, taking place at the time of research. In all primary schools, sensitization and information campaigns served to advise children about the threats of gender-based violence. These campaigns took place outside of the schools, under large trees. An estimated 100 students attended each workshop, which lasted about two to three hours. Aid workers from different agencies took part, and put emphasis on holding child-friendly presentations about risks and protection services. After the information sessions came to an end, the children were allowed to ask brief questions—but few did. It seemed not so much that the children dared not raise questions but more that the subject was nothing new to them. Most, rather, appeared to already be well aware of the risks of gender-based violence. Of course, they had to pass the signposts mentioned earlier in order to enter the school every day, after all.

In February 2014, different aid agencies collaboratively organized a conference for women leaders in Kyaka II. Under the title of "Change Begins at Home," the conference targeted these individuals with information about prevention and protection mechanisms, and offered support with regard to women's empowerment.[47] The invitation for women leaders was based on the assumption that they were to act as multipliers, and thus share the gained knowledge with other women in their communities. The conference started with the singing of the national anthem and of the women's anthem, then an aid worker said

---

[47] See Chapter 4 about gender relations for 'bottom-up' reflections on whether and how women support and achieve their own empowerment in Kyaka II.

Christian prayers and laid out the 'ground rules' of participation: "minimal movements, phones on vibrate, talk by raising hands, respect each other's ideas, time keeping, [and] observe discipline"—as written on a large piece of paper and hung up in front. Afterward, several aid workers gave presentations about education and health, the rights of women, and economic empowerment, during the course of which gender-based violence was a continuously cited theme. The time remaining was used for discussions in which women were allowed to address and elaborate on specific challenges as well as on ways to overcome them. During these discussions, violence was a key issue that these women raised time and again.

This conference's focus on women was critical, as it was ultimately about informing *women* about *their* rights. As multipliers, the *women* were supposed to share *their knowledge* with *other women*; men were neither allowed to participate nor considered future recipients of the information shared. Moreover, the aid workers who gave presentations repeatedly emphasized the various risks to women due to gender-based violence. They also continually stressed women's roles in the home, and their domestic duties as 'good mothers' caring for children and especially 'good wives' having to satisfy their husbands. This reveals diverse contradictions, including imbalances of knowledge among different groups as well as women's rights versus patriarchal values. Participating women were thus 'taught' not only that they are victims and how to be empowered and claim their rights, but also how important it is to fulfill traditional domestic roles. These conflicting roles stood out even more clearly in Kyaka II's women's empowerment projects, which I will discuss in due course.

Women/Victim Focus

The focus on women as (potential) victims cast its shadow over all projects tackling gender-based violence in Kyaka II that I learned about during my time there. Although it is clear that women and girls face particular risks, a one-sided approach in support of victims is unlikely to sufficiently respond to and prevent gender-based violence. Considering that employees of aid agencies were mostly of the opinion that women constitute victims and men perpetrators, plausible consequences hereof would be stricter law enforcement, involving men in projects against gender-based violence, and offering specific measures for them. However, during my research stay only one police officer was present in Kyaka II—with this individual meant to oversee security in the entire camp, which, as noted, then hosted more than 20,000 refugees (not including Ugandans living close by). I neither came across any projects, workshops, or campaigns about gender-based violence or women's rights specifically for men in Kyaka II, nor offers of psycho-social counseling for perpetrators (whether men or women).

When I asked aid workers whether men are involved in projects countering gender-based violence or about women's rights, they mentioned different degrees of engagement. This ranged from explicitly stressing that "men participate in trainings, sensitizations"[48] to remarking "[f]or a [women's] empowerment project to succeed, there must be male involvement because some of these women are married—and hence need the support and involvement of their husbands to attend and benefit from the project."[49] Others vaguely noted that "men are somehow involved"[50] or simply said: "No, they are not."[51] Many—if not most—men in Kyaka II would probably agree with that last quote, as a number of those spoken with were to criticize their lack of involvement, stressing among other reasons for this that "only women get more help, not us men."[52] This perspective is supported in the above-discussed findings of the survey with 400 participants.

The women/victim focus reflects how the local understandings of aid workers transmitted to their projects partly maintained and promoted, but partly also contradicted and contested, global norms regarding protection. While global policies also promote the idea of working with community figureheads such as women leaders and propose collaborative measures so as to create awareness and counteract gender-based violence (UNHCR 2008a: 43, 53, 87, 213), they nevertheless explicitly state the relevance of including men and various other groups therein (UNHCR 2008a: 55ff; 2011b: 14–19).

Moreover, although aid workers continuously stressed the importance of the protection, empowerment, and self-determination of the woman during this conference and although they 'gave' the participating ones the chance to speak, the event was carried out with strict hierarchies; staff from the various agencies planned and implemented

---

[48] Female aid worker, interview, April 22, 2014.
[49] Female aid worker, interview, May 11, 2014.
[50] Female aid worker, interview, April 2, 2014.
[51] Female aid worker, interview, April 14, 2014.
[52] Discussion with local leaders, March 20, 2014, Base Camp.

it, whereas women leaders were merely allowed to take part (not, as noted, even the case for men). The women/victim focus, thus, exemplifies how local interpretations of protection in Kyaka II reinforced inequalities, an observation that Bonacker and Heusinger (2017) also note in the context of development aid in Cambodia.

"Women are taught to be respectful and submissive": Empowering Vulnerable Women

Campaigns such as this conference for women served not only to counteract gender-based violence and inform people about humanitarian protection structures, but also to support women's empowerment. The international genesis of 'empowerment' has led to an institutionalized yet inconsistent concept (on the broader development discourse, see Calvès 2009), one that has since undergone change in global refugee policies and protection regimes (e.g., UNHCR 2001d, 2001b; 2004a: 3; 2008a: 39-54; 2017c: 24). In UNHCR's *Handbook for the Protection of Women and Girls*, empowerment has come to revolve around power relations and seeks to promote women's equal access to and participation in local decision-making structures (UNHCR 2008a: 39–44). To this end, UNHCR lists:

> *initiatives to prevent and respond to SGBV [...]; creating a space for women and girls and strengthening their public voice so that they can participate meaningfully in and influence societal decision-making processes, including camp management [...]; enhancing their equal access to [...] services and their economic empowerment [...], and working to achieve a shift in power relations between women and men, girls and boys towards equality, including in traditional roles inside the home.* (UNHCR 2008a: 15)

In Kyaka II, aid workers explained how they strategically support women's empowerment "with knowledge and skills to report [violence] and protect themselves."[53] The aim in empowerment, therefore, exceeded information campaigns, including "skills training for income-generating activities" such as tailoring and sewing[54]—thus fields typical for women and their domestic tasks. Some saving and credit projects were also offered to women.[55] Women's hardships and

---

[53] Female aid worker, interview, May 11, 2014.
[54] Female aid worker, interview, April 22, 2014.
[55] Male aid worker, interview, April 10, 2014.

suffering appeared to be the crucial argument underpinning the articulated need for such empowerment projects. One aid worker stressed that such saving and credit projects for women, for example, served "to help empower the refugees, and help them to forget the torture of the war."[56] Concerning empowerment more generally, another emphasized that "women are strongly psychologically tortured by the high level of poverty in their homes, they need to be empowered in order to reduce the dependency syndrome."[57] In essence, the projects were delivered so that women would be "able to look after themselves"[58] and "empowered with defensive and protective skills."[59]

These and other statements by the aid workers spoken with show that empowerment was diversely interpreted and contested in Kyaka II. From the interviews, four interdependent issues came to light: (1) Empowerment was inherently entangled with vulnerability but also (2) economic performance, translating into support for survivability, which (3) imposed various roles on the women, and (4) resonated with the neoliberal paradigm and biopolitical transfer of responsibilities.

Empowerment, Vulnerability, and Economic Performance

First, empowerment projects were said to support women's livelihoods, income-generation, and ability for self-protection in Kyaka II. While these approaches to safety, economic practice, and access to services broadly correspond with global norms (UNHCR 2008a: 15, 39–44), women's meaningful participation in and influence of societal decision-making processes—as highlighted by UNHCR (2008a: 15)—appeared less central in Kyaka II. Rather, empowerment projects were inherently rooted in the very idea of vulnerability. The apparent helplessness and subsequent vulnerabilization of women thus constituted the basic point of departure and the assumed status quo meant to be overcome through projects like these. Bluntly put, as vulnerable, powerless victims, women were seen to require external assistance to arrive at empowerment.

Second, the projects sought specifically to promote women's livelihoods and thus economic performance as the key way to resolve their vulnerable state. Women were therefore made responsible for being

[56] Male aid worker, interview, March 14, 2014.
[57] Male aid worker, interview, April 14, 2014.
[58] Female aid worker, interview, April 2, 2014.
[59] Female aid worker, interview, May 11, 2014.

less vulnerable to risks of gender-based violence by being taught to defend themselves and by being tasked with increasing their financial income. This is contradictory, and shows that empowerment projects at the time of research essentially sought to support women's survivability. Yet such a responsibility of becoming less vulnerable was not only regarding their own positions; women's empowerment for survivability also extended to their social networks. Responding to the question of how gender roles are regarded within empowerment projects, one aid worker addressed the key roles of women in the community and in families:

Women are good counselors of girls, especially when they are faced with a lot of SGBV challenges. They play a very strong role in family development, especially in bringing up children as they are very close to them. Women are productive in the community, as they are everywhere in work that involves being in a group.[60]

Another, whose job was to manage gender-related projects in Kyaka II, explained:

Women are taught to be respectful and submissive to their husbands, and to tolerate them. Men are seen as strong and having to take responsibility for their homes; that is, their wives and children. Projects are driven toward changing the attitudes of both men and women, so that women are taught to be self-sufficient and self-reliant—for instance via skills training. Sensitization about women's rights is done with emphasis on the duties and responsibilities of parents.[61]

Despite this aid worker's reference to the underlying intention of also changing the attitudes of men, no evidence for such projects was found during my time in the camp.

The focus of empowerment measures on women's individual responsibilities for themselves and their social networks indicates, third, how aid workers simultaneously promoted 'traditional' domestic roles of women as 'good wives, mothers, and caretakers' but added components of 'providers' of safety in communities and breadwinners in families, too. This signified women suddenly obtaining a great mixture of different, and contradictory, domestic, social, and economic roles—a tendency that corresponds with other studies about women's various

---

[60] Male aid worker, interview, April 10, 2014.
[61] Female aid worker, interview, April 22, 2014.

imposed roles (see Olivius 2014; Grabska 2011; Szczepaniková 2005). While global policies also promote the variety of roles women—as well as others—have (UNHCR 2008a: 39–44), the localization of this idea and thus the roles ascribed to women in Kyaka II led to difficulties. One aid worker said with concern that "many times women become the sole providers and protectors of the homes," and reflected on the effects hereof for men (not for women); she explained that "men run away due to overwhelming demands, as they can neither do that [protect the family] nor have money for business."[62] However, the roles for women promoted by empowerment projects also entailed difficulties for women themselves; in a discussion, a group of them addressed their various responsibilities and criticized how some came to feel overburdened and how men contributed insufficiently.[63] Hence, in lieu of the aim to make women responsible for overcoming their vulnerabilities through empowerment, these were partly increased. Moreover, relating to my argument above, this suggests that the women/victim focus not only in protection but also in empowerment projects in Kyaka II ultimately reinforced inequalities.

But whom did these projects actually address? In light of the collection of domestic, social, and economic roles noted, such projects did not appear to be directed at all women in the camp. Instead, these roles reveal how empowerment was concentrated on a specific group among the women—those who were married, had families and children, and were involved in community matters. This likely limited the group to people in an age range of about their early twenties to mid-forties in order to ensure that all characteristics were met —and, importantly, it was about those women whom aid workers could actually reach. Inequality was, therefore, reinforced among the women too. Fiddian-Qasmiyeh similarly highlights how aid in Sahrawi refugee camps targeted only certain groups, "thereby systematically failing to identify or address the needs and rights of social groups which have been marginalized from view" (2010a: 83).

Fourth, the survivability approach and transfer of responsibilities along with the aim to 'sensitize' and 'teach' women in Kyaka II reveals empowerment to be part of the prevailing neoliberal paradigm. Women were shown and taught 'how to be empowered' as 'providers'

---

[62] Female aid worker, interview, May 11, 2014.
[63] Discussion 1 with female refugees, March 12, 2014, Base Camp.

and 'protectors' in addition to being 'good wives, mothers, and care-takers' due to their ascribed vulnerability. With a view on Burmese refugees in Thailand and Bangladesh, Olivius also identifies the influence of such a neoliberal paradigm (2013) and notes elsewhere in a similar fashion: "Appealed to as mothers and carers, refugee women are made responsible for the welfare and development of their families and community" (2014: 50). Yet while global norms stipulate "[e]mpowerment is not something that is done to women" but instead represents "a participatory process" (UNHCR 2008a: 41), in Kyaka II roles were primarily 'given' to women. In an almost biopolitical sense, a one-dimensional process appeared to be in play—with aid agencies providing and women receiving these roles. In other words: Women, as the prime target group of empowerment projects, were generally believed to be powerless and vulnerable, and only capable of being empowered with the support of (the powerful) humanitarian agencies.

Quo Vadis? Critical Reflections on Humanitarian Biases and Categories

Concluding this section, we cannot proceed without noticing the remarkable resemblance between the protection and empowerment projects carried out in Kyaka II at the time of research and the objectives that earlier feminist scholars and activists pursued. In the second wave of feminism, the prominent slogan of 'The Private is Political' stressed the interdependence of women's personal experiences with the contemporary political, social, and legal structures in place. This spurred requests to promote women's roles, ensure their participation, and increase their protection in public and private spheres, and support processes toward gender equality by focusing on improving women's position in society (see Echols 1989; Ryan 1992; Evans 1995).

The second wave was mainly shaped by Western scholars and focused on Western hemispheres, but it did also affect developments globally (see Molony and Nelson 2019). The essentialist view on white, middle-class women prompted criticism, however, and paved the way for the following third wave with broader views (see Archer Mann and Huffman 2005). This third wave is also influenced by postcolonial scholars such as Spivak (1999), relates to global and local feminist movements and transnational politics, concerns itself with individuality and complexity, and intersects with numerous actors and issues (see Garrison 2007; Snyder 2008; Wessels 2018).

Had the above-discussed projects in Kyaka II been implemented in the 1970s or 1980s and had my analytical approach been mainly—or perhaps solely—shaped by the second wave's objectives, then my analysis would have likely turned out different, less critical, and more celebratory. It would have likely highlighted how women were indeed moved to the forefront of humanitarian and, thus, political attention; how the focus was placed on them, their safety, and their roles, with increased access to aid provided; and, how the second-wave feminists achieved their call for the private to be part of the public and the political. It would have likely stressed how the protection and empowerment projects in Kyaka II appeared to follow the feminist concepts of women's engagement and empowerment, and thus how these have done what feminists requested—albeit decades ago.

The latter aspect of earlier concepts still being followed at the time of research remains valid today, and it could be taken as a sign of earlier feminist research and activism having succeeded in prompting change within the humanitarian field of refugee protection. By this, I certainly do not want to imply that refugee aid specifically in Kyaka II was then 'backward' or that aid workers there were not up-to-date with current feminist or gender debates. Far from it, my research in connection with other recent studies pointing to similar tendencies (e.g., Fiddian-Qasmiyeh 2010a; Grabska 2011; Olivius 2014) leads to the question of how long it takes until debates in research—particularly in Social Science–related fields—enter those in operational areas such as refugee protection.

Since my analysis of the developments in Kyaka II takes place now and is, of course, influenced by the literature that I have read and the theories I have come across in the years since, the essentialist view on women—their vulnerability, protection, and empowerment—is certainly liable to provoke criticism. The focus on women produces imbalances, which can be understood as a structural disadvantage for, the exclusion of, or as discrimination against both women and men—as noted in Chapter 2, and further reflected on below. Women were primarily seen as vulnerable, a view that was generally not held toward men. Paradoxically, such a skewed perspective also indicates a continuation of male-dominated norms within refugee protection. Since the 1980s, feminist scholars have criticized how international refugee law is influenced by a 'gender bias,' 'male bias,' or even a 'male paradigm' (see, e.g., Indra 1987: 3; Greatbatch 1989: 518; Markard 2007: 377–378; Firth and Mauthe 2013: 475, 473).

This is not limited to law, but also applies to humanitarianism. Early on, Indra stressed that "gender is a central organizational element of humanitarian assistance and refugee lives"—but one that was being ignored, contributing to the "bureaucratic muting of women" (1989: 222). This had far-reaching effects, as everyday issues of women, such as sanitary pads, were rarely addressed (see Marshall 1995) in the male-dominated world of humanitarian aid for refugees. Much has certainly changed in the way aid is delivered since then, but the above analysis reveals that men were still seen as the powerful ones: the primary providers in families and communities. Men were, therefore, still the standard filter in humanitarian protection and assistance; women, in contrast, appeared to require externally provided protection and empowerment. This perpetuates the essentialization of gender differences, and mirrors the top-down structure found in Kyaka II.

Similar to vulnerability being an apparently clearly identifiable categorization, humanitarian agencies also defined what forms of gender-based violence were tackled as well as how protection and empowerment were to be achieved there. Such approaches bear the risk of reducing protection and empowerment to certain humanitarian criteria, therein neglecting the views, experiences, and capacities of women and others who are detached from aid structures—not to mention of creating binary categorizations of women and men as well as of vulnerable and empowered people.[64] The tensions between the different humanitarian ascriptions and categorizations imposed on women are also addressed by Fiddian-Qasmiyeh (2014a, 2010a), who demonstrates impressively how women in the Algerian Sahrawi refugee camps are considered prime examples of empowered 'ideal' women. The focus on prominently favored groups in Kyaka II, however, left other realities unnoticed; people outside the visible range of humanitarianism as well as the social hierarchies that formed among the people in the camp remained pretty much hidden in plain sight.

---

[64] This shares similarities with the self-reliance approach in Uganda's refugee protection, in which refugees also appear to only fulfill one of the categories (see Krause and Schmidt 2020).

Here I see strong influences of 'global' policies on the local projects —policies that are in fact embedded in Western politics. An analysis hereof would therefore be best facilitated by postcolonial reflections, which sadly are beyond the scope of my research in this book. Despite consideration in some studies (see Hyndman 1996; Peterson 2012; Mayblin 2017; Lingelbach 2020; Krause 2021b), postcolonial perspectives certainly need further academic attention in future explorations of refugee protection and politics more generally. Linked with debates about norm localization, postcolonial thought can help us to better understand the ways in which refugee aid is localized in the specific settings of refugee camps. Here, the local contestations between different actors—including aid and government staff as well as refugees—should receive particular consideration, so as to illuminate the local treatment of allegedly global concepts.

In Kyaka II, it was not only that "in SGBV projects women are given more priority and advantage over men,"[65] but the general focus of gender-related approaches and projects was on women and had little to do with the aim of promoting 'gender equality' in all its complexity. Interestingly, an example for actual equal access to aid was the distribution of farmland—thus, a form that did not specifically focus on gender. In Kyaka II, it was given to women and men alike; refugees received the same size of land depending on the size of households—whether headed by women or men. This represented great structural change to the social norms in DR Congo where land was primarily transferred patrilineally—therefore being passed down from fathers to sons, while girls had only limited rights. Some women in Kyaka II found this change an opportunity for them.

However, gender-related projects in the camp were found to be based on gender biases and to reinforce respective inequalities; 'vulnerable women' appeared to stand in contrast to (supposedly violent) men —who were rarely seen as vulnerable. Contrary to an alleged gender sensitivity, the approaches manifested the equation of 'gender=woman' (see Fiddian-Qasmiyeh et al. 2017; Krause 2017c); it excluded men in some areas, and denied them support based on their gender. This occurred regardless of whether or not they had committed or suffered violence, whether or not they were single fathers (as an equivalent to single mothers, who, as noted, are assumed to be 'especially

---

[65] Female aid worker, interview, April 22, 2014.

vulnerable'). Grabska also finds how humanitarian projects related to gender equality and women's empowerment focus on women, and how refugees perceive the projects and subsequently gender as "giving power to women" (2011: 88).

Although risks to men have been increasingly addressed in global refugee debates and policies since 2009 (see Edwards 2010: 40–41), there was, as noted, no evidence of related projects in Kyaka II (on Syrian men in Jordan, see Turner 2019). Yet that men constituted the norm in aid projects in Kyaka II is revealed in the fairly exclusive humanitarian categorizations of vulnerability and empowerment imposed on women. Women but also men had to meet attributes to prove their need for—or even their 'worthiness' of—specific aid in the camp.[66] This essentialized the complex experiences, needs, capacities, interests, and hopes of all people living there—not just women. Further, it scarcely considered individual and context-specific representations of own experiences in the still male-dominated asylum and protection discourse. It is, thus, not despite but because of the humanitarian focus on women in Kyaka II that women's anonymity was maintained and further intensified by approaching them as 'vulnerable protection objects' there. Defined by vulnerability, humanitarian agencies underlined the helplessness of women in the camp and subsequently vulnerabilized them—even in the course of projects that apparently sought to contribute to their empowerment.

Women's image thus seems clear: helpless and passive objects in the humanitarian apparatus, ones that (not who) required and relied on external support mechanisms for their safety. This is an image that now virtually demands a postcolonial reading. Following Spivak's seminal postcolonial critique that "white men are saving brown women from brown men" (1999: 284), humanitarian refugee aid—with its Western-style norms and principles—seems to have come to pursue the Western savior mentality (see also Fernando 2016), thus meaning that these aid agencies must step in to protect, save, heal, and empower women. In so doing, victimhood, powerlessness, and passivity become qualities inherently connected with women's refugeehood.

---

[66] Similarly in legal matters, women must comply with the cultural concepts and stereotypes of countries when seeking asylum (see Firth and Mauthe 2013: 482–483).

Linking Camp Structures, Humanitarian Aid, and Gender-Based Violence

In his book *Rethinking Refugees*, Nyers posits "Humanitarian violence? At first glance, the concept seems to be an oxymoron, an almost insulting contradiction in terms" while then acknowledging the disjuncture (2006: 24). Not only are androcentric values and patriarchal structures reproduced in humanitarian refugee aid but, as Freedman postulates: "The type of processes established by the UNHCR and other agencies and NGOs in refugee camps to try and promote gender justice can also be seen to fail in some instances because they reproduce and normalise cultural differences, ascribing unequal gender relations and violence against women to the product of 'traditions' which cannot or should not be challenged" (2015a: 39). Such tensions form the basis of this third section in this chapter, concentrating on how camp structures, aid, and gender-based violence were interlinked in Kyaka II. It is asked: How is it possible that a number of projects were implemented to reduce the scope of gender-based violence, yet these risks still persisted? How was this violence associated with the way camps like Kyaka II function and humanitarian aid is delivered?

Of course, one could underline that it is up to the camp inhabitants themselves to stop or prevent such violence. Another perspective may be that this prevalent gender-based violence occurs due to inadequate or scarce protection, or even represents the failure of humanitarian actors (see also Olsen and Scharffscher 2004). Kyaka II encompasses, as noted, more than 80 km^2 however, and humanitarian agencies cannot be everywhere at the same time. While these arguments may appear logical, they overlook the complexity of the effects of the humanitarian regime per se on the people and the gender-based violence in the camp.

To explain how the camp structures and aid system in Kyaka II potentially contribute to such violence, I argue that: (1) some cases are perpetrated by aid workers themselves; (2) the camp landscape and local limitations generally bear risks; and, (3) humanitarian aid links with power practices and effects changes in gender relations, which can give rise to significant tensions. Each of these aspects makes clear that gender-based violence does not necessarily occur in spite of the camp conditions and aid structures in Kyaka II but also, indeed, because of them.[67]

"It is very inevitable [but hard to] prove": Aid Workers as Perpetrators of Violence?

In Chapter 2, I presented survey findings about the scope and structures of gender-based violence in Kyaka II. These results indicated participants' perceptions not only about the main groups of victims but also of perpetrators. Following all responses survey participants gave, 15.5 percent of the women and 8.3 percent of the men believed aid workers to be among the main perpetrator group of gender-based violence. Although this is much lower than the 77.9 percent of the women and 81.7 percent of the men who felt that these acts are primarily committed by male refugees (see Figure 2.2), the statistics regarding aid workers are still telling in themselves and should not be underestimated—as participants' responses likely reflected their own personal experiences. Dialogues, discussions, and journal writings provided more detailed accounts of gender-based violence committed by aid workers, revealing why more women than men assumed that aid workers were among the perpetrators hereof; it is mostly women who endured such experiences or who (dared to) speak about them.

A 28-year-old woman who had fled the genocide in Rwanda with her parents and sister vividly recalled incidents with one aid worker. When she was younger and in secondary school, she had a baby but not sufficient resources to support herself and her newborn child even despite help from her family. "Life was tough then" she said, before explaining that she decided to try and pursue her dream of becoming a nurse. To this end, she once applied for a scholarship to continue her education provided by an NGO in Kyaka II. However, she was confronted with an aid worker who asked for sexual favors in return.

The guy working there told me I can't have the scholarship unless I accepted to go with him. He told me he wanted to take me to Kampala, rent me a house and take care of me. He asked me not to tell my parents about it. To me that would have been a big risk, going with a man without my parents'

---

[67] Prior analyses on the effects of the humanitarian system on gender-based violence against women in Kyaka II were published (see Krause 2020), which this part now builds on and expands.

knowledge. Because I said no, he told me I would never go to school as long as I am in Kyaka II.

Describing her desperate situation and frustration, she continued: "I really, really wanted to go to school, because that was even the only way to better myself; it felt very belittling to tell me such a thing." At first she did not know what to do, but after several days she decided to go to OPM, report the case, and to seek assistance; it eventually worked, with her starting a different program at a private school.[68]

Other women shared similar stories, and such perpetration of violence corresponds with Galtung's form of direct and personal violence understood in a gender-sensitive conceptualization following Confortini. A number of adolescents furthermore underlined, as detailed in Chapter 2, the risks of sexual harassment and abuse by teachers. Schoolteachers may not always be assumed to be 'aid workers' in a narrow sense, but when employed in the camp they operate within its structures and humanitarian programs, and are at times paid by aid agencies. Their roles can therefore be understood as forming part of the humanitarian system unfolded on-site. Adolescents referred to sexual violence by teachers and said that "[s]tudents are forced into sexual intercourse by their lustful male teachers"[69] while "girls are harassed sexually by some male teachers and boys. This takes the form of rape, defilement, and other harassment."[70] It was also expressed that "female teachers [use] boys for sexual activities in school."[71] Moreover, an adolescent noted: "There is sexual harassment where girls are asked to give their private parts to officials during the time of asking [for] jobs."[72]

Such accounts reveal risks similar to Ferris's criticism that: "Humanitarian workers traded food and relief items for sexual favors. Teachers in schools in the camps exploited children in exchange for passing grades. Medical care and medicines were given in return for

---

[68] Female refugee, dialogue, March 18, 2014, Base Camp.
[69] Male adolescent, 19 years old, journal writing, April 3, 2014, Bujubuli Secondary School.
[70] Female adolescent, 17 years old, journal writing, April 3, 2014, Bujubuli Secondary School.
[71] Male adolescent, 15 years old, journal writing, April 3, 2014, Bujubuli Secondary School.
[72] Female adolescent, 15 years old, journal writing, March 5, 2014, Bujubuli Secondary School.

sex" (2007: 585). In recent years, sensitivity to these dangers in peace-keeping, relief provision, and development work has increased—not least after cases of violence committed by aid workers became public and were widely discussed (see UN 2018; Reuters 2019). These risks also occur in the context of refugee aid; UNHCR has already made such cases public almost 20 years ago (UNHCR 2002). Then as today, assessments of the situations ensue and regulations follow that seek to put in place better protection mechanisms (UNHCR and Save the Children 2002; UNHCR 2018d, 2019b). But do they help? Has awareness of these issues increased among staff worldwide?

Having asked aid workers about gender-based violence perpetrated by humanitarian staff in Kyaka II, it came as a surprise that their answers would demonstrate different and almost opposing tendencies. On the one hand, sex for favors was widely acknowledged to occur. Informants relayed, for example: "Yes, there exist such cases mostly for small favors like to get access to basic needs."[73] Another illuminating response was:

Sex for favors is usually in schools where pupils and students do it to find favor before their class teachers, so that they can be given more marks and helped to pass and also not to be frequently punished in school. This is also done by local community persons, where a leader can subject a member to sex so as to support them in one way or another.[74]

These statements reveal that these risks tend to be understood as an apparently unavoidable or normal part of people's everyday lives in Kyaka II, even that of children in schools. None of the interviewees seemed to problematize the risks or see needs to prevent them and assist victims. Not deeming such dangers as forms of gender-based violence resonates with similar findings by Izugbara et al. (2018) on refugee community workers' perceptions in Dadaab, Kenya.

On the other hand, most aid workers interviewed denied that any staff member in Kyaka II would commit or had committed gender-based violence against refugees. Only few addressed apparently rare cases hereof. Besides noting that there had been "one case" in the past and "the perpetrator was punished,"[75] another informant recounted that it happened and "[t]he most common scenarios and perpetrators

---

[73] Female aid worker, interview, April 22, 2014.
[74] Female aid worker, interview, May 11, 2014.
[75] Female aid worker, interview, March27, 2014.

were partner staff and government officials [police, guards, etc.]."[76] Only one interviewee underscored that "it is very inevitable to a great extent. Though this is often very hard to know, or even prove."[77]

This indicates an unknown scope to gender-based violence committed by humanitarian staff, as well as victims' potential complications in reporting violence and pursuing justice in such cases. These concerns also relate to the earlier statement made by the man who complained: "UNHCR is supposed to protect the refugees, but I do not see them playing that role."[78] This criticism, of course, cannot be limited to UNHCR alone, but should instead be directed at the wider 'aid community' in Kyaka II comprising various agencies—yet Janmyr (2014a) argues that UNHCR would be internationally responsible in cases of wrongful conduct of implementing partners.

Issues with handling cases perpetrated by aid workers and security personnel are immediately apparent; for example, even if police officers were to be involved in violence, they or their colleagues would still be the ones responsible for compiling reports and pursuing cases. If refugees were to report gender-based violence committed by aid workers, they or their colleagues would likely receive notice and be the ones providing assistance. Refugees would, therefore, likely worry about both the material and immaterial consequences thereof. These examples prompt questions about reporting and subsequent referral in Kyaka II because, similar to what Wirtz et al. found for refugees in Ethiopia, the structures in place appear to be "passive systems that rely on survivor-initiated reporting and service-seeking" (2013: 2).

"We refugees do not have a say in Kyaka": Structural Effects of the Humanitarian Aid System

Exploring the links of aid, encampment, and gender-based violence in Kyaka II must not only cover direct perpetration thereof but also effects of existing and insufficient aid and regulations. These effects of humanitarian practices (including aid projects), approaches, and power dynamics on the prevalence of gender-based violence—or how they present forms of violence—are at the core in this section.

---

[76] Female aid worker, interview, April 10, 2014.
[77] Female aid worker, interview, May 11, 2014.
[78] Male refugee, dialogue, March 28, 2014, Base Camp.

With the scholarly debate about encampment in mind, I found great similarities to other camps in Kyaka II; local conditions were embedded in the hierarchical decision-making processes of humanitarian agencies. Harrell-Bond (1986) discusses the "imposed" nature of aid, while Agier describes such agencies as "humanitarian governments" practicing power over the people and transforming in the process into a form of "totalitarianism" (2011: 196). Turner, McConnachie, Jaji, and others point to the contradictory nature of camps, with refugees being invisible in them while also simultaneously visible objects of humanitarian aid (Turner 2016a: 144); camps also presenting "sites characterized by restricted autonomy and by resilient agency" (McConnachie 2016: 407). Due to the power practices as well as 'containment politics' unfurled, camps essentially serve, as previously noted, as a technology of control over refugees (Jaji 2012).

In drawing on this literature and reflecting on the endemic issues encountered in Kyaka II, the effects of humanitarian regulations and practices on gender-based violence come to light. Aid agencies impose structures on the people through the various projects that they implement, which, in turn, defines the possibilities and limitations of the people's living conditions. And these influences can partly be understood as structural violence as well as conditions that contribute to tensions among refugees.

On the one hand, keeping the Galtungian understanding of violence complemented by Confortini's gendered conceptualization as outlined in Chapter 2 in mind, not only direct but also structural and cultural forms thereof are relevant. The neglect of men in humanitarian programs as well as the labeling of women as vulnerable present just two examples for forms of discrimination and thus structural violence committed against refugees as a part of the regular aid delivery. Moreover, one woman prominently criticized the insufficient room for participation within the humanitarian system on-site, noting that "we refugees do not have a say in Kyaka II. We are discriminated against and harassed a lot. Those organizations do not give us time and space to speak for ourselves. They say we refugees report and destroy their work."[79] Many others lamented the treatment of aid workers in a similar vein. This was linked to decision-making procedures in the camp, as discussed above and as revealed in the above-discussed survey

---

[79] Female refugee, dialogue, March 14, 2014, Base Camp.

findings. To recap, the latter showed that about two-thirds of the survey participants believed they cannot involve in the aid system, aid agencies as making all decisions, and women receiving more aid than men. Yet, more women than men felt ways to participate in the aid system did exist, likely being influenced by the earlier-discussed specific protection and empowerment projects that these agencies offered to women living in the camp.

If we understand such differential treatment as discrimination, exclusion or disadvantage, then these present forms of structural violence that primarily occur on the grounds of gender and respective ascriptions. Aid workers—consciously or unconsciously—perpetrated these forms by upholding and perpetuating patriarchal gender norms and exclusionary hierarchies, realizing aid projects in certain ways, and therewith contributing to difficult situations for men and women. Further exacerbating this is the fact also that raising complaints and initiating change would likely be difficult for refugees as well. It would have been them to approach and complain to aid workers—the very individuals in charge of the projects needing to be altered.

On the other hand, the asymmetries of power in Kyaka II are not 'natural' but rather materialize in aid projects and political regulations that can contribute to physical hardships, social and economic restrictions, and frustrations of the displaced. Again, the way in which the vulnerability concept was used in Kyaka II presents an insistent example: While women were generally believed to be vulnerable and thus received prioritized access to aid, men were largely excluded— both because they were women or men. Although some women described such aid projects as helpful due to access to land and equal rights,[80] skills and knowledge,[81] others perceived it as overwhelming,[82] because the implications were not only that they had to maintain traditionally ascribed roles of 'good mothers, wives, and caretakers' but also turn into 'breadwinners.' Men, however, viewed these prioritized measures for women and the respective social changes that they

---

[80] Female refugee, dialogue, February 25, 2014, Base Camp; female refugee, dialogue, March 14, 2014, Base Camp.
[81] Female refugee, dialogue, March 18, 2014, Base Camp.
[82] Discussion 1 with women, March 12, 2014, Base Camp.

contributed to critically,[83] while also complaining about their neglect in aid projects.[84]

In addition to this presenting gender-based discrimination, the differential treatment can produce deep tensions too. By turning themselves into the main providers, protectors, and decision-makers in Kyaka II, humanitarian agencies contributed to a new and *unfamiliar* imbalance of power within those gender relations between the displaced women and men, which cause frustration. Yet tensions among refugees not only result from these vulnerability ascriptions, gender-related projects and their subsequent effects but also more generally from the scope of and top-down approach to aid delivery. This is because humanitarian agencies inflicted decisions, created restrictions, and cast roles for women and men on-site, as well as because aid was insufficient, livelihoods limited, and circumstances restrictive and uncertain. This ultimately influenced the living conditions and social relations existing within the camp—and could contribute to irritations. How broad these were can be seen in the use of early and forced marriage due to economic motives, or in the increase of domestic violence during harvest seasons—forms of violence associated with the limitations in Kyaka II. Hence, humanitarian agencies can contribute to—or sometimes even foment—some of the dangers they are striving to reduce in the name of refugee protection and assistance.

"SGBV takes place almost every time of the day": Camp Landscape Bearing Risks

Linked with these perspectives on direct perpetration of gender-based violence by aid workers and the aid system producing frustration, the third connection between the camp structures, humanitarian system, and gender-based violence in Kyaka II was the camp landscape itself. More precisely, the camp architecture gave rise to elements of insecurity, which increased the likelihood of such violence occurring. Women and girls noted that they were attacked while collecting firewood, fetching water, or farming. For example, one adolescent said that her sister was raped "when she went to fetch water."[85] Then there is the

---

[83] Discussion with local leaders, March 20, 2014, Base Camp.
[84] Discussion with local leaders, March 20, 2014, Base Camp.
[85] Female adolescent, 18 years, journal writing, March 5, 2014, Bujubuli Secondary School.

story of another woman, already presented in Chapter 2: She was raped while collecting firewood. Two men approached her on a public but remote road and although she tried to run away, they were stronger than her and managed to capture her. She did not report the case afterward, because the men threatened to kill her if she went to the police.[86]

These risks were well known among aid workers, with one stressing that gender-based violence takes place any time of the day; however, "[at] night, there is a lot of rape and defilement as women return home from business, water points, and when children are returning home from school. In the gardens and forest areas, while young girls go out to fetch firewood, they are trapped by men and boys and defiled."[87] Whereas some of the areas visited to find firewood were outside of the camp, this was by no means always the case. Water-collection points and the land for farming were also within the camp boundaries, but at times far away from where these individuals lived. The required treks to accomplish their everyday work in these rather remote sites could turn out to be risky. As a result, maneuvering in and through the camp landscape presented dangers that these people, and especially women and girls, appeared to have to face and deal with in order to manage their daily work. This reality was not limited to Kyaka II; earlier studies and reports from elsewhere have portrayed similar risks, and with them protection projects, in other camps too (see UNHCR 2001a; Hyndman 2004).

Local limitations in the camp can also contribute to gender-based violence, as outlined in Chapter 2. To recap, as part of the survey a number of participants said they believed sexual as well as domestic violence to be committed due to 'drugs and alcohol' and a 'lack of work.' Moreover, when the women and men reflected on causes of gender-based violence in dialogues and discussions, they also referred to livelihood limitations, restrictions, and economic drivers.[88] Although this may not immediately relate to the features of the camp landscape, interdependences certainly existed. Insufficient opportunities for employment were linked with the chosen setup and location of

---

[86] Female refugee, dialogue, March 13, 2014, Bujubuli.
[87] Female aid worker, interview, May 11, 2014.
[88] Female adolescent, 17 years old, journal writing, March 5, 2014, Bujubuli Secondary School; female adolescent,15 years old, journal writing, March 5, 2014, Bujubuli Secondary School.

the camp, along with the decision-making of authorities (e.g., restrictions on movement); drug and alcohol consumption were likely associated then with conditions in the camp.

Such unfavorable circumstances can turn into contributing factors to structural violence against women and girls, such as the denial of resources and early/forced marriage. In the latter case, economic motives need to be considered—as the child brides' caretakers or families received 'bride prices'. As one adolescent explained: "There is forced marriage for girls where parents want to get money to care for the family."[89] Thus, related to the shortcomings in the camp, financial, material, or other forms of 'compensation' could be a decisive incentive for some parents or caretakers to agree to or even arrange girls' weddings.

Many research participants, furthermore, spoke about increased violence during the harvest season. Among them, one aid worker said, "when women and girls are going to fetch firewood/charcoal for cooking, collecting food on food distribution days, lots of domestic violence is reported after harvest season."[90] Other aid workers discussed this correlation similarly, noting "cases of SGBV are seasonal"[91] and explaining that:

SGBV takes place almost every time of the day. However, it's at its peak during and after the harvest season. This is when the man take the proceeds for selling [crops] without the consent of the wife, and drinks any money he has earned from it. When the wife asks for money and food etc., he gets angry and beats her and the children. When the men get money after the harvest, they become promiscuous and get involved in extramarital relationships—even with other people's wives. This causes internal and community instability.[92]

Quotes like these bring to light how the prevalence of gender-based violence also resulted from the local conditions found in Kyaka II. Key to note is that these conditions were part of the camp setting produced specifically by humanitarian regulations and practices. Moreover, these risks stand in stark contrast to the fundamental idea of the people

---

[89] Female adolescent, 17 years old, journal writing, March 5, 2014, Bujubuli Secondary School.
[90] Female aid worker, interview, April 10, 2014.
[91] Male aid worker, interview, March 18, 2014.
[92] Female aid worker, interview, May 11, 2014.

having to achieve self-reliance through farming in Uganda; the focus on agriculture created and maintained a specific level of risk.

The overall discussion in this third section has demonstrated how gender-based violence is connected with conditions in the camp as well as the system of humanitarian aid. In lieu of singular, clear-cut, and monocausal relations, various interdependent factors contribute to this encountered reality on the ground. The way aid is realized and camps are run, how women and men are treated, whether or not they are involved in decision-making, what opportunities they have available to them beyond aid projects, yet also the types of the latter offered as well as how cases of sexual abuse were prosecuted—all of these aspects can be linked to the prevalence of gender-based violence.

Brief Excursus: Reasonable Criticism in Light of Humanitarian Challenges?

In a similar vein to how I have criticized various aspects of how Kyaka II was run and aid delivered at the time of research, a broader related debate among scholars finds much to complain about too. Camps are discussed as places of "non-existence" (Agier 2011: 80) and "a form of human warehousing and 'storage' of refugees who are simultaneously perceived as victims and agents of insecurity" (Jaji 2012: 227). As a result of their leadership and acquisition of governmental functions, humanitarian agencies and camps are also described as 'surrogate states' (Deardorff Miller 2018; Kagan 2011). The effects on refugees are fundamental, as their lives are 'managed' by humanitarian agencies via what Foucault would describe as "discipline" and "governmental-ity"—the practices through which control is exercised (Hyndman 2000; Lippert 1999; Jaji 2012; Agier 2011).

The earlier-mentioned notion of vulnerability may at first seem to support a charitable, humanistic approach to 'helping' refugees in lieu of controlling them. However, as I have reflected on in this chapter, perceiving, presenting, and imagining refugees in general and women in particular as 'vulnerable victims' externally ascribes to these indi-viduals an identity constituted by passivity, political innocence, and disconnectedness from community structures, which reveals the "con-temporary narcissistic cult of victimisation" (Pupavac 2006: 14). As Indra already stressed in the late 1990s: "Western social issue and social problem-generated images of refugees as powerless victims of forces beyond their control are well entrenched" (1999b: xiv). Agamben (1998) refers to the reduction of the individual to its pure existence, "the bare life." Malkki (1995a: 11) compares the understanding of refugees within the humanitarian discourse as akin to that of helpless infants; Manchanda (2004: 4179) captures the framing of women as "non-person" similarly in an "infantilisation." Fassin (2009: 49) emphasizes the biopolitics that not only promote life, but also decide the kind that refugees can have; Fassin (2012) also elaborates on how camps act as both humanitarian shelters and sites of repression.

But are such criticisms reasonable? Or do humanitarian agencies merely serve as scapegoats for inadequate national policies and a lack of international cooperation and funding—all factors essential for providing (more and better) humanitarian support? Of course, the refugee camp imposes by its very nature various restrictions on the people living within its confines, and thus is not a suitable form of long-term accommodation. Over the past few years, UNHCR has been increasingly committed to finding and negotiating alternatives to camps so as to enable refugees to self-settle in countries of asylum (Crisp 2017; UNHCR 1997b, 2009a, 2014a). However, governments of asylum countries—who essentially decide about refugee policies within their territory—remain reluctant to genuinely entertain this self-settlement option (Kibreab 2007).

Moreover, humanitarian agencies as well as countries of asylum in regions of the Global South, where, as noted, the vast majority of refugees worldwide live, must confront the issue of chronic underfunding each year (see, e.g., Loescher et al. 2012: 96–100). This links with the much-debated issues of burden and responsibility sharing in the international community (e.g., Martin 1995; Gottwald 2014; Türk and Garlick 2016), and underfunding eventually leads not only to limited but ultimately insufficient aid. In line with this, most of the humanitarian staff in Kyaka II stressed the difficult funding situation, which created obstacles to realizing protection and assistance as needed in the camp. Critical statements made by interlocutors about "vast area[s] of operation, dealing with people who have been traumatized,"[93] "[i]nsufficient construction material[s] when it comes to sanitation; [a] lack of staffing with little salaries and accommodation

---

[93] Female aid worker, interview, April 10, 2014.

issues,"[94] "[p]oor road network[s] especially to the local villages, which affects efficient service delivery,"[95] and the lack of "funds to finish their activities as planned"[96] demonstrate how funding—or rather underfunding—gave rise to multiple and particular challenges in their aid work.

Thus, aid workers in Kyaka II were very critical of the humanitarian system itself with its shortcomings—especially in a financial sense—but they additionally also criticized 'the refugees' for their laziness or shortsightedness, as discussed earlier. This appears similar to shifting responsibility to refugees; and already over three decades ago, Waldron pointed out that "[t]he clue to the appearance of unfounded negative statements concerning the behaviour of the refugees in Somali camps lies in an inspection of the structure of the expatriate administration and the ways in which this conditioned the management and perception of those designated as refugees" (1987: 1). With reference to Waldron, Walkup reasoned that "to protect Self, they begin to rationalize failure by transferring the guilt away from themselves or the system, and by pointing the blame at other external factors" (1991: 9). Despite negative ascriptions of refugees expressed by aid workers, the empirical data collected in Kyaka II does not reveal whether or to what extent the aid workers interviewed there actually transferred guilt on refugees for the systematic problems experienced.

From a broader perspective, four issues come to light regarding this particular camp: contradictory ideas about gender roles; everyday workloads; humanitarian jobs; and, questions of power. First, a great number of humanitarian staff in Kyaka II were women, and several had decision-making positions within aid agencies. While this did not appear to be an issue for male colleagues in the camp, the ideas about gender relations that aid workers presented during interviews were strongly patriarchal. In Chapter 4, I will further discuss how female and male aid workers clung to gender stereotypes of men as decision-makers and women as responsible for the domestic spheres in the projects. The different perspectives that women held about being in power while also believing in strict gender hierarchies were contradictory, with female aid workers being confronted with various obstacles

---

[94] Female aid worker, interview, March 27, 2014.
[95] Female aid worker, interview, May 11, 2014.
[96] Female aid worker, interview, April 2, 2014.

and limitations even despite their leading positions. Some had to defend their professional and also social roles—partly indirectly, yet continuously—at work and in their families. As a result, it may be understandable why some of them focused specifically on women's protection and empowerment.

Second, aid workers' everyday work in Kyaka II was filled with the administrative duty of writing proposals and reports to keep donors and partner organizations satisfied, and thus to support the process of acquiring new funds. As a result, criticisms by refugees that aid workers were not doing their work and not providing protection as locally required[97] were likely not the whole story at least. Aid workers may not have been able to provide more than they already did. An example of this can be seen in UNHCR's publicly available funding statistics: Humanitarian operations for refugee aid throughout Uganda were largely underfunded by 66 percent in September of 2014 (UNHCR 2014e), thus shortly after the research was carried out in Kyaka II. This was by no means limited to this period; operations were also underfunded by 62 percent at the end of 2017, by 58 percent at the end of 2018, and by 60 percent at the end of 2019—while received funds were often earmarked (UNHCR 2017e, 2018f, 2019c).

Third, at the time of research all humanitarian staff in Kyaka II were Ugandan nationals, and for many of those spoken with employment in the camp constituted just that: a job. Of course, aid workers have to act in accordance with the rules and standards of humanitarian agencies (see Harrell-Bond et al. 2005: 292ff); thus, they should adhere to the humanitarian principles of humanity, neutrality, impartiality, and independence. Yet when I sat with the displaced women and men, as well as with aid workers in the evenings, and talked about life and work, the notion of their employment there merely constituting a job became clear. This contrasts with the possibly romantic or romanticized Western idea of humanitarianism. Many of the aid workers in Kyaka II undoubtedly wanted to do more to reduce the suffering of the people living there. However, they not only saw the structural (and financial) limitations faced, but were also frustrated by them—which can have serious consequences for one's mental health, such as burnout (see Strohmeier and Scholte 2015). Some were simply looking out for themselves meanwhile. With their families often living far from Kyaka

---

[97] Male refugee, dialogue, March 28, 2014, Base Camp.

II, mostly only seeing them on weekends, as well as their contracts merely lasting for the duration of project funding (often one or two years), some of the staff were just biding their time until a better employment opportunity arose. This caused high turnover rates among staff in camps like Kyaka II.

Linked to the necessary contextualization of charitable humanitarianism is, fourth, power. Delivering humanitarian services in whatever sector —be it education, medical support, food, or similar—put aid workers in powerful positions: They gave something that refugees received. Conversely, being on the receiving end, refugees therefore appeared powerless. Harrell-Bond (2002), Indra (1993), Barnett (2011), and others have discussed how the apparent altruism in 'humanitarian giving' links up with paternalism and hierarchical imbalances, which may ultimately lead to the question of who is deserving of aid. The correct humanitarian response, based on global (thus Western-influenced) policies, is probably 'the vulnerable,' which further cements the power of aid workers and the apparent helplessness of refugees. That some of the former indeed misused their power in going so far as to commit gender-based violence or request sexual favors in return for aid or good grades in school was discussed already. Yet it would be wrong to assume that all aid workers in Kyaka II or worldwide behaved or behave in such ways.

Contradictory ideas about gender relations and high staff turnovers, job-seeking, or insufficient funding situations are, however, certainly not justifications for strong restrictions on, the inadequate treatment of, or even violence against refugees. Are, then, the criticisms raised in this chapter reasonable in light of the manifest challenges that humanitarian agencies and their staff faced? I argue that, despite the challenging circumstances faced, they are, as revealed by the numerous empirical examples given. To delve even deeper into this thorny issue, it would also be worthwhile to further explore aid workers' own ideas about gender relations, so as to better understand the core premises of their projects as well as these individuals' chosen behaviors toward displaced women, men, and others. Gender ideas, roles, and relations will be the subject of discussion in Chapter 4.

In Conclusion: The Camp as a Site of Humanitarian Control?

This chapter has reflected closely on aid practices in Uganda's Kyaka II refugee camp. Following on from the introduction, in the first section

I discussed the general approach to development-oriented refugee aid on-site and critically addressed the promoted self-reliance strategy with it mainly focusing on farming. I further showed how refugees in Kyaka II were not treated as actors, but instead as 'protection objects.'

The second section about specific measures implemented against gender-based violence elaborated on the latter point, and revealed that women in particular were framed as 'vulnerable protection objects' by aid agencies working in Kyaka II. This chapter section paid attention to the way aid workers delivered reactive and preventative projects against such violence as well as measures to support empowerment, and how in the process they aligned to, contested, or went beyond related global norms. Importantly, I argued that the women/victim focus within protection and empowerment projects in Kyaka II actually reinforced existing inequalities between displaced women and men in lieu of promoting gender equality.

In the third section, I questioned how the very humanitarian structures put in place to protect and assist refugees can in fact contribute to the risks that they experience during encampment. I addressed three issues here: aid workers themselves committing gender-based violence; the camp landscape presenting risks; and, humanitarian aid contributing to social imbalances. As this chapter critiques at length the humanitarian practices encountered in Kyaka II during my time there, in the fourth section I questioned whether such criticism is ultimately reasonable and if the idea of humanitarianism should be deromanticized to some extent going forward. Despite inherent obstacles to the provision of aid such as limited funding and high staff turnovers, I argued that issues of violence, control, and strict power practices are highly problematic regardless of circumstance.

A significant body of research has developed in Forced Migration and Refugee Studies about encampment and humanitarian aid, on which I drew in this chapter and, of course, hope to contribute to. These works reflect on the humanitarian architecture of and in camps, their power structures, as well as on the projects implemented in order to help the displaced. In spite of the high volume of studies available, two concrete fields of research still requiring close attention must be pointed out here. First, while the local collaborations, procedures, projects, and strategies of aid agencies in refugee camps have been scrutinized, still little is known about how these are influenced by global or regional refugee policies and norms. While I addressed these influences and thus norm localizations, more research is necessary to divulge how local actors debate global norms, how they try to fit them into the normative order of the camp, or how they may perhaps only reproduce hollow ascriptions. Along with this, I believe postcolonial approaches would be valuable for nuanced analyses, as noted above. Second, via the example of Kyaka II, I showed that the camp is not only a conceived 'protection space' but also a site where aid measures and camp structures can contribute to or even cause risks. This corresponds with other studies, and exactly this link now needs further exploration, in order to thereafter develop ways to mitigate such effects.

4 | Changing Gender Relations in the Camp

For us Congolese, we know the man has to be on top and makes the final decision. The wife doesn't access anything, and everything belongs to the man. Now, we found things are different [in Kyaka II]. Man and woman are equal.[1]

In Congo, it is the man who carried out all the responsibilities, but in Kyaka II men and women share them. This is because men lost power in the home. In Congo, the man was the one responsible for looking for food and after everything in the home, but here in Kyaka II they all depend on UNHCR.[2]

These quotes from a Congolese woman and man foreshadow the tendencies—yet also contestations—of gender roles and relations that refugees would experience in Uganda's Kyaka II. Although both quotes similarly present the man as the dominant figure in gender systems and indicate changes during encampment compared to the situation prior to displacement, they also signify differences. The first quote by the woman implies that a certain level of gender equality had been reached in Kyaka II, whereas the second of the man reflects that men lost their social power there. Many women, men, adolescents, and aid workers spoken with in the camp expressed similar and additional views. But how did they perceive, challenge, negotiate, and make sense of the gender roles and relations, along with the changes occurring within them?

Much of the research on gender in Forced Migration and Refugee Studies attends to the risks, roles, and experiences primarily of women in refugee situations.[3] In recent years, scholars have also increasingly

[1] Female refugee, dialogue, March 27, 2014, Base Camp.
[2] Male refugee, dialogue, March 18, 2014, Base Camp.
[3] For more on this, see the literature cited in this book's chapters for related articles. Besides those, monographs and edited volumes are also available (e.g., Indra 1999b; Crawley 2001; Martin 2004; Hajdukowski-Ahmed et al. 2008b;

addressed those of men too.[4] These academic debates are highly relevant, and have contributed to our better understanding of gender-specific developments in such settings. They show that women and men experience displacement and life in exile differently, which ultimately reflects gendered processes in which roles and relations are renegotiated (Turner 1999: 1; Hans 2008: 69; Freedman 2015a: 33–34). However, the prevailing analytical view has been to examine either women or men. In order to trace and explore the indeed gendered processes, it is crucial to consider the roles and relations of both women and men of different age groups—which I strive to do in this chapter. As explained in Chapter 1, the research focuses on heterosexual relationships; homosexual ones are an unfortunate lacuna.

The perspective on changing gender systems and social (re)negotiations requires going beyond a focus on the camp alone and thus considering the life conditions of the displaced prior to flight too. Similar to the above quotes, many women and men shared stories about how they remembered gender relations in their countries of origin—often in comparison or even contrast to how they experienced them in Kyaka II. This is understandable, as most of the people who participated in the research spent parts of their lives in their countries of origin before fleeing violent conflicts there. Many had also been living in the artificially created camp for years. Although sites like Kyaka II are largely shaped by aid agencies and structures, these do not represent a humanitarian or social vacuum. Further to being influenced by local camp conditions, inhabitants also bring and call on their prior experiences, ideas, social structures, and practices there (see Inhetveen 2010: 271). To understand the changes the people referred to in their gender roles and relations, it is key to explore how they perceived them prior to as well as during life in the camp.

For the research in this chapter, Hearn's (2004, 2012, 2015) theory of the hegemony of men serves as its analytical matrix. Hearn approaches hegemony through patriarchy, in which social concepts

Martin and Tirman 2009; Mulumba 2010; Gerard 2014; Grabska 2014; Fiddian-Qasmiyeh 2014a; Freedman 2015a; Buckley-Zistel and Krause 2017).
[4] A steadily growing body of research concerns men and masculinities in Forced Migration and Refugee Studies (e.g., Turner 1999, 2004; Brun 2000; Jaji 2009a; Lukunka 2011; Kabachnik et al. 2013; Henry et al. 2013; Charsley and Wray 2015; Dolan 2014, 2017; Krause 2016e; Olivius 2016; Janmyr 2017; Suerbaum 2018; Turner 2018, 2019).

and power constellations of male dominance are anchored. Based on Critical Masculinity Studies, Hearn does not assume a monocultural, one-dimensional, or universal view on 'the one' masculinity—and neither do I. Instead he sees variations herein, and places a focus on 'men'—whom he understands as "both a social category formed by the gender system and dominant collective and individual agents of social practices" (Hearn 2004: 59). Just like men, 'women,' 'girls,' and 'boys' all present social categories relevant for intersectional gender systems too (Hearn 2013: 120); men, along with their roles and social practices, exist in relation to other men, to women, girls, and boys.

Neither these categories nor the gender systems are static worldwide, but rather exist as dynamic constructs. As Hearn notes, these social categories are "always open to interpretation, contestation and debate" but they affect "social distributions and arrangements" (2012: 596). Key for the hegemony of men, in particular, and gender systems, more broadly, are the social practices of members of these different categories, as occurring within certain social worlds. Categories can change within social worlds, and they are both influenced by and influential for gender systems—as agents with their social practices. Hearn (2004: 60–61) argues that specific social processes are decisive for the hegemony of men. These include that: men are accepted as a hegemonic category by men and those from other social categories; correlations between the formations of men in gender hierarchies exist, although they can deal with power differently; and, certain social practices of men are considered normal by actors from other categories and they support men's hegemony.

The relational approach that Hearn puts forward is crucial for my examination of life in Kyaka II, as it emphasizes the importance of social categories and practices, gender systems, and local social worlds (Hearn 2004: 59, 2012). It thus enables us to explore gender roles and relations of the different categories or groups within the social world of this camp. While Hearn concentrates on the hegemony of men in gender systems, I direct the focus in this chapter toward those systems. It is, therefore, not only or mainly about men; as noted above, to explore the *gendered* processes, I reflect how members of different social categories perceived and affected the gender systems in Kyaka II. The context-specific theoretical view of social worlds is crucial here, as it demands exploration of gender systems in the camp as a particular social world but also reflections of the previous ones. Moreover, within the camp, this context-specific view brings in aid workers as a social category given their influential roles.

The chapter thus addresses the perspectives of women and men, girls and boys, as well as of aid workers regarding gender roles and relations, changes therein after displacement, and the effects of the humanitarian system hereon.[5] The following section sheds light on how the displaced experienced gender roles and relations before flight. The subsequent one focuses on the gender roles and social practices that members of the different social categories expressed. Although men, women, youth, and aid workers all accepted the hegemony of men, contestations and variations in social practices nevertheless came to light. These also influence gender relations and their renegotiations in Kyaka II, which are explored in the third section.

Analyzing how those spoken with experienced gender roles and relations prior to flight in their countries of origin and how they changed in Kyaka II comes with difficulties. After all, the research was conducted in the specific context of the camp and at a certain point in time—and the analysis here centers on memories shared, recollections of past situations, and on the responsibilities and relationship patterns then practiced. It also revolves around informants' perceptions of the conditions they were currently experiencing on-site. Although memories can fade to some extent over time, the many narratives the people in Kyaka II offered revealed great similarities—these help to address how gender roles and relations were shaped and changed in the camp.

Gender Roles and Relations before Flight

When discussing gender roles and relations with people in Kyaka II, they frequently referred to the situation in DR Congo, how it was then, and how much things had changed in the camp. These considerations of erstwhile gender systems were brought forward by women and men, and often described as the 'normal' situation, as the way 'it should be'—but one that could hardly be practiced in the camp.

---

[5] Previous analyses of gender roles and relations focusing on women or on men in Kyaka II were published (see Krause 2015b, 2016e), which this chapter expands on.

"In Congo, women would listen and obey": Patriarchal Role Distribution

In reflections on gender roles and relations in DR Congo, the insights of women and men revealed a strong leaning toward strict patriarchal relations.[6] All narratives consistently portrayed the man as the dominant figure, to whom women and children were clearly subordinated. A group of men highlighted in a discussion that women were always at home in DR Congo. They were "not allowed to carry out any business" or to own land, but they were "led by the men"; one man stressed how "[i]n Congo, women would listen and would obey."[7] Men closely associated being a man with social dominance, which one explained as "[m]en are allowed to do wrong, and women are only allowed to do right"[8]—meaning that women had to follow men's commands, while the latter were able to do as they wished. A group of women likewise emphasized that men constituted the decision-makers at home in DR Congo—and they left no room for interpretation of that fact.[9] In line with the continuous references to the situation at home, gender roles were mainly explained with regard to families and private spheres—with women responsible for the household duties of cooking, cleaning, and parenting, while the man constituted the public figure, the breadwinner, the decision-maker. The divide between the public and private thus appeared to be a rigid one.

Age also played a crucial role in informants' narratives. Older men and partly also women were generally assumed to be authority figures who thus received respect, attention, and had powerful standing within the community. With men's generally authoritative social position, property rights and possessions were passed on from father to son—and therefore transferred patrilineally. These patriarchal structures limited women due to their lack of opportunities to own property, to participate, and their need to obey husbands or fathers. Yet the structures were also described as offering a certain level of support and protection in everyday life to women. This went beyond the inner family circle and also included communities; women widely agreed in a discussion that domestic violence was less intense in DR Congo because "men would fear the relatives of the wife, or even their own

[6] See also Freedman (2015b), who furthermore considers colonial influences.
[7] Discussion with male refugees, March 13, 2014, Base Camp.
[8] Discussion with local leaders, March 20, 2014, Base Camp.
[9] Discussion 1 with female refugees, March 12, 2014, Base Camp.

relatives" and because if livelihoods, such as those from the harvest. were low, "it was easy to borrow seeds from your neighbors, friends, or relatives."[10] Some men expressed a contrary position in a discussion, and highlighted that: "Domestic violence has reduced [in Kyaka II]."[11] While these differing perceptions are likely the result of personal experiences, other studies indicate a broad scope to domestic and intimate partner violence in DR Congo (see also Mulumeoderhwa 2020; Tlapek 2015; Kohli et al. 2015; Babalola et al. 2014; Kelly et al. 2012). In his study with adolescents in South Kivu, for example, Mulumeoderhwa (2020) finds that intimate partner violence against women is partly understood by men as a way of showing love and care.

Ethnic Groups and Gender Systems

In addition to these general explanations of gender roles and relations prior to flight, concrete features, differences, but also similarities were discussed as existing among ethnic groups. Many people found ethnic customs highly influential for the specific ways gender systems were practiced. How important ethnic belonging was to many people spoken with in Kyaka II was revealed by them not only identifying themselves as 'Congolese' when we first met but often as members of a particular ethnic group too. Most of the people in Kyaka II said they belonged to the Banyabwisha, Alur, Hema, and Munyanga, with a number of research participants addressing the gender systems within these DR Congo groups. In depth, they were reflected in a discussion with local leaders—thus forming the basis for the following overview,[12] being complemented with additional quotes from others.

Among Banyabwisha, wives were said to generally be considered the "first-born" and therefore viewed as having the social status of children. Men retained the right to discipline family members, for which resorting to violence was noted to be common. Roles were strictly defined, with men responsible for decision-making, farming, and hunting and women for cooking, cleaning, looking after the children, and collecting firewood. Disputes were first handled at the family level, and, if issues continue, then at the community one in consultation with relatives or elders. How close the family unit was among the

---

[10] Discussion 1 with female refugees, March 12, 2014, Base Camp.
[11] Discussion with male refugees, March 13, 2014, Base Camp.
[12] Discussion with local leaders, March 20, 2014, Base Camp.

people stood out in a dialogue with one woman, who noted, "the Banyabwisha, you can't know what's happening in their families. They decide as a family and settle the issues secretly."[13] Among Banyabwisha, women were said to not be allowed to have a say in matters or to acquire property except in cases where they inherited possessions or land from fathers or grandfathers. Yet they did not own it, and were not allowed to sell it. It was to be kept in the family, and believed to belong to fathers or brothers; when daughters married, they were at times able to take the property with them to the new family— where it then belonged to the husband. Banyabwisha were said to practice both monogamous and polygamous relationships, and marriages between family members such as cousins or nieces were accepted.

Polygamous relationships were noted as common among Alur and Hema. Moreover, among Alur, women were allowed to drink alcohol and cultivate their husbands' lands but men owned it; the latter also retained sole decision-making power in families and mainly also communities. As the head of the household, the man was responsible for providing for the family and had the right to inflict corporal punishment on his wife and children. It was said that the only power that women had was in the kitchen. In line with that, disputes were mainly solved within families and thus decided upon by men; but in the case of prolonged conflict, clan heads or church leaders were involved. Men had the sole right to speak in public, which was prohibited for women. An important identified custom among Alur was the bride price: grooms or their next of kin were to pay them to their brides' families. In cases where a marriage failed, the man could initiate divorce proceedings. In some instances, women were said to be able to divorce men as well, but they would then not receive support.

Among Hema, polygamous relationships appeared to be socially important as the more wives that a man had, the greater was his reputation. Existing under the leadership of men in all spheres of life, women assumed subordinate roles, but were considered superior to children—including boys. Disputes in families were tackled with the help of clan heads, who were said to be older men. Education was primarily granted to male offspring, while schooling for girls and women was widely looked down on or even forbidden—as they were

---

[13] Female refugee, dialogue, March 18, 2014, Base Camp.

seen as responsible for household tasks. Hema were traditionally cattle keepers, and both boys and girls were responsible for the herd. If a woman was unable to have children or had only girls, the man was allowed to "chase away" the wife or to marry an additional one.[14] Bride prices as well as early and arranged marriages for girls were common among Hema; one woman in a discussion detailed how the bride's family was to receive "20 cows in cash, or one can pay the money equivalent to 20 cows."[15] This was also known by one aid worker, who noted in an interview that the Hema "legalized marriage as early as aged 11, and also banked on marrying off their daughters when [they are] still very young as a source of income or wealth."[16]

Among Munyanga, finally, property rights were strictly handled, and only men were allowed to own land and other material possessions. However, it was the chief of a community alone who was said to be the one who decided on and distributed land. Men were responsible for heavy labor, and women for the household. Traditionally, after the wedding the woman entered the husband's family and had no right to thereafter support their birth one. As one woman noted in a discussion, wives were understood to be "the possession of husbands"[17] and thus they were believed to belong to the new family circles. In instances of dispute, each clan resolved them within its own groups. Husbands and wives reported to clan heads, and at times attended a 'Baraaza' (local church) where solutions were put forward. Girls were said to be forbidden access to the Baraaza.[18]

This overview, of course, only provides a snapshot of the differing and partly also overlapping views and customs vis-à-vis gender roles and relations prevalent among the ethnic groups. From a Eurocentric or Western perspective, the differences may appear minimal but such a judgment would be reductionist and highly problematic, as informants discussed these ethnic specifics as significantly shaping their lives, social practices, and gender relations in DR Congo prior to flight. The articulated ethnic structures indicate the different ways men exercised positions of power specifically over women there, ranging from structural subordination to physical force—largely perceived as a legitimate

---

[14] Discussion with local leaders, March 20, 2014, Base Camp.
[15] Discussion 1 with female refugees, March 12, 2014, Base Camp.
[16] Female aid worker, interview, May 11, 2014.
[17] Discussion 1 with female refugees, March 12, 2014, Base Camp.
[18] Discussion with local leaders, March 20, 2014, Base Camp.

means of enforcing authority. As I outline later, some men in Kyaka II appeared to have maintained such views.

Important to reiterate at this point, this summary of norms and customs regarding pre-flight gender roles and relations reveals how they represent context-specific social arrangements. Approximately half of Kyaka II's residents were over 18 years old at the time of research (for statistics, see UNHCR 2018a). They likely grew up within these social structures in their regions of origin. Most people who participated in the research even said that they had spent a good part of their adult lives in DR Congo, with many describing conditions there as the 'normal' way of life and gender relations.

Maintaining and Contesting Gender Roles and Practices in Kyaka II

After fleeing their regions of origin and arriving in Uganda and specifically Kyaka II, along with the social context, these individuals' family and community structures altered too. Since many had lost family members during the war and fled alone, with a few close relatives (often the nuclear family of partners, children, parents, or siblings), or with some community members, their known social support systems no longer existed when they reached the camp; they could not easily practice ethnic customs the same way they had done before either. Those in Kyaka II thus had to both cope with a foregone past and adjust to the new camp conditions, in which they relied on the then unknown, externally imposed power structures of on-site humanitarian agencies.

As part of their adjustment to the camp as their new (interim) social world, these individuals reconfigured among other things gender systems—marking displacement and exile gendered processes (see also Freedman 2015a: 32–34; Hans 2008: 69). The ways the women, men, girls, and boys in Kyaka II experienced and practiced gender roles as well as relations were, of course, inherently intertwined. Yet exploring these separately helps to distinguish which roles the people ascribed to certain groups (or, following Hearn's theory, to certain social categories), how they challenged them, as well as what patterns of relations formed in Kyaka II based on contestations of these roles. I will first discuss the roles here and turn to relations in the following section.

Interestingly, at first sight, great similarities appeared to exist in the narratives about gender roles in Kyaka II compared to in the time prior to flight. Women and men of different ages largely continued to recognize men as the dominant figures and held on to patriarchal role allocations, with differing private and public positions. Women were mainly explained to be responsible for taking care of domestic duties such as cleaning the home, cooking, collecting water, raising and caring for the children, and 'digging,' as noted before meaning farming. Men were said to be the heads of the household, decision-makers, providers, and in charge of financial matters—including paying school fees for children. While less strictly divided up, girls and boys were also ascribed gender-specific tasks within the household. While girls were to help clean the house, wash clothes, cook, and fetch water, boys were often supposed to help cultivate the field.[19] Thus, women's roles were primarily associated with private spheres, men's with public and decision-making ones.

Remarkable here is not only that these role distributions show similarities to those earlier practiced in DR Congo. They were also depicted in a way that portrayed them as 'traditional,' 'normal,' or even 'natural' gender roles, ones the women and men were seemingly 'born into' and innately supposed to fulfill; roles and role allocations as they apparently 'should be.' In stark contrast to this and the overarching tendency toward a public–private divide that the women and men commonly shared, gender roles in Kyaka II were not fixed but rather subject to critical reflection and dynamic change. When conversation partners went beyond listing what gender roles they ascribed to women or men in principle and reflected instead on their lives, they would address difficulties, note variations in the gender systems affecting them, and challenge 'traditional' roles.

In Kyaka II, the women and men furthermore paid significantly less attention to the particularities of the ethnic customs regarding gender systems—although many found these important in DR Congo and although many still identified themselves through ethnic belonging. In the camp, members of the different ethnic groups lived side-by-side, as well as in close proximity with Ugandans, for several years or even decades at the time of research. In a few instances, some people

---

[19] Discussions 1 and 2 with female refugees, March 12, 2014, Base Camp; discussion with male refugees, March 13, 2014, Base Camp.

explained this heterogeneous setting to generate frictions or to reduce violence.[20] For the most part, the social constellation in the camp contributed to adjustments and converging gender systems, making ethnic specifics less influential.

This indicates how those spoken with generally believed in 'traditional' gender roles while at the same time also contesting them due to the encountered heterogeneous social structures and humanitarian camp setup in Kyaka II. As a result, a complex composition of different perspectives and practices supporting and contradicting men's dominant and women's subordinate gender roles, men's public and women's private social positions were identified by those in the camp. This diversity of roles characterized the gender systems in Kyaka II and strongly contrasts with the seemingly 'natural' roles that women and men initially noted.

"The man is like the manager": Men's Hegemonic Roles and Violence as (Il)legitimate Practice

Even though male informants (as well as women, youth, and aid workers) largely portrayed men as decision-makers and as the providers for their families, some voiced differing views. In addition to noting they supported women's participation and safety,[21] some argued that "both man and woman" should mutually handle shortcomings in the camp "like food, medicines, clothing, education for their children."[22] A few also explained that they would share duties with their wife at home, including cooking, farming, and childcare.[23] In contrast, however, one man stated that the "sharing of rights in a home" can cause problems, specifically when women "want equal rights with their husbands. For example, when the wife wants to be the final decision maker in the home."[24]

---

[20] Among others, discussion with male refugees, March 13, 2014, Base Camp; male refugee, dialogue, March 18, 2014, Base Camp; female refugee, dialogue, March 27, 2014, Base Camp. On a reduction in domestic violence, discussion with religious leaders, March 19, 2014, Base Camp.

[21] Male refugee, dialogue, March 26, 2014, Base Camp.

[22] Male refugee, dialogue, March 18, 2014, Base Camp.

[23] Discussion with religious leaders, March 19, 2014, Base Camp.

[24] Male refugee, dialogue, March 18, 2014, Base Camp.

Men's Perceptions in Light of the Camp Difficulties

In line with the latter criticism, most men spoken with in Kyaka II held on to hegemonic roles for themselves—but also often complained that they were unable to fulfill these due to the previously discussed limitations faced in the camp, or that women at times did not sufficiently attend to 'their' domestic roles, with their noncompliance potentially leading to violence. These ambivalent attitudes stood out most concretely in a discussion with nine men;[25] taking a closer look at it allows us to scrutinize their perspectives. The discussion started with reflections on the conditions in Kyaka II, and quickly moved on to issues revolving around gender roles and gender-based violence. The participants widely agreed on the veracity of men's 'traditional' roles as breadwinners and decision-makers, which one informant articulated as follows: "The man is like the manager, the owner of the home. He does the planning for the family, sickness, school, etc., and makes decisions for all the issues concerning the family. But the biggest percentage of [them], they don't plan with their wives."

Yet many lamented insufficient food (distribution) and aid agencies' power within the camp. One worried that "[w]omen don't respect men if they do not provide"; another replied, "[w]e men, our only source of income is cultivation," noting that it is not enough to provide for families. A different informant added: "Parents are suffering to raise money for school fees for girls, and big men come and try to seduce the young girls." He argued that parents stayed silent and refrained from reporting cases because "parents are poor," and the "small gifts" these men gave met some of the "home needs."

As a result of such livelihood issues, one man stressed that men "have no value in this place. They feel they are useless, and because of that they behave recklessly. For example, they spend their money on alcohol and then also get as many women as they can." The impact of alcohol on discrimination and violence against women was also noted by female informants.[26] Other research participants of the discussion criticized how some women would "disobey" husbands and "[s]ome

---

[25] All the participating men originated from DR Congo and had been living in Kyaka II for several years. Seven were married, and all were middle-aged—with the exception of one who was 70 years old. Discussion with male refugees, March 13, 2014, Base Camp.

[26] Among many such references made, discussions 1 and 2 with female refugees, March 12, 2014, Base Camp.

women also do not help out at home, and this violates the men and they end up getting into fights."[27] Very similar views were shared in another discussion with local leaders, stating "women don't help men in domestic needs, which make men violent." One further argued that "[s]ome women are cooperative, others are not. That's why some men beat their wives, while others use peaceful means."[28] These quotes echo the views shared by many men in Kyaka II, showing how strongly many believed in men's hegemonic position as sole decision-makers— which women should comply with.

Violence as Legitimate Social Practice?

These quotes also hint at the belief of some men in Kyaka II that violence represented a legitimate means of enforcing dominance. This links with Galtung's understanding of direct, structural and cultural violence, and the gender-sensitive conceptualization following Confortini, as outlined earlier in the book. This furthermore corresponds with other studies about the link between adhered-to gender roles and the occurrence of domestic violence among displaced people in camps (see Horn 2010; Pittaway and Rees 2006; Carlson 2005; Khawaja 2004). In their research into intimate partner violence against women in three refugee camps in Iraq, Kenya, and South Sudan respectively, Wachter et al. illustrate the influence of gendered social norms and ascribed gender roles on the scope of violence experienced —noting that "men abused the power ascribed to them by their traditional roles" (2018: 293). Focusing on camps in Jordan meanwhile, Khawaja et al. (2007) find that many women and men spoken with as part of their study consider 'wife beating' acceptable in certain circumstances (also Khawaja 2004).

By no means did all men in Kyaka II advocate using force against women in domestic spheres. Yet in various dialogues and discussions men shared perspectives both justifying and partly rejecting violence, specifically as a social practice for defending, maintaining, or regaining their hegemonic roles. Returning to the earlier-mentioned discussion with nine men, the contrasting views articulated show how these individuals made sense of violence as an (il)legitimate social practice

---

[27] Discussion with male refugees, March 13, 2014, Base Camp.
[28] Discussion with local leaders, March 20, 2014, Base Camp.

in varying ways.[29] One criticized, "women suffer violence," and that "[m]en are mistreating women. Women have no voice to suggest anything at home. They are beaten like a drum." He reasoned: "As refugees in Kyaka II, we cannot have liberty to own everything we need; this is pushed onto women through [their] mistreatment." This resonates with the previously discussed limited livelihoods in the camp, with frustration, disputes, and violence said to arise especially when women asked for household items that men could not afford. As one noted:

Some women are developmental, and others are not. Sometimes a woman wants to have all the money used to buy good food and clothes, and they forget about doing developmental investments. In this case, some men beat their wives when they try to complain in such situations. And there are two ways men can deal with their wives. The ones [who are violent and the ones] who cannot beat them up, they decide to keep quiet and do their things quietly. Sometimes they can move out of the home, and when they do the women then complain and this starts the quarrel.

Another narrated that women were confronted with physical violence when they did not submit to men's hegemony and rules:

We beat women because some disobey. They don't understand. They want to talk and talk and do everything. Some men can see far, and women don't agree. For example, a Congolese man in Sweswe [Zone] who was tortured by the wife['s arguments] decided to save his money and then that they move back to DR Congo. He now beats his wife like a drum, and she cannot do anything because the law is not effective in Kyaka II.

In addition to such positions tending to justify violence as legitimate social practice due to men's struggle to maintain their dominance, counter women's claims, and overcome difficult camp conditions, some participants also stressed the relevance of 'culture' as a way to limit abusive tendencies. In that regard, they referred to the otherwise rarely noted weight of the ethnic customs practiced prior to flight. As one man explained:

We should maintain our culture, and that will reduce violence against women. In DR Congo, women were not allowed to carry out any business. They were not allowed to go out, they stayed home, and would be led by the

---

[29] Discussion with male refugees, March 13, 2014, Base Camp.

men. Here in Uganda, women are given their rights. They can move and carry out business in any way [they want]. Women are listened to more than men in Kyaka II, and I think this is a violation of us also.

Later in the discussion he would emphasize that "the woman [should] follow her husband's culture if she wants to stay safe," noting also that "[a] woman has no power over the man, even the Bible supports this, and the government doesn't say a woman should behave badly toward a man." Paradoxically, practices regarding gender roles were here not only presented as 'normal' but also as a way to reduce practices of violence, although it was said that violence by men against women was common in different ethnic groups in DR Congo. This man's statements further connect with Galtung's forms of violence and Confortini's gender-sensitive conceptualization thereof in contradictory ways: On the one hand, his perception of being violated as a result of aid agencies not listening to the needs of men resonates with structural violence, read as a gender-based form of discrimination. On the other hand, the man in question approves of structural and cultural violence against women—indirectly even physical one, when it comes to ensuring obedience—to reinforce men's domination over women and to legitimize patriarchy.

Other participants broadly agreed with his position during the discussion; one explained he found his role as a father being to "counsel my girls," telling them: "There is a day when you will get married; what I advise you is to do what they do in that culture. Go as an empty jerrican. Don't carry our culture with you in your marriage, and then you will be loved there." Although not explicitly stated, his words implied that girls were likely to face physical violence if they did not obey their husbands' 'culture,' which similarly reflects a legitimation of physical, structural, and cultural violence against women to maintain men's hegemony.

Moreover, another of these nine men reasoned that the "different mixture of cultures" in Kyaka II sparked "problems." He expressed how Hema were originally cattle keepers in DR Congo, but now had to engage in farming. He stressed that "girls" married men belonging to other ethnic groups, who might "force her to dig, and yet she doesn't even know how to"—eventually remarking "our girls don't dig." Yet another of the men pointed at women mingling with Ugandan women as an issue: "[I]f a Ugandan woman sees a Congolese woman, they tell them 'you have no freedom. You need to get some liberty,' and this acquisition of wrong ideas changes our women and brings violence."

Although most of the nine men participating in the discussion widely acknowledged gender-based violence against women—and for the most part justified it for the outlined reasons—one of them voiced contrasting views. He emphasized that men always have choices as to whether they want to use force or "treat women as human beings." He argued that "[w]e are able to change," and drawing on the debate about 'culture,' noted that "[we] can also copy the good cultural practices." He cited how "Hema now take their girls to school, and that wasn't the case in DR Congo."[30]

Such effects were similarly expounded in a discussion with religious leaders, who widely agreed that people in Kyaka II "mixed with other tribes"—leading to changes and shared responsibilities among men and women in the home and possibly a reduction of force against women.[31] Moreover, one man posited that it would be a "personality issue" if a man was to use violence against a woman to enforce his dominance and narrated in a dialogue how: "The ones who beat their wives, most of them, they were also beating their wives back home. I don't think this camp situation is the one that has changed their behavior. If the man was good and used to respect the wife and share the little [he has] with her, he will still be nice here."[32]

Such statements put the widespread use of violence by men against women, along with the justifications for it, into perspective. They ultimately show how diversely men interpreted what it means to be a man, and subsequently undertook varying roles and practices—even though, as noted, most research participants clearly supported men's hegemony, including violence as a legitimate social practice. Moreover, the references to 'culture'—despite the differing tendencies—indicate how influential some of the former ethnic customs and gender systems in DR Congo continued to be for some in Kyaka II.

The views of men about gender roles and systems resonate with the reflections of Hearn that the hegemony of men requires "social processes by which there is a hegemonic acceptance of the category of

---

[30] Discussion with male refugees, March 13, 2014, Base Camp.
[31] Discussion with religious leaders, March 19, 2014, Base Camp.
[32] Male refugee, dialogue, March 5, 2014, Kaborogota Zone.

men" and that "distinctions and categorizations between different forms of men and men's practices [exist] to women, children and other men" (2004: 60). Explaining the resort to violence, Hearn notes the "variations in violence[s]," "plural ways of being men that perpetuate violence" (or, contrariwise, refute it), and, consequently, the "multiple, and sometimes contradictory, rationales within men's accounts" (2012: 599–600). The initially stated domestic duties some men said they take on—thus those not perceived as men's 'traditional' roles—as well as the latter narratives rejecting abusive practices reveal how violence does not necessarily represent an inherent part of the hegemonic gender roles and social practices of all men in Kyaka II. Differences certainly existed. Nonetheless, violence against women was prevalent, and most men participating in the research made sense of it as a routine social practice to defend, uphold, or regain hegemonic roles by blaming the difficult camp conditions or women's disobedience. That men's hegemony and their violent practices were widely accepted in Kyaka II is, then, likely linked to the gender systems learned before flight.

"Women do a lot more": Women's Roles (Not Only) as Carer

Women widely accepted and reinforced men's dominant roles, but also acknowledged changes occurring therein within Kyaka II. A key example is the quote cited at the beginning of this chapter by the woman who asserted: "For us Congolese, we know the man has to be on top and makes the final decision. The wife doesn't access anything, and everything belongs to the man." Yet in Kyaka II, she added, "things are different. Man and woman are equal."[33] Another woman ascribed men primarily roles of providing for women and families, explaining: "It is ok if a man has other women as long as he still provides for you equally. If he buys food for all of you in equal amounts and clothes, then there would be no problem."[34] While such statements supporting men's roles as decision-makers and providers were common among many, they were also challenged by others.

---

[33] Female refugee, dialogue, March 27, 2014, Base Camp.
[34] Female refugee, dialogue, March 25, 2014, Base Camp.

Criticism of Violence and Imposed Subordination

Some women recognized that men could not solely provide for their families due to the challenging camp conditions and that they consequently shared responsibilities and jointly generated income.[35] Others criticized how men could but did not support their families, failed to share resources, and were violent, forcing women to take on more responsibilities.[36] One woman stated: "Life in Kyaka II is hard, and my husband doesn't really provide for me." She dealt with the situation by working as a community health worker for an NGO. "That's how I can get some little money," she said. Despite the small amounts she earned, she could take care of herself and especially also her children.[37] A frequent example for not sharing resources was the use of crop yields; as previously discussed, men would sell the harvest, spend the money on alcohol, deny women access to both, and often react violently when the latter tried to claim their share.[38] One woman stressed:

Domestic violence is common in Kyaka II, and especially done by Congolese men who have never considered women to be people. They normally deny their children education, and especially the girls. Their wives are to be their workers, and even only sex objects. Women are not involved in family issues. They are always under the men, and there is even a church that promotes such violence. Women are beaten and forced to have sex in their own homes. They are made to work for nothing by their husbands. Not even the food is enough. They are harassed and seen as helpless people in society.[39]

Although this woman would also largely concur with men's dominant social position, by criticizing the role expectations for women as well as the dismissive treatment by and violence of men, she strongly contested the 'traditional' gender roles of being an obedient and submissive wife existing under the husband's hegemony. Another woman correspondingly both recognized women's various roles and

---

[35] Female refugee, dialogue, March 18, 2014, Base Camp; discussion 2 with female refugees, March 12, 2014, Base Camp.

[36] Discussions 1 and 2 with female refugees, March 12, 2014, Base Camp.

[37] Female refugee, dialogue, March 18, 2014, Base Camp.

[38] Discussion 1 with female refugees, March 12, 2014, Base Camp; discussion with Refugee Welfare Council, March 19, 2014, Base Camp; female aid worker, interview, May 20, 2014.

[39] Female refugee, dialogue, March 11, 2014, Bukere Zone.

simultaneously criticized men's behavior, even describing it as slave-like treatment:

Women do a lot more than men—like paying school fees for their children, helping them with homework. And so you see that women do the work that is supposed to be done by men. Actually men just disrespect them. They think women are lazy and can't do anything. They take it as the way it is in the Bible that women are supposed to be dull and men be heads. They tend to take their wives as slaves. Actually some churches support that, and have caused violence to increase in Kyaka II.[40]

Both of these quotes illustrate in a particularly compelling way the interrelated risks of violence connected to gender roles and relations that many women faced in Kyaka II. Again, drawing on Galtung's forms of violence complemented by Confortini's gender-sensitive reading, these women complained about physical abuse in domestic spheres, which served men as a way to maintain social control. The women furthermore lamented men's structural domination and dehumanizing practices—even comparing them to slave-like treatment or that of sex objects—which the cultural environment supported. This resonates with Confortini's analysis that "[v]iolence is both made *possible* by the existence of power/gender relations, and power/gender relations *rely on* violence for their reproduction. Violence and gender are involved in a relationship of mutual constitution" (2006: 355). Yet, the quotes furthermore demonstrate how these women strongly criticized and protested the conditions—and hence challenged such a 'mutual constitution.'

In a similar vein, other women did not passively submit to men's violent dominance but railed against it by reporting cases of abuse, seeking justice afterward, or alternatively deliberately adopting responsibilities. While a few women additionally acknowledged that "strong women" would fight back and also use force against their husbands,[41] most reflected on preventive approaches. As a part of their commitment to reduce violence and manifest a more peaceful ethos in the home and with partners, several women in a discussion explained how they initiated conversations with their husbands. By trying to take on

---

[40] Female refugee, dialogue, March 18, 2014, Base Camp.
[41] Female refugee, dialogue, March 18, 2014, Base Camp; see also female refugee, dialogue, March 5, 2014, Kaborogota Zone; female refugee, dialogue, March 18, 2014, Sweswe Zone; female refugee, dialogue, March 23, 2014, Base Camp.

mediating roles, they hoped that "there may be peace and a change at least in the way things are done, so that men may start to listen to women and consult them via more peaceful means."[42]

In light of these contestations, it may come unexpected that many women also saw themselves as holding important roles in the domestic spheres. This included running the household and caring for families and especially children, with female informants ascribing great meaning to their offspring's good upbringing. Time and again women spoke of the importance of raising children, both boys and girls, in a way that fostered violence-free relationships based on mutual respect. Most concretely, women widely agreed in a discussion that they strove to "groom their children, especially their sons, so that they may grow into respectful men who will not beat their wives; [they also] advise their daughters to love education, since it is the key to the future."[43]

Women's Various Roles

When the discussions of women's perceptions of their gender roles moved away from questions of direct entanglement in gender systems and families and toward the gender roles that women (as women) adopted more generally, they referred to a number of responsibilities they took on and enterprises they initiated—not necessarily because they had to, but more because they wanted to. This was often about how they perceived their social (gender) roles, supported each other, and pursued self-reliance—not always being immediately associated with men, and women's dependencies on men. Such narratives connect with women's agency and especially also empowerment—understood, per feminist research, as the bottom-up processes by which women move toward autonomy, self-determination, social change, and social justice (see Deveaux 1994; Parpart 2010).[44]

As Logie and Daniel (2016) discuss in their study of internally displaced in Haiti, women's agency is evident in intrapersonal processes of gaining knowledge and confidence, interpersonal ones of

---

[42] Discussion 2 with female refugees, March 12, 2014, Base Camp.

[43] Discussion 2 with female refugees, March 12, 2014, Base Camp.

[44] Empowerment is thus not seen here as something given to 'the disempowered' by dominant actors or as the institutionalized concept prevalent among political, economic, and humanitarian institutions vis-à-vis improving women's position in society (on broader development discourse, see Calvès 2009), as addressed in Chapter 3 in the context of humanitarian aid in Kyaka II.

speaking with each other, relational ones of mutual support, and collective ones toward creating awareness. The participating women not only showed strength in but also drew strength from these various processes. With regard to women's own capacities and agency, Deveaux (1994) refers to Foucault to underline the decisive link between power and freedom. She elaborates how "[w]omen's 'freedom' does not simply refer to objective possibilities for maneuvering or resisting within a power dynamic but concerns whether a woman *feels* empowered in her specific context" (Deveaux 1994: 234).

These feelings—and thus women's own self-perceptions—are vital for understanding how the women spoken with in Kyaka II saw, reasoned about, and made sense of their social and gender positions. This relates not only to what gender roles they ascribed to women, but more comprehensively to how they viewed their roles, which social practices they employed, and what levels of power and freedom they felt themselves to enjoy. It was evident from the research undertaken that creating livelihoods and engaging in social structures represented two critical areas for examining women's very own role and empowerment perceptions within Kyaka II, as local conditions were shaped by poverty and camp limitations while the women themselves stemmed from contexts where patriarchal systems prevailed. While women's activities for coping are analyzed in more detail in Chapter 5, I now address women's perceptions of their roles, freedom, and power.

The first key area of livelihoods meant to women "to be self-reliant, for example where they can at least own some business so that they can be less dependent on their husbands," as one woman argued in a discussion.[45] Female informants widely rued economic restraints, often lamenting "digging" being the only source of income in Kyaka II.[46] Yet some saw receiving farmland as an opportunity, which structurally differed from their rights in DR Congo. One woman who had lost her first husband during the war in DR Congo and fled to Uganda with her three children stressed that her life was hard in Kyaka II. She remarried, had two more children, and noted that they "have little food; the children do not have clothes." Yet she found her life "better" than before in DR Congo. "When someone has children, they give you at least three acres of land for digging and living." She said it enabled

---

[45] Discussion 1 with female refugees, March 12, 2014, Base Camp.
[46] Female refugee, dialogue, March 11, 2014, Base Camp.

women to "dig and get beans and maize, which they can sell and get money. They did not get that in DR Congo."[47] Thus, like her, some women used farming to enter into further economic practice.

In her study on other refugee camps in Uganda, Mulumba also found that women's access to land for farming was perceived as liberating by some women as it crossed cultural boundaries regarding patrilineal practices of land ownership. However, she states that "gender conflicts" can arise as "men [wish] to be in control of resources" (Mulumba 2010: 275). Moreover, the author questions how sustainable such empowering changes ultimately are considering refugees' only temporary stays in Uganda. It remains uncertain from the literature how women's positions may alter upon their return to countries of origin.

Women also established diverse other forms of livelihood through economic networks within and beyond Kyaka II. Besides selling the harvest, they traded food such as prepared meals, oil or fish, everyday materials such as fabric for clothing, established small saloons and braided hair, and more. Also being allowed and able to build their own homes was associated with the individuals feeling some level of autonomy. One woman, who described herself as "a businesswoman" selling foods in the camp, said: "Women now build houses, and that was not the case in DR Congo. [. . .] For myself, I would say I have learned things for the better."[48] Such economic activities reveal the great variety of roles women took on to self-determine their lives. Crucial was not only the feeling of independence from their husbands —as "[w]hen we earn money, we do not need men anymore to support us"[49]—but many also stressed how they enjoyed having (established) something on their own.[50] Yet they still sensed restrictions due to the patriarchal role allocations, noting "some husbands would never allow [women] to work or own businesses" or they would "even take her money."[51]

For the second key area of women involving themselves in social and thus also power structures, many noted the restraints imposed by patriarchal gender systems and humanitarian agencies. Much of life

---

[47] Female refugee, dialogue, February 25, 2014, Base Camp.
[48] Female refugee, dialogue, March 5, 2014, Base Camp.
[49] Female refugee, dialogue, March 17, 2014, Sweswe Zone.
[50] Discussions 1 and 2 with female refugees, March 12, 2014, Base Camp.
[51] Discussion 1 with female refugees, March 12, 2014, Base Camp.

in the camp was said to be regulated by these agencies, or limited by men's decision-making. Nonetheless, women proactively engaged in processes to promote local social justice and resolve disputes in the community. Leadership functions were mainly restricted to men prior to displacement, but in Kyaka II women strove to make their voices heard and participate in decision-making—especially with the aim of reducing the scope of the violence many women were exposed to.

In addition to the above-noted conversations initiated with their husbands, some women—especially older ones—also raised awareness about violence within their communities.[52] The woman who was generally accepting of men's hegemony, quoted at the beginning of this chapter saying "we know the man has to be on top," later in our conversation criticized violence against women in Kyaka II. She described how some women made themselves and their security concerns heard at the community level. Whereas there used to be only discussions among male elders in cases of violence in families or communities, she said that this had changed. After separate discussions among men and women, "mixed" ones started to take place. Despite the prevalence of violence, she noted that the level of it "[had] reduced due to this arrangement. There is a very big change."[53]

Despite these various responsibilities women took on, the different examples addressed above reveal how women in Kyaka II widely accepted men's hegemonic roles, being seen as ones with which women should comply—a factor that Hearn (2004: 61) finds crucial for the (continued) hegemony of men. Yet they also divulge how women contested and countered the imposed roles of submissive wife, and created and reproduced their own meaningful ones through economic livelihoods, political and social participation, and ownership of property. The surrounding camp conditions and structures both supported and hindered women's very own empowerment processes. Although those circumstances partly enabled change, and despite women portraying their practices as facilitating greater autonomy and self-determination, many also commented how they perceived the conditions in Kyaka II through the lens of a certain helplessness.[54] Structural and social factors were named time and again as hampering women's

---

[52] Female refugee, dialogue, March 18, 2014, Base Camp.
[53] Female refugee, dialogue, March 27, 2014, Base Camp.
[54] Female refugee, dialogue, March 18, 2014, Base Camp; female refugee, dialogue, March 11, 2014, Bukere Zone.

opportunities for self-directed and independent lives. One woman stressed that "most men tend to despise women when they are given the same rights"[55]; another noted, as recounted in Chapter 3: "Everyone should make decisions because we all have equal rights, but we refugees do not have a say in Kyaka II. We are discriminated against and harassed a lot. Those organizations do not give us time and space to speak for ourselves."[56]

Thus, the limitations that female informants encountered in their daily life were not only the result of patriarchal gender relations, with men restricting women's practicing of their freedoms, but also of humanitarian agencies' measures and regulations hampering women's autonomy.

"Boys and girls are the same and equal": Teenagers' Equality But Adults' Patriarchal Roles

Following Hearn (2004: 59,2012), not only men's outlooks but also those of members of other social categories are, as noted, important for the hegemony of men. Youth certainly constitute one such decisive social category. From the information that adolescents in Kyaka II shared during journal writing, some rather unexpected tendencies occurred. When youth reflected on the gender roles, practices, and hierarchies of adult women and men, they clearly tended toward supporting patriarchal structures—with men being widely accepted as carrying hegemonic social roles. Yet when they addressed the gender roles, practices, and hierarchies of teenagers both female and male, they broadly referred to equality and shared responsibilities. Although variations occurred of course, girls and boys thus distinguished between their own age group and adults—ascribing each different roles and levels of power, most likely as the result of learned practices from families and communities.

Equal Roles among Teenagers?

In more detail, most of the adolescent research participants broadly shared similar inclinations toward equality with regard to boys' and girls' gender roles and social practices; they also articulated certain

---

[55] Female refugee, dialogue, March 17, 2014, Sweswe Zone.
[56] Female refugee, dialogue, March 14, 2014, Bujubuli.

differences however. Among those differences, several indicated varying "private parts" or "body parts"[57] (as synonyms for sex organs), that girls received specific support including "sanitary towels,"[58] the social difficulties encountered with girls' restricted access to education due to parental decisions,[59] as well as how "boys do not suffer like girls do at home"[60] as a result of domestic violence. However, when participating youth somewhat disregarded physical features, or external conditions, they widely agreed on commonalities and equal abilities. For example, a male teenager stated that "both boys and girls are the same and equal"[61] while a female peer noted, "they are equal because they all need the same rights, and they should be given their rights equally. For example, education should be given to both boys and girls."[62]

Although another male adolescent generally agreed with such similarities existing, he still noted how "boys are meant to do heavy work [more] than girls."[63] One female teenager narrated this differently:

At home, girls and boys do the same work like cooking, fetching water, and sweeping. Academically, girls and boys are the same like in S.2 [secondary school], the person who is first is either a girl or a boy. Girls and boys are not different at all. Girls take part in ruling the school for example, as prefects, class monitors—the same as boys.[64]

Such perspectives were also shared by other teenagers. Interestingly, the domestic roles of boys and girls were portrayed differently by adults, as noted earlier—with the latter distinguishing mainly between

---

[57] Male adolescent, 16 years old, journal writing, March 26, 2014, Bujubuli Secondary School; female adolescent, 17 years old, journal writing, March 26, 2014, Bujubuli Secondary School.

[58] Female adolescent, 16 years old, journal writing, March 26, 2014, Bujubuli Secondary School.

[59] Female adolescent, 16 years old, journal writing, March 26, 2014, Bujubuli Secondary School.

[60] Male adolescent, 18 years old, journal writing, March 26, 2014, Bujubuli Secondary School.

[61] Male adolescent, 16 years old, journal writing, March 26, 2014, Bujubuli Secondary School.

[62] Female adolescent, 16 years old, journal writing, March 26, 2014, Bujubuli Secondary School.

[63] Male adolescent, 18 years old, journal writing, March 26, 2014, Bujubuli Secondary School.

[64] Female adolescent, 16 years old, journal writing, March 26, 2014, Bujubuli Secondary School.

'traditional' female duties for girls, including cooking and cleaning, and tasks such as harvesting crops for boys. Another deviation from adults' views concerned violence. As part of their perceived somewhat equal roles, a number of boys critically reflected on the risks of gender-based violence for girls—indicating their disapproval of such practices. Many lamented "early marriage"[65] or "forced marriage of girls,"[66] as well as girls being "beaten,"[67] "raped," and "harassed."[68] Also forced school dropouts were captured as distinct forms of violence against girls.[69]

While the participating teenagers thus acknowledged difficult context conditions and imposed social norms beyond the physical differences, they broadly believed the roles of girls and boys to be similar. Since both used the term "equal" quite frequently, they did not appear to perceive potential hierarchies among girls and boys as decisive—instead emphasizing their equivalent abilities to fulfill tasks and accomplish goals.

Patriarchal Roles among Adults?

In stark contrast, youth presented strongly differing views regarding adults. Regardless of their being girls or boys, they generally accepted and supported the prevailing role allocations of men as decision-makers and of women as subordinately responsible for domestic duties—in other words, views broadly in line with the positions of men and women. Yet, youth also voiced critical perceptions hereof.

Supporting patriarchal structures, one female adolescent stated that "[t]he man should make decisions in a home, because most of them know how to rule a home" and because he is "respected" by all family members. She further remarked: "It is easy for a man to make

---

[65] Male adolescent, 17 years old, journal writing, March 5, 2014, Bujubuli Secondary School.

[66] Female adolescent, 17 years old, journal writing, March 5, 2014, Bujubuli Secondary School.

[67] Male adolescent, 19 years old, journal writing, March 5, 2014, Bujubuli Secondary School.

[68] Male adolescent, 18 years old, journal writing, April 3, 2014, Bujubuli Secondary School.

[69] For example, male adolescent, 17 years old, journal writing, March 5, 2014, Bujubuli Secondary School; male adolescent, 18 years old, journal writing, April 3, 2014, Bujubuli Secondary School; female adolescent, 17 years old, journal writing, April 3, 2014, Bujubuli Secondary School.

decisions. In many families, men are educated more than women and if you are educated, it is too easy to make a good decision."[70] In a similar vein, a male teenager emphasized men's power in the following way: "[The] father is responsible for making decisions in a home because he is the one who makes a living for the family. A father is very important at home in terms of making decisions because he provides basic needs, good quality education to his children—therefore he is the head of the family."[71] Another male adolescent added: "When a woman at home makes decisions, other people will start abusing the man that his wife rules him—which will cause violence in the home."[72] A female teenager also supported men's powerful roles, even explaining that "we say that women are always under the men."[73]

In contrast, other teenagers—echoing the sentiments of their peer group at large—posited that men and women should share duties and decision-making at home. Among others, one male adolescent emphasized that children, mothers, and fathers all have their rights and freedoms:

Mums also have their rights and freedoms in the home. For example her husband must not mistreat her because he is not superior to her, so they must be equal and share household work. Dads have also their rights and freedoms. For example men should not be abused because they have not given full basic needs to their children and their wives, yet their pockets are also demanding or bankrupt. So all family members must be treated equally.[74]

A female teenager stated meanwhile:

I think both the man and the woman should together make decisions in a home because you may find that if a man or woman decides, the other one may not agree. And in an actual sense, no one can manage to care for a

---

[70] Female adolescent, 16 years old, journal writing, March 26, 2014, Bujubuli Secondary School.

[71] Male adolescent, 18 years old, journal writing, March 26, 2014, Bujubuli Secondary School.

[72] Male adolescent, 17 years old, journal writing, March 26, 2014, Bujubuli Secondary School.

[73] Female adolescent, 16 years old, journal writing, March 26, 2014, Bujubuli Secondary School.

[74] Male adolescent, 16 years old, journal writing, March 26, 2014, Bujubuli Secondary School.

family without a helper. So a man should join hands to make decisions in the home.[75]

Such references to mutual dependence and meeting basic needs connect gender roles with the previously outlined limited livelihoods and financial instability that many people in Kyaka II were confronted with. The diverging positions that adolescents articulated about gender roles among adults reveal how they supported but also partly contested men's hegemony and patriarchal structures. Again, what stands out in the narratives of youth is the different roles and hierarchies that they ascribed to their own age group and to adults respectively. Whether and how these variations may be indicative of more sustainable change occurring—also concerning the possible reduced use of violence as then illegitimate social practice—cannot be discerned at this stage, and would require further research being conducted with the same group over the course of several years. Yet the widely shared views of equal gender roles for girls and boys certainly indicate change was afoot.

"Men obviously make more decisions": Aid Workers' Representations of Patriarchal Structures

In addition to the perceptions and practices of the people in Kyaka II, the humanitarian camp structures externally affected the way they enacted gender roles too. How, then, did humanitarian staff perceive such gender roles among the people living in Kyaka II?

Whether women or men, aid workers shared the view of men representing the dominant actor to whom women should subordinate themselves. They thus upheld patriarchal gender roles. Among others, one female aid worker said that "men are supposed to bear the bigger responsibilities; for example they pay school fees, take care of the whole family. Normally it is men who make the decisions."[76] A male colleague summarized, "men construct houses, and provide security while women look for food and prepare it for the whole family [and] care for sanitation in the home."[77]

---

[75] Female adolescent, 16 years old, journal writing, March 26, 2014, Bujubuli Secondary School.
[76] Female aid worker, interview, April 14, 2014.
[77] Male aid worker, interview, April 14, 2014.

Reflecting on who should have decision-making roles, only one male out of all 28 aid-worker interviewees said that women and men were "alike for decisions."[78] Two female colleagues noted that it depends on the field in question, for example: "Sometimes it's the woman who makes more decisions than a man, and in other instances it's the man. However, to a larger extent, men make more decisions than women."[79] Only one aid worker acknowledged that gender roles and responsibilities change over time: "At the time of entering Uganda, most decisions are made by men. Women only stand by and watch or listen, but rarely actively contribute. As the stay in Uganda lengthens, women slowly by slowly start making more decisions—especially those concerning the welfare of their families."[80]

All other interviewees stressed men's hegemonic roles, and left little room for alternative possibilities. Even an aid worker supporting projects tackling gender-based violence subscribed to patriarchal role allocations:

Men obviously make more decisions given the fact that the society here is a patriarchal one, where women are receivers and actors while men are instructors and commanders. Women are socialized to be submissive and never to challenge their husbands or male counterparts, lest it be seen as disrespect and insubordination—hence leading to punishment in the form of physical or psychological abuse.[81]

Moreover, a female aid worker estimated:

Some 95 percent of the men got their wives here, because in most cases, for the woman who lost her husband, she is usually overwhelmed by responsibilities like taking care of her children, paying for school fees—among other things. Therefore, this woman is forced to get another man to take care of her needs.[82]

The apparent 'need' for women to find new partners as well as the clear division of roles between men and women reproduced the private–public binary of the former being responsible for public representations and economic income whereas the latter were "supposed to remain at

---

[78] Male aid worker, interview, April 3, 2014.
[79] Female aid worker, interview, May 20, 2014.
[80] Female aid worker, interview, April 10, 2014.
[81] Female aid worker, interview, May 11, 2014.
[82] Female aid worker, interview, March 26, 2014.

home."[83] Aid workers inherently tended toward representing women as not only subordinate but vulnerable, as discussed before, which led to varying offers of humanitarian support to them. One interviewee emphasized that "[w]omen now are more recognized than men because of their rights [and] because most organizations that come [here] target women and not men."[84] How this translates into aid projects and affects gender relations is dealt with in Chapter 3.

Briefly summing up reflections about gender roles in Kyaka II, it has been shown that women and men, teenage girls and boys, as well as aid workers widely supported the hegemonic social positions of men and the subordinate ones of women. However, they also raised issues with and challenged the strictly patriarchal gender constellations. Following Hearn (2004: 60–61), this support despite contestations is crucial for the hegemony of men; it reveals how members of different social categories broadly accepted that hegemony but also distinguished variations and differing practices. How important the local contextualization of gender systems in the social world of Kyaka II was can be seen in the influence the camp conditions were said to exert on the people, in the gender roles upheld there, and in the similarities to 'traditional' practices and role allocations in DR Congo. While the customs in the latter were still perceived as the 'normal' ones, the 'social camp world' and heterogeneous setting nevertheless triggered changes herein.

Negotiating Gender Relations under Humanitarian Influence

The ascribed and widely shared, yet also contested, gender roles influenced how the people spoken with practiced gender relations in Kyaka II. Of course, as such roles were maintained, challenged, and redefined continuously, so were such relations. Some studies depict that gender relations alter in refugee situations (e.g., Grabska 2011; Mulumba 2010; Szczepaniková 2005; Al-Ali 2002; on migration and transnationalism see Erdal and Pawlak 2018). Yet what new or different forms thereof may evolve in specific local settings has rarely been explored. Despite variations and individual practices, tendencies toward three main patterns of changing gender relations could be discerned in

---

[83] Female aid worker, interview, April 2, 2014.
[84] Male aid worker, interview, March 18, 2014.

Kyaka II from the various women's and men's narratives (see also Krause 2015b: 249–256). These included a patriarchal pattern characterized by male dominance, a relatively equal one signifying shared responsibilities, and a supposedly independent one vis-à-vis single women with children. The latter two patterns were less common compared to the widespread patriarchal one.

"Things are different": Patterns of Gender Relations

Although the woman quoted at the beginning of this chapter stated, "things are different [in Kyaka II]. Man and woman are equal,"[85] most people actually claimed to maintain patriarchal gender relations. This reveals similarities to the gender relations upheld in DR Congo before flight, but ethnic particularities were referred to significantly less often and thus appeared to be less influential for the people in Kyaka II— even if, as mentioned earlier, their own ethnic identities remained strong. Nonetheless, the patriarchal pattern was said to be based on 'traditional' gender roles. Both men and women of different age groups (and thus also teenagers) frequently portrayed, as noted, this patriarchal structure as the way it should be, the 'normal' form of relationships. One man explained that women "are always under men's control; here I mean women are not given the chance to be involved in decision-making in the home"—also because "most ladies are not educated."[86] In a discussion, one woman stated: "Men are the decision makers in the home. They do not consult their wives over anything, but mainly act as they wish." Other women agreed, with one responding, "they believe that they are always right on anything, and if a woman tries to challenge them, they can beat her up [in order to make her obey]."[87] How widely shared these perspectives were among the people in Kyaka II is revealed in the above-discussed gender roles.

In line with these statements, violence was noted to be quite common within this pattern of relations, with some men justifying the use of force by way of women's disobedience. Hence, in addition to structurally subordinating women, men also used direct physical forced as a means of social control, corresponding with the understanding of violence used in this book. Although women were often critical of such

---

[85] Female refugee, dialogue, March 27, 2014, Base Camp.
[86] Male refugee, dialogue, March 18, 2014, Base Camp.
[87] Discussion 1 with female refugees, March 12, 2014, Base Camp.

violence,[88] many recounted that they had stayed with violent partners regardless—that because they still believed the latter to provide a degree of protection against attacks by strangers, and also due to fears of even worse violence or social exclusion in the event of separation.[89] One woman correspondingly explained: "Violence is not reported, because women fear losing their families and husbands. They do not want to be separated from them."[90] Another commented: "He doesn't provide for me, [but] I just made up my mind to stay with him because it is the right thing to do. I didn't want to act like an uneducated woman."[91] Such statements reflect that some women may feel they have no other choice but to endure violent relationships or that they seek to comply with social norms.

In relatively equal relationships, meanwhile, women and men tended to engage in decision-making, household tasks, and childrearing together. These relations were said to be rarely arranged by families, less shaped by violence, and leaned toward collaboration and sharing power.[92] This pattern was primarily found among young couples in their mid-twenties or younger, with some of them having spent most of their lives in Kyaka II. Considering this age group, this pattern links with the earlier-mentioned gender roles tending toward equality and commonalities that most youth posited with regard to their peers. It appears that the views widely shared among younger people had translated into social practices, and shaped the way younger women and men enacted gender relations.

In more detail, a woman who was in her early twenties explained that she took care of the household with her husband and they would "share the money." When she is tired from working in the field, "he takes the baby so I can cook, or he cooks. He also does the building of the house." They furthermore "started a business together" to generate income by selling fish and occasionally other foods and products. Yet when she became pregnant, the situation changed. "There is also little

---

[88] Discussion 1 with female refugee, March 12, 2014, Base Camp; discussion with male refugees, March 13, 2014, Base Camp; female refugee, dialogue, March 11, 2014, Bukere Zone.

[89] Discussion 1 with female refugees, March 12, 2014, Base Camp.

[90] Female refugees, March 12, 2014, Bukere Zone.

[91] Female refugee, dialogue, March 18, 2014, Base Camp.

[92] Female refugee, dialogue, March 18, 2014, Base Camp; discussion 2 with female refugees, March 12, 2014, Base Camp.

time because of the baby." Her husband took over the business and then started to become more hesitant about her involvement, as "he thinks men will sleep with me." Yet the woman said she still involved herself in the business regardless.[93]

Her story exemplifies how this pattern of gender relations implies more freedoms and participation for women away from 'traditional' roles and strict power allocations; most of the women who noted being in such relationships still perceived them not as 'normal' ones however. That this pattern was seen as something irregular or unusual was also evident in a discussion with local leaders; one explained that: "For me, I cook sometimes if my wife is doing other things like taking care of the baby. Even if other people may think you are bewitched, I do it."[94] One woman who also recorded sharing much of the labor with her husband reflected on the level of mutual access to resources critically: "Much as husbands allow them to work, they always want to have full control over their money or even want to have the bigger percentage of it—or else they stop [women] from working."[95] Not only the question of resources but also her emphasis on women being 'allowed' to work reveals constraints.

The third and final identified pattern relates to women who lived independently and alone with their children in Kyaka II. These particular informants stressed that staying single was their own conscious decision, which may appear confounding to prevailing gender relations or perhaps to constitute a form of 'nonrelations.' Yet taking the views that women (and men) shared seriously, and seeking to scrutinize how they perceived and made sense of their respective situations, encounters, and practices, I understand their decision to remain single as a pattern rooted in both prior and current experiences. While I did not meet any men in Kyaka II who expressed such choices, this does not mean that they did not exist. The women I spoke with mutually underlined that they preferred to manage the household by themselves, ensure income, raise the children, and make their own decisions. This indicates freeing themselves from 'traditional' social structures, conventions, and norms; these women nevertheless also stated that men 'normally' constitute the dominant figures in gender relations.

---

[93] Female refugee, dialogue, March 18, 2014, Base Camp.
[94] Discussion with local leaders, March 20, 2014, Base Camp.
[95] Discussion 2 with female refugees, March 12, 2014, Base Camp.

Yet past and current life conditions must be taken into account here. On the one hand, in spite of the range of responsibilities faced, they primarily reasoned that a new husband or partner would not necessarily offer support and protection. Instead, they would likely increase insecurities for them and their children due to the prevalence of domestic violence and sexual abuse. However, single women were also partly perceived as threats by others. One woman, as recounted in Chapter 2, noted in a discussion that: "When single, the rest of the women in the community tend to think that you want to snatch their husbands."[96] On the other hand, many of the women who decided against new partners had lost their husbands during the war. They had often witnessed their murder, or been the one to find their bodies. Some informants may have still been suffering from trauma and its after-effects, and their wish to remain single thus could suggest emotional withdrawal and possible unresolved fears of renewed loss.

One woman who rejected the idea of having a new partner was very active in her community trying to help others, and was well-recognized in Kyaka II. Although she appeared confident, her decision to remain single not only evolved from her own empowerment based in freeing herself from social norms relating to women having to have husbands. She had fled the war in DR Congo with her children in the year 2000, finally coming to Kyaka II in 2003. In the course of our dialogue she spoke of adversities, how she was raped during the war, how her husband and son were killed, how she found their bodies—and how she was raped again in Kyaka II, consequently having a baby. She recalled when the war reached her village:

I was working in a restaurant and my husband was at the hospital. [...] One day, they killed my husband and my 15-year-old son. My husband was in the store preparing medicine together with my son when they were killed. It was around 9pm at night when I heard the bullets; I switched off the lights and ran away to hide in the bush. When I came back in the morning, I found blood all over the house and two dead bodies.

After those events, she fled to Uganda. She first said that she was unable to have a new partner after recalling the bitter memories of rape in Kyaka II and noting worries about the pregnancy. She had left

---

[96] Discussion 1 with female refugees, March 12, 2014, Base Camp; female refugee, dialogue, February 18, 2014, Base Camp.

the market and was attacked during the day. She collapsed, woke up "in the bush," and said "I later realized I was pregnant. I reported the matter to OPM, they know about it. They gave me some support with the child." Then she paused for a while, before saying with lowered voice but great certainty: "I cannot have another husband. I feel I cannot have another husband, because I saw my husband killed."[97] The line of thought, the pause, the way she spoke of these events indicate that social conventions and the traumatic nature of her experiences influenced her decision to remain single. She still grieved her husband's death, and was trying to cope with painful memories. She furthermore felt ashamed of what had happened, of not fulfilling the ideal of being a 'good wife and mother' as social conventions dictated —that due to the rape, and the baby born of it. This is also evident in her words: "[H]ere I have a child without a clan. The child has no father." The lack of a social network to rely on while also unable to give the child a father led her to blame herself for the circumstances. Her relationship decision was ultimately thus as much about staying single as it was about not remarrying.

"We are able to change": Negotiations of Gender Relations

Although none of these three patterns of gender relations were fixed— as the male religious leader quoted earlier emphasized, "[w]e are able to change"[98]—and variations within them occurred, the question arises of how they developed in the first place. Hearn (2004: 60) describes the acceptance of the hegemony of men as a social process. In line with this, the social practices, norms, and constellations that shape gender systems constitute social processes, which the (re)negotiations of gender relations in Kyaka II reveal. These are not linear and short-term but rather dynamic, ongoing, and part of people's lives in the camp and beyond. The narratives of those in Kyaka II show that these processes were influenced by past practices and experiences, as well as by life within multi-ethnic groups and polyhierarchical humanitarian structures inside the camp. The processes went hand-in-hand with supporting and contesting men's hegemony, women's subordination, and other gender roles contributing to the way that gender relations were performed on-site.

---

[97] Female refugee, dialogue, March 18, 2014, Base Camp.
[98] Discussion with male refugees, March 13, 2014, Base Camp.

Holding on to known patriarchal power relations as the 'normal' ones, what I previously called *familiar* gender relations (see Chapters 2 and 3), appeared to have given some people in Kyaka II a feeling of stability and some degree of certainty in times of displacement and change—or multidimensional uncertainties, as I discuss in Chapter 5. While this tendency is most discernable in the patriarchal pattern, which can be seen as an attempt to maintain previously known gender relations, the one of relative equality might be interpreted as a pattern to create new norms; women choosing to stay single may be considered withdrawing from social gender norms. Yet the situation was more complex than this.

Negotiations not only occurred between couples, but also concerned the ways in which individuals navigated the multifaceted, complicated social settings and changes in search for establishing their own social roles. Negotiations also took place in the community, in families, and among women as well as men. Negotiations of gender relations were thus shaped individually and collectively, homosocially and heterosocially, as well as intergenerationally over time. The humanitarian structures and hierarchies, the ideas of aid workers about gender relations, furthermore affected these negotiations externally. Due to their level of power in the camp, these became influential for the people.

Within the groups of women and men spoken with, perceptions of gendered power structures were impacted by their interactions as well as by considerations of age-related status. Regarding interactions, it was not only those forming part of people's everyday lives—for example, in neighborhoods, among friends, or when working together—that contributed to changes in gender relations but people also reflected proactive initiatives. Some men noted having intervened in disputes between couples in public, trying to influence other men's behavior.[99] Others remarked that the heterogeneous social setting of different ethnic groups within the camp contributed to alterations, as women and men reproduced varying practices and customs.[100] Some women recounted how they had proactively founded groups to discuss their experiences of violence with other women, to elaborate on ways to handle hostile partners, and to protect each other. Yet men partly

---

[99] Male refugee, dialogue, March 26, 2014, Base Camp.
[100] Discussion with religious leaders, March 19, 2014, Base Camp.

also criticized such interactions, saying women would get "wrong ideas"[101] or "copy bad characteristics from their friends [...], and that brings violence."[102]

Turning to the role of age, particularly elderly women well-respected by others took up initiatives and engaged in sensitizing younger women or communities to violence between couples, to help reduce it.[103] Children and youth were generally expected to respect adults and obey them and elders especially, who constituted authority figures due to their age. This social norm was explained to have predated displacement. Furthermore, as noted above, both women and men in Kyaka II sought to influence perspectives on gender roles and relations among the next generation. While some women strove to raise their children to be "respectful,"[104] one man stressed—as mentioned earlier—the importance of "culture," explaining how he counseled his girls to obey their future husbands and follow their "culture"; they should "[g]o as an empty jerrican."[105] Such influences also existed in polygamous relationships, wherein older wives were generally assigned more power although men were said to maintain overarching decision-making power.[106] Elders thus presented key figures also for adults; as one woman explained: "Usually the elderly in the community will try to advice or counsel the women and men on how to handle marriage issues."[107]

Finally, the importance of continuity and change over time is revealed in the repeatedly raised comparisons between gender roles and relations before flight and during encampment. For example, some women portrayed a certain level of security and protection from relatives and in the community in DR Congo, whereas they believed in Kyaka II "husbands are not accountable to anyone." Due to the absence of long-developed community and family structures, men were said to "feel at liberty to just do as they please."[108] One man stated, meanwhile, "[w]omen in DR Congo were undermined," but that in

---

[101] Discussion with male refugees, March 13, 2014, Base Camp.
[102] Male refugee, dialogue, March 18, 2014, Base Camp.
[103] Female refugee, dialogue, March 18, 2014, Base Camp.
[104] Discussion 2 with female refugees, March 12, 2014, Base Camp.
[105] Discussion with male refugees, March 13, 2014, Base Camp.
[106] Female refugee, dialogue, March 11, 2014, Base Camp; male refugee, dialogue, March 18, 2014, Base Camp.
[107] Discussion 1 with female refugees, March 12, 2014, Base Camp.
[108] Discussion 1 with female refugees, March 12, 2014, Base Camp.

Uganda "now there is some gender balance—although the man is the head of the family."[109] These parallels between the past and the present echo the great number of narratives shared by people in Kyaka II, showing how earlier and current experiences simultaneously affect their negotiations of gender roles and relations.

"Women are given many favors in Kyaka II": Impact of Humanitarian Aid and Actors

The man quoted in the beginning of the chapter also compared how it was men in DR Congo "who carried on all the responsibilities, but in Kyaka II men and women share them." In addition to reasoning "men [had] lost power in the home," he remarked that "here in Kyaka II they all depend on UNHCR."[110] Another man correspondingly found men to be the decision-makers in DR Congo but in light of the limited livelihoods in Kyaka II he said: "Men do not have more power than women [in the camp]." Instead, he posited: "Women have more power than men [now]. Women are given many favors in Kyaka II compared to men."[111] These references to dependence on and favors through aid agencies indicate the structural impact that humanitarian system and projects have also on the negotiations of gender relations within the camp. Men repeatedly relayed feeling like they had "no power" and that "women have taken over [in Kyaka II]."[112] Such perceptions of lost social status related to what the individuals had learned and believed it to mean to be a man or a husband. While they strongly associated being 'a real man' with making decisions and providing for their wives and families, as practiced in DR Congo, displacement and encampment imposed restrictions on them.

This resonates with other studies on effects of humanitarian structures. Dolan (2009: 191ff) discusses how refugee protection can turn into a form of humiliation in camps and contribute to profound changes in gender relations, which he depicts as a collapse of masculinity. He attributes alcoholism and domestic violence to men's failure to realize their ideals of masculinity as husbands, fathers, and breadwinners. Turner (1999) explores the situation of young men from Burundi in a refugee camp in Tanzania, and the challenges many face

---

[109] Discussion with local leaders, March 20, 2014, Base Camp.
[110] Male refugee, dialogue, March 18, 2014, Base Camp.
[111] Male refugee, dialogue, March 17, 2014, Sweswe Zone.
[112] Discussion with religious leaders, March 19, 2014, Base Camp.

in finding their role within the social structures. This is marked by humanitarian agencies' power, which triggers men to lose economic, social, and political status. "UNHCR is a better husband" (Turner 1999: 2) is a powerful quote that the author cites to illustrate the changing power structures men experienced in the camp studied. Lukunka also depicts how Burundian men perceived dependence within a Tanzanian refugee camp, noting how such circumstances "caused a socio-psychological crisis for refugee men that took the form of a gender identity crisis, specifically, emasculation" (2011: 2). To counteract this, men would resort to violence.

Other studies also refer to 'emasculation' of men in refugee situations (see, e.g., Ritchie 2018; Griffiths 2015; Thornhill 2012), and the above statements by men in Kyaka II feeling powerless and unable to head families could be seen as indications supporting such assumptions. However, as a description for the social degradation (of men) resulting from the conditions within refugee camps, the term poses certain issues. It risks focusing mainly or perhaps solely on how humanitarian structures and life in the camp affect men and their social positions, portraying these effects as substantial. This could lead to paying little to no attention to the effects on women or to subconsciously anticipating an innate accompanying empowerment process for the latter. Moreover, the term 'emasculation' risks displaying the effects as a change from patriarchal structures assumed to be the ordinary ones—the standard— thus normalizing men's hegemony, women's subordination, and gender inequalities at large. Schulz remarks similar critique regarding this term in addition to 'feminization' and 'homosexualization' to describe sexual violence against men, arguing that underlying assumptions "in many ways rely upon (implicit and explicit) misogyny, gender essentialism and homophobia" (2018a: 1105).

Instead, I believe taking a broader approach is crucial to consider and reflect the gendered influences and power structures of aid and 'camp life' as they impact on the identities and gender relations among inhabitants. All those living in refugee camps like Kyaka II are affected by the humanitarian settings and structures in gender-specific ways; social degradation or other forms of humiliation are certainly not limited to men alone. Earlier discussions about gender roles in this chapter and humanitarian aid in Chapter 3 signify this.

As shown above, aid workers in Kyaka II widely ascribed women submissive, nurturing roles, being responsible for the household but not for decision-making, and men hegemonic ones, as heads of house-holds and providers for families but disregarding their vulnerabilities. That these and other attributions that aid workers articulated not only reflected their personal opinions but also translated into their practices and aid projects is evident in the way the latter were delivered. This *modus operandi* influenced women and men of different ages individu-ally, as groups, and their gender relations too. In Chapter 3, I argued that refugees were generally treated as 'protection objects' and women specifically as 'vulnerable protection objects.' This perpetuated top-down aid provision and decision-making, and left little room for the displaced to influence the aid projects. Despite the aim of promoting gender equality, women were prioritized in many areas and received specialized support. While men criticized their neglect, women were 'vulnerabilized,' pushed into roles of being 'good wives and mothers,' and expected to be economically active, which some found overwhelm-ing or were ashamed of if they could not fulfill them. Moreover, both women and men spoken with addressed difficulties with the various humanitarian approaches taken. In addition to insufficient aid[113] and the gender biases in aid delivery,[114] the imposed structures were lamented. Among others, one woman criticized being a refugee means "they cannot make decisions," which humanitarian and political authorities do for them,[115] while one man said, "refugees do not depend on themselves. A refugee feels helpless."[116]

The camp conditions, aid, and especially humanitarians' practices therefore complicated the lives of women and men in Kyaka II and affected their negotiations of gender relations, which essentially led to paradoxes arising. On the one hand, aid workers' beliefs in men being the powerful leaders and women the vulnerable subordinates contrib-uted to the preservation of patriarchal gender orders, and aid projects inadvertently simultaneously reinforced gender inequalities, which cor-responds with scholarly debates (see among others Grabska 2011; Fiddian-Qasmiyeh 2010a). The critical factor here is that aid staff

---

[113] Male refugee, dialogue, March 28, 2014, Base Camp.
[114] Discussion with religious leaders, March 19, 2014, Base Camp; discussion with local leaders, March 20, 2014, Base Camp; female refugee, dialogue, March 18, 2014, Base Camp.
[115] Female refugee, dialogue, March 27, 2014, Base Camp.
[116] Discussion with male refugees, March 13, 2014, Base Camp.

and projects assigned roles but at the same time hindered men and women in fulfilling them.

On the other hand, the way the projects were delivered contributed to aid workers obtaining the roles of protector, provider, and decision-maker to support specifically the 'helpless women'—and more generally, the refugees. As the new hegemon, aid workers thus figuratively became part of the gender systems on-site, and to some extent replaced the roles men used to have—although perhaps unwittingly and unintentionally. However, this adoption of power by aid agencies occurred while employees continued to believe that men represented the (sole) decision-makers and providers in families—despite these being roles they could hardly fulfill due to the conditions, limitations, and regulations encountered in the camp.

In Conclusion: Changing Gender Relations in an Interim Social World

This chapter has explored how women and men of different age groups remembered gender roles and relations in DR Congo, and how they maintained, contested, and altered these roles and relations in Uganda's Kyaka II. Their narratives indicated an interdependence with local conditions in the camp; the people's perceptions of social, cultural, political, and economic circumstances; and, the influence of humanitarian structures and regulations. First and foremost, this underlines how gender relations—like all social ones—are determined by the experiences and contexts of (new) coexistence within given environments. Due to gender-specific experiences pre-flight and during encampment, along with a changing locale and specific living conditions, the displaced could no longer exercise familiar gender roles and relations also shaped by ethnic customs. Instead, they had to be (re)negotiated. Gender roles and relations are thus revealed to be context-specific, and inherently influenced by the social practices of women, men, girls, and boys. Through these interdependencies, (re)negotiations of gender relations not only took place among those living in the camp but were also influenced by humanitarian aid and agencies—and, of course, their staff.

The recounted narratives of women and men, girls and boys, as well as of aid workers reveal many assumed patriarchal gender structures to be the 'normal' ones—despite concurrent contestations thereof.

The influence of aid workers in perpetuating such notions was critical, as they believed in these patriarchal structures and imposed roles but nevertheless limited the women's and men's capacities to fulfill those as a result of the projects offered—with aid workers instead taking on, even inadvertently, the roles of decision-makers themselves.

What became clear through many of the perspectives shared by informants is how strongly the past—and thus learned gender roles—shaped their ideas of gender roles and relations in Kyaka II. While the local social world of the refugee camp affected all parts of their lives, and thus also their gender roles and relations, this social world was characterized by spatial and temporal limitations. Many of these people grew up in DR Congo, where they practiced certain gender roles and relations prior to flight. Moreover, they were well aware that the camp was only an interim place of settlement for them—albeit a very long-term one over many years. While the narratives of youths showed prevailing perceptions of patriarchal structures among adults, differing tendencies were articulated with a view to their own age group—namely, toward equal gender roles and partly relations. Yet this being only an interim social world may ultimately complicate sustainable change occurring toward less strict gender orders going forward.

Analytically, drawing on Hearn's theory has facilitated the shedding of light on the parallel, varying, and also conflicting perceptions that interlocutors had on gender roles and relations within Kyaka II. For future research, taking broad approaches by considering prior and current conditions and gender systems appears a useful way to explore what changes occur, how, and why. Longitude studies on life conditions, gender roles and relations in regions of origin, in exile and post-displacement may be difficult, but would certainly be insightful. While I myself relied on memories shared about gender systems in DR Congo, studying the local constellations on-site both pre- and post-displacement would allow for more comprehensive insights into how the change of location, respective experiences, and differing living conditions may affect the perspectives and practices of the people on gender systems.

5 | Coping with the Difficult Life in the Refugee Camp

Although life is harder [in Kyaka II], it is better than home [...] because you are not worried about being killed. You sleep comfortably, without the fear of being attacked and killed.[1]

This quote is by a woman who had fled her home in DR Congo with her three children due to the war there. Her husband was abducted by rebels, and she said she waited for more than a year hoping he was still alive and would return but then the security situation worsened. She felt she had to leave to protect herself and her children. Yet during their flight to Uganda, she was raped by strangers who were also in the process of escaping the war. After having arrived and lived in Uganda's refugee camp Kyaka II for some time, she remarried and had two more children. She explained that her new husband had also lost his family during the war in DR Congo, witnessing rebels murder his first wife and their children. They shared the sorrow of lost loved ones, and dealt with the terrible memories of wartime violence together. However, the woman also explained in dialogue their challenging daily life in the camp. They were confronted with diverse difficulties and frequent concerns about food, clothing, childcare, and finances. In spite of these problems, she highlighted that aspects of Kyaka II had helped her and her family to move forward; that "life was harder" but also better than in DR Congo, because she was no longer afraid of imminent wartime danger.

This woman's story is expressive of the ways in which she coped but also the grave difficulties that she encountered, and this was revealed in most of the narratives those in Kyaka II shared. These difficulties are unquestionably present for refugees all over the world, but mere focus on problems such as violence and restrictions in the camp risks produc-ing and reproducing a victimizing, objectifying, and depoliticizing

[1] Female refugee, dialogue, February 25, 2014, Base Camp.

notion of such individuals—and of women especially. Over the past years, scholars have criticized how refugees are described as "incapacitated children" in the humanitarian discourse (Malkki 1995a: 11), "innocent victims, stripped of political subjectivity" (Turner 2010: 155), "the undesirable and rejectable" (Agier 2011: 19), and "habitually portrayed as if they are without agency, like corks bobbing along on the surface of an unstoppable wave of displacement" (Gatrell 2013: 9). Women, in particular, are presented as "an almost madonnalike figure" (Malkki 1995a: 11) and "the label 'refugee woman' becomes a marker of their exploitability and denies them the expression of other identities" (Pittaway and Pittaway 2004: 131), reduced to stock images of 'womenandchildren' in humanitarian discourses (Fiddian-Qasmiyeh 2014a: 4–7; Johnson 2011: 1032; in line with Enloe 2014: 1). From such a top-down perspective on refugees as voiceless aid beneficiaries and helpless victims (see Nyers 2006; Hyndman and Giles 2011)—or, as argued in Chapter 3, as 'vulnerable protection objects'—these individuals appear unable to make decisions and survive on their own; instead they appear to require a strong 'humanitarian protector' to be on their side. This thrusts a label on them that denies subjective and individual identities and experiences; widely ignores their diverse social, cultural, economic, and political interests as well as backgrounds; and, presents them as subjected to—instead of agents of—the future (Harrell-Bond 2002; Lubkemann 2008a: 16; Turner 2010: 3). Displayed as devoid of agency in humanitarian and political discourses, refugees' own capacities, activities, and coping strategies become pushed into the shadows—and this remains critical despite and due to the current trend in these discourses toward promoting refugees' resilience (see Krause and Schmidt 2020).

When placing the views, narratives, and strategies of the refugees themselves at the center of research, however, problematic conditions during conflict, flight, and encampment prompt the question of how they cope with the manifold issues arising—and strive to improve their lives in camps like Kyaka II, as well as other sites of settlement. For many years now, and increasingly in recent times, scholars have paid attention to refugees' agency and coping strategies (see Hutchinson and Dorsett 2012; Gladden 2012; Seguin and Roberts 2017). Psychologists have been exploring coping and resilience based on the "cognitive turn" already since the 1970s, seeking to nurture the inner strength of refugees and offer suitable therapeutic interventions for dealing with traumatic experiences (see Dember 1974; Droždek, 2015). In the Social Sciences, scholars have shed light on various strategies to handle challenges. They have explored, for example, how specific groups deal with dangers or risky living conditions in exile (Thomson 2013; Erdener 2017; Krause 2016d; Krause and Schmidt 2018); how refugees in protracted situations contribute to home-making (Korac 2009; Brun 2015a; Boer 2015; Omata 2016); how they handle uncertainty about their future (Golooba-Mutebi 2004; Dryden-Peterson 2006; Horst and Grabska 2015; Grabska and Fanjoy 2015); or how they see themselves as refugees (Clark-Kazak 2014; Krause 2016f). In these studies, scholars have revealed factors hindering coping strategies like discrimination and external labeling as well as supportive ones such as adaptability, optimism, and (religious) belief. In addition to individual initiatives, social networks to support, help, and protect each other are noted to be important for being able to deal with difficult experiences and conditions (see Hutchinson and Dorsett 2012).

This chapter hence draws on and seeks to contribute to this body of literature on coping strategies of refugees living in camps. It illustrates that women as well as other actors are the ones who initiate ways to cope with obstacles, deficits, and risks, not only so as to survive but also in order to improve the daily circumstances that shape their lives. It ultimately portrays refugees' coping as the practicing of agency both despite and due to adversities. Maintaining the orientation of the previous chapters, this one also places special attention on the perceptions of women as well as of men and adolescents, seeking to shed light on how they made sense of the conditions and coped with them.

Lister's (2004) agency theory serves as the analytical framework here. She focuses on marginalized actors living in poverty who are confronted with diverse restrictive structures that limit but also enable or elicit strategies to deal with those difficulties. This already indicates parallels to the conditions that refugees encounter in camps such as Kyaka II. Drawing on long-standing theoretical debates about agency in the Social Sciences as well as her work on poverty, human rights, and citizenship, Lister (2004: 124–130) interdependently links structures and actors with their actions. Agency generally refers to the ability of actors to reflect on their position and to design subsequent strategies for action, while structures mainly capture the surrounding social, political, and economic conditions as well as regulations and processes—in Lister's own work, as primarily influenced by and influencing poverty. Specifically, she develops four main scopes of action signifying agency: "getting by," "getting out," "getting (back) at," and "getting organized." These cover everyday, personal, strategic, and political possibilities for action.

"Getting by" largely represents the diverse actions that individuals employ to cope with poverty, limitations, and accompanying everyday problems. Lister (2004: 130) argues that this form of agency can be so commonplace that it may remain unnoticed but is nonetheless still key for individuals' routine coping. "Getting out" captures personal and strategic actions aimed at changing everyday living conditions. Individuals undertake a 'quasi-exit' from the current conditions to negotiate courses of action—although, following Lister (2004: 145), these are produced by structural factors that both support and hinder the exercising of agency. "Getting (back) at" refers to the practices that individuals use to respond to perceived unjust and inappropriate conditions. Lister describes such strategic and political practices as "acts of everyday resistance" (2004: 144). Finally, "getting organized" signifies collective, strategic, and partly political actions that people employ together in order to cope—and perhaps even bring about structural change.

This analytical matrix suits the investigation of coping strategies as forms of agency among women and men in Kyaka II, and has been employed in similar studies with marginalized groups of displaced people—most notably by Clark-Kazak (2014; see also Aaltonen 2013; Redmond 2009; Coulthard 2012). Lister's reference to poverty and structural restrictions reveals parallels to the conditions encountered in the refugee camp, where the experienced marginalization evolves out of its isolated location, structural limitations, and various forms of violence.

The chapter contains two main sections: one about coping with violence and the other about coping with camp conditions. The first addresses how the displaced seek to deal with and reduce the prevalence of violence during conflict, flight, and encampment. It treats fleeing wartime violence as a deliberate decision, and reflects on, among other means, conscious silence, mutual protection, and involvement in community structures as coping strategies. The second main section then turns to everyday life in the camp. It explores the strategies that individuals and collectives use to generate livelihoods, claim their rights, create normalcy and belonging despite multidimensional uncertainties, and generate hope and belief in a better future as drivers for coping. Throughout the chapter, I seek to not only reflect which coping strategies women and men use, but also how existing issues affect or even hamper their strategies.

Coping with Violence during Conflict, Flight, and Encampment

Insecurities and particularly different forms of gender-based violence posed widespread risks to most of the research participants. Chapter 2 revealed that many informants experienced prevalent threats of gender-based violence during the conflict in their country of origin, during flight, and later during their stay in Kyaka II too. Fears as well as experiences of sexual abuse, domestic violence, structural risks of discrimination, and other forms of this violence complicated the lives of many people living there. But how did they deal with these traumatic events and memories?

"The war in Congo made me flee": Decisions to Leave Conflict *and other Difficult Contexts*

During the conflict in DR Congo, women and men were exposed to a wide variety of risks. As a result, one woman highlighted: "The war in Congo made me flee"—a statement that many others similarly expressed in conversations.[2] In light of the dangers of the war, and the chosen wording of it "making" people leave, conflict-induced displacement may appear a seemingly unconscious passive reaction— an inherent reflex to external threat. Of course, ensuring one's survival is a fundamental impulse; however, the survival strategies that the affected establish and use are not accidental. Instead, fear of violence, loss of community structures, lack of livelihoods, seeking safe surroundings—all of these aspects and others influenced these people's decisions to leave the war behind.

Fearing, Experiencing, and Moving Away from Violence

Many research participants shared vivid memories of the war, and most narrated that they had fled due to intensifying violence. For women, however, it was often their direct exposure to violence that

---

[2] Female refugee, dialogue, March 26, 2014, Bukere Zone.

triggered their decision to leave their homes and seek safety elsewhere. One woman who had arrived in Uganda in 2008 with her children explained that she escaped "because of the war" in DR Congo. The specific moment that prompted her decision to leave was the fateful day when she was attacked and raped in her own home. Her husband was away for work, while her children were able to take cover and remain unharmed. The woman continued to be in great fear after the "soldiers" had left, and she subsequently tried to seek help from her community. As she recalled: "That morning I went to the chairman [of the village], but nothing could be done." Friends then took her and her children to the nearby village where her mother lived, but she said: "The soldiers were still disrupting the village, and so I decided to run to Uganda."

She had left DR Congo without being able to speak with her husband first. For a long time, she thought he had been murdered. After some time living in Kyaka II, she found a new partner with whom she had twins. However, later she later found out that her first husband was still alive:

He came [to Kyaka II] looking for me in 2012. He found me with the young twins, which he definitely knew didn't belong to him. He was sad that I had taken on another man. I told him the whole story of how I had been raped. My husband said he came to take me with him back to DR Congo but now that I had twins he couldn't. I begged him to take me with him, but he refused because I had another man. He said that maybe since I was raped, maybe I am always concentrating on men.[3]

Her story reveals the human tragedies and complex aftermaths that conflict, violence, and forced migration can have. It also demonstrates the issues of sexism and ingrained biases vis-à-vis stigmatization and rejection that women are often confronted with after being raped; they are at times directly or indirectly blamed for the abuse suffered, which can increase the already heavy burdens they have to carry (see also Albutt et al. 2017; Kennedy and Prock 2018; on effects on male victims, see Schulz 2018b; Onyango and Hampanda 2011; Christian et al. 2011).

The effects of violence also extend to family members and one's social circle. In this vein, the woman quoted at the beginning of this

---

[3] Female refugee, dialogue, March 5, 2014, Kaborogota Zone.

chapter recounted how after her husband's abduction she first decided to stay. She said she "waited with the mother-in-law for one and a half years" for his return, but when the security situation worsened, she felt the only option was to flee to protect their children especially. She noted that even after all these years she still did not know whether her husband was dead or alive.[4]

Another woman shared her story about the intense levels of violence enacted against herself and her family. She stressed, as also quoted above: "The war in Congo made me flee." She explained that rebels murdered her husband, father, mother, sisters, and brothers, and how "[m]y child, a very young boy was beaten." She feared "[t]hey wanted to kill me," and said, "I ran with my three children." Only one brother had survived the attack, but she was not sure if he was now still alive. During flight, she was raped and said she barely survived. But, "[w]e persevered and walked until we got to Uganda." There, they initially stayed in Kampala. Although hoping for a place of safety and security for her children and herself, she was also confronted with violence in the capital and then contacted the authorities to take her to a camp. Life continued to be difficult in Kyaka II; it was not only the violence on-site but especially also the memories of earlier forms of violence that she had to cope with. After a long pause in our dialogue, she quietly said: "I cannot sleep at all, I just lie awake all the time. I keep thinking about the issues, and I also get scary dreams about the incidents. I also over-worry about life in this camp."[5] This reveals the long aftermath experiences of violence can unfold.

In a vein similar to how these women told of flight being a protection strategy particularly for children, many men who had families also remarked that they decided to leave to keep their families safe after early indications of the violence worsening. Among them was a man who escaped DR Congo "when there was a war between the Lendu and Hema in 2002. It was at night in March 2002 when people were sounding the alarm. There were gunshots everywhere." He paused and added: "When I heard of the war, I fled with my wife and our child. I didn't carry any property." To get some food and little money, he explained he made "chapatis" to survive the journey. Although they managed to leave the conflict zone, they were attacked by rebels close

[4] Female refugee, dialogue, February 25, 2014, Base Camp.
[5] Female refugee, dialogue, March 26, 2014, Bukere Zone.

to the border and robbed of the few things they had. While he identified himself as a "businessman in DR Congo" he later explained how he "became a pastor" in Kyaka II, seeking to help others cope.[6]

Many others decided to flee by themselves either because they felt it was the only choice left for them with family members having been murdered or because they feared attack and so left quickly without notifying their next of kin. One man who experienced both of these realities explained that his father was the head of a farmer's organization in DR Congo. Rebels then accused his father of overseeing a "rebel organization," and so murdered him. "I was part of my father's organization, and had to flee for my life. They also killed my elder brother and two of my uncles." Later in our dialogue, the man said: "I cannot go back to DR Congo, because all our land was taken by the people that were trying to kill us. I know that if I try to set foot in the country I will be dead. I will never go back."[7]

Another man who fled alone made the decision to do so when rebels stepped up the forceful recruitment of young men into their ranks. He said: "I fled out of fear, because I did not want to be enlisted." This fear was articulated by several other men spoken with too. He left alone also because he worried the rebels would harm his family if he was caught with them. He remembered flight as long and exhausting, often avoiding movement during daytime and trying to find his way at night. After reaching Uganda, he went to a "police station, where I had to report since I had no papers." Then he was brought to Kyaka II. Being separated from his family was and remained painful for him, but he noted "they are still alive there in Goma," which he knew as they communicated on the phone. "Somehow my family survived the attacks, because they ran to another place and later went back home when the situation was calm but found everything looted."[8]

As in the women's narratives above, many other people were also not able to stay in touch with family members who remained in DR Congo. The uncertainty of not knowing whether they were still alive and well was very worrying for them too. This was the case for one man who, as mentioned in Chapter 2, had fled alone because he feared rebels wanted to kill him. He recounted: "I looked for a bush where

[6] Male refugee, dialogue, March 27, 2014, Base Camp.
[7] Male refugee, dialogue, March 5, 2014, Kaborogota Zone.
[8] Male refugee, dialogue, March 28, 2014, Base Camp.

I had to hide. The place I was hiding was away from our zone." He then mainly moved at night, under the shelter of darkness. He said he survived the flight by continuously trying to circumvent attacks, and by "eating fruits and yellow bananas from gardens. [...] I would carry those that were not ripe with me to eat them later." With a despondent tone in his voice, he said: "I have not heard from my family ever since, and I am not sure if they are still alive or not. After I disappeared I never received any information about them."[9]

Waiting, Leaving, Moving Again

These individual stories shared by female and male informants bring to light their difficult experiences of violence, the personal losses suffered as a result of the war, and the continued risks that these individuals faced even after leaving their homes in DR Congo. The stories also reflect the heavy burdens of memory that these people still felt and carried with them daily, even years afterward. Moreover, these accounts indicate how flight did not constitute a 'passive survival reflex.' Instead, these people's diverse and personal experiences, fears and life conditions, but also hopes of reaching a safe place represented core reasons for fleeing—thus existing as conscious decisions, as deliberate choices that they took.

Moore and Shellman (2004, 2006), Bohra-Mishra and Massey (2011), Adhikari (2012, 2013), and others also argue that conflict-induced flight represents such an intentional choice. Taking choice-centered approaches, they examine why and under which conditions people decide to leave behind violent conflict and unrest to seek safety elsewhere. Such research corresponds with Lister's earlier-mentioned agency theory, and particularly the "getting out" form thereof—as "[i]ndividuals exercise their strategic agency in negotiating [...] routes, but the routes themselves are forged by structural and cultural factors, which can assist or obstruct the exercise of that agency" (2004: 145). While Lister attends to routes out of poverty, these physically and symbolically also apply to flight. It is about refusing to submit to the presenting challenging conditions, and resisting in one way or another (Lister 2004: 144). Focusing on the decisions to flee is not to trivialize the severe impacts of conflict-related violence, with its gender-specific direct, structural, and cultural forms following Galtung and

---

[9] Male refugee, dialogue, March 27, 2014, Base Camp.

Confortini, by supposing that the affected people had various freedoms to easily choose outcomes or do as they wished. Of course, issues are intense and people may not feel they have any alternatives—but this does not denote passivity. Nor should the focus on choice obscure the fact that people in conflict zones can encounter "involuntary immobility," which Lubkemann (2008b) explains as occurring when security-related, financial, social, or infrastructural circumstances restrict mobilities.

Instead, choice-centered approaches consider the problems that the affected face and explore their agency both despite and due to these challenges. The value of such approaches is their clear renunciation of assumptions of passivity among people afflicted by conflict, and the attention paid to the various actions that they undertake so as to cope with issues that arise—the central such action here being the decision to leave. As Schon posits: "Rather than migration timing being the outcome of binary choices of whether to fight or whether to flee—fight or flight—people select from large repertoires of protection strategies such as daily movement, bribery, or protest" (2019: 12).

In line with that, the accounts the people in Kyaka II shared regarding flight reveal their decisions being important protection strategies. They indicate how women and men decided to flee the war depending on the scope and level of violence they experienced or feared, and the safety concerns they had for their families as reasons for persevering and staying longer or alternatively moving away sooner. Many relayed having made the choice to leave in light of immediate threats or attacks, having heard shooting or encountered violence. Protecting not only themselves but especially also their families was crucial; some waited for abducted relatives to return, some moved instantly to protect children especially, and some chose to leave alone to reduce risks for themselves and partly also their families. In order to escape, they employed various strategies *en route* in seeking safety and survival. Some took cover and hid from rebels, navigated dangerous surroundings mainly, or only, at night, or used the scant resources available to meet basic needs such as nourishment.

Choosing to get out and move is not limited to the exact moment of leaving homes in conflict zones or the process of flight, but also captures decisions to find places of safety and security—which can be taken again and again, even after arriving at certain sites of destination. Similar to the above stories, a number of other research participants also recalled that they initially moved to Kampala—often arbitrarily, as they did not know where to go (see also Krause and Gato 2019). Some said officials then took the decision for them to settle in Kyaka II. Among others, one woman who had fled violence and a dangerous husband in South Sudan first registered and stayed in Kampala; but "[a]fter three months, they said we want to take you to Kyaka II. So they brought me here."[10]

Others stayed in Kampala longer and tried to make a living in the city, often without registering as refugees, but later decided to go to the authorities and move to a camp in order to gain access to aid services.[11] This was the case for one woman who had escaped the war in DR Congo with her children after her husband was murdered. After arriving in Uganda, she first chose to live in Kampala—where she would stay for about two years. She said she did not register in the capital due to fear of being relocated, but this resulted in trouble finding formal employment. She only gained limited income by selling homemade bracelets and traditional fabric, *chitenge*. The money was not enough for the life of her family in the city, and their everyday challenges were worsened by increasing poverty. Besides the initial problems of a language barrier and difficult public transport, she worried a lot about her children. They were unable to attend school, and rarely had enough food. She furthermore relied on harsh landlords, who she lamented increased the rent suddenly, unannounced, or even demanded sexual favors in return. To herself and her children, the situation became so difficult that she decided to get out, go to the police in Kampala, register as a refugee, and then move to a camp. By the time we met, she had lived in Kyaka II for six years. Although she experienced 'camp life' as difficult, she said she managed better there compared to the city, also because she was able to build a social support network.[12]

---

[10] Female refugee, dialogue, March 18, 2014, Base Camp.

[11] Drawing on this study as well as a subsequent research project, together with Joshua Gato, I analyzed refugees' choices regarding staying in the camp or the city. We found that many who chose the latter were strongly influenced therein by the desire to avoid the former; however, a clear separation of camps or cities as sole sites of residence could not be drawn. Instead, refugees dealt with issues strategically in both sites, for which their mobilities were key in improving livelihoods (Krause and Gato 2019).

[12] Female refugee, dialogue, February 18, 2014, Base Camp.

Thus, in lieu of understanding forced migration as merely a passive and linear process from a place of danger to one of safety, it must rather be seen as a phenomenon encompassing many active choices and coping strategies of great complexity and variety. Based on her research with Angolan refugees in Zambian camps, Inhetveen also refers to "tours and detours" (2010: 215, my translation) in explaining such variations in mobilities. What decisions and practices like these have in common is that they are strategic movements, through which those affected resist difficulties and leave sites of violence and hardship in order to find ways to establish better lives.

Voice and Silence to Cope with Gender-Based Violence in the Camp

When reflecting on the scopes of gender-based violence in Kyaka II in light of the impact of conditions and humanitarian aid on-site, as addressed in the previous chapters, the question arises of how refugees cope with these experiences and risks. Moreover, it can be asked whether committing violence and using acts of force represent particular coping strategies in themselves. Without doubt, the latter is a controversial question because by understanding violence as a way of coping it might also be seen as an ordinary part of life—and thus not so much a specific problem that the women and men in Kyaka II sought to cope with. Yet I would like to start this section by briefly addressing exactly this question.

Informants in Kyaka II said that some men had lost their dominant social roles as a result of displacement, the conditions in the camp and the effects of the humanitarian system. Some were unable to care for their wives and families, and therefore said to feel useless and helpless. In response to these changes and conditions in the camp, some men lamented how women disobeyed them—and thus used violence against the latter to regain or defend their position of power.[13] As discussed in Chapter 4, some men found the use of force against women a legitimate social practice to maintain their dominance. Yet difficulties and changes were certainly not limited only among men. Women also experienced various changes of circumstance and often took on new

---

[13] Discussion with male refugees, March 13, 2014, Base Camp; discussion 1 with female refugees, March 12, 2014, Base Camp.

responsibilities—being overwhelming for some. Violence perpetrated by women was also said to partly occur due to local conditions. For example, one explained: "Some women are very strong, they have energy and some men are very weak. They can beat their husbands." She added that these men "cannot tell people. The men will keep quiet."[14] At times violence among co-wives was noted to take place to defend hierarchical roles within polygamous relationships, whereas that against strangers—mainly women—was said to occur to guard relationships, keep other women away, or punish them for interacting with husbands.[15] Thus, being violent can in some cases be understood as a practice that people used to deal with the conditions they encountered in Kyaka II.

But how did women and men in Kyaka II both cope with violence and seek to reduce the risks of it occurring? Regarding war zones and refugee camps, studies in Psychology rightly point to the likelihood and dangers of trauma as well as of re-traumatization among those affected (see, e.g., Flatten et al. 2013: 4; Karunakara et al. 2004; Nagai et al. 2008). This applies similarly to those living in Kyaka II. As portrayed in previous chapters, gender-based violence prevailed during conflict, flight, and encampment—posing almost ubiquitous risks. This emphasizes the need for psychosocial care for those affected both directly and indirectly (i.e., those experiencing, witnessing, or fearing attack). Supporting this, one man underscored the intense effects of violence during the war in DR Congo, noting "some [women] were raped and [are] now sick, also men were tortured." He reasoned that "these people need comfort and good care because they have got psychological problems. Here in Kyaka II life is difficult for all refugees; they can never access good food for their diet, medication, and counseling. People are sick psychologically, and need counselors who can bring them back to their moods of normal people or bring back hope."[16]

Although humanitarian agencies provided psychosocial counseling for victims of gender-based violence and women especially, access to this was complicated due to difficulties in the referral system, as previously discussed. Correspondingly, one woman pointed out that

[14] Female refugee, dialogue, March 18, 2014, Base Camp.
[15] Female refugee, dialogue, March 26, 2014, Bukere Zone; male refugee, dialogue, March 18, 2014, Base Camp; discussion 1 with female refugees, March 12, 2014, Base Camp.
[16] Male refugee, dialogue, March 18, 2014, Base Camp.

"[t]he organizations are not giving good mental and medical care"[17]—also because aid agencies insufficiently attended to refugees' problems and police would request fees for following up on incidents. Even if victims did receive access, some explained their refraining from using these services—as counseling mainly took place in offices shared by several aid workers and thus lacked the necessary privacy to discuss highly traumatic experiences.[18] Furthermore, many noted that those affected by violence deliberately avoided reporting cases due to fear of stigmatization, social exclusion, and increased violence, among other things.[19]

Such reservations about reporting cases of gender-based violence to the police, to government and humanitarian agencies, may appear to display a certain degree of intimidation, reticence, or resignation on the part of victims, being a way of giving in or even giving up—and therefore representing alleged 'non-actions.' However, rather than interpreting a lack of reporting as indicative of passivity and victims surrendering of the situation, which would at the same time increase focus on perpetrators' power over them, it is crucial to take into account the variety of coping strategies used. This requires recognizing strategies of women and men that represent not only immediately visible public and proactive ones such as open resistance, but also everyday actions of getting by such as silence or also waiting; Brun (2015b), for example, theorizes "active waiting" as a form of agency in protracted displacement based on her research with internally displaced Georgians. Such 'hidden' actions may remain invisible at first sight, but what must not be overlooked regardless is how they serve particular purposes for those who use them. These actions are deliberately taken, and therefore represent agency.

Hence, both the act of and the desistance from reporting cases of violence are revealing of concrete coping strategies. No matter how 'passive' remaining quiet may appear to be at first glance, "silence also 'speaks'" (Hajdukowski-Ahmed 2003: 216)—and hence is expressive

---

[17] Female refugee, dialogue, March 14, 2014, Bujubuli.
[18] Discussion 1 with female refugees, March 12, 2014, Base Camp; female refugee, dialogue, March 18, 2014, Base Camp; male refugee, dialogue, March 18, 2014, Base Camp; two aid workers, interview, February 24, 2014.
[19] Female refugee, dialogue, March 17, 2014, Bujubuli; discussion with religious leaders, March 19, 2014, Base Camp; female aid worker, interview, April 10, 2014; female aid worker, interview, April 22, 2014.

in itself. Silence reflects actions people take to cope with issues, protect themselves, and/or move forward. Other scholars in Forced Migration and Refugee Studies and beyond have also discussed the power that silence can carry for individuals, and women in particular, vis-à-vis coping (see Hajdukowski-Ahmed 2003; Tankink and Richters 2007; Campbell and Mannell 2016; Ussher et al. 2017; Lazreg 2018; Parpart and Parashar 2019). Among others, Parpart (2010: 1) argues that alongside choosing to voice one's perspective, being silent and secretive signal agency too. As speaking out can be difficult or have its limits, secrecy and silence thereby become "crucial survival strategies, offering protection and sometimes spaces for renegotiating harmful gender relations and practices. While ideally voices should be heard and challenges launched, voice is not the only weapon available" (Parpart 2010: 5).

Following Lister's (2004: 130–144) agency theory, decisions for and against reporting violence to authorities represent actions of "getting by" and "getting back at"—thus being practices used to strategically maneuver and resist adverse local conditions. These are both influenced by and influential for the encountered structural contexts. On the one hand, by reporting cases those involved may purposefully seek to access external protection, assistance, and justice; protest the prevalence of violence that shapes camp conditions; and therefore also seek to change it. Although voicing issues may appear a strong marker of agency, those affected may also lack viable alternatives to seeking support elsewhere—as the violence might have reached unbearable levels for them. This indicates how acutely structural conditions can require certain actions to be taken (here, reporting incidents) but this still denotes agency.

On the other hand, by refraining from reporting cases of attack or abuse, those affected may seek, as noted, to avoid feared risks of increased violence or stigmatization. Moreover, they may pursue other concerns such as livelihoods, blame themselves, or have doubts about receiving protection. Abstaining from reporting cases is, therefore, entangled in an interdependent mixture of 'choosing to be silent' and 'being silenced'—neither inherently denoting passivity or resignation, but instead the decisions that people take as influenced by and influential for the structural conditions they live under.

The tense fusion of 'silence/d' was evident in a discussion with women in Kyaka II. Several conveyed not reporting attacks so as to avoid their husbands "beating them even harder," or because they had threatened to do so. One added: "When you report your husband, he can chase you away from the house or even stop providing for the family completely." Some women thus tended to get by through hanging on, or prioritizing the little support that men still offered despite violence. The women widely agreed with one who stressed: "If the woman cannot tolerate being beaten, she will have to separate from the husband and live alone."[20] That such silence does not inevitably mean surrendering but is a strategic action is also evident in the research of Thomson (2013), who reveals how young Somali women in Nairobi, Kenya, use "muted voices" and silence as problem-solving strategies.

In addition, one middle-aged woman spoke about how she was raped by a stranger in Kyaka II while farming. She distantly described the rape as "that problem," and blamed herself for it. As she narrated, "the day I got that problem, that one I can say that it was my foolishness and I did not know better. That thing happens all the time [in Kyaka II]." Yet, her decision against reporting it and hence in favor of staying silent not only stemmed from her blaming herself but was also "because some people were saying that those ones who have problems like rape, they can get support, but here we don't see it."[21] Her silence, thus, also resulted from believing she would not receive help. Others, likewise, addressed the lack of protection and assistance provided in Kyaka II, which meant not merely choosing silence; some also spoke up but were nevertheless ignored by humanitarians.[22] One woman recalled encounters she made while still attending school in Kyaka II, noting "my teachers would harass me so much" and neither physicians nor aid workers helped even though she approached them for that.[23] Another woman went so far as to say: "Refugees are chased [away] when they come and report violence." She explained how she had tried to report attacks by her husband, but "they chased me away because I couldn't pay the fees to the police."[24] In addition to women who suffered in silence; as reflected in Chapter 2, one aid worker said

[20] Discussion 1 with female refugees, March 12, 2014, Base Camp.
[21] Female refugee, dialogue, March 18, 2014, Base Camp.
[22] Among others, female refugee, dialogue, April 12, 2014, Bujubuli; discussion 2 with female refugees, March 12, 2014, Base Camp; male refugee, dialogue, February 28, 2014, Bukere Zone.
[23] Female refugee, dialogue, March 18, 2014, Base Camp.
[24] Female refugee, refugee, dialogue, March 14, 2014, Bujubuli.

of men "[they] suffer silently, at times they are not heard."[25] Aid workers and structural conditions in Kyaka II consequently not only contributed to such silencing by failing to recognize certain forms of violence, but also by ignoring and not assisting those in need. The latter must be seen as forms of gender-based structural and cultural violence according to Galtung and Confortini.

Resonating with Nabukeera (2015: 133) who attests that "[a] feminist dialogical approach to practice considers 'silence' to be a rational response to mistrust of authority and fear of torture," the narratives of the refugees in Kyaka II depict both 'choosing to be silent' and 'being silenced' as forms of agency. This applies to both women and men. As Hajdukowski-Ahmed argues: "Silence is imposed by power, by the necessity to survive, or it is self-imposed through an internalized discourse" (2003: 217). Imposed and self-imposed silence are often closely intertwined, due to the strong effects of external conditions—leading some to perceive themselves as having few or no other options. Yet no matter how narrow they found the space to be in which they could maneuver and get by, adhering to imposed silence as well as using self-imposed silence still represent important coping and protection strategies employed depending on the situation at hand. This also corresponds with the research by Erdener about Yezidi women in Diyarbakir refugee camp, Turkey, which highlights how "women found their solidarity in silence for sexual attacks" (2017: 67).

Single Actions, Mutual Support, and Involving Themselves against Violence in the Camp

The phenomenon of women engaging in (new) relationships with men in Kyaka II, addressed in Chapter 4 in the context of patterns of gender relations, might be dismissed as the former's giving in or apparent non-action; instead, however, it constitutes actions related to these individuals' security drivers or dilemmas. While a number of women said they wanted to remain single and decided against pursuing new relationships not least due to the widespread risk of domestic violence and prior experiences of attack, many others entered into new partnerships or stayed in violent ones on the grounds of protection and

---

[25] Male aid worker, interview, April 4, 2014.

sociocultural conventions. During a discussion, a number of women agreed that many would stay with "ruthless husbands" because they still provided a degree of support and protection. Women who had separated and lived on their own "risked being raped" by strangers and former husbands "sending other men to rape or even kill them," as one conversation partner highlighted.[26] In another discussion, one woman criticized that "[t]he biggest problem is that you can marry a man thinking he is going to help you, but later he marries another woman and then you are chased out of the house and left to be homeless."[27]

In addition to these risks, the woman quoted earlier about how she left DR Congo without having any contact with her husband until he came looking for her in 2012 stated that she had earlier decided to remarry so as "to get some help [for] family expenses. It is also to get someone to sleep with in the house. I am always scared when I am alone since I was raped. When I have a man in the house, I feel safe and secure. Also when I was living alone, everyone would keep asking me why I was."[28] Her choices and actions to find a new partner and share a home thus not only served her desire for safety; social conventions surrounding women being seen as having to have husbands also affected her decision-making. She, thus, navigated both explicit and implicit gender norms that women (and men) had internalized—with being single and living alone considered a social stigma.

This importance of learned gender norms stands out even more distinctly in the narrative of one woman who, as recounted in Chapter 4, had fled violence in Rwanda as a child with her parents and siblings before later experiencing attacks in Kyaka II. Although she noted that her husband was violent and hardly supported her and the two children, she reasoned: "I just made up my mind to stay with him because it was the right thing to do. I didn't want to act like an uneducated woman. I decided to have all my children with one man. After all, I think I can work and take care of my children and myself."[29]

Female informants also relayed engaging in other individual and collective strategies to bolster against and reduce the risks of violence.

[26] Discussion 1 with female refugees, March 12, 2014, Base Camp.
[27] Discussion 2 with female refugees, March 12, 2014, Base Camp.
[28] Female refugee, dialogue, March 5, 2014, Kaborogota Zone.
[29] Female refugee, dialogue, March 18, 2014, Base Camp.

A key example of collective strategies, or more concretely of strategies aiming at collectives and communities, concerns older women widely respected in the communities of Kyaka II. Several such women involved themselves proactively in raising awareness about violence against women. They sought to educate members of their communities, sensitize them to related issues and means of protection, and by that contribute to decreasing the risks hereof. Their engagement was often preventive, and therefore not about helping address particular cases of gender-based violence. Importantly, their engagement in community support was directed at women as well as men of different age groups. Through various forms of communication, they acted as 'community educators' and 'advisors'—the latter by guiding (potential) victims of violence on how and where they could receive support.

Moreover, one woman stressed the relevance of peace education. The segregation and violence in the camp encouraged her "to be a community educator, so I can teach people to stop [resorting to violence]." She described how she wanted to engage in this field to help "bring peace to other people. That peace begins with you." She furthermore took up counseling. Because of the violence many people had experienced during the war in DR Congo as well as in Kyaka II, she remarked "I believe general counseling is important for the community." She described how she had recently helped a young man to handle his testing positive for HIV, as well as a woman who was constantly scared due to wartime trauma to deal with her fears and thereby become more sociable.[30]

Such local engagement primarily of older women was so wide-ranging in Kyaka II that humanitarian agencies were well aware of it. For her community engagement, one elder was the current 'woman of the year' in Kyaka II at the time of research. An aid worker explained that she had suffered much violence and the loss of part of her family in DR Congo, but how in Kyaka II she was deeply committed to helping others—and especially those also affected by various forms of violence. He emphasized how "she takes care of pregnant women, takes care of the sick, and does all this work voluntarily. Her selfless nature earned her best woman 2013."[31] Of course, one may wonder why—if they did indeed acknowledge the significance of and need for these

---

[30] Female refugee, dialogue, March 27, 2014, Base Camp.
[31] Male aid worker, interview, March 14, 2014.

actions—humanitarian agencies did not increase cooperation with such women and men, and pay them for the work they did. While several agencies worked with refugees as 'local community workers,' I was unable to discern why there was a lack of further cooperation in this particular case.

Collective strategies among women in Kyaka II furthermore targeted mutual protection through the power of groups and alliances. Lister (2004: 149–156) refers to "getting organized" as a form of agency that among other things strives for the building of social networks for self-help. In Kyaka II, female adolescents said they drew on group support to protect each other during everyday tasks. One young woman who had recently finished secondary school in Kyaka II highlighted, for example, how "[i]t is easy to avoid the boys and men that try to touch me, because I always move with my young siblings. We fetch water quickly, and leave for home. When these boys tried to touch me, I tell my friend."[32] This was similarly explained in relation to going to school together with siblings or friends, so as to avoid possible attacks by strangers.

Adult women also consciously formed support groups to discuss their experiences and elaborate on ways of providing mutual protection.[33] These groups varied in terms of setup and size. Some were of a fairly fixed nature, with regular appointments to meet and only women participating; other groups originated out of the friendship circles that these women had created. In these informal gatherings, the women came together to speak with each other and give each other encouragement—sometimes while also going about everyday tasks such as cooking. What they provided to one another was rarely about material assistance, being mostly rather about moral support, listening and being listened to, coming to know that they are not alone, and empathy through having experienced and endured similar situations.

Such collective support not only existed among women but also among men and in mixed collectives. In the section about sexual and domestic violence against men in Chapter 2, I mentioned self-help groups that were supported by the Refugee Law Project in Uganda, most notably the Men of Hope Association. The initial group of three

---

[32] Female refugee, dialogue, April 2, 2014, Base Camp.
[33] Discussion 1 with female refugees, March 12, 2014, Base Camp.

men was founded in Kampala in 2012 and grew to forty members already in the same year; over time, it started to involve other individuals as well as clients of the Refugee Law Project (Edström et al. 2016; see also Edström and Dolan 2018). A key part of this self-help initiative was to create surroundings in which survivors can speak safely with each other, but also engage in advocacy and outreach and offer further help such as accompanying others to hospitals, giving financial support in times of crisis, or contributing to peer counseling (Edström et al. 2016: 14). During research in Kyaka II, we did not come in contact with any members of the Men of Hope Association and were hesitant to push forward extensively due to the outlined tense political situation at that time. Yet informants insinuated that such self-help groups specifically for men were also active in the camp.

Linking up with such formal and informal assemblies, neighborhood collectives were especially important. Although women and men sometimes spoke of conflicts with neighbors,[34] women, in particular, helped each other handle the everyday work of, for example, farming, taking care of children, and the like as part of such neighborhood collectives. Support of this nature furthermore served as a local system of protection, helping intervene in cases of attack by strangers and to provide assistance in cases of conflict within families.

While local conflict-resolution mechanisms were mainly based around male elders, clan, or village leaders in DR Congo, with female elders not always involved, such structures would change in Kyaka II. Women initiated ways to be involved in local decision-making and social orders so as to promote social justice and make their voices heard, as indicated in Chapter 4. For example, one woman, who generally believed in patriarchal gender relations and men's hegemonic roles, criticized the scope of violence against women in Kyaka II before then describing how things were slowly changing. In addition to her own commitment to peace education, as noted above, she explained how women increasingly made themselves and their security concerns heard on the community level. She conveyed that in the beginning there were only discussions among male elders in cases of violence within families or communities, but now:

---

[34] Discussions 1 and 2 with female refugees, March 12, 2014, Base Camp; discussion with Refugee Welfare Council, March 19, 2014, Base Camp.

We are doing proper discussion, like talk just on the way [and] debate in the village. First, they would be men only and then they discuss, and, after that, then you come with ideas. The second group is women to women. The final one is mixed. We still have cases of violence, but they have reduced due to this arrangement. There is a very big change.[35]

The powerful support of community and social collectives such as those made up of family, friends, and neighbors therefore represents a key strategy for coping with traumatic events and for providing protection, as well as for dealing with other limitations of camp life (more below). Across various disciplines and cases all over the world, scholars have also recognized the importance of collective coping, support, and protection among refugees (see among others Alzoubi et al. 2019; Logie and Daniel 2016; Gladden 2013; Stewart et al. 2008; Khawaja et al. 2008; Farwell 2001).

However, it would be erroneous to see these narratives as signaling a mere 'collectivization' of coping in Kyaka II. Such collective and social coping strategies were inherently intertwined with informants' very own practices of dealing with risks of violence and giving support and protection. Individuals came together and helped each other, and involvement in the collectives rested on these individuals' notions of shared safety and mutual support.

To conclude this section, these individual and collective practices reveal how women and men used conscious strategies to both prevent and react to violence as well as other issues experienced. They strove to counteract gender-based violence by seeking or avoiding relationships with men, by staying silent or raising their voices, by creating awareness, and by moving in groups when navigating the camp landscape. Such groups were also important for responding to attacks, as women helped each other, involved themselves proactively on the community level, and came together in seeking justice. As shown, it is not only "through voice and voicing that agency and power are reclaimed by marginalized groups, particularly women" (Hajdukowski-Ahmed et al. 2008a: 13) but also via silence being chosen as "a form of opposition or of resisting discourse, a means by which refugee women reclaim their agency" (Hajdukowski-Ahmed 2008: 47).

---

[35] Female refugee, dialogue, March 27, 2014, Base Camp.

Coping with Difficult Camp Conditions and an Uncertain Future

Time and again throughout the book, I quote refugees who criticized the challenging circumstances that they experienced in Kyaka II. It was not only the broad scope of gender-based violence that affected the women, men, girls, and boys living in the camp but also limited livelihoods, a lack of opportunities to further their personal education and skills, uncertainties regarding their future, and the hierarchical humanitarian structures.

The various problems that arise for refugees during encampment have also been explored in other studies.[36] A prevailing issue often addressed in research constitutes refugees' dependency on humanitarian and governmental structures within camps, which concerns not only material handouts but also, as outlined in Chapter 3, top-down decision-making power. Yet, already in the early 1990s, Kibreab shed light on the "myth of dependency among camp refugees in Somalia," underscoring that "refugees managed their own affairs by relying on their own traditional coping mechanisms, creativity and private arrangements with the local population" (1993: 322). In his recent book about self-reliance in a Liberian refugee camp, Omata (2017) also illustrates the various strategies employed to improve economic lives and overcome hardships.

Taking up the baton, how then did women and also men in Kyaka II cope with camp conditions and humanitarian structures? Contrary to the prevailing humanitarian portrayal of refugees in general and women in particular as passive aid recipients and helpless victims, those in Kyaka II did not merely submit to humanitarian rules and regulations or give in to the limitations encountered in the camp. Instead, they pursued economic independence, consciously claimed their rights, created spheres of belonging as well as normalcy despite

---

[36] Among the early seminal works hereon are certainly *Imposing Aid* by Harrell-Bond (1986) as well as *Purity and Exile* by Malkki (1995a). Since then, the body of research on these challenges has grown considerably, with the following list exemplifying just some of the monographs published in the past ten years: see Turner (2010); Inhetveen (2010); Mulumba (2010); Agier (2011); Jansen (2011); Clark-Kazak (2011); Fiddian-Qasmiyeh (2014a); McConnachie (2014); Janmyr (2014b); Holzer (2015); Purdeková (2015); Hovil (2016); Grayson (2017); Omata (2017); Deardorff Miller (2018); Glasman (2019).

multidimensional uncertainties, and remained hopeful—all of which are strategies that will now be examined.

"Refugees do not depend on themselves": Pursuing Economic Independence in the Camp

Those living in Kyaka II widely lamented camp conditions. Informants noted that they could barely lead an entirely self-sufficient life, because "refugees do not depend on themselves"[37] and "do not have work in Kyaka II, and cannot depend on food delivery because it is not enough."[38] Considering the diverse hardships of everyday life in terms of insufficient food, employment, and livelihoods, economic strategies for coping were especially important. Yet, seeking to live self-sufficient lives and be independent from humanitarian structures is not limited to just pursuing economic security. It furthermore includes various social, political, and cultural factors regarding the ways in which these people wanted to live their lives, the social networks they wanted to engage in, and the social orders and representations they wanted to see in place.

Mobilities, Trade, and Income-Generation as Individual and Collective Economic Practices

With a focus on women's engagement in local social orders, the earlier-discussed initiatives regarding making their voices heard show their proactive engagement in community-based political structures in lieu of simply waiting for the 'humanitarian hegemon' to step in and solve issues. References to women's perceptions of having the right to own land to generate harvest and income, live more independently from husbands' rulings, and improve subsistence were also illustrated in Chapter 4. In addition, women—as well as men—established economic cooperation to find work, generate income, or trade goods. To this end, they left the camp and traveled back and forth between Kyaka II and other refugee camps, smaller cities nearby, or Kampala (about four to five hours away by car at the time of research).

Refugees took such trips on a regular basis, which lasted a few days up to a month—mostly without a permit from camp authorities (more below)—before eventually returning to their families in Kyaka II. To

---

[37] Discussion with male refugees, March 13, 2014, Base Camp.
[38] Female refugee, dialogue, March 17, 2014, Sweswe Zone.

find employment and establish economic cooperation in cities or elsewhere, the people used local social networks in the respective destinations—which largely consisted of displaced people of the same nationality there.[39] This indicates the importance of mobilities to the women and men living in the confined surroundings of the refugee camp, not only being mobile and able to travel (i.e., also afford to) but also using mobility as a source of income-generation. Moreover, these travels point to the social process of coping—as such networks were not limited to economic collaboration, but had a strong component of mutual support too. This corresponds with other studies referring to the relevance of collectives, social support, and belongings to clan, religious, and/or ethnic groups (e.g., Grabska 2006; Stewart et al. 2008; Hussain and Bhushan 2010; Clark-Kazak 2011; Ager et al. 2015; Lyytinen 2017). Mobilities may thus be understood as a "livelihood asset," following Omata (2017: 38–39). Economically driven networks also emerge transnationally, as illustrated by Horst (2006, 2008) and Lindley (2010) in exploring the day-to-day routines and practices of Somali refugees in Kenya. They show the importance of remittances as well as diverse mobilities of goods, people, and information within the Somali diaspora.

Viewing such travels, economic initiatives, collaborations, as well as social support through Lister's (2004: 124–156) theoretical lens reveals that they correspond with all four forms of agency that she identifies. "Getting by" in difficult conditions and establishing ways of handling them, "getting out" of such circumstances by drawing on and creating means of improving them, "getting organized" to make use of mutual support and collaboration in order to gain benefits, as well as "getting back at" humanitarian restrictions by using, bypassing, or even challenging them.

In Kyaka II, women's and men's economic coping strategies were diverse. Returning to the example of a young couple trading fish cited in Chapter 4, the woman explained confidently what she had achieved both on her own and together with her husband. They would travel to another refugee camp in eastern Uganda to buy fish there, mostly tilapia as it is quite common in Uganda, and then return to Kyaka II to sell it. They had initiated networks with displaced people from DR Congo in that other camp years ago, and since fish was rare in Kyaka II

---

[39] Female refugee, dialogue, March 11, 2014, Base Camp.

their business was successful. Yet cold storage of the fresh fish was difficult, so they had to rush back to Kyaka II after acquiring it. After they married and had a baby, her husband managed most of the business and became more reluctant to involve her. However, the woman explained how important the business was to her and how she defended her place in it, at times even traveling alone to buy the fish.[40] And similar insights were shared by others regarding foods or products they traded.

The woman referred to earlier in the context of her having made a little money by selling homemade bracelets and chitenge in Kampala had established a similar business on her own in Kyaka II. There, she drew on her networks in DR Congo and Kampala to buy those traditional fabrics. Chitenge are used for both everyday and festive clothing, and come in various print designs. In addition to managing to have fabric sent to meeting points close to the camp where she would pick them up, she regularly traveled to Kampala and sometimes even to the border with DR Congo to buy new stock. With the insufficient and often only sporadic income many people in Kyaka II were confronted with, the woman gave her customers the possibility to pay in installments.[41]

Economic networks did not always exceed the boundaries of Kyaka II. Although employment opportunities were rare in the camp, some people sold harvest on the markets or found short-term work with humanitarian agencies or in farming for other refugees or Ugandans.[42] One particular field constituted the production of so-called MakaPads; these are sanitary pads for women and girls made in the camp from local materials, especially papyrus. The factory in Kyaka II opened in 2007 and has offered employment to a varying number of refugees over the years (see Musaazi 2014). Women and men also engaged economically within the camp—for example, by being part of a local savings group. Such groups were both mixed as well as women or men only. They were founded by displaced people to pursue the common aim of generating income, but they also had a social component in providing comfort as well as a security network in cases of emergency,

---

[40] Female refugee, dialogue, March 18, 2014, Base Camp.
[41] Female refugee, dialogue, March 18, 2014, Sweswe Zone.
[42] Male refugee, dialogue, March 27, 2014, Base Camp; female refugee, dialogue, February 18, 2014, Base Camp; female refugee, dialogue, March 27, 2014, Base Camp.

such as serious illness. Members helped each other by means of credit schemes, through which all of them regularly paid in a certain amount of money and with the member in need receiving the funds at once (see also Schmidt and Krause 2019).[43]

Supporting and Driving Factors for Economic Practices

These social components of comfort and security were often essential for economic practice. Similar to mutual protection strategies, women and men here drew on and engaged in social collectives and support systems, and underlined the importance of family members, friends, communities, and religious groups (see also Hutchinson and Dorsett 2012: 60–61; Gladden 2012: 190–191; Seguin and Roberts 2017: 8, 13). In Kyaka II, it was often the nearest community that represented an important network for individuals; neighbors developed shared routines through which they established distinct support systems also of economic value. Whether about aspects of everyday life such as raising children or collecting firewood together, these collectives served to provide mutual support. By working together in the context of agriculture, they shared the hard labor and were more likely to reduce shortcomings in food—and thus to survive off farming, despite its previously discussed shortcomings in this context.

Yet economic coping neither only serves survival nor does it merely rest on social collaboration. Drawing on a research project about refugee-led community-based organizations, which I carried out with Hannah Schmidt subsequent to the project this book centers on,[44] we have shed light on the social value that economic practices have for refugees in Kyaka II (Schmidt and Krause 2019). They not only mobilize resources for themselves but those resources are also crucial for others. In addition to being able to increase income by working together and employing others, and thus providing jobs, people become experts on economic strategies and local systems, and can share their knowledge with others. This can be mutually beneficial, as increasing collaborations can arise. Moreover, whether through formal or informal assemblies, socioeconomic networks such as the

---

[43] Discussion 1 with women, March 12, 2014, Base Camp.

[44] Entitled 'Global Refugee Protection and Local Refugee Engagement. Scope and Limits of the Agency of Refugee-Led Community-Based NGOs' (2016–2020), the project used Kyaka II and Kampala as case studies and was funded by the Gerda Henkel Foundation.

above-noted savings groups or joint farming can serve as risk-absorbing strategies by providing material and immaterial support.

A particular driver for taking up economic practices was their children, and specifically parents' responsibilities and available opportunities to care for them. For example, women and men worried about the poor education that their children received in Kyaka II and that they could not afford access to school.[45] They depicted children as their priority, seeking to "give them a quality life"[46] and remarking that "I dig and get food for my children; I don't have any other assistance but I try."[47] One woman spoke about the various difficulties she encountered in Kyaka II, also from having a husband who did not support the family. Yet she found employment in the aid sector as a community health worker. She explained: "I earn UGX 120,000 [circa USD 50 in 2014] a month. It is little, but it helps me settle some of my financial problems and take care of my children."[48]

Surviving or Thriving? Navigating the Limitations and Risks of Informal Economies

The presented findings about individual and collective economic activities for coping in Kyaka II resonate with a range of empirical studies partly signifying refugee camps as flourishing economic zones with markets and trade systems (e.g., Callamard 1994; Dalal 2015; Betts et al. 2017a). Remittances are certainly an important part of such economic practices in camps and beyond (see Horst 2008; Lindley 2010; Jacobsen et al. 2014). Although tensions and conflicts can arise, the displaced are discussed as also collaborating with nationals living in the vicinity of camps as part of seeking to enter into trade and generate income (see Oka 2014; Alloush et al. 2017; Loschmann et al. 2019). Of note, and with case studies in Uganda, Betts et al. have addressed such 'refugee economies,' examined the economic-immanent value of refugees' practices, and "identified a significant minority of

---

[45] Female refugee, dialogue, March 11, 2014, Bukere Zone; female refugee, dialogue, March 4, 2014, Bujubuli; male refugee, dialogue, March 18, 2014, Base Camp.
[46] Female refugee, dialogue, February 18, 2014, Base Camp.
[47] Female refugee, dialogue, March 27, 2014, Base Camp.
[48] Female refugee, dialogue, March 18, 2014, Base Camp.

refugee entrepreneurs who had established successful businesses, often employing others" (2017a: 729).

Despite the various economic initiatives refugees undertake in camps, it must be noted that they are compelled 'to be creative' and find ways forward due to the very camp conditions that were actually put in place to protect and assist them. Further to that, mere focus on economic capabilities risks trivializing camp conditions as 'not that bad'—since refugees prove they can move forward and somehow make it. Such a focus could furthermore lead to the perpetuation of the neoliberal frame, whereby it is no longer primarily about government and humanitarian agencies being responsible for providing protection and assistance for refugees but about how the latter are expected to and made responsible for contributing to local economies and finding solutions in restrictive camps. This tendency is evident in current humanitarian policies promoting refugees' self-reliance and resilience (Krause and Schmidt 2020).

Crucially, many of the individual and collective economic practices of refugees that are detailed in the academic literature, and that I addressed above too, take place in informal sectors—often for the reason that formal ones, and especially also sustainable and safe forms of employment, are scarcely accessible for refugees living in camps. The discussion among scholars of "refugee economies" thus largely revolves around informal economic practices (critical see Werker 2007; Oka 2011). This produces risks related to social stability, security, and services—for example, in times of sickness—and frequently leaves refugees in unprotected working arrangements in which they can rarely claim employment rights. As such, even though these informal economic practices signify such people's coping strategies and persistence, they in fact frequently constitute the only available and viable option for refugees to maneuver locally established restrictions and power structures. Some of these practices can therefore be understood as one way refugees pursue 'survivability.'

Survival Sex, Sex for Favor, and Other Risky Practices Imposed by the Informal Economy

Exactly this link between actions in informal economies and survivability is evident most overtly in transactional sexual intercourse and prostitution or, as it was at times called in Kyaka II, "commercial sex"—which some women practiced to generate income. Although it was not discussed by informants as frequently as other issues and practices, it was still used in response to camp conditions. "Women in Kyaka II have started practicing prostitution in order to survive," remarked an elderly woman. She reasoned that this was due to the limited opportunities and the focus on agriculture there, also noting that: "Women from DR Congo, very few can do hard work like digging."[49] One man further highlighted that "[p]rostitution in Kyaka, much is caused by poverty"; the people "have no jobs, and they don't want to dig but can only sell their bodies."[50]

This was not limited to financial returns; others—and women of different age groups in particular—also saw no other way forward but to exchange sex for goods or support; they were either directly forced by perpetrators or indirectly by their challenging living situation to do so. This links with the gender-specific forms of direct, structural, and cultural violence following Galtung and Confortini. An example for direct force placed on someone to engage in "sex for favors" was noted in Chapter 3 with regard to the woman who recalled bitter memories of applying for a scholarship to continue her education and become a nurse. She explained that an aid worker had demanded her "to go with him" in order to get the scholarship, which, however, she declined and reported to the authorities.[51] Another woman shared that some of her friends occasionally "come to Bukere [Zone], they sleep there and they give them money or food."[52]

Porter et al. (2008: 240) also outline prostitution among Liberian refugees in Buduburam refugee camp, Ghana. They argue that prostitution is perceived to be the only viable option for some girls regarding supporting their families. At times, the latter are aware of and accept it; the issue nevertheless caused significant distress among those living in the camp. These findings about the pressure arising from having no suitable alternatives correspond with the situation faced by some women in Kyaka II too. Both teenage girls and boys lamented that some fathers would "chase" girls "to go for prostitution and earlier marriages when they are still young,"[53] or recounted that the rape and

---

[49] Female refugee, dialogue, March 11, 2014, Bukere Zone.
[50] Male refugee, dialogue, March 18, 2014, Base Camp.
[51] Female refugee, dialogue, March 18, 2014, Base Camp.
[52] Female refugee, dialogue, March 18, 2014, Base Camp.
[53] Male adolescent, 17 years old, journal writing, March 5, 2014, Bujubuli Secondary School.

defilement of girls would cause "unwanted pregnancies and dropping out of school. This makes them desperate and hate their lives, hence resorting to prostitution."[54]

Prostitution, commercial sex, sex for favors, or survival sex—while each of these terms carries different connotations, all such forms of sexual intercourse in return for financial or material goods represent strategies that are structurally and physically highly risky for those who practice them, or who are forced to do so (Martin and Tirman 2009; Williams et al. 2018).

Bypassing and Challenging Restrictions

Both women and men also shared that there were many restrictions especially from the aid systems that they had to cope with, but that also hindered their coping, in Kyaka II—whereas women additionally had to handle restrictions imposed by men. In a discussion, women explained how husbands at times reacted violently if they "found out" that women were economically active via earning income and running businesses. One woman explained: "The husband might come back and demand that money. If the woman refuses to give them that money, they just beat her." Moreover, the regularly discussed topics of domestic violence and the harvest were also addressed. A female informant explained even if it is women who "harvest and sell their crops, the husband will steal their money—and when the woman finds out and tries to ask why, she will be beaten."[55] Within family circles, women's economic practices can thus be confronted with restrictions— even though they may contribute to the well-being and coping of the whole family.

In addition to the limitations that women experienced interpersonally, particularly from husbands, the aid system also produced constraints for them and men too. They highlighted, as noted previously, that as refugees "[we] cannot make decisions of our own" and relied on government and aid agencies.[56] Aid workers were seen to be "corrupt, and this makes services very expensive"[57]—while also

---

[54] Female adolescent, 17 years old, journal writing, April 3, 2014, Bujubuli Secondary School.

[55] Discussion 1 with female refugees, March 12, 2014, Base Camp.

[56] Female refugee, dialogue, March 27, 2014, Base Camp.

[57] Female refugee, dialogue, February 28, 2014, Bukere Zone.

insufficiently attending to these people's problems.[58] Correspondingly, it was rued how "[s]ome aid workers together with OPM have disappointed refugees by telling them that they are going to remove them here. [...] People don't get help."[59] Also humanitarians' exclusive positions of power and refugees' lack of participation in decision-making were criticized: "Aid workers do not give us democracy. They violate us so much. We do not have enough of anything, and they harass us."[60]

The latter feeling of "not having enough of anything" was most likely a significant driving force behind many of those living in Kyaka II engaging in (informal) economic practices, thus occurring in order to create some level of stability for themselves, their families, and especially their children. Not least because of the restrictions of the aid system, their various economic practices entailed going beyond humanitarian regulations. By starting businesses, they bypassed humanitarian objectives of achieving self-reliance mainly through agricultural productivity—which many said to not be enough to survive on. Although Uganda's Refugee Act generally grants these individuals "the right to have access to employment opportunities and engage in gainful employment" (Uganda 2006: art. 29 e vi), government and humanitarian strategies maintained and reinforced agricultural practice specifically. Furthermore, finding employment within the confines of the camp was fairly difficult for most spoken with.

In order to run businesses or pursue other interests, as outlined earlier, traveling to more attractive economic regions in Uganda for a short time to find jobs or collect goods before returning to the camp was crucial. These trips actually required prior authorization to leave the camp however. One aid worker casually stated: "Refugees have freedom of movement and the right to work anywhere in the country. All they need is to have a movement permit, which is free of charge [and serves] to identify them in case they get into trouble."[61] However, on the basis of the accounts shared by informants, it was by no means that simple in reality. Receiving permission to leave took weeks, and applications were at times declined—so many people decided to travel

---

[58] Female refugee, dialogue, March 14, 2014, Bujubuli.
[59] Female refugee, dialogue, March 11, 2014, Base Camp.
[60] Female refugee, dialogue, March 12, 2014, Bukere Zone.
[61] Female aid worker, interview, April 10, 2014.

without them. In a similar vein to many others spoken with in Kyaka II, one religious leader explained:

We are not allowed to move out of the settlement. If you want to move out of Kyaka II, you have to ask for permission and explain how long you will be away and give reasons why you are going. At times, your request is rejected. That is why some people in Kampala and Mubende just left without permission.[62]

The trips, therefore, frequently meant bypassing or disobeying regulations, as a way to consciously and strategically navigate the camp administration. As a result, such trips and economic practices signify how refugees 'silently' revolted against the camp's perpetuation of confinement.

"Refugees are having their rights denied": Consciously Claiming Rights

The strong criticisms articulated about how aid workers imposed decisions, provided insufficient support, or allowed little room for refugees' participation indicate how the women and men in Kyaka II stood up for themselves, contested wrongdoing and with it structural, cultural, and physical violence, as well as sought ways forward. Following Lister's (2004: 140–144) agency theory, they partly "got back at" the injustice they experienced. Moreover, highlighting themselves how they had certain rights as refugees, albeit ones that were not always met, demonstrates a legal consciousness of refugee law in Uganda existing among these individuals.

Despite extensive academic debate about legal consciousness and how people in different situations perceive and access legal structures and justice having occurred in recent years (see, e.g., Grechin 1983; Merry 1990; Silbey 2005; Harding 2010; Halliday 2019; Chua and Engel 2019; Hertogh 2018), this topic has only slowly been picked up on in Forced Migration and Refugee Studies (see Sandvik 2008; Holzer 2013; Galli 2019; Koçak 2020). Sandvik (2008), for example, draws on research with refugees in Kampala, demonstrating the strategies through which they present their personal experiences in legal terms. In her research with refugees in Buduburam camp, Ghana, Holzer

---

[62] Discussion with religious leaders, March 19, 2014, Base Camp.

underlines that many understand themselves "as rights holders under the protection of the international community—a legal consciousness that inspired some to claim rights in large-scale social movement activism in 2007–2008" (2013: 839).

Analyses of refugees' legal consciousness are highly relevant, as they often find themselves in particularly restrictive situations. They may originate from countries where they encountered limited access to rights, potentially resulting in their flight and creating distrust in legal systems, or they may struggle to obtain the legal status of refugee in countries of asylum. Being aware of and claiming their rights can thus form a crucial coping strategy. Following Silbey, such consciousness reveals individuals' awareness of and participation in the "social production of ideology and hegemony"—thus contributing to "the very same structures that are also experienced as external and constraining." By "both thinking and doing," legal consciousness constitutes a "social practice, in the sense that it both reflects and forms social structures" (Silbey 2005: 333–334). These social practices resonate with agency, and how actors are both affected by and affect structures (Lister 2004: 125–127).

Refugees' Criticisms of Rights Abuses in the Camp

In Kyaka II, this awareness of legal norms was evident in women and men of different age groups regularly referring to their rights, to issues of insufficient access to the law, and to ways of claiming rights. Importantly, they raised such issues on their own without the research team explicitly asking about legal norms and practices, thus indicating how central these rights were to them. Among the teenage girls and boys who took part in the research, not only their rights per se but especially also rights abuses that minors experienced in Kyaka II represented subject matters that they would continuously bring up.

Youth often addressed denial of access to education as an "abuse of children's rights,"[63] and issues of violence as particular rights violations. One teenage girl pointed out "[v]iolence is mistreating and disrespecting of human rights," and later lamented how "some parents

---

[63] Male adolescent, 18 years old, journal writing, April 3, 2014, Bujubuli Secondary School; female adolescent, 19 years old, journal writing, April 3, 2014, Bujubuli Secondary School; female adolescent, 16 years old, journal writing, March 5, 2014, Bujubuli Secondary School; male adolescent, 19 years old, journal writing, April 3, 2014, Bujubuli Secondary School.

give corporal punishment to their children, for example they burn them, beat them heavily, and sometimes deny them their right to education, right to eat, right to play."[64] Another commented: "There are so many kinds of violence that are being brought up by some teachers and some students too. Violence is the mistreatment of human beings and denying them their rights." She then added how common violence against girls is.[65] This corresponds with statements shared by several others, and teenagers furthermore referred to children's freedom of religion and the right to movement,[66] their right to participate in school and the community,[67] and the right for girls to marry as adults instead of being "married when they are still young."[68]

In addition to elaborating their own rights, violence against women was partly described as the abuse of rights. As one teenager stated: "Women's rights are being violated in the way they are being beaten, humiliated, and other sorts of injustice."[69] Some adults also argued that women are discriminated against by means of violence.[70] Yet, others noted, "men beat their wives more often [in Kyaka II than in DR Congo] because the law is not strict [here],"[71] or, contrariwise, that "because of the law in Uganda, the man wouldn't hit [the woman]."[72] In addition to laws, religious beliefs were also at times addressed as quasi-legal norms justifying patriarchal gender systems and the subsequent need for women to obey men, as well as the latter's apparent rights to use force against the former. As reflected in Chapter 4, a man stated, "[a] woman has no power over the man, even the Bible supports this"[73] and a woman criticized that men would

---

[64] Female adolescent, 17 years old, journal writing, March 5, 2014, Bujubuli Secondary School.

[65] Female adolescent, 17 years old, journal writing, April 3, 2014, Bujubuli Secondary School.

[66] Male adolescent, 19 years old, journal writing, April 3, 2014, Bujubuli Secondary School.

[67] Female adolescent, 19 years old, journal writing, April 3, 2014, Bujubuli Secondary School.

[68] Male adolescent, 18 years old, journal writing, April 3, 2014, Bujubuli Secondary School.

[69] Male adolescent, 19 years old, journal writing, March 5, 2014, Bujubuli Secondary School.

[70] Discussion with male refugees, March 13, 2014, Base Camp; discussion 1 with female refugees, March 12, 2014, Base Camp.

[71] Female refugee, dialogue, March 18, 2014, Base Camp.

[72] Male refugee, dialogue, March 5, 2014, Base Camp.

[73] Discussion with male refugees, March 13, 2014, Base Camp.

"take it as the way it is in the Bible that women are supposed to be dull and men be heads."[74]

Among adults, key references made to their rights were furthermore directly related to issues faced with the aid system in Kyaka II. In a similar vein to the above-noted criticisms, refugees highlighted that there is "no strict law enforcement here,"[75] "refugees are having their rights denied,"[76] or aid agencies "are supposed to help us, [but] are not really doing their work."[77] Such appraisals of insufficient access to their rights, protection, and assistance were not only brought forward by informants during dialogues and discussions held as a part of the research; aid workers also spoke of refugees protesting when the delivery of food was delayed.[78] Others mentioned that refugees approached them, complained, and asked for improvements, or that they lied about their living conditions in order to "falsely" claim additional food aid like maize and posho.[79]

While the people in Kyaka II rarely noted using 'creative' narratives to receive support and thus have their rights met, other scholars elaborate how refugees at times criticize aid structures and stress their helplessness to evoke compassion and benefit. Some explore how they reproduce the humanitarian language of vulnerability, which serves to legitimize the provision of aid in the first place (Inhetveen 2006: 11; Turner 2010: 58). Others address how refugees strategically 'cheat' humanitarian staff to negotiate and gain improved access to resources (Kibreab 2004; Jansen 2008). This has been partly captured as a form of entrepreneurship (Kumsa 2006: 251), or "as evidence of the re-development of 'solidarity' among these populations [in camps]" (Harrell-Bond 2004: 28).

Fearing and Contradicting Forced Repatriation

For some of the women and men spoken with in Kyaka II, living at the mercy of humanitarian and government decisions despite their rights

---

[74] Female refugee, dialogue, March 18, 2014, Base Camp.
[75] Female refugee, dialogue, March 18, 2014, Base Camp.
[76] Male refugee, dialogue, March 18, 2014, Base Camp.
[77] Male refugee, dialogue, March 28, 2014, Base Camp.
[78] Female aid worker, interview, April 2, 2014; female aid worker, interview, April 22, 2014.
[79] Female aid worker, interview, May 11, 2014; male aid worker, interview, March 19, 2014.

created acute fears. One woman pointed out, as noted before, that the agencies can take decisions on them "anytime," noting that "a national living here cannot be removed, they will refuse; but for a refugee, they will say 'get your property and leave.' And you will go."[80]

The fear of "being removed" or of receiving less or even no humanitarian aid produced great uncertainty, and was prominent primarily among refugees of nationalities other than Congolese—mostly those from Rwanda and Burundi. At the time of research, such fears resulted from rumors of refugees having to leave Uganda and return to their countries of origin.[81] These anxieties were not unjustified; only four years earlier, in 2010, the Government of Uganda forcefully repatriated refugees from the refugee camps Nakivale and Kyaka II to Rwanda. This operation was criticized by UNHCR (UN 2010). During a discussion with religious leaders who had all been in Kyaka II for several years, one man recalled painful memories of that operation:

One day, they told Rwandese to go to the store to get food. When they were already in the store they were locked inside the gate, forced [out of the camp], and taken back to Rwanda. [. . .] We saw policemen in the store. The children got lost, some people tried to jump over the fence and hurt themselves trying to run away. It is not allowed for someone who has left his country to be forced to go back home. The soldiers included Rwandese and Ugandan ones. [. . .] It was a weekday, and UNHCR looked on and didn't do anything. This operation actually took time. It was actually not the first time [it happened].[82]

---

[80] Female refugee, dialogue, March 27, 2014, Base Camp.

[81] Of the three durable solutions, the Government of Uganda generally gives little attention to the local integration of refugees with prospects for citizenship. Resettlement is meanwhile principally only offered to a small number of refugees, and it is the countries admitting them—not Uganda—who decide about how many can move there. The Government of Uganda has thus been focusing on repatriation as the preferred durable solution, but security has to first be reinstated and ensured in the countries of origin in order for people to return there. Yet since conflicts have tended to last for years or even decades in countries of origin—with the war in the Kivu regions of DR Congo being paradigmatic, having erupted time and again since the 1990s (Breytenbach et al. 1999; Reyntjens 2009; Doevenspeck 2016)—the majority of displaced people in Uganda cannot return but are to remain in protracted situations for indefinite and uncertain periods of time.

[82] Discussion with religious leaders, March 19, 2014, Base Camp.

With rumors about (forceful) repatriation circulating again, one man underlined: "I also feel unhappy when there are always threats of repatriation. Rwandese refugees cannot stay stable because they know, from time to time, they are to go back to their country. Rwandese cannot make permanent plans because of repatriation threats. Discrimination based on tribe or nationality also makes me unhappy, because I feel isolated from others."[83] The religious leaders spoken with also stressed the worries of many people in the camp. However, they were well aware of their rights as refugees and that forceful repatriation was against international law.

To cope with these fears and threats and thus 'get back at' the challenging system encountered, one such informant emphasized that "[s]ome dodged their nationalities to be Congolese" and that the only alternative to avoiding forceful repatriation was to bribe officials. "If they know you are Rwandese or Burundian, you will pay about UGX 100,000 [circa USD 40 in 2014] to OPM to be given a Congolese status. If you have a big family, you may have to pay even UGX 1.5 Million [circa USD 590 in 2014]."[84]

Yet such fears and rumors also extended to refugees regardless of their nationality in Kyaka II; teenagers shared being afraid that "they want to take us back to DR Congo" or of "being chased away from Uganda."[85] According to one religious leader: "[N]ow even us the Congolese live in fear, because if it can happen to the Rwandese then it can also happen to us—so we must work to stop it."[86] At the time of research, the main practice employed "to stop it" and cope was changing or adjusting personal stories and histories with an eye to the rules and laws of humanitarian and governmental agencies.

Creating Normalcy and Belonging Despite Multidimensional Uncertainties

From a humanitarian perspective, camps may not only be understood as purposefully created sites of protection, assistance, and shelter but

[83] Male refugee, dialogue, March 18, 2014, Base Camp.
[84] Discussion with religious leaders, March 19, 2014, Base Camp.
[85] Female adolescent, 16 years old, journal writing, March 5, 2014, Bujubuli Secondary School; female adolescent, 17 years old, journal writing, March 5, 2014, Bujubuli Secondary School.
[86] Discussion with religious leaders, March 19, 2014, Base Camp.

also as ones of belonging for refugees. These people seem to be out of place; they have reached a new national or territorial context to which they do not appear to belong. Their dislocation or deterritorialization from the country of origin to the one of asylum signifies a certain reterritorialization, a social construction of a new affiliation, an affiliation as 'refugees' (legally, should they even receive that status). Camps may subsequently represent the territorial component of these refugees belonging in the new country; on the one hand, a lack of belonging that legitimizes their encampment and, on the other hand, an artificial creation of belonging existing under the supervision of humanitarian and government agencies (Brun 2001: 17). Camps thus appear to establish sites of exception to 'facilitate' refugees to be 'among their peers'—or actually, to be kept there (Krause 2018b: 492). In this regard, Malkki (1995b: 514) discusses the contradictions of the not belonging, dehistoricization, and depoliticization of refugees in camps, Turner (2016a: 144) their inclusion and exclusion due to encampment in host countries, and Agier (2002: 322) refugees' lack of social and political existence in camps.

However, beyond reading camp features through humanitarian lenses, these sites also constitute the living spaces of many refugees worldwide; they, of course, also shape the structures there. In Kyaka II, I witnessed how refugees went about their everyday lives, created families, and handled issues. Interestingly, such practices among women and men, girls and boys strongly overlapped and did not reveal stark differences.

Everyday Life and Belonging

"Life goes on in camps—albeit a life that is affected by the camp," as Turner (2016a: 139) writes. It is the protracted situation of many camps worldwide—with Kyaka II being no exception—that requires refugees to develop an everyday life, a normalcy, there. Such a normalcy is also portrayed when Agier (2002: 326) describes the various coffee shops, video stores, hairdressing salons, and photo studios in the Dadaab refugee complex and Oka (2014) the role of consumption in Kakuma refugee camp, both in Kenya. Inhetveen (2010: 188, 351) depicts wedding ceremonies in Zambian refugee camps, while Jansen (2011: 123) writes about people watching football together in Kakuma. Jolliffe (2015) furthermore explains what people in camps in Thailand do after dark, how some meet in the early-evening hours, and how others only leave their homes under the shelter of darkness.

That life goes on in camps also applies to the women and men, girls and boys in Kyaka II. Although their lives were embedded in the confined humanitarian camp, these people certainly also produced a normalcy and shaped their lives through their various everyday practices. During research in Kyaka II, I saw numerous situations reflecting exactly this normalcy—of girls and young women meeting and doing their hair, children playing with skipping ropes, adolescents listening to music and playing billiards in the youth center, women and men selling and buying products at the market, going to different religious celebrations, socializing at home or in bars. People established economic opportunities and livelihoods, developed social collectives to help and protect each other, as well as engaged in local decision-making structures. They furthermore created daily routines, cared for relatives, started families, raised and worried about children, cooked, slept, ate, worked, or socialized with friends. Even their often long times of waiting in front of aid-worker offices to voice their concerns appeared to have become 'normal.'

No matter how banal these examples may appear to be, they are part of the everyday lives of the women and men in Kyaka II and thus relevant for understanding the local context and their coping within it. Because creating and maintaining routines helps to regain a degree of stability, even as uncertainty about the future continues to prevail. Notable about such normalcy is how people create sites of belonging through their social practices. In lieu of only understanding refugee camps as artificially created sites of (not) belonging, the people in Kyaka II actually developed many different social spheres in which they felt comfortable and could enjoy a sense of community.

Although as refugees they may not legally 'belong' to the host country in terms of citizenship, and despite their encampment symbolizing tensions between belonging versus separation and inclusion versus exclusion, refugees were still able to create and draw on mutual social support in Kyaka II—and to some extent, contribute to feelings of belonging. Yet these feelings were also restricted by the camp setting itself, as an omnipresent reminder of refugees' uncertainty over the future. This tension of (not) belonging was explicitly revealed in narratives shared. On the one hand, women's but also men's everyday practices often aimed to create social spheres of belonging for and among themselves and their families, especially for their children. On the other hand, women and men stressed how humanitarian structures hampered belonging. This can be exemplified by one woman's statement about the treatment by aid workers, as noted earlier in the book. She said: "[It] seems you don't have identity, you don't belong. You are just there, like just something."[87]

Creating normalcy and belonging not only constituted actions of coping—and following Lister (2004: 130–140, 149–156), ways of "getting by" and "getting organized" in the face of difficulties in the camp; they ultimately also served as sources and drivers of nourishment for other coping strategies. The latter rest, among other things, on people's social support, which has become common over time, as well as their knowledge and awareness about the regular conditions in Kyaka II, such as where they can gather certain goods or sell them at market, get help in times of need, or how local social structures function in order to make their voices heard. Understood as a process, the women and men thus create daily routines as coping strategies—but also use those routines as a foundation for coping with other issues.

Social belonging was often recognized through the lens of wider family and community circles and ethnic affiliations, ones that were, however, disrupted due to war and forced migration. In Kyaka II, it was not only newly established friendships and locally founded communities that often received much esteem among informants but so did the nuclear family. Among others, one woman explained that her family was only her and her children when she arrived in Kyaka II—but then in the camp she found her elder sister. She added:

My mother and my brother later came to Uganda too. They came in through Kihihi, near the border town of Butogota. They called me, and I had to go there and pick them up. My mother was old and weak. When they got here, my sister asked to have them [living] at her house—since for her, she has been here for a longer time and she is also the eldest.[88]

The woman then described how the family grew very close, took care of each other and especially the brother, who "got so sick even before the war, getting some paralysis that left one of his arms lame." Living

---

[87] Female refugee, dialogue, March 27, 2014, Base Camp.
[88] Female refugee, dialogue, March 5, 2014, Kaborogota Zone.

near each other, even only in a nuclear family circle, created a sphere of trust and belonging for them.

Moreover, for many people it was important to create a 'home' as part of a daily routine, which reflects the pursuit of a certain normalcy as well as of stability and belonging (see the related special issue of Refuge, Doná 2015). Due to uncertainty about their future as well as prevalent domestic violence, creating a home in which the people feel comfortable and feel they belong may initially appear an impossible task. This challenge is not only relevant to refugees in Kyaka II but indeed worldwide. Omata (2016) explores how Lebanese refugees established a home that was meaningful to them and eventually affected their decision about whether or not to repatriate to their country of origin. Brun (2015a) stresses the critical value of acquaintances and relatives, buildings and their surroundings, for the creation of a home of displaced people in Georgia.

A point of criticism that informants in Kyaka II raised time and again, and widely, was the local decision taken by camp authorities at the time of research that they were not allowed to use metal sheets as roofs, as discussed in Chapter 3.[89] This practice would not only have provided better protection from the weather; it was also about being able to pursue, build, and have their own homes as set up in a way of their own choosing. Instead, being forbidden to install these roofs represented a constant reminder that their homes and thus their presence were only temporary—that regardless of the actual duration of their stay in Kyaka II.[90]

This friction between provisional setup and protracted situations of refuge is a core issue when it comes to creating normalcy, and one that stood out in my own research in Kyaka II too—as an impermanent yet challenging context. Refugees there employed various strategies to navigate the aid landscape and used resources emanating from the camp environment, by which they also influenced the camp setting.[91] Their "gardens" (as people called the fields in which they farmed), their marketplaces, their homes built with mud so they reflected the different red and brown colors of the soil, and at times words written on the

---

[89] Discussion with local leaders, March 19, 2014, Base Camp; discussion 1 with female refugees, March 12, 2014, Base Camp.

[90] Discussion with religious leaders, March 19, 2014, Base Camp.

[91] See also my other publications about refugees' coping on the basis of case studies in Uganda (Krause 2016d; Krause and Gato 2019; Krause and Schmidt 2018).

outside walls of homes, are just a few examples of how these individuals made the camp a living environment.

Dealing with Multidimensional Uncertainties

However, the camp itself—and along with it, the diverse local limitations—continued to signify this space being a temporary site wherein the people were forever reminded of their uncertain futures. This 'temporary' situation is paradigmatic for the provisional setup of refugee camps per se; other scholars have also reflected on the role of temporality and uncertainty in displacement (see Lems 2018; Turner 2016b; Horst and Grabska 2015; Brun 2015b; Golooba-Mutebi 2004). Horst and Grabska (2015) emphasize the effects of uncertainty for refugees who fled violent conflicts. These scholars hone in on fragmentary knowledge and the unpredictable futures of refugees to explain uncertainty—life aspects that affect them radically and immediately, but nevertheless also over a longer period of time. Brun meanwhile explains "how people simultaneously move on, feel stuck in the present, and still actively relate to alternative and changing notions of the future during such displacement" (2015b: 20), existing as agency-in-waiting in protracted situations. Turner introduces the concept of "dia-placement" to portray how Burundian refugees in a camp in Tanzania and in Nairobi, Kenya are influenced by past experiences while striving for better futures, and thus how they aim to move from "being" at a place to "'becoming' someone in the future" (2016b: 38).

In Kyaka II, informants were confronted with similar issues—which I capture as multidimensional uncertainties, thus those that occurred across time and space and in different areas of their lives. These were about where their future might lie and how to cope with the past, how to generate income to improve the future, how to ensure children being able to (continue to) attend school, whether family members who stayed in DR Congo are still alive, how social structures in Kyaka II may change, what local restrictions government and aid agencies might impose, and similar. One stark example of the fears that this uncertainty can give rise to relates to those stemming from the aforementioned rumors about forced repatriation. In comparison, the socioeconomic problems and restrictive humanitarian structures encountered on a daily basis in the camp rather constituted more subconscious ongoing uncertainties—but ones that nevertheless produced acute feelings of anxiety and insecurity.

While refugees found ways to cope with these manifold issues, the latter simultaneously also hampered their practices to establish an everyday life. For some, this meant trying to accept the camp's living conditions in their vagueness and uncertainty even despite their long-standing nature. This was the approach that the woman who I early explained to have engaged in peace education and counseling in Kyaka II took. She commented: "I depend on the decisions of the government; I am living in a foreign country, and have to live under the government's decisions. I have to just accept them."[92] In contrast, one man who had been in the camp for 12 years still found the conditions limiting to such an extent that he would describe living Kyaka II as akin to incarceration: "[Being here] makes you feel like you are in a prison of some sort."[93]

Not only despite some people's perception of life in the camp as prisonlike but also because of it, activities to create normalcy were thus key in coping strategies, handling issues faced, and for being able to remaining hopeful. Such activities often had a strong orientation toward the future, specifically a better one.

"I hope for a better future": The Power of Belief in Better Times to Come

"I don't feel threatened here in Kyaka, but I am always scared. I only fear to be alone, but I hope for a better future."[94] With these words, one woman described her situation of living between fear and hope in displacement. She was referencing not only her past experiences of war and her current situation of encampment as creating feelings of being lost, but her uncertain future ahead doing so too. In spite of her experiences and worries, she said she remained hopeful for better times to come.

In light of this impermanence and deficiency as well as the protracted situation in Kyaka II, remaining hopeful and believing in a better future to come was key for being able to move forward and cope with fears and worries. For some, this meant hoping for resettlement to a safe place in a third country. At the time of research, a resettlement program to the United States was in operation. A UNHCR employee

---

[92] Female refugee, dialogue, March 27, 2014, Base Camp.
[93] Male refugee, dialogue, March 27, 2014, Base Camp.
[94] Female refugee, dialogue, March 5, 2014, Kaborogota Zone.

interviewed women and men, and went through a number of questions to determine whether candidates did indeed meet the eligibility criteria. The employee then forwarded information to the UNHCR country office in Kampala. This process attracted a lot of attention from those in Kyaka II, as many hoped for a positive answer.

Through his research in Kakuma, Jansen (2008) reveals a similar situation there and explains how refugees at times present themselves in certain ways in order to improve their chances of resettlement. I did not inquire about what refugees said in their interviews for the resettlement process in Kyaka II, but a number of research participants nevertheless addressed the process on their own and expressed their hope of being accepted. Some even portrayed resettlement as the only imaginable way forward, because they could not return to their country of origin and saw no prospects in Kyaka II or Uganda more generally. As one woman noted:

Actually the only hope of finding a place like home is when you are resettled. When you are here, the decision might be to take you back to your home country anytime. I don't believe I will go back to DR Congo because of my past experiences. Maybe if I get resettlement I can live well.[95]

Such a perspective of resettlement being the main, or perhaps even only, alternative to camp life was also revealed by one man who strongly complained about the poor conditions in Kyaka II and voiced concerns about the tensions that can arise among the people affected when decisions about resettlement are made:

Families who are ready to go to other countries or who have got resettlement begin bragging that they are going, and that can cause violence in people. Everyone living in Kyaka II aspires to go to another country, so when they hear that there is one family going they become jealous and feel like bewitching them so that they might fail to go.[96]

In contrast, a young man voiced his continued hope. He had become separated from his family during the conflict in DR Congo and stayed alone there for some time before learning from clan members that his mother and sister were still alive, living in Kyaka II. Soon after, he came there and reunited with them. He was among those hoping for

---

[95] Female refugee, dialogue, March 27, 2014, Base Camp.
[96] Male refugee, dialogue, March 18, 2014, Base Camp.

family resettlement.[97] At the end of my research in Uganda, he called me to tell me that their application was unfortunately not successful. I assumed that this message would dispirit him, but he remained very hopeful. He expressed his maintenance of a positive attitude, and said he was sure that a new possibility would arise "so God wills."[98]

His reference to God leads us to the strong relevance of hope and especially also spiritual and religious hope and belief as drivers in learning to cope with highly challenging situations. Even the man whom I quoted earlier saying he felt "unhappy" because of repatriation threats eventually underlined: "Now for me, it is prayers and having hope in God that have sustained me."[99] In a similar vein, many women and men in Kyaka II highlighted their trust in a better future stemming from their religious faith—which gave them strength to move on and helped them endure and get by the various difficulties in both their past and current situations. Important to note, this comprised individuals adhering to different orientations of the Christian and Muslim faiths as well as local religions, all existing side-by-side in Kyaka II.

A quote that mirrors the narratives about religious hope of many women and men in Kyaka II was one given by a woman who had lost her husband and son during the war in DR Congo, personally suffered violence, and decided against remarrying and thus in favor of staying by herself. She said "[w]e just live by God's grace," but added "life is not good."[100] This nexus between worry and belief was commonplace. One adolescent explained her worries of perhaps not being allowed to finish school, "but when I read the Bible it brings me hope"[101]; a man expressed his concerns, but also hope that "[my] daughter gets married, you can just thank God for it";[102] a young women described how "God helped me, and I escaped" from her violent husband and the dangers in South Sudan.[103]

---

[97] Male refugee, dialogue, February 25, 2014, Base Camp.
[98] Male refugee, phone call, April 21, 2014.
[99] Male refugee, dialogue, March 18, 2014, Base Camp.
[100] Female refugee, dialogue, March 18, 2014, Base Camp.
[101] Female adolescent, 16 years old, journal writing, March 5, 2014, Bujubuli Secondary School.
[102] Male refugee, dialogue, March 5, 2014, Kaborogota Zone.
[103] Female refugee, dialogue, March 18, 2014, Base Camp.

The importance of faith for informants resonates with other studies too. Among others, Gladden (2013: 77) discusses how religious faith gives women in Kakuma emotional support not only from believing in a higher power but also trusting and having faith that change may come. Studies in Psychology similarly support the finding that religious belief and spirituality help refugees cope with their situation and focus on the future (see Tippens 2017; Bentley et al. 2014; Khawaja et al. 2008; Schweitzer et al. 2007). However, research also indicates that coping is not limited to spirituality and religious faith; education plays an important role in optimism and hopefulness too (see Seguin and Roberts 2017: 12; Gladden 2013: 77–78).

The significance of education and gaining skills was especially noted by younger people in Kyaka II, with them often expressing their hopes for a better future not only through faith but particularly through opportunities. These included hopes for finishing school and going to college to become a "water engineer or civil engineer," "nurse," "primary school teacher," "doctor," or "policeman."[104] Such hopes of younger people show a clear concentration on the future, involving potentially leaving the camp. Interestingly, they also divulge adhered-to gender roles—as most young men hoped for occupations as providers and protectors, and young women for jobs in socially supportive spheres. These articulated hopes especially also illustrated realms of endeavor that these informants saw as being insufficiently attended to within the camp.

This valuing of and hope for education was underlined by nearly all secondary school students who took part in the journal writing. As one wrote:

Kyaka II seemed to be interesting on arriving in it. This was because in my home country everything I had was lost, so Kyaka II has been my hope and given me confidence to go with life. But in Kyaka II, I have got something special that I am afraid of losing and this is education. This has been so because surely education has given and embraced me with knowledge, which I always admired. When I was still young it was portrayed to me what life means to be and life is what we make it, not only that but also how we can go on through good and bad times. But sometimes I wonder how am I going to

---

[104] Male refugee, dialogue, April 4, 2014, Base Camp; female refugee, April 2, 2014, Base Camp; female refugee, April 1, 2014, Base Camp; male refugee, dialogue, April 3, 2014, Base Camp; male refugee, dialogue, March 31, 2014, Base Camp.

continue with it, because nowadays education is becoming expensive and I am a poor refugee girl with no parents and reliabilities for it in spite of there has been some help from UNHCR. So my biggest prayer is to go on with education, because I may not be a moon to light the whole world but I may want to be a candle to light my own room, in other words, fulfill my dreams, and the only thing to achieve all those is education, but it is as if am soon losing it. Finally in spite of that, I have always had hope in something so I hope possibly by God I will attain it. Education is the life that I see sincerely. I deserve it if I am to live a happy life in the future, because my role models are all educated and things that I admire are for the educated.[105]

With these powerful words, this female informant echoes various statements shared by other adolescents in Kyaka II who likewise had endured experiences of war and violence, now worried about their current situation of confinement in the camp, as well as continued to preoccupy themselves with the uncertain futures ahead. Despite and perhaps because of these circumstances, they still clung to hope for, belief in, and working toward education and better futures for themselves and often their families too.

Although a number of adults in Kyaka II expressed, meanwhile, that they perceived their situation as hopeless due to the camp limitations, this did not mean that they 'gave up' hope. In contrast, as revealed above, they widely described the violence they suffered in the past, criticized the hardships they faced in the camp, but also nevertheless explained how they still actively sought ways forward. The women and men commonly shared a focus on the future through which their hopes, dreams, and prayers for, as well as beliefs in, a better future became drivers of their various coping strategies. This is because hope was not a passive or silent act, but supported their optimism. It also translated into actions striving to achieve better livelihoods, continue education so as to be able to go to college, or committed to helping their children have better lives in the future.

"Witchcraft is done for good and bad reasons": Witchcraft as Means to Rationalize Issues

Related to the value of beliefs and especially religious beliefs that informants shared in Kyaka II, the spiritual meaning of witchcraft is

---

[105] Female adolescent, 16 years old, journal writing, March 5, 2018, Bujubuli Secondary School.

also of importance. Witchcraft has received attention in diverse fields of the Social Sciences, also beyond Forced Migration and Refugee Studies, ever since the 1960s (see, e.g., Middleton and Winter 1963; Geschiere 1997; Pavanello 2017; on refugees see Brinkman 2000; Schnoebelen 2009; Apter 2012; Luongo 2015). Murrey (2017) explores the academic literature about witchcraft in Geography, and argues, among other things, that respective studies tend to reproduce colonial Othering and treat witchcraft as a peripheral or marginal subject. While this cannot be entirely applied to Forced Migration and Refugee Studies as an interdisciplinary field, I still take this criticism seriously and want to draw on it. I thus aim now to elucidate how research participants understood and used witchcraft, and what role it played as one of several components in their coping strategies.

Although those in Kyaka II also referred to witchcraft as a belief system, it differs from religious faith—the latter being mainly portrayed as gaining the necessary strength to handle obstacles that people encountered in the present and also foresaw in the future. In contrast, refugees discussed witchcraft mainly as sense-making vis-à-vis various difficult situations. Witchcraft therefore served as a means of finding and establishing relatable explanations for issues, explanations that were meaningful to them. This corresponds with other studies on the practice (see Ramsay 2016; Apter 2012). The difficulties that people in Kyaka II rationalized through witchcraft primarily revolved around violence, death, or sickness, and thus potentially life-changing issues, but also varied to include behavioral patterns as well.

In a discussion with religious leaders, one narrated how witchcraft was all about spiritual belief, noting: "Witchcraft is done for good and bad reasons." In addition to using witchcraft to heal or cure, for example, sicknesses, he addressed harmful intentions at length. "The witch will cooperate with demons to do something to you. They will invoke the evil spirit to attack their subject. For bad things, the witch may send diseases which can cause death," so he explained. Another discussant added: "Some herbalists can give you an herb and say this one can protect you. Or this one can harm someone." Others gave examples of how water spilled a certain way or herbs and other items thrown on the ground could bewitch people.[106] An aid worker expounded meanwhile: "Witchcraft is considered to be some kind of

---

[106] Discussion with religious leaders, March 19, 2014, Base Camp.

supernatural 'magic,' and can be used by one party against the other for any reason, imagined or real."[107]

Those spoken with in Kyaka II rarely reflected on how witchcraft heals people, largely addressing its harmful impact instead. Making sense of violence within families and between intimate partners, people argued it resulted from limited resources like the harvest,[108] men discriminating against or disrespecting women,[109] or women's disobedience.[110] Several women and men furthermore said violence was caused by witchcraft. One woman explained that men would become violent if they "drink a lot of alcohol and practice witchcraft."[111] Yet, one man stated, "[w]itchcraft is done by women" who used it as "poison of any kind to kill husbands."[112] As cited in Chapter 4, one man who relayed being in a somewhat equal relationship with his wife, sharing the domestic duties with her and caring for the baby, explained how he had chosen to proceed in this manner "[e]ven if other people may think you are bewitched."[113]

Another recounted that when he was younger and his father remarried, his stepmother would mistreat him. "That woman, she hates me so much," he said. While he had a close relationship with his father when his mother was still alive, he reasoned: "That woman, I am sure she bewitched my father. My father doesn't love me at all. He doesn't even care about my other siblings. He even chased me away from home."[114] One woman elaborated how, due to witchcraft, "[a]t times people just run mad; others die in a minute." She noted: "People like to bewitch. When they see you doing better [than they are], they may bewitch you. Some do not have a reason why they do it. They will just want to kill you, so they do it."[115] Then there is the man quoted earlier about how people may "feel like bewitching" others who were

[107] Female aid worker, interview, April 10, 2014.
[108] Discussion 1 with female refugees, March 12, 2014, Base Camp; discussion with Refugee Welfare Council, March 19, 2014, Base Camp; female aid worker, interview, May 20, 2014.
[109] Female refugee, dialogue, March 18, 2014, Base Camp; female refugee, dialogue, March 11, 2014, Bukere Zone.
[110] Discussion with male refugees, March 13, 2014, Base Camp.
[111] Female refugee, dialogue, February 25, 2014, Base Camp.
[112] Male refugee, dialogue, March 18, 2014, Base Camp.
[113] Discussion with local leaders, March 20, 2014, Base Camp.
[114] Male refugee, dialogue, March 5, 2014, Sweswe Zone.
[115] Female refugee, dialogue, March 18, 2014, Base Camp.

accepted for resettlement, "so that they may fail to go."[116] One of the religious leaders furthermore argued in a discussion: "Most families are suffering because of witchcraft." He recalled an incident prior to flight of a young man "who studied in France and Germany, but never sent his uncle help back in DR Congo and the uncle sent him witchcraft. Now he is back in DR Congo, and very poor."[117]

Although these narratives touch on diverse subjects such as family patterns, jealousy among community members, gender relations, and poverty, they have in common that the people referred to and used witchcraft as a source of rationalization. The young man for example reasoned the rejection of his father so, and the subsequent emotional distance that arose. The woman, ipso facto, explained mental illnesses and tensions in the community. The religious leader justified a man's poverty despite having studied in Europe on this basis. It seemed that making sense through witchcraft of situations that were worrisome and difficult to contemplate helped some people to justify developments, cope with issues, and thus get by and move forward.

In spite of witchcraft being said to be associated with "good and bad,"[118] that is healing and harming, the practice was mostly linked with danger and it generated fear within the community (see also Apter 2012). One adolescent explicitly noted: "I fear witchcraft of people."[119] Security personnel and aid workers also spoke of cases of violence being caused by witchcraft. One aid worker said "most witchcraft cases have ended up as security cases,"[120] which one security personnel also recognized while stating that "witchcraft is not a crime in Ugandan law"[121] so the security personnel were rarely in the position to pursue cases. What such information indicates, however, is that witchcraft may not only serve as a vehicle to rationalize developments but that it could also be used as ways of inflicting harm on people. While I cannot draw conclusions based on the insights that informants in Kyaka II shared about how closely witchcraft was indeed linked to violence, some studies indicate that this can occur

---

[116] Male refugee, dialogue, March 18, 2014, Base Camp.
[117] Discussion with religious leaders, March 19, 2014, Base Camp.
[118] Discussion with religious leaders, March 19, 2014, Base Camp.
[119] Male adolescent, 15 years old, journal writing, March 5, 2014, Bujubuli Secondary School.
[120] Female aid worker, interview, April 10, 2014.
[121] Security personnel, interview, February 26, 2014.

and result in discrimination, social exclusion, and stigmatization as well as physical force against both alleged witches and those bewitched (see Schnoebelen 2009; Brinkman 2000). These risks in countries of origin may furthermore cause people to seek asylum elsewhere (Luongo 2015).

In Conclusion: The Various Facets of Coping

Without doubt, encampment was difficult for the women and men living in Kyaka II. Research participants expressed worries, revealed shortcomings in their livelihoods, and at times articulated feelings of helplessness. However, they neither passively waited for aid agencies to provide assistance nor submissively obeyed humanitarian rules and regulations. On the contrary, as has been shown in this chapter, the women and men of different age groups employed a variety of strategies to navigate the camp landscape and administration, gain income, and use available resources. They sought ways to protect themselves, called on the power of social support, and believed in better futures to come.

To explore how women and men in Kyaka II coped with the conditions that they were confronted with, I drew on Lister's (2004) agency theory with the forms of "getting by," "getting out," "getting (back) at," and "getting organized." This revealed how practices of coping were directly associated with surrounding structures. The people were not only limited by the structures but they also used, bypassed, and challenged them. The first main section of this chapter addressed people's reasons for fleeing the conflict in DR Congo, which I discussed as representing conscious decisions. Of course, the war had far-reaching consequences and witnessed a broad scope of violence, disrupting social, political, and economic structures. Flight nevertheless constituted a choice. Some moved quickly to protect themselves and their families; others stayed longer, often to await the return of family members. Following Lister's agency theory, flight represents then a way of 'getting out' of the war zone and actively changing living conditions, undertaking a 'quasi-exit' to seek betterment elsewhere.

Following that, against the backdrop of prevalent gender-based violence in Kyaka II, I conveyed what women especially but also men did to protect themselves. In addition to mutual support, raising awareness in communities, and involving themselves in local decision-making structures, I explored the role of voice and silence. In contrast to understanding silence as a symbol of passivity, the narratives of the women in Kyaka II indicated how—self-imposed as well as complying with externally imposed—silence was strategically used to cope with and seek to reduce the scope of attacks. The diverse strategies utilized in these regards show how the people employed particularly practices of "getting by" and "getting organized" to protect themselves and each other.

The second section of this chapter then focused on ways of coping with the camp conditions. By going beyond humanitarian and governmental regulations, informants not only established strategies to advance their livelihood opportunities; they also countered and resisted structural regulations. Based on the stories the women and men shared, mobilities were found to be crucial to create livelihoods. The great majority of economic practices discussed occurred in informal sectors though, which left these individuals in risky situations. Claiming rights was furthermore found to be among their key coping strategies. With these strategies, the women and men bred normalcy and social spheres of belonging in the camp despite its temporality and multidimensional uncertainties. Remaining hopeful and believing in better times to come gave strength for persisting and continuing to move forward. By that, informants' coping in Kyaka II demonstrates how they simultaneously "got organized" at times to "get by," "get out," or "get back at" the manifold challenges faced.

6 | Conclusions

In this book, I set out to explore the interrelated subjects of gender-based violence, humanitarian aid, gender roles and relations, as well as coping strategies of displaced women especially but also men in encampment. Drawing on empirical research mainly with Congolese refugees that I carried out together with a team in Uganda's camp Kyaka II in 2014, each chapter focuses on one of these four key subject areas; nevertheless, they are in fact inherently connected, and build on each other. The interconnectedness of these subjects is also evident in the book's core interest in women and their lived experiences in the camp, which I could only explore by also taking into account those of men (as well as of female and male youth) because displacement and encampment affects all people in gender-specific ways. In this conclusion, I seek to sum up the main findings, reflect the role of time and space, and point to some crucial areas for further research arising from my work.

Despite the specific focus areas of the respective chapters, all key subject matters run through the book. Chapter 2 addressed scope, conditions, and forms of the gender-based violence experienced during encampment as well as conflict and flight, and noted the pivotal effects hereon of unfamiliar gender relations and humanitarian aid structures. The latter formed the central focus of Chapter 3, which explored not only how humanitarian aid is delivered—in part, to prevent such violence—but also how it can contribute to risks for refugees as a result of how it impacts them, including on their upheld gender roles. These roles, along with gender relations, were discussed in Chapter 4, which revealed how women, men, youth, and aid workers perceived gender roles on-site in Kyaka II and how the violence experienced there was entangled with local gender systems. Finally, Chapter 5 elucidated refugees' strategies to cope with violence, humanitarian restrictions, poor camp conditions, and limiting social roles.

More concretely, Chapter 2 showed how the lives of women and men of different age groups in Kyaka II and in DR Congo prior to flight were heavily affected by gender-specific direct, structural, and cultural risks. With regard to the conflict, refugees recalled diverse risks of murder, theft, and discrimination in addition to sexual abuse of women and militarized abduction and forced recruitment of men, as specific prevailing dangers. Fears and experiences of violence frequently influenced their decisions to leave and seek safety elsewhere, thus striving to protect themselves and particularly their families. However, flight and encampment proved to have their own dangers too. After leaving homes *en route* to Uganda, they continued to face risks similar to those in the conflict zones. In the camp, women and men were exposed to sexual and domestic abuse, structural and cultural violence, and militarized dangers to varying degrees and in gender-specific ways. As a result of this prevalence of violence, I went beyond the exile-oriented approach persistently used in Forced Migration and Refugee Studies and argued that women and men were exposed to a continuum of gender-based violence across all of conflict, flight, and encampment.

These issues of enduring and endemic violence stand in stark contrast to the camp having being established to protect and assist refugees, as investigated in Chapter 3. Although support was delivered that some refugees perceived as helpful, many others rued the aid conditions in Kyaka II being limiting and poor. The camp governance and aid system inflicted regulations on refugees, mainly treating them as 'protection objects.' This resonates with academic debate about refugee camps per se; among others, Agier (2011: 182) points to the biopolitical nature of aid in camps and Harrell-Bond (1986) even titled her book *Imposing Aid*. As women in Kyaka II were primarily defined through vulnerability, I found that aid agencies approached them as 'vulnerable protection objects' whom they strove to teach how to be empowered while not only maintaining typical roles as 'good wives and mothers' but also making them responsible for economic survivability. Through the various aid measures undertaken, these humanitarian agencies adopted positions of provider and powerbroker—while leaving refugees little room to participate in decision-making processes. This led to frustration among the displaced, and some—particularly men—felt discriminated against and undermined. The humanitarian structures furthermore partly contributed to the prevalence of gender-based violence, directly through the occasional committing of abuse by aid workers or indirectly through the insidious effects of aid and the difficult camp landscape.

Chapter 4 scrutinized gender roles and relations in encampment. Due to the changes occurring as a result of conflict and displacement, as well as the challenging conditions in the camp, the women and men in Kyaka II could no longer practice the gender roles and relations they were familiar with in DR Congo, rather having to renegotiate them. Many had lost husbands, wives, or other family and community members during conflict and flight, while often relying on external aid in the camp itself. Contributing to research debates about changing gender relations in exile (see, e.g., Szczepaniková 2005; Grabska 2011), it was thus illustrated how social practices of renegotiation took place in interactions between women and men—while also being significantly influenced by the humanitarian structures in Kyaka II. New gender roles and patterns of relations evolved as a consequence, but women and men also often referred to or partly tried to preserve 'traditional' ones that they found 'normal.'

Despite and due to these fears and risks of violence, humanitarian regulations and restrictions, limited livelihoods, and changing gender roles and relations, the women and men established diverse strategies for coping. These were explored in Chapter 5, which divulged how these strategies incorporated a wide range of economic, social, political, religious, and other means to generate income, protect themselves, their families (especially their children), and each other, deal with traumatic memories and current risks, push back against the inflicted humanitarian limitations, claim their rights, and to create everyday normalcy despite multidimensional uncertainties. These ultimately illustrate the many ways in which the women and men spoken with practiced agency. However, this did not suddenly make them entirely resilient; instead, the coping strategies of these women, men, girls, and boys signify individual and social mechanisms employed continuously over time in pursuit of moving forward, managing challenges, and, especially, handling the manifold uncertainties that they were confronted with. Hope for and belief in a better future was not only a coping strategy in itself, but also served as a driver for other strategies. Moreover, these practices were not limited to the camp itself; refugees used multiple forms of mobilities to leave sites of danger such as conflict regions and to create ways to access and use resources or help and protect themselves and each other both within and outside of the camp.

Associated with the interrelated core themes of the book is the role of time and space, running as an undercurrent throughout. Although my empirical research focused on a particular moment in Uganda's refugee camp Kyaka II, each chapter indicated how we can only understand the issues that refugees encounter, and therefore figuratively see 'where they are coming from,' by going beyond the specific temporally and spatially defined situation of a given camp or other location. Without having theorized the exact meanings of time and space in the book, prevailing tendencies can still be said to have come to light. On the one hand, the chapters about gender-based violence, gender relations, and coping reveal just how influential past experiences in regions of origin occurring in the time prior to displacement were, how these people (continued to) experience violence, how they were strongly guided by gender systems they had learnt much earlier, and how they coped with issues of the past and present in seeking to create a better future. This all corresponds with recent research about time and space, the entanglement of past, present, and future in displacement (see Horst and Grabska 2015; Brun 2015b; Turner 2016b; Ramsay 2018) and regarding questions of belonging, place-making, and spatial structures (see Ramadan 2013; Doná 2015; Hartmann 2017; Lems 2018).

On the other hand, the third chapter about refugee aid in Kyaka II conveyed three differing meanings of time and space as related to the on-site humanitarian apparatus specifically. First, similar to many other refugee camps worldwide, Kyaka II was originally established as a provisional space of protection and settlement of refugees for only a transitional and interim period of time, but would ultimately turn into a protracted situation of refuge—one ongoing since the 1980s (and counting). Second, aid projects revolved around refugees living in the camp space (though partly also accessible for Ugandan nationals). They were largely delivered on a short-term basis of one or two years' duration and then renewed, while the overall development-oriented approach to refugee aid in Uganda sought the sustainable use of services even after refugees repatriated. Third, 'local' aid projects and humanitarian practices in Kyaka II were influenced by 'global' refugee policies and norms, the nature and implications of which have thus far rarely been researched in Forced Migration and Refugee Studies. These apparently 'global' policies and norms were, of course, developed in a certain local space at a specific time, yet they are assumed to be 'global' and enduring due to the actors who established them (e.g., international organizations or the international community) and the intentions behind them appropriate for ongoing use worldwide. The 'global' norms and the knowledge that they carry traveled to and were 'localized' in Kyaka II. This localization took place mainly among aid workers, was contested, and affected the women and men in Kyaka II differently. This links with literature on norm localization in International Relations as well as in the interdisciplinary fields of Peace and Conflict, Humanitarian, and Development Studies (see, e.g., Bonacker et al. 2017; Zimmermann 2016; Acharya 2004).

Not only do those norm localization processes require further research to better understand how global norms are put into practice in specific contexts, and therewith, importantly, what roles refugees play in them. Gender-based violence representing a continuum across conflict, flight, and encampment as well as gender roles and relations changing in the refugee camp while continuing to be influenced by prior experiences and 'traditional' paradigms also stand out as key areas in need of further close investigation. In relation to this, there is a need to move beyond the exile-oriented research approach hitherto often adopted in Forced Migration and Refugee Studies. 'Exile,' 'refugee situations,' or 'refugee camps' do not constitute isolated sites or times, but are influenced by prior and likely also ensuing circumstances—taking these into account is of key relevance if we are also to understand the 'here and now.'

In addition, gender-related research should continue to receive ongoing attention. Much of the literature about refugees with a distinct gender focus revolves around women. My initial aim for this book was also to concentrate on women—and women alone. However, the more the various chapters came together, the more I found myself trying to maintain an artificial boundary between social perspectives and systems that were actually inherently intertwined. I thus decided to turn to exploring how women but also men of different age groups experience and perceive local processes, how their encounters are interconnected, and how they make sense of their situations from gendered perspectives. This does not mean that I find research specifically on displaced women irrelevant; far from it. Women are often exposed to explicit risks and limitations in exile because they are identified as women—something that should also be explored going forward.

Yet this point applies to other social groups too, due to their own specific experiences and ascriptions. Research on men and masculinity, forced migration, and encampment is certainly growing, albeit slowly (see, e.g., Turner 1999, 2004; Jaji 2009a; Lukunka 2011; Suerbaum

2018; Turner 2019)—but much more needs to be done. This is also—and perhaps even much more so—the case for LGBTIQ+ people. While I was unable to explore risks and conditions for LGBTIQ+ people in Kyaka II due to the political situation at the time of research, it is crucial to move beyond the perspective on women and men also maintained in this book and engage with all social groups and their gender-specific experiences and relations so as to better understand how forced migration represents a gendered process.

Finally, there are the refugees themselves, the very people spoken with and whose experiences are at the heart of this book. Broad segments of the Forced Migration and Refugee Studies literature echo critical perspectives on political structures, governance, (lack of) aid, and camps, as well as reflect on refugees' own capacities to cope with, use, bypass, and challenge humanitarian regulations and camp conditions (among some of the recent monographs, see Turner 2010; Agier 2011; Jansen 2011; Fiddian-Qasmiyeh 2014a; McConnachie 2014; Omata 2017). My research in Kyaka II has illuminated how humanitarian and government agencies may seek to promote refugees' empowerment, self-reliance, and resilience, and thus also independence from aid, but do so within structures that ultimately actually limit these women and men. Whereas I discussed various strategies the women and men used to navigate the camp landscape, cope with conditions, and mobilize resources, these aid practices can produce further risks and challenges for them. Continuing research from different disciplinary perspectives into how refugees practice agency is of scientific relevance. However, it would be far better, besides, if we did not even need to carry out such research—that is, if countries of asylum finally enabled refugees to access their rights and self-settle, and if the international community provided quicker access to durable solutions, and particularly if people did not have to flee in the first place.

As things stand, there are not (m)any indications of change being underfoot in the conditions refugees continue to be confronted with all over the world. Scholars emphasizing refugees' various 'creative' coping strategies may be academically relevant but simultaneously bear the risk of perpetuating the neoliberal frame that makes them responsible for contributing to national interests. A further danger is of portraying refugees' situations as manageable, as 'not that bad' since they somehow seem to make it, which I criticized in Chapter 5. However 'not that bad' is still bad and a long road from stable living conditions with access to rights, livelihoods, and overall security—and the difficult life in Kyaka II was even described as akin to incarceration by one informant.[1] Closing with the words of someone who endured such conditions thus seems apposite. During a dialogue, one elderly Congolese woman shared her experiences about the war, how she lost family members, but also how she gained strength from active involvement in community issues in Kyaka II. When we met, she had been living in Kyaka II for more than a decade already. She criticized the prevalent violence and many difficulties encountered as part of everyday life in the camp, noting the insufficient food supply and lack of common goods. As she would lament, "life is not good. We need changes."[2]

---

[1] Male refugee, dialogue, March 27, 2014, Base Camp.
[2] Female refugee, dialogue, March 18, 2014, Base Camp.

Bibliography

Aaltonen, Sanna (2013), '"Trying to Push Things Through": Forms and Bounds of Agency in Transitions of School-Age Young People', *Journal of Youth Studies*, 16 (3), 375–390.

Abdi, Awa M. (2006), 'Refugees, Gender-Based Violence and Resistance: A Case Study of Somali Refugee Women in Kenya', in Evangelia Tastsoglou and Alexandra Dobrowolsky (eds.), *Women, Migration and Citizenship* (Hampshire: Ashgate), 231–251.

Acharya, Amitav (2004), 'How Ideas Spread: Whose Norms Matter? Norm Localization and Institutional Change in Asian Regionalism', *International Organization*, 58 (2), 239–275.

Achvarina, Vera and Reich, Simon F. (2006), 'No Place to Hide: Refugees, Displaced Persons, and the Recruitment of Child Soldiers', *International Security*, 31 (1), 127–164.

Adelman, Howard (1998), 'Why Refugee Warriors Are Threats', *Journal of Conflict Studies*, 18 (1), n/a.

Adhikari, Prakash (2012), 'The Plight of the Forgotten Ones: Civil War and Forced Migration', *International Studies Quarterly*, 56 (3), 590–606.

—— (2013), 'Conflict-Induced Displacement, Understanding the Causes of Flight', *American Journal of Political Science*, 57 (1), 82–89.

Agamben, Giorgio (1998), *Homo Sacer: Sovereign Power and Bare Life*, trans. Daniel Heller-Roazen (Stanford: Stanford University Press).

Ager, Joey, Fiddian-Qasmiyeh, Elena, and Ager, Alastair (2015), 'Local Faith Communities and the Promotion of Resilience in Contexts of Humanitarian Crisis', *Journal of Refugee Studies*, 28 (2), 202–221.

Agier, Michel (2002), 'Between War and City: Towards an Urban Anthropology of Refugee Camps', *Ethnography*, 3 (3), 317–341.

—— (2011), *Managing the Undesirables. Refugee Camps and Humanitarian Government* (Cambridge: Polity Press).

Ahlborn, Christiane (2011), 'The Normative Erosion of International Refugee Protection through UN Security Council Practice', *Leiden Journal of International Law*, 24 (4), 1009–1027.

Ainamani, Herbert E., Elbert, Thomas, Olema, David Kani, and Hecker, Tobias (2017), 'PTSD Symptom Severity Relates to Cognitive and

Psycho-social Dysfunctioning—A Study with Congolese Refugees in Uganda', *European Journal of Psychotraumatology*, 8 (1), 1–10.

(2020), 'Gender Differences in Response to War-Related Trauma and Posttraumatic Stress Disorder—A Study among the Congolese Refugees in Uganda', *BMC Psychiatry*, 20 (1), 1–9.

Akello, Vanessa (2009), 'Uganda's Progressive Refugee Act Becomes Operational', *UNHCR News Stories* (www.unhcr.org/4a3f9e076 .html).

Al-Ali, Nadje (2002), 'Gender Relations, Transnational Ties and Rituals among Bosnian Refugees', *Global Networks*, 2 (3), 249–262.

Albutt, Katherine, Kelly, Jocelyn, Kabanga, Justin, and VanRooyen, Michael (2017), 'Stigmatisation and Rejection of Survivors of Sexual Violence in Eastern Democratic Republic of the Congo', *Disasters*, 41 (2), 211–227.

Alden, Amie (2010), 'A Continuum of Violence: A Gendered Analysis of Post Conflict Transformation', *POLIS Journal*, 3, 1–37.

Alloush, Mohamad, Taylor, J. Edward, Gupta, Anubhab, Rojas Valdes, Ruben Irvin, and Gonzalez-Estrada, Ernesto (2017), 'Economic Life in Refugee Camps', *World Development*, 95, 334–347.

Alzoubi, Fatmeh Ahmad, Al-Smadi, Ahmed Mohammad, and Gougazeh, Yazeed Mohammad (2019), 'Coping Strategies Used by Syrian Refugees in Jordan', *Clinical Nursing Research*, 28 (4), 396–421.

Apter, Andrew (2012), 'Matrilineal Motives: Kinship, Witchcraft, and Repatriation among Congolese Refugees', *The Journal of the Royal Anthropological Institute*, 18 (1), 22–44.

Araujo, Juliana de Oliveira, Souza, Fernanda Mattos de, Proença, Raquel, Bastos, Mayara Lisboa, Trajman, Anete, and Faerstein, Eduardo (2019), 'Prevalence of Sexual Violence among Refugees: A Systematic Review', *Revista de Saúde Pública*, 53, 1–15.

Archer Mann, Susan and Huffman, Douglas J. (2005), 'The Decentering of Second Wave Feminism and the Rise of the Third Wave', *Science & Society*, 69 (1), 56–91.

Asgary, Ramin, Emery, Eleanor, and Wong, Marcia (2013), 'Systematic Review of Prevention and Management Strategies for the Consequences of Gender-Based Violence in Refugee Settings', *International Health*, 5 (2), 85–91.

Autesserre, Séverine (2008), 'The Trouble with Congo: How Local Disputes Fuel Regional Conflict', *Foreign Affairs*, 87 (3), 94–110.

(2010), *The Trouble with the Congo: Local Violence and the Failure of International Peacebuilding* (Cambridge Studies in International Relations; Cambridge; New York: Cambridge University Press).

Babalola, Stella, Gill-Bailey, Amrita, and Dodo, Mathurin (2014), 'Prevalence and Correlates of Experience of Physical and Sexual

Intimate Partner Violence among Men and Women in Eastern DRC', *Universal Journal of Public Health*, 2 (1), 25–33.

Bakewell, Oliver (2007), 'Editorial Introduction: Researching Refugees: Lessons from the Past, Current Challenges and Future Directions', *Refugee Survey Quarterly*, 26 (3), 6–14

Bank, André, Fröhlich, Christiane, and Schneiker, Andrea (2017), 'The Political Dynamics of Human Mobility: Migration Out of, as and into Violence', *Global Policy*, 8, 12–18.

Barnett, Michael (2011), *Empire of Humanity: A History of Humanitarianism* (Ithaca, New York: Cornell University Press).

Bartels, Susan A., Michael, Saja, Roupetz, Sophie, Garbern, Stephanie, Kilzar, Lama, Bergquist, Harveen, Bakhache, Nour, Davison, Colleen, and Bunting, Annie (2018), 'Making Sense of Child, Early and Forced Marriage among Syrian Refugee Girls: A Mixed Methods Study in Lebanon', *BMJ Global Health*, 3 (1), 1–12.

Baxi, Pratiksha (2014), 'Sexual Violence and Its Discontents', *Annual Review of Anthropology*, 43 (1), 139–154.

Beaudou, Alain, Cambrézy, Luc, and Zaiss, Rainer (2003), *Geographical Information System, Environment and Camp Planning in Refugee Hosting Areas. Approach, Methods and Application in Uganda* (Bondy: Institut de recherche pour le développement (IRD); www .cartographie.ird.fr/refugies/rapuga/1_intro.pdf).

Bentley, Jacob, Ahmad, Zeba, and Thoburn, John (2014), 'Religiosity and Posttraumatic Stress in a Sample of East African Refugees', *Mental Health, Religion & Culture*, 17 (2), 185–195.

Berwouts, Kris (2017), *Congo's Violent Peace: Conflict and Struggle Since the Great African War* (London: Zed Books).

Beswick, Stephanie (2001), '"If You Leave Your Country You Have No Life!" Rape, Suicide, and Violence: The Voices of Ethiopian, Somali, and Sudanese Female Refugees in Kenyan Refugee Camps', *Northeast African Studies*, 8 (3), 69–98.

Betts, Alexander (2014), 'From Persecution to Deprivation: How Refugee Norms Adapt at Implementation', in Alexander Betts and Phil Orchard (eds.), *Implementation and World Politics: How International Norms Change Practice* (Oxford: Oxford University Press), 29–49.

Betts, Alexander and Durieux, Jean-François (2007), 'Convention Plus as a Norm-Setting Exercise', *Journal of Refugee Studies*, 20 (3), 509–535.

Betts, Alexander, Omata, Naohiko, and Bloom, Louise (2017a), 'Thrive or Survive? Explaining Variation in Economic Outcomes for Refugees', *Journal on Migration and Human Security*, 5 (4), 716–743.

Betts, Alexander, Bloom, Louise, Kaplan, Josiah, and Omata, Naohiko (2017b), *Refugee Economies: Forced Displacement and Development* (Oxford: Oxford University Press).

Block, Karen, Riggs, Elisha, and Haslam, Nick (eds.) (2013), *Values and Vulnerabilities. The Ethics of Research with Refugees and Asylum Seekers* (Toowong: Australian Academic Press).

Boer, Roselinde Den (2015), 'Liminal Space in Protracted Exile: The Meaning of Place in Congolese Refugees' Narratives of Home and Belonging in Kampala', *Journal of Refugee Studies*, 28 (4), 486–504.

Bogic, Marija, Njoku, Anthony, and Priebe, Stefan (2015), 'Long-Term Mental Health of War-Refugees: A Systematic Literature Review', *BMC International Health and Human Rights*, 15 (1), 1–41.

Bohnet, Heidrun, Cottier, Fabien, and Hug, Simon (2018), 'Conflict-Induced IDPs and the Spread of Conflict', *Journal of Conflict Resolution*, 62 (4), 691–716.

Bohra-Mishra, Pratikshya and Massey, Douglas S. (2011), 'Individual Decisions to Migrate During Civil Conflict', *Demography*, 48 (2), 401–424.

Bonacker, Thorsten and Heusinger, Judith von (2017), 'How the Localization of Macrocultural Concepts Can Reinforce Gender Inequalities: A Case Study on the Localization of Reproductive Health in Cambodia', in Thorsten Bonacker, Judith von Heusinger, and Kerstin Zimmer (eds.), *Localization in Development Aid. How Global Institutions Enter Local Lifeworlds* (London, New York: Routledge), 91–114.

Bonacker, Thorsten, Heusinger, Judith von, and Zimmer, Kerstin (eds.) (2017), *Localization in Development Aid. How Global Institutions Enter Local Lifeworlds* (London, New York: Routledge).

Breytenbach, Willie, Chilemba, Dalitso, Brown, Thomas A., and Plantive, Charlotte (1999), 'Conflicts in the Congo: From Kivu to Kabila', *African Security Review*, 8 (5), 33–42.

Brinkman, Inge (2000), 'Ways of Death: Accounts of Terror from Angolan Refugees in Namibia', *Africa: Journal of the International African Institute*, 70 (1), 1–24.

Brown, Jennifer and Walklate, Sandra (eds.) (2012), *Handbook on Sexual Violence* (London: Routledge).

Brown, Sara E. (2014), 'Female Perpetrators of the Rwandan Genocide', *International Feminist Journal of Politics*, 16 (3), 448–469.

Brun, Cathrine (2000), 'Making Young Displaced Men Visible', *Forced Migration Review*, 9, 10–12.

(2001), 'Reterritorializing the Relationship between People and Place in Refugee Studies', *Geografiska Annaler: Series B, Human Geography*, 83 (1), 15–25.

(2015a), 'Home as a Critical Value: From Shelter to Home in Georgia', *Refuge*, 31 (1), 43–54.

(2015b), 'Active Waiting and Changing Hopes: Toward a Time Perspective on Protracted Displacement', *Social Analysis*, 59 (1), 19–37.

Brun, Cathrine and Fábos, Anita (2015), 'Making Homes in Limbo? A Conceptual Framework', *Refuge*, 31 (1), 5–17.

Buckley-Zistel, Susanne, Krause, Ulrike, and Loeper, Lisa (2014), 'Sexuelle und geschlechterbasierte Gewalt an Frauen in kriegsbedingten Flüchtlingslagern. Ein Literaturüberblick', *Peripherie: Zeitschrift für Politik und Ökonomie in der Dritten Welt*, 34 (133), 71–89.

Buckley-Zistel, Susanne and Krause, Ulrike (eds.) (2017), *Gender, Violence, Refugees* (Studies in Forced Migration, 37; New York, Oxford: Berghahn).

Büschel, Hubertus (2014), *Hilfe zur Selbsthilfe. Deutsche Entwicklungsarbeit in Afrika 1960–1975* (Frankfurt: Campus Verlag).

Buscher, Dale (2009), 'Women, Work, and War', in Susan F. Martin and John Tirman (eds.), *Women, Migration, and Conflict. Breaking a Deadly Cycle* (Heidelberg, London, New York: Springer), 87–106.

(2017), 'Formidable Intersections: Forced Migration, Gender and Livelihoods', in Susanne Buckley-Zistel and Ulrike Krause (eds.), *Gender, Violence, Refugees* (Studies in Forced Migration, 37; New York, Oxford: Berghahn), 152–170.

Callamard, Agnès (1994), 'Refugees and Local Hosts: A Study of the Trading Interactions between Mozambican Refugees and Malawian Villagers in the District of Mwanza', *Journal of Refugee Studies*, 7 (1), 39–62.

Calvès, Anne-Emmanuèle (2009), 'Empowerment: The History of a Key Concept in Contemporary Development Discourse', *Revue Tiers Monde*, 4 (20), 735–749.

Campbell, Catherine and Mannell, Jenevieve (2016), 'Conceptualising the Agency of Highly Marginalised Women: Intimate Partner Violence in Extreme Settings', *Global Public Health*, 11 (1–2), 1–16.

Čapo, Jasna (2015), '"Durable Solutions," Transnationalism, and Homemaking among Croatian and Bosnian Former Refugees', *Refuge*, 31 (1), 19–29.

Care International (2011), *Reported Cases of Sexual Violence Have Quadrupled among Refugees* (Care International; www .careinternational.org.uk/news-and-press/latest-press-releases/1805-reported-cases-of-sexual-violence-have-quadrupled-among-refugees).

Carlson, Sharon (2005), 'Contesting and Reinforcing Patriarchy: Domestic Violence in Dzaleka Refugee Camp', *RSC Working Paper Series*, No. 23.

Carney, Michelle, Buttell, Fred, and Dutton, Don (2007), 'Women Who Perpetrate Intimate Partner Violence: A Review of the Literature with Recommendations for Treatment', *Aggression and Violent Behavior*, 12 (1), 108–115.

Carpenter, R. Charli (2006), 'Recognizing Gender-Based Violence against Civilian Men and Boys in Conflict Situations', *Security Dialogue*, 37 (1), 83–103.

Chandler, David (2012), 'Resilience and Human Security: The Post-interventionist Paradigm', *Security Dialogue*, 43 (3), 213–229.

Charsley, Katharine and Wray, Helena (2015), 'Introduction: The Invisible (Migrant) Man', *Men and Masculinities*, 18 (4), 403–423.

Chiu, William (2009), 'Refugees and Asylum', in Wayne Sandholtz and Kendall Stiles (eds.), *International Norms and Cycles of Change* (Oxford: Oxford University Press), 237–262.

Christian, Mervyn, Safari, Octave, Ramazani, Paul, Burnham, Gilbert, and Glass, Nancy (2011), 'Sexual and Gender Based Violence against Men in the Democratic Republic of Congo: Effects on Survivors, Their Families and the Community', *Medicine, Conflict and Survival*, 27 (4), 227–246.

Chua, Lynette J. and Engel, David M. (2019), 'Legal Consciousness Reconsidered', *Annual Review of Law and Social Science*, 15 (1), 335–353.

Chynoweth, Sarah K. (2017), *'We Keep It in Our Heart'—Sexual Violence against Men and Boys in the Syria Crisis* (Geneva: UNHCR).

Cipriani, Linda (1993), 'Gender and Persecution: Protecting Women under International Refugee Law', *Georgetown Immigration Law Journal* 7 (3), 511–548.

Clark-Kazak, Christina R. (2010a), 'The Politics of Formal Schooling in Refugee Contexts: Education, Class, and Decision Making among Congolese in Uganda', *Refuge*, 27 (2), 57–64.

  (2010b), 'The Politics of Protection: Aid, Human Rights Discourse, and Power Relations in Kyaka II Settlement, Uganda', *Disasters*, 34 (1), 55–70.

  (2011), *Recounting Migration: Political Narratives of Congolese Young People in Uganda* (Montreal, Kingston, London, Ithaca: McGill-Queen's University Press).

  (2014), '"A Refugee Is Someone Who Refused to Be Oppressed": Self-Survival Strategies of Congolese Young People in Uganda', *Stability: International Journal of Security and Development*, 3 (1), Art. 13.

Coady, Cecil A. J. (2007), *Morality and Political Violence* (Cambridge: Cambridge University Press).

Cockburn, Cynthia (2004), 'The Continuum of Violence—A Gender Perspective on Violence and Peace', in Werona Giles and Jennifer Hyndmann (eds.), *Sites of Violence—Gender and Conflict Zones* (Berkeley, Los Angeles: University of California Press), 24–44.

Coen, Alise (2019), 'Can't Be Held Responsible: Weak Norms and Refugee Protection Evasion', *International Relations*, published online first, doi: 10.1177/0047117819884613.

Confortini, Catia C. (2006), 'Galtung, Violence, and Gender: The Case for a Peace Studies/Feminism Alliance', *Peace & Change*, 31 (3), 333–367.

Coulter, Chris (2008), 'Female Fighters in the Sierra Leone War: Challenging the Assumptions?', *Feminist Review*, 88 (1), 54–73.

(2011), *Bush Wives and Girl Soldiers: Women's Lives through War and Peace in Sierra Leone* (Ithaca, London: Cornell University Press).

Coulthard, Sarah (2012), 'Can We Be Both Resilient and Well, and What Choices Do People Have? Incorporating Agency into the Resilience Debate from a Fisheries Perspective', *Ecology and Society*, 17 (1), 4, doi: 10.5751/ES-04483-170104.

Crawley, Heaven (2001), *Refugees and Gender: Law and Process* (Bristol: Jordan Publishing).

Crawley, Heaven, Düvell, Franck, Jones, Katharine, McMahon, Simon, and Sigona, Nando (2016), 'Destination Europe? Understanding the Dynamics and Drivers of Mediterranean Migration in 2015', *MEDMIG Final Report*, .

Crisp, Jeff (2000), 'Africa's Refugees: Patterns, Problems and Policy Challenges', *New Issues in Refugee Research*, No. 28.

(2017), 'Finding Space for Protection: An Inside Account of the Evolution of UNHCR's Urban Refugee Policy', *Refuge*, 33 (1), 87–96.

Dalal, Ayham (2015), 'A Socio-economic Perspective on the Urbanisation of Zaatari Camp in Jordan', *Migration Letters*, 12 (3), 263–278.

Danish Refugee Council (2018), *'To Have Peaceful Coexistence, People Need to Have Full Stomachs'. Rapid Conflict Assessment in Kyaka II Refugee Settlement, Uganda* (https://drc.ngo/media/4585938/drc-may-2018-kyaka-ii-rapid-conflict-assessment_for-release.pdf).

Darling, Jonathan (2014), 'Emotions, Encounters and Expectations: The Uncertain Ethics of "The Field"', *Journal of Human Rights Practice*, 6 (2), 201–212.

Davies, Sara E. and True, Jacqui (2015), 'Reframing Conflict-Related Sexual and Gender-Based Violence: Bringing Gender Analysis Back In', *Security Dialogue*, 46 (6), 495–512.

De Alwis, Malathi (2004), 'The "Purity" of Displacement and the Reterritorialization of Longing: Muslim IDPs in Northwestern Sri Lanka', in Wenona Giles and Jennifer Hyndman (eds.), *In Sites of*

Violence: Gender and Conflict Zones (Berkeley: University of California Press), 213–231.

de Laine, Marlene (2000), *Fieldwork, Participation and Practice: Ethics and Dilemmas in Qualitative Research* (London: Sage).

de Neef, C. E. J. and de Ruiter, S. J. (1984), *Sexual Violence against Women Refugees: Report on the Nature and Consequences of Sexual Violence Suffered Elsewhere* (Amsterdam; http://repository.forcedmigration.org/show_metadata.jsp?pid=fmo:3842).

Deardorff Miller, Sarah (2018), *UNHCR as a Surrogate State: Protracted Refugee Situations* (London, New York: Routledge).

Deitelhoff, Nicole and Zimmermann, Lisbeth (2018), 'Things We Lost in the Fire: How Different Types of Contestation Affect the Robustness of International Norms', *International Studies Review*, 22 (1), 51–76.

Dember, William N. (1974), 'Motivation and the Cognitive Revolution', *American Psychologist*, 29 (3), 161–168.

Denov, Myriam (2010), *Child Soldiers: Sierra Leone's Revolutionary United Front* (Cambridge: Cambridge University Press).

Derluyn, Ilse, Vandenhole, Wouter, Parmentier, Stephan, and Mels, Cindy (2015), 'Victims and/or Perpetrators? Towards an Interdisciplinary Dialogue on Child Soldiers', *BMC International Health and Human Rights*, 15 (1), 28.

Deveaux, Monique (1994), 'Feminism and Empowerment: A Critical Reading of Foucault', *Feminist Studies*, 20 (2), 223–247.

Dilts, Andrew, Winter, Yves, Biebricher, Thomas, Johnson, Eric Vance, Vázquez-Arroyo, Antonio Y., and Cocks, Joan (2012), 'Revisiting Johan Galtung's Concept of Structural Violence', *New Political Science*, 34 (2), e191–e227.

Doevenspeck, Martin (2016), 'Territoriality in Civil War: The Ignored Territorial Dimensions of Violent Conflict in North Kivu, DRC', in Annika Björkdahl and Susanne Buckley-Zistel (eds.), *Spatializing Peace and Conflict: Mapping the Production of Places, Sites and Scales of Violence* (Basingstoke: Palgrave), 41–59.

Dolan, Chris (2009), *Social Torture. The Case of Northern Uganda, 1986–2006* (New York, Oxford: Berghahn).

(2014), 'Into the Mainstream: Addressing Sexual Violence against Men and Boys in Conflict', *Briefing Paper Prepared for the Workshop Held at the Overseas Development Institute, London, 14 May 2014* (London: ODI).

(2017), 'Hidden Realities: Screening for Experiences of Violence amongst War-Affected South Sudanese Refugees in Northern Uganda', *Refugee Law Project Working Paper*, No. 25.

Doná, Giorgia (2007), 'The Microphysics of Participation in Refugee Research', *Journal of Refugee Studies*, 20 (2), 210–229.

(2015), 'Making Homes in Limbo: Embodied Virtual "Homes" in Prolonged Conditions of Displacement', *Refuge*, 31 (1), 67–73.

Drożđek, Boris (2015), 'Challenges in Treatment of Posttraumatic Stress Disorder in Refugees: Towards Integration of Evidence-Based Treatments with Contextual and Culture-Sensitive Perspectives', *European Journal of Psycho-Traumatology*, 6, 1–8.

Dryden-Peterson, Sarah (2006), '"I Find Myself as Someone Who Is in the Forest": Urban Refugees as Agents of Social Change in Kampala, Uganda', *Journal of Refugee Studies*, 19 (3), 381–395.

Dyregrov, Kari, Dyregrov, Atle, and Raundalen, Magne (2000), 'Refugee Families' Experience of Research Participation', *Journal of Traumatic Stress*, 13 (3), 413–426.

Easton-Calabria, Evan E. (2015), 'From Bottom-Up to Top-Down: The "Pre-History" of Refugee Livelihoods Assistance from 1919 to 1979', *Journal of Refugee Studies*, 28 (3), 412–436.

Easton-Calabria, Evan E. and Omata, Naohiko (2018), 'Panacea for the Refugee Crisis? Rethinking the Promotion of "Self-Reliance" for Refugees', *Third World Quarterly*, 39 (8), 1458–1474.

Easton-Calabria, Evan and Skran, Claudena (eds.) (2020), *Journal of Refugee Studies. Special Issue: Rethinking Refugee Self-Reliance* (33 (1)).

Echols, Alice (1989), *Daring to Be Bad: Radical Feminism in America, 1967–1975* (London: University of Minnesota Press).

Edström, Jerker and Dolan, Chris (2018), 'Breaking the Spell of Silence: Collective Healing as Activism amongst Refugee Male Survivors of Sexual Violence in Uganda', *Journal of Refugee Studies*, 32 (2), 175–196.

Edström, Jerker, Dolan, Chris, Shahrokh, Thea, and David, Onen (2016), 'Therapeutic Activism: Men of Hope Refugee Association Uganda Breaking the Silence over Male Rape in Conflict-related Sexual Violence', *IDS Evidence Report*, No. 182.

Edwards, Alice (2010), 'Transitioning Gender: Feminist Engagement with International Refugee Law and Policy 1950–2010', *Refugee Survey Quarterly*, 29 (2), 21–45.

Eifler, Christine and Seifert, Ruth (eds.) (1999), *Soziale Konstruktionen— Militär und Geschlechterverhältnis* (Münster: Verlag Westfälisches Dampfboot).

El-Bushra, Judy, Myrttinen, Henri, and Naujoks, Jana (2013), *Renegotiating the 'Ideal' Society. Gender Relations in the Wake of Conflict and Displacement in Uganda* (London: International Alert; www.international-alert.org/sites/default/files/Gender_%20RenegotiatingIdealSocietyUganda_EN_2013_0.pdf).

Ellis, B. Heidi, Kia-Keating, Maryam, Yusuf, Siraad Aden, Lincoln, Alisa, and Nur, Abdirahman (2007), 'Ethical Research in Refugee Communities and the Use of Community Participatory Methods', *Transcultural Psychiatry*, 44 (3), 459–481.

Enloe, Cynthia (2014), *Bananas, Beaches and Bases: Making Feminist Sense of International Politics* (2nd revised and updated edn.; Berkeley, Los Angeles, London: University of California Press).

Ensor, Marisa O. and Gozdziak, Elzbieta (eds.) (2016), *Children and Forced Migration: Durable Solutions during Transient Years* (Cham: Palgrave Macmillan).

Erdal, Marta Bivand and Pawlak, Marek (2018), 'Reproducing, Transforming and Contesting Gender Relations and Identities through Migration and Transnational Ties', *Gender, Place & Culture*, 25 (6), 882–898.

Erdener, Eda (2017), 'The Ways of Coping with Post-war Trauma of Yezidi Refugee Women in Turkey', *Women's Studies International Forum*, 65, 60–70.

Eriksson Baaz, Maria and Stern, Maria (2009), 'Why Do Soldiers Rape? Masculinity, Violence, and Sexuality in the Armed Forces in the Congo (DRC)', *International Studies Quarterly*, 53 (2), 495–518.

(2013a), *Sexual Violence as a Weapon of War? Perceptions, Prescriptions, Problems in the Congo and Beyond* (Africa Now, London: New York Zed Books).

(2013b), 'Fearless Fighters and Submissive Wives: Negotiating Identity among Women Soldiers in the Congo (DRC)', *Armed Forces & Society*, 39 (4), 711–739.

Ermann, Michael (2005), 'Trauma und Traumafolgen aus psychodynamischer Sicht', *Psychotherapeut*, 50 (3), 209–228.

Evans, Brad and Reid, Julian (2013), 'Dangerously Exposed: The Life and Death of the Resilient Subject', *Resilience*, 1 (2), 83–98.

Evans, Judith (1995), *Feminist Theory Today: An Introduction to Second-Wave Feminism* (London, Thousand Oaks, New Delhi: Sage).

Farmer, Alice (2006), 'Refugee Responses, State-like Behavior, and Accountability for Human Rights Violations: A Case Study of Sexual Violence in Guinea's Refugee Camps', *Yale Human Rights and Development Journal*, 9 (1), 44–84.

Farwell, Nancy (2001), '"Onward through Strength": Coping and Psychological Support among Refugee Youth Returning to Eritrea from Sudan', *Journal of Refugee Studies*, 14 (1), 43–69.

Fassin, Didier (2009), 'Another Politics of Life Is Possible', *Theory, Culture & Society*, 26 (5), 44–60.

(2012), *Humanitarian Reason: A Moral History of the Present Times* (Berkeley: University of California Press).

Fernando, Nilmini (2016), 'The Discursive Violence of Postcolonial Asylum in the Irish Republic', *Postcolonial Studies*, 19 (4), 393–408.

Ferris, Elizabeth G. (1990), 'Refugee Women and Violence', *World Council of Churches* (Geneva).

(2007), 'Women in Refugee Camps. Abuse of Power: Sexual Exploitation of Refugee Women and Girls', *Signs: Journal of Women in Culture and Society*, 32 (3), 584–591.

Fiddian-Qasmiyeh, Elena (2010a), '"Ideal" Refugee Women and Gender Equality Mainstreaming in the Sahrawi Refugee Camps: "Good Practice" for Whom?', *Refugee Survey Quarterly*, 29 (2), 64–84.

(2010b), 'Concealing Violence against Women in the Sahrawi Refugee Camps: The Politicization of Victimhood', in Hannah Bradby and Gillian L. Hundt (eds.), *Global Perspectives on War, Gender and Health: The Sociology and Anthropology of Suffering* (Farnham: Ashgate), 99–110.

(2014a), *The Ideal Refugees: Gender, Islam, and the Sahrawi Politics of Survival* (New York: Syracuse University Press).

(2014b), 'Gender and Forced Migration', in Elena Fiddian-Qasmiyeh, Gil Loescher, Katy Long, and Nando Sigona (eds.), *The Oxford Handbook of Refugee and Forced Migration Studies* (Oxford: Oxford University Press), 395–408.

Fiddian-Qasmiyeh, Elena, Lewis, Chloé, and Cole, Georgia (2017), '"Faithing" Gender and Responses to Violence in Refugee Communities: Insights from the Sahrawi Refugee Camps and the Democratic Republic of Congo', in Susanne Buckley-Zistel and Ulrike Krause (eds.), *Gender, Violence, Refugees* (Studies in Forced Migration, 37; New York, Oxford: Berghahn), 127–151.

Figley, Charles R. (ed.) (2012), *Encyclopedia of Trauma* (London: Sage).

Finnemore, Martha and Sikkink, Kathryn (1998), 'International Norm Dynamics and Political Change', *International Organization*, 52 (4), 887–917.

Firth, Georgina and Mauthe, Barbara (2013), 'Refugee Law, Gender and the Concept of Personhood', *International Journal of Refugee Law*, 25 (3), 470–501.

Flatten, Guido, Gast, Ursula, Hofmann, Arne, Knaevelsrud, Christine, Lampe, Astrid, Liebermann, Peter, Maercke, Andreas, Reddemann, Luise, and Wöller, Wolfgang (2013), *Posttraumatische Belastungsstörungen. Leitlinien und Quellentexte* (Stuttgart: Schattauer).

Forced Migration Review (FMR) (2002), 'Displaced Children and Adolescents: Challenges and Opportunities', *Forced Migration Review*, 15.

Freedman, Jane (2015a), *Gendering the International Asylum and Refugee Debate* (Basingstoke, Hampshire: Palgrave Macmillan).

(2015b), *Gender, Violence and Politics in the Democratic Republic of Congo* (Farnham: Ashgate).

(2016a), 'Engendering Security at the Borders of Europe: Women Migrants and the Mediterranean "Crisis"', *Journal of Refugee Studies*, 29 (4), 568–582.

(2016b), 'Sexual and Gender-Based Violence against Refugee Women: A Hidden Aspect of the Refugee "Crisis"', *Reproductive Health Matters*, 24 (47), 18–26.

(2019), 'The Uses and Abuses of "Vulnerability" in EU Asylum and Refugee Protection: Protecting Women or Reducing Autonomy?', *Papeles del CEIC, International Journal on Collective Identity Research*, 2019 (1), 1–15.

Fresia, Marion (2014), 'Building Consensus within UNHCR's Executive Committee: Global Refugee Norms in the Making', *Journal of Refugee Studies*, 27 (4), 514–533.

Friedman, Amy R. (1992), 'Rape and Domestic Violence', *Women & Therapy*, 13 (1–2), 65–78.

Galli, Chiara (2019), 'The Ambivalent U.S. Context of Reception and the Dichotomous Legal Consciousness of Unaccompanied Minors', *Social Problems*, published online first, doi: 10.1093/socpro/spz041.

Galtung, Johan (1969), 'Violence, Peace, and Peace Research', *Journal of Peace Research*, 6 (3), 167–191.

(1990), 'Cultural Violence', *Journal of Peace Research*, 27 (3), 291–305.

(2004), 'Violence, War, and Their Impact: On Visible and Invisible Effects of Violence', *Polylog: Forum for Intercultural Philosophy* (https://them.polylog.org/5/fgj-en.htm).

(2010), 'Direct, Structural, and Cultural Violence', in Nigel J. Young (ed.), *The Oxford International Encyclopedia of Peace* (Oxford: Oxford University Press), 312–316.

Galtung, Johan and Höivik, Tord (1971), 'Structural and Direct Violence: A Note on Operationalization', *Journal of Peace Research*, 8 (1), 73–76.

Garrison, Ednie Kaeh (2007), 'Contests for the Meaning of Third Wave Feminism: Feminism and Popular Consciousness', in Stacy Gillis, Gillian Howie, and Rebecca Munford (eds.), *Third Wave Feminism: A Critical Exploration* (London: Palgrave Macmillan UK), 24–36.

Gatrell, Peter (2008), 'Refugees and Forced Migrants during the First World War', *Immigrants & Minorities*, 26 (1–2), 82–110.

(2013), *The Making of the Modern Refugee* (Oxford: Oxford University Press).

Gerard, Alison (2014), *The Securitization of Migration and Refugee Women* (Abingdon: Routledge).

Geschiere, Peter (1997), *The Modernity of Witchcraft: Politics and the Occult in Postcolonial Africa* (Charlottesville: University of Virginia Press).

Giles, Wenona and Hyndman, Jennifer (eds.) (2004), *Sites of Violence. Gender and Conflict Zones* (Berkeley, Los Angeles, London: University of California Press).

Girtler, Roland (2001), *Methoden der Feldforschung* (4th edn.; Wien, Köln, Weimar: UTB).

Gladden, Jessica (2012), 'The Coping Skills of East African Refugees: A Literature Review', *Refugee Survey Quarterly*, 31 (3), 177–196.

(2013), 'Coping Strategies of Sudanese Refugee Women in Kakuma Refugee Camp, Kenya', *Refugee Survey Quarterly*, 32 (4), 66–89.

Glasman, Joël (2019), *Humanitarianism and the Quantification of Human Needs: Minimal Humanity* (London, New York: Routledge).

Golooba-Mutebi, Frederick (2004), 'Refugee Livelihoods—Confronting Uncertainty and Responding to Adversity: Mozambican War Refugees in Limpopo Province, South Africa', *New Issues in Refugee Research*, No. 105.

Goodman, Ryan and Jinks, Derek (2008), 'Incomplete Internalization and Compliance with Human Rights Law', *European Journal of International Law*, 19 (4), 725–748.

Gottschalk, Noah (2007), 'Giving Out Their Daughters for Their Survival: Refugee Self-Reliance, "Vulnerability", and the Paradox of Early Marriage', *Refugee Law Project Working Paper Series*, No. 20.

Gottwald, Martin (2014), 'Burden Sharing and Refugee Protection', in Elena Fiddian-Qasmiyeh, Gil Loescher, Katy Long, and Nando Sigona (eds.), *The Oxford Handbook of Refugee and Forced Migration Studies* (Oxford: Oxford University Press), 525–539.

Government of Uganda, The World Bank, and United Nations (2017), *Refugee and Host Population Empowerment (ReHoPE) Strategic Framework, 03 February 2017* (Kampala: Government of Uganda).

Grabska, Katarzyna (2006), 'Marginalization in Urban Spaces of the Global South: Urban Refugees in Cairo', *Journal of Refugee Studies*, 19 (3), 287–307.

(2011), 'Constructing "Modern Gendered Civilised" Women and Men: Gender-Mainstreaming in Refugee Camps', *Gender & Development*, 19 (1), 81–93.

(2014), *Gender, Identity, Home: Nuer Repatriation to South Sudan* (New York: James Currey).

Grabska, Katarzyna and Fanjoy, Martha (2015), '"And When I Become a Man": Translocal Coping with Precariousness and Uncertainty among Returnee Men in South Sudan', *Social Analysis*, 59 (1), 76–95.

Gray, Harriet, Stern, Maria, and Dolan, Chris (2020), 'Torture and Sexual Violence in War and Conflict: The Unmaking and Remaking of Subjects of Violence', *Review of International Studies*, 46 (2), 197–216.

Grayson, Catherine-Lune (2017), *Children of the Camp: The Lives of Somali Youth Raised in Kakuma Refugee Camp, Kenya* (New York, Oxford: Berghahn).

Greatbatch, Jacqueline (1989), 'The Gender Difference: Feminist Critiques of Refugee Discourse', *International Journal of Refugee Law*, 1 (4), 518–527.

Grechin, A. S. (1983), 'A Sociological Study of Legal Consciousness', *Soviet Law and Government*, 22 (2), 23–32.

Griffiths, Melanie (2015), '"Here, Man Is Nothing!": Gender and Policy in an Asylum Context', *Men and Masculinities*, 18 (4), 468–488.

Groß, Lisa (2015), 'The Journey from Global to Local: Norm Promotion, Contestation and Localisation in Post-war Kosovo', *Journal of International Relations and Development*, 18 (3), 311–336.

Haer, Roos and Hecker, Tobias (2018), 'Recruiting Refugees for Militarization: The Determinants of Mobilization Attempts', *Journal of Refugee Studies*, 32 (1), 1–22.

Hajdukowski-Ahmed, Maroussia (2003), 'At the Borders of Language, Language without Borders: Non-verbal Forms of Communication of Women Survivors of Torture', in Magda Stroinska and Vittorina Cecchetto (eds.), *Exile, Language and Identity* (Frankfurt a.M.: Peter Lang), 213–229.

(2008), 'A Dialogical Approach to Identity and Its Implications for Refugee Women', in Maroussia Hajdukowski-Ahmed, Nazilla Khanlou, and Helene Moussa (eds.), *Not Born a Refugee Woman. Contesting Identities, Rethinking Practices* (Studies in Forced Migration; New York, Oxford: Berghahn), 28–54.

Hajdukowski-Ahmed, Maroussia, Khanlou, Nazilla, and Moussa, Helene (2008a), 'Introduction', in Maroussia Hajdukowski-Ahmed, Nazilla Khanlou, and Helene Moussa (eds.), *Not Born a Refugee Woman. Contesting Identities, Rethinking Practices* (Studies in Forced Migration; Oxford, New York: Berghahn), 1–23.

Hajdukowski-Ahmed, Maroussia, Khanlou, Nazilla, and Moussa, Helene (eds.) (2008b), *Not Born a Refugee Woman. Contesting Identities, Rethinking Practices* (Studies in Forced Migration, 24; Oxford, New York: Berghahn).

Halliday, Simon (2019), 'After Hegemony: The Varieties of Legal Consciousness Research', *Social & Legal Studies*, 28 (6), 859–878.

Hans, Asha (2008), 'Gender, Camps and International Norms', *Refugee Watch*, (32), 64–73.

Hansen, Art (1979), 'Once for Running Stops: Assimilation of Angolan Refugees into Zambian Border Villages', *Disasters*, 3 (4), 369–374.

Happold, Matthew (2008), 'Child Soldiers: Victims or Perpetrators', *University of La Verne Law Review*, 29, 56–87.

Harding, Rosie (2010), *Regulating Sexuality: Legal Consciousness in Lesbian and Gay Lives* (New York: Routledge).

Harrell-Bond, Barbara E. (1986), *Imposing Aid. Emergency Assistance to Refugees* (Oxford Medical Publications; Oxford, New York, Nairobi: Oxford University Press).

(1999), 'The Experience of Refugees as Recipients of Aid', in Alastair Ager (ed.), *Refugees: Perspectives on the Experience of Forced Migration* (London: Continuum International Publishing Group Ltd), 136–168.

(2000), 'Are Refugee Camps Good for Children?', New Issues in Refugee Research, No. 29.

(2002), 'Can Humanitarian Work with Refugees Be Humane?', *Human Rights Quarterly*, 24 (1), 51–85.

(2004), 'Weapons of the Weak', *Journal of Refugee Studies*, 17 (1), 27–28.

Harrell-Bond, Barbara E. and Voutira, Eftihia (2007), 'In Search of "Invisible" Actors: Barriers to Access in Refugee Research', *Journal of Refugee Studies*, 20 (2), 281–298.

Harrell-Bond, Barbara E., Verdirame, Guglielmo, Lomo, Zachary, and Garry, Hannah (2005), *Rights in Exile—Janus-faced Humanitarianism* (New York, Oxford: Berghahn).

Harrison, Wendy C. (2006), 'The Shadow and the Substance. The Sex/ Gender Debate', in Kathy Davis, Mary Evans, and Judith Lorber (eds.), *Handbook of Gender and Women's Studies* (London, Thousand Oaks, New Delhi: Sage), 35–52.

Hart, Jason (2014), 'Children and Forced Migration', in Elena Fiddian-Qasmiyeh, Gil Loescher, Katy Long, and Nando Sigona (eds.), *The Oxford Handbook of Refugee and Forced Migration Studies* (Oxford: Oxford University Press), 383–394.

Hartmann, Melanie (2017), 'Spatializing Inequalities: The Situation of Women in Refugee Centres in Germany', in Susanne Buckley-Zistel and Ulrike Krause (eds.), *Gender, Violence, Refugees* (Studies in Forced Migration, 37; New York, Oxford: Berghahn), 102–126.

Hearn, Jeff (2004), 'From Hegemonic Masculinity to the Hegemony of Men', *Feminist Theory*, 5 (1), 49–72.

(2012), 'A Multi-faceted Power Analysis of Men's Violence to Known Women: From Hegemonic Masculinity to the Hegemony of Men', *The Sociological Review*, 60 (4), 589–610.

(2013), 'Vernachlässigte Intersektionalitäten in der Männerforschung: Alter(n), Virtualität, Transnationalität', in Helma Lutz, María Teresa Herrera Vivar, and Linda Supik (eds.), *Fokus Intersektionalität* (Geschlecht und Gesellschaft, 47: Springer Fachmedien Wiesbaden), 115–135.

(2015), *Men of the World: Genders, Globalizations, Transnational Times* (London: Sage).

Hecker, Tobias, Fetz, Simon, Ainamani, Herbert, and Elbert, Thomas (2015), 'The Cycle of Violence: Associations between Exposure to Violence, Trauma-Related Symptoms and Aggression—Findings from Congolese Refugees in Uganda', *Journal of Traumatic Stress*, 28 (5), 448–455.

Hedlund, Anna (2018), '"We Are Not Part of Their War": Hutu Women's Experiences of Rebel Life in the Eastern DRC Conflict', in Mary Michele Connellan and Christiane Fröhlich (eds.), *A Gendered Lens for Genocide Prevention* (London: Palgrave Macmillan UK), 111–132.

Henry, Shayne, Rizvi, Farha, and Tchoukleva, Ioana (2013), 'Promoting Accountability for Conflict-Related Sexual Violence Against Men: A Comparative Legal Analysis of International and Domestic Laws Relating to IDP and Refugee Men in Uganda', *Refugee Law Project Working Paper Series*, No. 24, 1–83.

Hertogh, Marc (2018), *Nobody's Law: Legal Consciousness and Legal Alienation in Everyday Life* (London: Palgrave Macmillan UK).

Heusinger, Judith von (2017), *Kulturelle Konflikte in der Entwicklungszusammenarbeit: Eine Analyse von Programmen im Bereich der reproduktiven Gesundheit* (Wiesbaden: Springer).

Hilhorst, Dorothea and Jansen, Bram J. (2010), 'Humanitarian Space as Arena: A Perspective on the Everyday Politics of Aid', *Development and Change*, 41 (6), 1117–1139.

Hilhorst, Dorothea, Porter, Holly, and Gordon, Rachel (2018), 'Gender, Sexuality, and Violence in Humanitarian Crises', *Disasters*, 42 (S1), S3–S16.

Hirschauer, Sabine (2014), *The Securitization of Rape: Women, War and Sexual Violence* (Basingstokeact: Palgrave Macmillan).

Holzer, Elizabeth (2013), 'What Happens to Law in a Refugee Camp?', *Law & Society Review*, 47 (4), 837–872.

(2015), *The Concerned Women of Buduburam: Refugee Activists and Humanitarian Dilemmas* (Ithaca: Cornell University Press).

Honwana, Alcinda (2011), *Child Soldiers in Africa* (Philadelphia: University of Pennsylvania Press).

Horn, Rebecca (2010), 'Exploring the Impact of Displacement and Encampment on Domestic Violence in Kakuma Refugee Camp', *Journal of Refugee Studies*, 23 (3), 356–376.

Horst, Cindy (2006), *Transnational Nomads: How Somalis Cope with Refugee Life in the Dadaab Camps of Kenya* (Oxford: Berghahn).

   (2008), 'The Transnational Political Engagements of Refugees: Remittance Sending Practices amongst Somalis in Norway', *Conflict, Security & Development*, 8 (3), 317–339.

Horst, Cindy and Grabska, Katarzyna (2015), 'Flight and Exile: Uncertainty in the Context of Conflict-Induced Displacement', *Social Analysis*, 59 (1), 1–18.

Hovil, Lucy (2016), *Refugees, Conflict and the Search for Belonging* (Cham: Palgrave Macmillan).

Hugman, Richard, Pittaway, Eileen, and Bartolomei, Linda (2011), 'When "Do No Harm" Is Not Enough: The Ethics of Research with Refugees and Other Vulnerable Groups', *British Journal of Social Work*, 41 (7), 1271–1287.

Human Rights Watch (2017), *Heavy Fighting in Eastern DR Congo, Threats to Civilians Increase* (www.hrw.org/blog-feed/democratic-republic-congo-crisis#blog-309854).

   (2018), *DR Congo: Mass Rape Trial Crucial for Justice* (www.hrw.org/news/2018/11/29/dr-congo-mass-rape-trial-crucial-justice).

Hussain, Dilwar and Bhushan, Braj (2010), 'Cultural Factors Promoting Coping among Tibetan Refugees: A Qualitative Investigation', *Mental Health, Religion & Culture*, 14 (6), 575–587.

Hutchinson, Mary and Dorsett, Pat (2012), 'What Does the Literature Say about Resilience in Refugee People? Implications for Practice', *Journal of Social Inclusion*, 3 (2), 55–78.

Hyndman, Jennifer (1996), Geographies of Displacement: Gender, Culture and Power in UNHCR Refugee Camps, Kenya, DPhil Thesis, Department of Geography, University of British Columbia.

   (1997), 'Refugee Self-management and the Question of Governance', *Refuge*, 16 (2), 16–22.

   (2000), *Managing Displacement. Refugees and the Politics of Humanitarianism*, eds. David Campbell and Michael J. Shapiro (Borderlines, 16; Minneapolis, London: University of Minnesota Press).

   (2004), 'Refugee Camps as Conflict Zones. The Politics of Gender', in Wenona Giles and Jennifer Hyndman (eds.), *Sites of Violence—Gender and Conflict Zones* (Berkeley, Los Angeles: University of California Press), 193–212.

Hyndman, Jennifer and Giles, Wenona (2011), 'Waiting for What? The Feminization of Asylum in Protracted Situations', *Gender, Place & Culture*, 18 (3), 361–379.

IASC (2015), *Guidelines for Integrating Gender-Based Violence Interventions in Humanitarian Action: Reducing Risk, Promoting Resilience and Aiding Recovery* (Geneva: IASC).

Ilcan, Suzan and Rygiel, Kim (2015), '"Resiliency Humanitarianism": Responsibilizing Refugees through Humanitarian Emergency Governance in the Camp', *International Political Sociology*, 9 (4), 333–351.

Indra, Doreen Marie (1987), 'Gender: A Key Dimension of the Refugee Experience', *Refuge*, 6 (3), 3–4.

(1989), 'Ethnic Human Rights and Feminist Theory: Gender Implications for Refugee Studies and Practice', *Journal of Refugee Studies*, 2 (2), 221–242.

(1993), 'The Spirit of the Gift and the Politics of Resettlement: The Canadian Private Sponsorship of South East Asians', in Vaughan Robinson (ed.), *The International Refugee Crisis: British and Canadian Responses* (London: Palgrave Macmillan UK), 229–254.

(1999a), 'Not a "Room of One's Own". Engendering Forced Migration Knowledge and Practice', in Doreen Marie Indra (ed.), *Engendering Forced Migration: Theory and Practice* (New York, Oxford: Berghahn Books), 1–22.

Indra, Doreen Marie (ed.) (1999b), *Engendering Forced Migration: Theory and Practice* (Refugee and Forced Migration Studies, 5; New York, Oxford: Berghahn).

Inhetveen, Katharina (2006), '"Because We Are Refugees": Utilizing a Legal Label', *New Issues in Refugee Research*, No. 130.

(2010), *Die Politische Ordnung des Flüchtlingslagers. Akteure - Macht - Organisation. Eine Ethnographie im Südlichen Afrika* (Bielefeld: Transcript Verlag).

Iyakaremye, Innocent and Mukagatare, Claudine (2016), 'Forced Migration and Sexual Abuse: Experience of Congolese Adolescent Girls in Kigeme Refugee Camp, Rwanda', *Health Psychology Report*, 4 (3), 261–271.

Izugbara, Chimaraoke, Muthuri, Stella, Muuo, Sheru, Egesa, Carolyne, Franchi, Giorgia, Mcalpine, Alys, Bacchus, Loraine, and Hossain, Mazeda (2018), '"They Say Our Work Is Not Halal': Experiences and Challenges of Refugee Community Workers Involved in Gender-Based Violence Prevention and Care in Dadaab, Kenya', *Journal of Refugee Studies*, published online first, doi: 10.1093/jrs/fey055.

Jacobsen, Karen, Ayoub, Maysa, and Johnson, Alice (2014), 'Sudanese Refugees in Cairo: Remittances and Livelihoods', *Journal of Refugee Studies*, 27 (1), 145–159.

Jaji, Rose (2009a), 'Masculinity on Unstable Ground: Young Refugee Men in Nairobi, Kenya', *Journal of Refugee Studies*, 22 (2), 177–194.

(2009b), Refugee Woman and the Experiences of Local Integration in Nairobi, Kenya, PhD Thesis, BIGSAS, Bayreuth University.

(2012), 'Social Technology and Refugee Encampment in Kenya', *Journal of Refugee Studies*, 25 (2), 221–238.

Janmyr, Maja (2014a), 'Attributing Wrongful Conduct of Implementing Partners to UNHCR: International Responsibility and Human Rights Violations in Refugee Camps', *Journal of International Humanitarian Legal Studies*, 5 (1–2), 42–69.

(2014b), *Protecting Civilians in Refugee Camps. Unable and Unwilling States, UNHCR and International Responsibility* (Leiden: Brill).

(2017), 'Military Recruitment of Sudanese Refugee Men in Uganda: A Tale of National Patronage and International Failure', in Susanne Buckley-Zistel and Ulrike Krause (eds.), *Gender, Violence, Refugees* (Studies in Forced Migration, 37; New York, Oxford: Berghahn), 219–238.

Jansen, Bram (2008), 'Between Vulnerability and Assertiveness: Negotiating Resettlement in Kakuma Refugee Camp, Kenya', *African Affairs*, 107 (429), 569–587.

(2011), The Accidental City: Violence, Economy and Humanitarianism in Kakuma Refugee Camp Kenya, PhD Thesis, Wageningen School of Social Sciences, University of Wageningen.

Johnson, Heather L. (2011), 'Click to Donate: Visual Images, Constructing Victims and Imagining the Female Refugee', *Third World Quarterly*, 32 (6), 1015–1037.

Johnson, Howard and Thompson, Andrew (2008), 'The Development and Maintenance of Post-traumatic Stress Disorder (PTSD) in Civilian Adult Survivors of War Trauma and Torture: A Review', *Clinical Psychology Review*, 28 (1), 36–47.

Johnson, Kirsten, Scott, Jennifer, Brughita, Bigy, Kisielewski, Michael, Asher, Jana, Ong, Ricardo, and Lawry, Lynn (2010), 'Association of Sexual Violence and Human Rights Violations With Physical and Mental Health in Territories of the Eastern Democratic Republic of the Congo', *Journal of the American Medical Association*, 304 (5), 553–562.

Johnsson, Anders B. (1989), 'The International Protection of Women Refugees A Summary of Principal Problems and Issues', *International Journal of Refugee Law*, 1 (2), 221–232.

Jolliffe, Pia (2015), 'Night-Time and Refugees: Evidence from the Thai-Myanmar Border', *Journal of Refugee Studies*, 29 (1), 1–18.

Kabachnik, Peter, Grabowska, Magdalena, Regulska, Joanna, Mitchneck, Beth, and Mayorova, Olga V. (2013), 'Traumatic Masculinities: The Gendered Geographies of Georgian IDPs from Abkhazia', *Gender, Place & Culture*, 20 (6), 773–793.

Kagan, Michael (2011), '"We Live in a Country of UNHCR" The UN Surrogate State and Refugee Policy in the Middle East', *New Issues in Refugee Research*, No. 201.

Kaiser, Tania (2000), 'UNHCR's Withdrawal from Kiryandongo—Anatomy of a Handover', *New Issues in Refugee Research*, No. 32.

(2005), 'Participating in Development? Refugee Protection, Politics and Developmental Approaches to Refugee Management in Uganda', *Third World Quarterly*, 26 (2), 351–367.

(2006), 'Between a Camp and a Hard Place: Rights, Livelihood and Experiences of the Local Settlement System for Long-Term Refugees in Uganda', *The Journal of Modern African Studies*, 44 (4), 597–621.

Karunakara, Unni, Neuner, Frank, Schauer, Maggie, Singh, Kavita, Hill, Kenneth, Elbert, Thomas, and Burnha, Gilbert (2004), 'Traumatic Events and Symptoms of Post-traumatic Stress Disorder amongst Sudanese Nationals, Refugees and Ugandans in the West Nile', *African Health Sciences*, 4 (2), 83–93.

Kelly, Jocelyn, Kabanga, Justin, Cragin, Will, Alcayna-Stevens, Lys, Haider, Sadia, and Vanrooyen, Michael J. (2012), '"If Your Husband Doesn't Humiliate You, Other People Won't": Gendered Attitudes towards Sexual Violence in Eastern Democratic Republic of Congo', *Global Public Health*, 7 (3), 285–298.

Kelly, Liz (2013), *Surviving Sexual Violence* (Cambridge, Oxford: Polity Press).

Kelly, Liz, Burton, Sheila, and Regan, Linda (1996), 'Beyond Victim or Survivor: Sexual Violence, Identity and Feminist Theory and Practice', in Lisa Adkins and Vicki Merchant (eds.), *Sexualizing the Social: Power and the Organization of Sexuality* (London: Palgrave), 77–101.

Kennedy, Angie C. and Prock, Kristen A. (2018), '"I Still Feel Like I Am Not Normal": A Review of the Role of Stigma and Stigmatization among Female Survivors of Child Sexual Abuse, Sexual Assault, and Intimate Partner Violence', *Trauma, Violence, & Abuse*, 19 (5), 512–527.

Keygnaert, Ines, Vettenburg, Nicole, and Temmerman, Marleen (2012), 'Hidden Violence Is Silent Rape: Sexual and Gender-Based Violence in Refugees, Asylum Seekers and Undocumented Migrants in Belgium and the Netherlands', *Culture, Health & Sexuality*, 14 (5), 505–520.

Khawaja, Marwan (2004), 'Domestic Violence in Refugee Camps in Jordan', *International Journal of Gynecology & Obstetrics*, 86 (1), 67–69.

Khawaja, Marwan, Linos, Natalia, and El-Roueiheb, Zeina (2007), 'Attitudes of Men and Women towards Wife Beating: Findings from Palestinian Refugee Camps in Jordan', *Journal of Family Violence*, 23 (3), 211–218.

Khawaja, Nigar G., White, Katherine M., Schweitzer, Robert, and Greenslade, Jaimi (2008), 'Difficulties and Coping Strategies of Sudanese Refugees: A Qualitative Approach', *Transcultural Psychiatry*, 45 (3), 489–512.

Kibreab, Gaim (1993), 'The Myth of Dependency among Camp Refugees in Somalia 1979–1989', *Journal of Refugee Studies*, 6 (4), 321–349.

——— (2004), 'Pulling the Wool over the Eyes of the Strangers: Refugee Deceit and Trickery in Institutionalized Settings', *Journal of Refugee Studies*, 17 (1), 1–26.

——— (2007), 'Why Governments Prefer Spatially Segregated Settlement Sites for Urban Refugees', *Refuge*, 24 (1), 27–35.

Koçak, Mert (2020), 'Who Is "Queerer" and Deserves Resettlement?: Queer Asylum Seekers and Their Deservingness of Refugee Status in Turkey', *Middle East Critique*, 29 (1), 29–46.

Kohli, Anjalee, Perrin, Nancy, Mpanano, Remy Mitima, Banywesize, Luhazi, Mirindi, Alfred Bacikenge, Banywesize, Jean Heri, Mitima, Clovis Murhula, Binkurhorhwa, Arsène Kajabika, Bufole, Nadine Mwinja, and Glass, Nancy (2015), 'Family and Community Driven Response to Intimate Partner Violence in Post-conflict Settings', *Social Science & Medicine*, 146, 276–284.

Korac, Maja (2009), *Remaking Home: Reconstructing Life, Place and Identity in Rome and Amsterdam* (Studies in Forced Migration, 26; New York, Oxford: Berghahn).

Krause, Ulrike (2013), *Linking Refugee Protection with Development Assistance. Analyses with a Case Study in Uganda* (Baden-Baden: Nomos).

——— (2015a), 'A Continuum of Violence? Linking Sexual and Gender-Based Violence during Conflict, Flight, and Encampment', *Refugee Survey Quarterly*, 34 (4), 1–19.

——— (2015b), 'Zwischen Schutz und Scham? Flüchtlingslager, Gewalt und Geschlechterverhältnisse', *Peripherie: Zeitschrift für Politik und Ökonomie in der Dritten Welt*, 35 (138/139), 235–259.

——— (2016a), 'Limitations of Development-Oriented Assistance in Uganda', *Forced Migration Review*, 52, 51–53.

——— (2016b), 'Ethische Überlegungen zur Feldforschung. Impulse für die Untersuchung konfliktbedingter Flucht', *CCS Working Paper Series*, No. 20.

——— (2016c), 'Konflikt-Flucht-Nexus: Globales Ausmaß, genderbezogene Auswirkungen und politische Relevanz', *S&F Sicherheit und Frieden*, 34 (1), 46–51.

(2016d), 'Wie bewältigen Flüchtlinge die Lebensbedingungen in Flüchtlingslagern? Ergebnisse aus einer empirischen Analyse zu kongolesischen Flüchtlingen in Uganda', *Zeitschrift für Friedens- und Konfliktforschung*, 5 (2), 189–220.

(2016e), 'Hegemonie von Männern? Flüchtlingslager, Maskulinitäten und Gewalt in Uganda', *Soziale Probleme*, 27 (1), 119–145.

(2016f), '"It Seems Like You Don't Have Identity, You Don't Belong." Reflexionen über das Flüchtlingslabel und dessen Implikationen', *Zeitschrift für Internationale Beziehungen*, 23 (1), 8–37.

(2017a), 'Escaping Conflicts and Being Safe? Post-conflict Refugee Camps and the Continuum of Violence', in Susanne Buckley-Zistel and Ulrike Krause (eds.), *Gender, Violence, Refugees* (Studies in Forced Migration, 37; New York, Oxford: Berghahn), 173–196.

(2017b), 'Researching Forced Migration. Critical Reflections on Research Ethics during Fieldwork', *RSC Working Paper Series,* No. 123.

(2017c), '*Die* Flüchtling—der Flüchtling als Frau. Genderreflexiver Zugang', in Cinur Ghaderi and Thomas Eppenstein (eds.), *Flüchtlinge: Multiperspektivische Zugänge* (Wiesbaden: Springer), 79–93.

(2018a), 'Gewalterfahrungen von Geflüchteten', State-of-Research Papier, No. 03, Verbundprojekt 'Flucht: Forschung und Transfer' (Osnabrück: Institut für Migrationsforschung und Interkulturelle Studien (IMIS) der Universität Osnabrück, Bonn: Internationales Konversionszentrum Bonn (BICC)).

(2018b), 'Protection | Victimisation | Agency? Gender-Sensitive Perspectives on Present-Day Refugee Camps', *Zeitgeschichte*, 45 (4), 483–506.

(2019a), 'Gender Relations in Confined Spaces. Conditions, Scope and Forms of Sexual Violence against Women in Conflict-Related Refugee Camps', *Forschung DSF*, No. 50 (Osnabrück: Deutsche Stiftung Friedensforschung; https://bundesstiftung-friedensforschung.de/blog/for schung-dsf-no-50/).

(2019b), 'Geflüchtete und ihre Sicherheit: humanitärer Schutz vs. Handlungen der Geflüchteten', *L.I.S.A. Das Wissenschaftsportal der Gerda Henkel Stiftung* (https://lisa.gerda-henkel-stiftung.de/gefluech tete_und_ihre_sicherheit_humanitaerer_schutz_vs._handlungen_der_ gefluechteten?nav_id=8017).

(2020), 'Violence against Women in Camps? Exploring Links between Refugee Camp Conditions and the Prevalence of Violence', in Katharina Crepaz, Ulrich Becker, and Elisabeth Wacker (eds.), *Health in Diversity—Diversity in Health: (Forced) Migration, Social Diversification, and Health in a Changing World* (Wiesbaden: Springer), 187–208.

(2021a), '(Un)sichtbar und (un)sicher? Humanitäre Politiken und Praktiken um Frauen in Flüchtlingssituationen', in Antje Daniel, Rirhandu Mageza-Barthel, Melanie Richter-Montpetit, and Tanja Scheiterbauer (eds.), *Gewalt, Krieg und Flucht. Feministische Perspektiven auf Sicherheit* (Opladen: Verlag Barbara Budrich) , 159–179.

(2021b), 'Colonial Roots of the 1951 Refugee Convention and Its Effects on the Global Refugee Regime', *Journal of International Relations and Development* , published online first, doi: 10.1057/s41268-020-00205-9.

(forthcoming), 'Kontinuitäten von Gewalt auf der Flucht mit Fokus auf Unterkünfte und Aufnahmelagern', in J. Olaf Kleist, Dimitra Dermitzaki, Bahar Oghalai, and Sabrina Zajak (eds.), *Gewaltschutz in Geflüchtetenunterkünften: Theorie, Empirie, Praxis* (Bielefeld: transcript).

Krause, Ulrike and Gato, Joshua (2019), 'Escaping Humanitarian Aid in Camps? Rethinking the Links between Refugees' Encampment, Urban Self-settlement, Coping and Peace', *Friedens-Warte*, 92 (1/2), 76–97.

Krause, Ulrike and Schmidt, Hannah (2018), '"Being Beaten Like a Drum" Gefahren, Humanitarismus und Resilienz von Frauen in Flüchtlingssituationen', *GENDER. Zeitschrift für Geschlecht, Kultur und Gesellschaft*, 2018 (2), 47–62.

(2019), '"Refugee-led CBOs": Gruppen und Organisationen von Geflüchteten und ihre Rolle für Schutz- und Unterstützungsleistungen', L.I.S.A. Das Wissenschaftsportal der Gerda Henkel Stiftung (https://lisa.gerda-henkel-stiftung.de/refugee_led_cbos_gruppen_und_organisationen_von_gefluechteten_und_ihre_rolle_fuer_schutz_und_unterstuetzungsleistungen).

(2020), 'Refugees as Actors? Critical Reflections on Global Refugee Policies on Self-reliance and Resilience', *Journal of Refugee Studies*, 33 (1), 22–41.

Krause, Ulrike and von Denkowski, Cordula (2020), 'Transfer of Knowledge for and with Whom? Ethical Reflections on Participatory Research with Displaced People', in Monika Gonser, Karin Zimmer, Nichola Mühlhauser, and Danielle Gluns (eds.), *Wissensmobilisierung und Transfer in der Fluchtforschung: Kommunikation, Beratung und gemeinsames Forschungshandeln* (Münster: Waxmann Verlag), 137–149.

Krause, Ulrike and Williams, Timothy (2020), 'Flexible Ethikgremien. Impulse zur Institutionalisierung ethisch verantwortlicher Feldforschung in der Konflikt- und Fluchtforschung', *Soziale Probleme*, published online first, doi: 10.1007/s41059-020-00072-z.

Kuckartz, Udo (2014), *Qualitative Text Analysis: A Guide to Methods, Practice & Using Software* (London: SAGE).

Kumsa, Martha Kuwee (2006), '"No! I'm Not a Refugee!" The Poetics of BeLonging among Young Oromos in Toronto', *Journal of Refugee Studies*, 19 (2), 230–255.

Laudati, Ann and Mertens, Charlotte (2019), 'Resources and Rape: Congo's (toxic) Discursive Complex', *African Studies Review*, 62 (4), 57–82.

Lazreg, Marnia (2018), *The Eloquence of Silence: Algerian Women in Question* (New York: Routledge).

Lecadet, Clara (2016), 'Refugee Politics: Self-organized "Government" and Protests in the Agamé Refugee Camp (2005–13)', *Journal of Refugee Studies*, 29 (2), 187–207.

Lee, Ah-Jung (2009), 'Understanding and Addressing the Phenomenon of 'Child Soldiers'—The Gap between the Global Humanitarian Discourse and the Local Understandings and Experiences of Young People's Military Recruitment', *RSC Working Paper Series*, No. 52.

Leenders, Reinoud (2009), 'Refugee Warriors or War Refugees? Iraqi Refugees' Predicament in Syria, Jordan and Lebanon', *Mediterranean Politics*, 14 (3), 343–363.

Lems, Annika (2018), *Being-Here: Placemaking in a World of Movement* (New York, Oxford: Berghahn).

Lindley, Anna (2010), *The Early Morning Phone Call: Somali Refugees' Remittances* (Studies in Forced Migration, 28; New York, Oxford: Berghahn).

Lindorfer, Simone (2009), *Verletzlichkeit und Macht. Eine psycho-soziale Studie zur Situation von Faruen und Mädchen im Nachkriegsliberia* (Köln: medica mondiale).

Lingelbach, Jochen (2020), *On the Edges of Whiteness: Polish Refugees in British Colonial Africa during and after the Second World War* (New York, Oxford: Berghahn).

Lippert, Randy (1999), 'Governing Refugees: The Relevance of Governmentality to Understanding the International Refugee Regime', *Alternatives: Global, Local, Political*, 24 (3), 295–328.

Lischer, Sarah K. (2005), *Dangerous Sanctuaries: Refugee Camps, Civil War, and the Dilemmas of Humanitarian Aid* (Ithaca: Cornell University Press).

——— (2007), 'Causes and Consequences of Conflict-Induced Displacement', *Civil Wars*, 9 (2), 142–155.

Lister, Ruth (2004), *Poverty* (Cambridge: Polity Press).

Ljungdell, Stina (1989), *Refugees? Female Asylum Seekers and Refugee Status: Guidelines for Assistance* (Geneva: UNHCR).

Loescher, Gil and Milner, James (2005), 'Protracted Refugee Situations: Domestic and International Security Implications', *The Adelphi Papers*, 45 (375), 7–84.

Loescher, Gil, Betts, Alexander, and Milner, James (2012), *UNHCR: The Politics and Practice of Refugee Protection* (2nd edn.; London, New York: Routledge Global Institutions).

Logie, Carmen H. and Daniel, CarolAnn (2016), '"My Body Is Mine": Qualitatively Exploring Agency among Internally Displaced Women Participants in a Small-Group Intervention in Leogane, Haiti', *Global Public Health*, 11 (1–2), 122–134.

Lombard, Nancy (ed.) (2018), *The Routledge Handbook of Gender and Violence* (Routledge Handbooks, Abingdon; New York: Routledge).

Lomo, Zachary (2000), 'The Struggle for Protection of the Rights of Refugees and IDPs in Africa: Making the Existing International Legal Regime Work', *Berkeley Journal of International Law*, 18 (2), 268–284.

Lorenz, Daniel F. and Dittmer, Cordula (2016), 'Resilience in Catastrophes, Disasters and Emergencies: Socio-scientific Perspectives', in Martin Endreß and Andrea Maurer (eds.), *Resilience in Social and Economic Spheres* (New York: Springer), 25–59.

Loschmann, Craig, Bilgili, Özge, and Siegel, Melissa (2019), 'Considering the Benefits of Hosting Refugees: Evidence of Refugee Camps Influencing Local Labour Market Activity and Economic Welfare in Rwanda', *IZA Journal of Development and Migration*, 9 (1), 1–23.

Lubkemann, Stephen C. (2008a), *Culture in Chaos. An Anthropology of the Social Condition in War* (Chicago: University of Chicago Press).

    (2008b), 'Involuntary Immobility: On a Theoretical Invisibility in Forced Migration Studies', *Journal of Refugee Studies*, 21 (4), 454–475.

Lukunka, Barbra (2011), 'New Big Men: Refugee Emasculation as a Human Security Issue', *International Migration*, 50 (5), 130–141.

Luongo, Katherine (2015), 'Allegations, Evidence, and Evaluation. Asylum Seeking in a World of Witchcraft', in Iris Berger, Tricia Redeker Hepner, Benjamin N. Lawrance, Joanna T. Tague, and Meredith Terretta (eds.), *African Asylum at a Crossroads. Activism, Expert Testimony, and Refugee Rights* (Athens: Ohio University Press), 182–202.

Lwambo, Desiree (2013), '"Before the War, I Was a Man": Men and Masculinities in the Eastern Democratic Republic of Congo', *Gender & Development*, 21 (1), 47–66.

Lyytinen, Eveliina (2017), 'Informal Places of Protection: Congolese Refugees' "Communities of Trust" in Kampala, Uganda', *Journal of Ethnic and Migration Studies*, 43 (6), 991–1008.

Mackenzie, Catriona, McDowell, Christopher, and Pittaway, Eileen (2007), 'Beyond "Do No Harm": The Challenge of Constructing Ethical Relationships in Refugee Research', *Journal of Refugee Studies*, 20 (2), 299–319.

MacKenzie, Megan (2012), *Female Soldiers in Sierra Leone: Sex, Security, and Post-conflict Development* (New York, London: New York University Press).

Maedl, Anna (2010), Towards Evidence-Based Post War Reconstruction, Doctoral Thesis, Fachbereich Psychologie, Universität Konstanz.

Maercker, Andreas (2009), 'Symptomatik, Klassifikation und Epidemiologie', in Andreas Maercker (ed.), *Posttraumatische Belastungsstörungen* (Berlin, Heidelberg: Springer), 13–32.

Malkki, Liisa H. (1995a), *Purity and Exile: Violence, Memory, and National Cosmology among Hutu Refugees in Tanzania* (Chicago, London: The University of Chicago Press).

(1995b), 'Refugees and Exile: From "Refugee Studies" to the National Order of Things', *Annual Review of Anthropology*, 24, 495–523.

Manchanda, Rita (2004), 'Gender Conflict and Displacement: Contesting "Infantilisation" of Forced Migrant Women', *Economic and Political Weekly*, 39 (37), 4179–4186.

Mann, Gillian (2012), 'Beyond War: "Suffering" among Displaced Congolese Children in Dar es Salaam', *Development in Practice*, 22 (4), 448–459.

Markard, Nora (2007), 'Fortschritte im Flüchtlingsrecht? Gender Guidelines und geschlechtsspezifische Verfolgung', *Kritische Justiz: Vierteljahresschrift für Recht und Politik*, 27 (4), 373–390.

Marshall, Ruth (1995), 'Refugees, Feminine Plural', *Refugees* 100 (i), 3–9.

Martin, Guy (1995), 'International Solidarity and Co-operation in Assistance to African Refugees: Burden-Sharing or Burden-Shifting?', *International Journal of Refugee Law*, 7 (Special Issue), 250–273.

Martin, Susan F. (2004), *Refugee Women* (2nd edn.; Lantham: Lexington Books).

(2017), 'UNHCR Policy on Refugee Women: A 25-Year Retrospective', in Susanne Buckley-Zistel and Ulrike Krause (eds.), *Gender, Violence, Refugees* (Studies in Forced Migration, 37; New York, Oxford: Berghahn), 21–43.

Martin, Susan F. and Tirman, John (2009), *Women, Migration, and Conflict: Breaking a Deadly Cycle* (Heidelberg, London, New York: Springer).

Mayblin, Lucy (2017), *Asylum after Empire: Colonial Legacies in the Politics of Asylum Seeking* (Kilombo: international relations and colonial questions; London; New York: Roman & Littlefield International).

McConnachie, Kirsten (2012), 'Rethinking the "Refugee Warrior": The Karen National Union and Refugee Protection on the Thai–Burma Border', *Journal of Human Rights Practice*, 4 (1), 30–56.

(2014), *Governing Refugees: Justice, Order and Legal Pluralism* (Abingdon: Routledge).

(2016), 'Camps of Containment: A Genealogy of the Refugee Camp', *Humanity: An International Journal of Human Rights, Humanitarianism, and Development*, 7 (3), 397–412.

McGinnis, Rachel E. (2016), 'Sexual Victimization of Male Refugees and Migrants: Camps, Homelessness, and Survival Sex', *Dignity: A Journal on Sexual Exploitation and Violence*, 1 (1), 1–8.

Meger, Sara (2010), 'Rape of the Congo: Understanding Sexual Violence in the Conflict in the Democratic Republic of Congo', *Journal of Contemporary African Studies*, 28 (2), 119–135.

Merry, Sally E. (1990), *Getting Justice and Getting Even: Legal Consciousness among Working-Class Americans* (Chicago, London: University of Chicago Press).

Mertens, Charlotte (2016), 'Sexual Violence in the Congo Free State: Archival Traces and Present Reconfigurations', *Australasian Review of African Studies*, 37 (1), 6–20.

(2019), 'Undoing Research on Sexual Violence in Eastern Democratic Republic of Congo', *ACME: An International E-journal for Critical Geographies*, 18 (3).

Meyer, Sarah (2006), 'The "Refugee Aid and Development" Approach in Uganda: Empowerment and Self-reliance of Refugees in Practice', *New Issues in Refugee Research*, No. 131.

Middleton, John and Winter, Edward Henry (1963), *Witchcraft and Sorcery in East Africa* (London, New York: Routledge).

Milner, James (2005), 'The Militarization and Demilitarization of Refugee Camps in Guinea', in Nicolas Florquin and Eric G. Berman (eds.), *Armed and Aimless. Armed Groups, Guns, and Human Security in the ECOWAS Region* (Geneva: Small Arms Survey), 144–179.

(2009), 'Refugees and the Regional Dynamics of Peacebuilding', *Refugee Survey Quarterly*, 28 (1), 13–30.

(2014), 'Protracted Refugee Situations', in Elena Fiddian-Qasmiyeh, Gil Loescher, Katy Long, and Nando Sigona (eds.), *The Oxford Handbook of Refugee and Forced Migration Studies* (Oxford: Oxford University Press), 151–162.

Molony, Barbara and Nelson, Jennifer (eds.) (2019), *Women's Activism and "Second Wave" Feminism: Transnational Histories* (London, Oxford, New York, New Delhi, Sydney: Bloomsbury Academic).

MONUSCO and OHCHR (2016), Accountability for Human Rights Violations and Abuses in the DRC: Achievements, Challenges and Way forward (1 January 2014–31 March 2016) (www.ohchr.org/Documents/Countries/CD/UNJHROAccountabiliteReport2016_en.pdf).

Mookherjee, Nayanika (2015), *The Spectral Wound: Sexual Violence, Public Memories, and the Bangladesh War of 1971* (Durham: Duke University Press).

Moore, Will H. and Shellman, Stephen M. (2004), 'Fear of Persecution: Forced Migration, 1952–1995', *Journal of Conflict Resolution*, 48 (5), 723–745.

(2006), 'Refugee or Internally Displaced Person? To Where Should One Flee?', *Comparative Political Studies*, 39 (5), 599–622.

Moser, Caroline N. O. and Clark, Fiona (eds.) (2001), *Victims, Perpetrators or Actors? Gender, Armed Conflict and Political Violence* (London, New York: Zed Books).

Mourtada, Rima, Schlecht, Jennifer, and DeJong, Jocelyn (2017), 'A Qualitative Study Exploring Child Marriage Practices among Syrian Conflict-affected Populations in Lebanon', *Conflict and Health*, 11 (1), 27.

Muggah, Robert (2006a), 'Protection Failures: Outward and Inward Militarization of Refugee Settlements and IDP Camps in Uganda', in Robert Muggah (ed.), *No Refuge: The Crisis of Refugee Militarization in Africa* (London, New York: Zed Books in Association with BICC and Small Arms Survey), 89–136.

Muggah, Robert (ed.) (2006b), *No Refuge: The Crisis of Refugee Militarization in Africa* (London, New York: Zed Books in Association with BICC and Small Arms Survey).

Mulumba, Deborah (2010), *Women Refugees in Uganda: Gender Relations, Livelihood Security, and Reproductive Health* (Kampala: Fountain Publishers).

Mulumeoderhwa, Maroyi (2020), '"A Slap of Love": A Way of Showing Love and Resolving Conflict Among Young People in South Kivu, Democratic Republic of Congo', *Journal of Interpersonal Violence*, published online first, doi: 10.1177/0886260519897335.

Murrey, Amber (2017), 'Decolonising the Imagined Geographies of "Witchcraft"', *Third World Thematics: A TWQ Journal*, 2 (2–3), 157–179.

Musaazi, Moses (2014), 'Technology, Production and Partnership Innovation in Uganda', *Forced Migration Review*, Supplement Issue on Innovation and Refugees, 14.

Nabukeera, Christine (2015), A Feminist Dialogic Encounter with Refugee Women, DPhil Thesis, Faculty of Graduate Studies, York University.

Nagai, Mari, Karunakara, Unni, Rowley, Elizabeth, and Burnham, Gilbert (2008), 'Violence against Refugees, Non-refugees and Host Populations in Southern Sudan and Northern Uganda', *Glob Public Health*, 3 (3), 249–270.

Nissim-Sabat, Marilyn (2009), *Neither Victim nor Survivor: Thinking toward a New Humanity* (Lanham: Lexington Books).

Nyanzi, Stella and Karamagi, Andrew (2015), 'The Social-Political Dynamics of the Anti-homosexuality Legislation in Uganda', *Agenda*, 29 (1), 24–38.

Nyers, Peter (2006), *Rethinking Refugees: Beyond States of Emergency* (New York: Routledge).

OHCHR (2011), *Report of the Panel on Remedies and Reparations for Victims of Sexual Violence in the Democratic Republic of Congo to the High Commissioner for Human Rights* (Geneva: OHCHR; www.refworld.org/docid/4d708ae32.html).

(2019), *55 Sentenced to Life Imprisonment: A Victory against Impunity in DRC* (www.ohchr.org/EN/NewsEvents/Pages/AvictoryagainstimpunityinDRCongo.aspx).

Oka, Rahul C. (2011), 'Unlikely Cities in the Desert: The Informal Economy as Causal Agent for Permanent "Urban" Sustainability in Kakuma Refugee Camp, Kenya', *Urban Anthropology and Studies of Cultural Systems and World Economic Development*, 40 (3–4), 223–262.

(2014), 'Coping with the Refugee Wait: The Role of Consumption, Normalcy, and Dignity in Refugee Lives at Kakuma Refugee Camp, Kenya', *American Anthropologist*, 116 (1), 23–37.

Olivius, Elisabeth (2013), 'Gender Equality and Neo-liberal Governmentality in Refugee Camps', *St Antony's International Review*, 9 (1), 53–69.

(2014), '(Un)Governable Subjects: The Limits of Refugee Participation in the Promotion of Gender Equality in Humanitarian Aid', *Journal of Refugee Studies*, 27 (1), 42–61.

(2016), 'Refugee Men as Perpetrators, Allies or Troublemakers? Emerging Discourses on Men and Masculinities in Humanitarian Aid', *Women's Studies International Forum*, 56, 56–65.

Olsen, Odd Einar and Scharffscher, Kristin S. (2004), 'Rape in Refugee Camps as Organisational Failures', *The International Journal of Human Rights*, 8 (4), 377–397.

Oltmer, Jochen (2017), 'Protecting Refugees in the Weimar Republic', *Journal of Refugee Studies*, 30 (2), 318–336.

Omata, Naohiko (2016), 'Home-Making during Protracted Exile: Diverse Responses of Refugee Families in the Face of Remigration', *Transnational Social Review*, 6 (1–2), 26–40.

(2017), *The Myth of Self-Reliance. Economic Lives Inside a Liberian Refugee Camp* (Oxford, New York: Berghahn).

Onyango, Monica Adhiambo and Hampanda, Karen (2011), 'Social Constructions of Masculinity and Male Survivors of Wartime Sexual Violence: An Analytical Review', *International Journal of Sexual Health*, 23 (4), 237–247.

Ozcurumez, Saime, Akyuz, Selin, and Bradby, Hannah (2020), 'The Conceptualization Problem in Research and Responses to Sexual and Gender-based Violence in Forced Migration', *Journal of Gender Studies*, published online first, doi: 10.1080/09589236.2020.1730163.

Pacéré, Titinga Frédéric (2007), *Progress Report Submitted by the Independent Expert on the Situation of Human Rights in the Democratic Republic of the Congo* (New York: UNGA; A/62/313; www.refworld.org/docid/47331a612.html).

Parpart, Jane L. (2010), 'Choosing Silence: Rethinking Voice, Agency, and Women's Empowerment. With Comments and Reply by Naila Kabeer',

Gender Perspectives on International Development, Working Paper, No. 297.

Parpart, Jane L. and Parashar, Swati (eds.) (2019), *Rethinking Silence, Voice and Agency in Contested Gendered Terrains* (Gender in a Global/Local World, London: Routledge).

Pasha, Suraina (2020), 'Developmental Humanitarianism, Resilience and (Dis)empowerment in a Syrian Refugee Camp', *Journal of International Development,* 32 (2), 244–259.

Patel, Sheetal H., Sewankambo, Nelson K., Muyinda, Herbert, Oyat, Geoffrey, Atim, Stella, and Spittal, Patricia (2012), 'In the Face of War: Examining Sexual Vulnerabilities of Acholi Adolescent Girls Living in Displacement Camps in Conflict-Affected Northern Uganda', *BMC International Health and Human Rights,* 12 (38), 22.

Pavanello, Mariano (ed.) (2017), *Perspectives on African Witchcraft* (London, New York: Routledge).

Perera, Suda (2013), 'Alternative Agency: Rwandan Refugee Warriors in Exclusionary States', *Conflict, Security & Development,* 13 (5), 569–588.

Peterson, Glen (2012), 'The Uneven Development of the International Refugee Regime in Postwar Asia: Evidence from China, Hong Kong and Indonesia', *Journal of Refugee Studies,* 25 (3), 326–343.

Pittaway, Eileen and Pittaway, Emma (2004), 'Refugee Woman: A Dangerous Label. Opening a Discussion the Role of Identity and Intersectional Oppression in the Failure of the International Refugee Protection Regime for Refugee Women', *Australian Journal of Human Rights,* 10 (1), 119–135.

Pittaway, Eileen and Rees, Susan (2006), 'Multiple Jeopardy: Domestic Violence and the Notion of Cumulative Risk for Women in Refugee Camps', *Women Against Violence: An Australian Feminist Journal,* (18), 18–25.

Porter, Gina, Hampshire, Kate, Kyei, Peter, Adjaloo, Michael, Rapoo, George, and Kilpatrick, Kate (2008), 'Linkages between Livelihood Opportunities and Refugee–Host Relations: Learning from the Experiences of Liberian Camp-based Refugees in Ghana', *Journal of Refugee Studies,* 21 (2), 230–252.

Pratt, Marion and Werchick, Leah (2004), *Sexual Terrorism: Rape as a Weapon of War in Eastern Democratic Republic of Congo—An Assessment of Programmatic Responses to Sexual Violence in North Kivu, South Kivu, Maniema, and Orientale Provinces* (USAID/DCHA; http://pdf.usaid.gov/pdf_docs/PNADK346.pdf).

Pupavac, Vanessa (2006), 'Refugees in the "Sick Role": Stereotyping Refugees and Eroding Refugee Rights', *New Issues in Refugee Research,* No. 128.

Purdeková, Andrea (2015), *Making Ubumwe: Power, State and Camps in Rwanda's Unity-Building Project* (Studies in Forced Migration, 34; New York, Oxford: Berghahn).

Ramadan, Adam (2013), 'Spatialising the Refugee Camp', *Transactions of the Institute of British Geographers*, 38 (1), 65–77.

Ramsay, Georgina (2016), 'Avoiding Poison: Congolese Refugees Seeking Cosmological Continuity in Urban Asylum', *Social Analysis: The International Journal of Social and Cultural Practice*, 60 (3), 112–128.

(2018), *Impossible Refuge: The Control and Constraint of Refugee Futures* (New York: Routledge).

Redmond, Gerry (2009), 'Children as Actors: How Does the Child Perspectives Literature Treat Agency in the Context of Poverty?', *Social Policy and Society*, 8 (4), 541–550.

Refugee Studies Centre (2007), 'Ethical Guidelines for Good Research Practice', *Refugee Survey Quarterly*, 26 (3), 162–172.

Reuters (2019), 'Rise in Sexual Abuse Cases in Aid Groups as More Victims Speak Up', *Reuters News,* (www.reuters.com/article/us-global-aid-har assment/rise-in-sexual-abuse-cases-in-aid-groups-as-more-victims-speak-up-idUSKCN1Q000X).

Reyntjens, Filip (2009), *The Great African War. Congo and Regional Geopolitics, 1996–2006* (Cambridge: Cambridge University Press).

Ritchie, Holly A. (2018), 'Gender and Enterprise in Fragile Refugee Settings: Female Empowerment amidst Male Emasculation—A Challenge to Local Integration?', *Disasters*, 42 (S1), S40–S60.

Robbers, Gianna Maxi Leila and Morgan, Alison (2017), 'Programme Potential for the Prevention of and Response to Sexual Violence among Female Refugees: a Literature Review', *Reproductive Health Matters*, 25 (51), 69–89.

Rosen, David M. (2005), *Armies of the Young: Child Soldiers in War and Terrorism* (New Brunswick, London: Rutgers University Press).

Ryan, Barbara (1992), *Feminism and the Women's Movement: Dynamics of Change in Social Movement Ideology and Activism* (New York, London: Routledge).

Salehyan, Idean (2007), 'Refugees and the Study of Civil War', *Civil Wars*, 9 (2), 127–141.

(2014), 'Forced Migration as a Cause and Consequence of Civil War', in Edward Newman and Karl DeRouen (eds.), *Handbook of Civil Wars* (New York: Routledge), 267–278.

Sandholtz, Wayne (2008), 'Dynamics of International Norm Change: Rules against Wartime Plunder', *European Journal of International Relations*, 14 (1), 101–131.

Sandvik, Kristin Bergtora (2008), 'The Physicality of Legal Consciousness: Suffering and the Production of Credibility in Refugee Resettlement', in Richard D. Brown and Richard Ashby Wilson (eds.), *Humanitarianism and Suffering: The Mobilization of Empathy* (Cambridge: Cambridge University Press), 223–244.

Schattle, Hans and McCann, Jennifer (2014), 'The Pursuit of State Status and the Shift toward International Norms: South Korea's Evolution as a Host Country for Refugees', *Journal of Refugee Studies*, 27 (3), 317–337.

Schmidt, Hannah and Krause, Ulrike (2019), '(Zu) Versorgende Geflüchtete? Analyse der sozialen Bedeutungen ökonomischer Praktiken von Geflüchteten in Uganda', *Soziale Welt*, 70 (2), 200–230.

Schneiker, Andrea (2017), 'NGOs as Norm Takers: Insider–Outsider Networks as Translators of Norms', *International Studies Review*, 19 (3), 381–406.

Schnoebelen, Jill (2009), 'Witchcraft Allegations, Refugee Protection and Human Rights: A Review of the Evidence', *New Issues in Refugee Research,* No. 169.

Schon, Justin (2016), 'The Centrality of Checkpoints for Civilians during Conflict', *Civil Wars*, 18 (3), 281–310.

(2019), 'Motivation and Opportunity for Conflict-induced Migration: An Analysis of Syrian Migration Timing', *Journal of Peace Research*, 56 (1), 12–27.

Schulz, Philipp (2018a), 'Displacement from Gendered Personhood: Sexual Violence and Masculinities in northern Uganda', *International Affairs*, 94 (5), 1101–1119.

(2018b), 'The "Ethical Loneliness" of Male Sexual Violence Survivors in Northern Uganda: Gendered Reflections on Silencing', *International Feminist Journal of Politics*, 20 (4), 583–601.

Schweitzer, Robert, Greenslade, Jaimi, and Kagee, Ashraf (2007), 'Coping and Resilience in Refugees from the Sudan: A Narrative Account', *Australian and New Zealand Journal of Psychiatry*, 41 (3), 282–288.

Seguin, Maureen and Roberts, Bayard (2017), 'Coping Strategies among Conflict-Affected Adults in Low- and Middle-Income Countries: A Systematic Literature Review', *Global Public Health*, 12 (7), 811–829.

Seifert, Ruth (1996), 'The Second Front: The Logic of Sexual Violence in Wars', *Women's Studies International Forum*, 19 (1–2), 35–43.

Shepherd, Laura J. (2019), *Handbook on Gender and Violence* (Cheltenham, Northampton: Edward Elgar).

Sieber, Joan E. (2008), 'Protecting the Vulnerable: Who Are They?', *Journal of Empirical Research on Human Research Ethics*, 3 (1), 1–2.

Silbey, Susan S. (2005), 'After Legal Consciousness', *Annual Review of Law and Social Science*, 1 (1), 323–368.

Sivakumaran, Sadesh (2007), 'Sexual Violence against Men in Armed Conflict', *European Journal of International Law*, 18 (2), 253–276.

Sjoberg, Laura and Gentry, Caron E. (2008), *Mothers, Monsters, Whores: Women's Violence in Global Politics* (London, New York: Zed Books).

Skjelsbæk, Inger (2006), 'Victim and Survivor: Narrated Social Identities of Women Who Experienced Rape during the War in Bosnia-Herzegovina', *Feminism & Psychology*, 16 (4), 373–403.

Snyder, R. Claire (2008), 'What Is Third-Wave Feminism? A New Directions Essay', *Signs: Journal of Women in Culture and Society*, 34 (1), 175–196.

Spivak, Gayatri Chakravorty (1999), *A Critique of Postcolonial Reason: Toward a History of the Vanishing Present* (Cambridge: Harvard University Press).

Squire, Vicki, Dimitriadi, Angeliki, Perkowski, N., Pisani, M., Stevens, D., and Vaughan-Williams, N. (2017), *Crossing the Mediterranean Sea by Boat: Mapping and Documenting Migratory Journeys and Experiences* (Coventry: University of Warwick).

Stevenson, August (ed.) (2010), *Oxford Dictionary of English* (3rd edn., Oxford: Oxford University Press).

Stewart, Miriam, Anderson, Joan, Beiser, Morton, Mwakarimba, Edward, Neufeld, Anne, Simich, Laura, and Spitzer, Denise (2008), 'Multicultural Meanings of Social Support among Immigrants and Refugees', *International Migration*, 46 (3), 123–159.

Strohmeier, Hannah and Scholte, Willem F. (2015), 'Trauma-Related Mental Health Problems among National Humanitarian Staff: A Systematic Review of the Literature', *European Journal of Psychotraumatology*, 6 (1), 1–16.

Suerbaum, Magdalena (2018), 'Defining the Other to Masculinize Oneself: Syrian Men's Negotiations of Masculinity during Displacement in Egypt', *Signs: Journal of Women in Culture and Society*, 43 (3), 665–686.

Suhrke, Astri and Berdal, Mats R. (eds.) (2012), *The Peace in Between: Post-War Violence and Peacebuilding* (London: Routledge).

Szczepaniková, Alice (2005), 'Gender Relations in a Refugee Camp: A Case of Chechens Seeking Asylum in the Czech Republic', *Journal of Refugee Studies*, 18 (3), 281–298.

Tankink, Marian and Richters, Annemiek (2007), 'Silence as a Coping Strategy: The Case of Refugee Women in the Netherlands from South-Sudan Who Experienced Sexual Violence in the Context of War', in Boris Drožđek and John P. Wilson (eds.), *Voices of Trauma: Treating Psychological Trauma Across Cultures* (New York: Springer), 191–210.

Temple, Bogusia and Moran, Rhetta (eds.) (2011), *Doing Research with Refugees: Issues and Guidelines* (Bristol: The Policy Press).

Thomson, Susan (2013), 'Agency as Silence and Muted Voice: The Problem-Solving Networks of Unaccompanied Young Somali Refugee Women in Eastleigh, Nairobi', *Conflict, Security & Development*, 13 (5), 589–609.

Thomson, Susan, Ansoms, An, and Murison, Jude (eds.) (2013), *Emotional and Ethical Challenges for Field Research in Africa: The Story Behind the Findings* (Basingstoke: Palgrave Macmillan).

Thornhill, Kerrie (2012), 'You Must Sit on the Old Mat to Ply the New One', in Jane Freedman (ed.), *Engaging Men in the Fight against Gender Violence* (New York: Palgrave Macmillan), 69–100.

Tippens, Julie A. (2017), 'Urban Congolese Refugees in Kenya: The Contingencies of Coping and Resilience in a Context Marked by Structural Vulnerability', *Qualitative Health Research*, 27 (7), 1090–1103.

Tlapek, Sarah Myers (2015), 'Women's Status and Intimate Partner Violence in the Democratic Republic of Congo', *Journal of Interpersonal Violence*, 30 (14), 2526–2540.

Türk, Volker and Garlick, Madeline (2016), 'From Burdens and Responsibilities to Opportunities: The Comprehensive Refugee Response Framework and a Global Compact on Refugees', *International Journal of Refugee Law*, 28 (4), 656–678.

Turner, Lewis (2018), Challenging Refugee Men: Humanitarianism and Masculinities in Za'tari Refugee Camp, PhD Thesis, Department of Politics and International Studies, SOAS, University of London.

(2019), 'Syrian Refugee Men as Objects of Humanitarian Care', *International Feminist Journal of Politics*, 21 (4), 595–616.

Turner, Simon (1999), 'Angry Young Men in Camps: Gender, Age and Class Relations Among Burundian Refugees in Tanzania', *New Issues in Refugee Research*, No. 9.

(2004), 'New Opportunities—Angry Young Men in a Tanzanian Refugee Camp', in Philomena Essed, Georg Frerks, and Joke Schrijvers (eds.), *Refugees and the Transformation of Societies—Agency, Policies, Ethnics and Politics* (New York, Oxford: Berghahn), 94–105.

(2010), *Politics of Innocence. Hutu Identity, Conflict and Camp Life* (Studies in Forced Migration, 30; New York, Oxford: Berghahn).

(2016a), 'What Is a Refugee Camp? Explorations of the Limits and Effects of the Camp', *Journal of Refugee Studies*, 29 (2), 139–148.

(2016b), 'Staying Out of Place: The Being and Becoming of Burundian Refugees in the Camp and the City', *Conflict and Society*, 2016 (2), 37–51.

Turner, Thomas (2007), *The Congo Wars. Conflict, Myth and Reality* (London, New York: Zed Books).

Turshen, Meredeth, Alidou, Oousseina, and De Marcellus, Olivier (2000), 'Commentary', *Race & Class*, 41 (4), 81–99.

Turshen, Meredeth, Meintjes, Sheila, and Pillay, Anu (eds.) (2001), *The Aftermath: Women in Postconflict Transformation* (London: Zed Books).

Uganda (1960), 'Control of Alien Refugees Act, Cap. 64', (Acts of Parliament Act, section 12; Kampala: Government of Uganda).

(2006), 'The Refugees Act 2006', (8, *Uganda Gazette* No. 47 Volume XCVIX dated 4 August 2006; Kampala: Government of Uganda).

UN (2010), 'UN Agency Deplores Forced Returns of Rwandan Refugees from Uganda', *UN News Service,* (www.refworld.org/docid/4c4562cc1c.html).

(2018), 'UN Recorded 64 New Allegations of Sexual Exploitation or Abuse in the Past Three Months', *UN News* (news.un.org/en/story/2018/11/1024972).

UNHCR (1969), 'Report of the United Nations High Commissioner for Refugees to the General Assembly. Supplement No. 11 (A/7211)', *A/7211* (New York: United Nations).

(1970), 'Report of the United Nations High Commissioner for Refugees to the General Assembly. Supplement No. 12 (A/7612)', *A/7612* (New York: United Nations).

(1985), 'Report of the United Nations High Commissioner for Refugees to the General Assembly. Supplement No. 12 (A/40/12)', *A/40/12* (New York: United Nations).

(1990), *UNHCR Policy on Refugee Women* (Geneva: UNHCR).

(1991), *UNHCR Guidelines on the Protection of Refugee Women* (Geneva: UNHCR).

(1992), *A Framework for People-Oriented Planning in Refugee Situations Taking Account of Women, Men and Children* (Geneva: UNHCR).

(1994), 'UNHCR Activities financed by Voluntary Runds: Report for 1993–1994 and Proposed Programmes and Budget for 1995. Part I Africa. Section 20—Uganda (submitted by the High Commissioner)', *A/AC.96/825/Part I/20* (New York: United Nations).

(1997a), *UNHCR Policy on Harmful Traditional Practices* (Geneva: UNHCR).

(1997b), *UNHCR Comprehensive Policy on Urban Refugees* (Geneva: UNHCR).

(2001a), 'Evaluation of the Dadaab Firewood Project, Kenya', *UNHCR Evaluation,* conducted by CASA Consulting; EPAU/2001/08 (www.unhcr.org/research/evalreports/3b33105d4/).

(2001b), *UNHCR's Commitments to Refugee Women* (Geneva: UNHCR; www.refworld.org/docid/479f3b2a2.html).

(2001c), *Prevention and Response to Sexual and Gender-based Violence in Refugee Situations* (Geneva: UNHCR).

(2001d), *A Practical Guide to Empowerment: UNHCR Good Practice on Gender Equality Mainstreaming* (Geneva: UNHCR).

(2002), 'Extensive Abuse of West African Refugee Children Reported', UNHCR News, (www.unhcr.org/news/press/2002/2/3c7bf8094/exten sive-abuse-west-african-refugee-children-reported.html).

(2003a), 'Hundreds of Congolese Refugees in Uganda Move to Inland Settlement', UNHCR News, (www.unhcr.org/news/latest/2003/8/ 3f311aa37/hundreds-congolese-refugees-uganda-move-inland-settlement.html?query=).

(2003b), *Sexual and Gender-Based Violence against Refugees, Returnees and Internally Displaced Persons. Guidelines for Prevention and Response* (Geneva: UNHCR).

(2004a), *Poverty Reduction Strategy Papers: A Displacement Perspective* (Geneva: UNHCR).

(2004b), *2003 Global Refugee Trends* (Geneva: UNHCR).

(2005a), 'Ugandan Settlement Struggles to Accommodate New Arrivals from DRC', UNHCR News (www.unhcr.org/news/latest/2005/2/ 421f352d4/ugandan-settlement-struggles-accommodate-new-arrivals-drc.html?query=).

(2005b), *2004 Global Refugee Trends* (Geneva: UNHCR).

(2006), *2005 Global Refugee Trends* (Geneva: UNHCR).

(2007a), *Handbook for Emergencies* (3rd edn.; Geneva: UNHCR).

(2007b), *2006 Global Trends: Refugees, Asylum-Seekers, Returnees, Internally Displaced and Stateless Persons* (Geneva: UNHCR).

(2008a), *UNHCR Handbook for the Protection of Women and Girls* (Geneva: UNHCR).

(2008b), *2007 Global Trends: Refugees, Asylum-Seekers, Returnees, Internally Displaced and Stateless Persons* (Geneva: UNHCR).

(2009a), *UNHCR Policy on Refugee Protection and Solutions in Urban Areas* (Geneva: UNHCR).

(2009b), *2008 Global Trends: Refugees, Asylum-Seekers, Returnees, Internally Displaced and Stateless Persons* (Geneva: UNHCR).

(2010), *2009 Global Trends: Refugees, Asylum-Seekers, Returnees, Internally Displaced and Stateless Persons* (Geneva: UNHCR).

(2011a), *Global Trends 2010: 60 Years and Still Counting* (Geneva: UNHCR).

(2011b), *Action against Sexual and Gender-Based Violence: An Updated Strategy* (Geneva: UNHCR).

(2011c), *Working with Lesbian, Gay, Bisexual, Transgender & Intersex Persons in Forced Displacement* (Geneva: UNHCR).

(2012), *Global Trends 2011: A Year of Crises* (Geneva: UNHCR).

(2013a), *Global Trends 2012. Displacement: The 21st Century Challenge* (Geneva: UNHCR).

(2013b), *UNHCR Global Report 2012, Uganda* (Geneva: UNHCR; www .refworld.org/docid/51befdd816.html).

(2014a), *UNHCR Policy on Alternatives to Camps* (Geneva: UNHCR).

(2014b), *UNHCR Uganda. SGBV Fact Sheet, Southwest Uganda, 2014* (data2.unhcr.org/en/documents/details/48494).

(2014c), *Global Trends 2013: War's Human Cost* (Geneva: UNHCR).

(2014d), *UNHCR Global Report 2013, Uganda* (Geneva: UNHCR; www .unhcr.org/publications/fundraising/539809f1b/unhcr-global-report-2013-uganda.html).

(2014e), *Uganda Factsheet, September 2014* (data2.unhcr.org/en/docu ments/details/29559).

(2014f), *Kyaka II. Fact Sheet 2014* (Kampala: UNHCR; data2.unhcr.org/ en/documents/details/48486).

(2015a), *Global Appeal 2015, Update—Uganda* (Geneva: UNHCR).

(2015b), *Global Trends 2014: World at War* (Geneva: UNHCR).

(2015c), *Protecting Persons with Diverse Sexual Orientations and Gender Identities. A Global Report on UNHCR's Efforts to Protect Lesbian, Gay, Bisexual, Transgender, and Intersex Asylum-Seekers and Refugees* (Geneva: UNHCR).

(2015d), *Uganda: South-Western Region—Location of UNHCR Presence, Refugee Locations and Entry Points (as of 28 August 2015)* (UNHCR; www.refworld.org/docid/55e563404.html).

(2016a), *Global Trends. Forced Displacement in 2015* (Geneva: UNHCR).

(2016b), *Uganda—Weekly Sector Indicators Matrix for South Sudan Refugees, 24 November 2016* (UNHCR; data2.unhcr.org/en/docu ments/details/52480).

(2017a), *Fresh Congo Violence Fuels Displacement to Uganda* (www .unhcr.org/news/briefing/2017/12/5a3cced54/fresh-congo-violence-fuels-displacement-uganda.html.

(2017b), *Global Trends. Forced Displacement in 2016* (Geneva: UNHCR).

(2017c), *UNHCR's Strategic Directions 2017–2021* (Geneva: UNHCR).

(2017d), *Uganda Refugee Response Monitoring Settlement Fact Sheet: Oruchinga—December 2017* (UNHCR; data2.unhcr.org/en/docu ments/details/63292).

(2017e), *UNHCR Uganda: 2017 Funding Update (as of 12 December 2017)* (reliefweb.int/report/uganda/unhcr-uganda-2017-funding-update-12-december-2017).

(2018a), *Demographics, Uganda and Kyaka II Refugee Settlement* (popstats.unhcr.org/en/demographics?year=2014%26cor=UGA).

(2018b), *Uganda Refugee Response Monitoring Settlement Fact Sheet: Kyaka II, March 2018* (Kampala: UNHCR; data2.unhcr.org/es/docu ments/download/63276).

(2018c), *Global Trends: Forced Displacement in 2017* (Geneva: UNHCR).

(2018d), 'Our Fight against Sexual Misconduct', *2018 in Review* (www .unhcr.org/5c51a5d34.pdf).

(2018e), *DRC Congo Violence Sees Surge in Refugees Fleeing Eastwards* (www.unhcr.org/news/briefing/2018/1/5a7037ab4/drc-congo-violence-sees-surge-refugees-fleeing-eastwards.html).

(2018f), *UNHCR Uganda: 2018 Funding Update (as of 5 November 2018)* (reliefweb.int/report/uganda/unhcr-uganda-2018-funding-update-5-november-2018).

(2019a), *Global Trends. Forced Displacement in 2018* (Geneva: UNHCR).

(2019b), 'Evaluative Review of UNHCR's Policies and Procedures on the Prevention of and Response to Sexual Exploitation and Abuse', *UNHCR Evaluation*, conducted by Sarah Bond, Paul Nolan, Laura Nyirinkindi, Elayn M. Sammon, Katie Tong, Jeanne Ward; ES/2019/03 (www.unhcr.org/5d5bb2637.pdf).

(2019c), *Uganda Operational Update, November 2019* (data2.unhcr.org/en/documents/details/73478).

(2020a), *Uganda—Refugee Statistics January 2020 —Kyaka II* (Kampala: UNHCR; data2.unhcr.org/fr/documents/download/73984).

(2020b), *Demographics, Uganda and Kyaka II Refugee Settlement* (popstats.unhcr.org/en/demographics?year=2014%26cor=UGA).

(2020c), *UNHCR Uganda Operational Update January 2020* (Kampala: UNHCR; data2.unhcr.org/en/documents/details/74074).

(2020d), *Demographics, Uganda* (popstats.unhcr.org/en/demographics?cor=UGA).

UNHCR and Save the Children (2002), *Sexual Violence & Exploitation: The Experience of Refugee Children in Guinea, Liberia and Sierra Leone* (www.alnap.org/help-library/sexual-violence-and-exploitation-the-experience-of-refugee-children-in-guinea-liberia).

UNHCR and OPM (2004), *Self-Reliance Strategy (1999–2003) For Refugee Hosting Areas in Moyo, Arua and Adjumani Districts, Uganda* (Report of the Mid-term Review, April 2004, RLSS Mission Report 2004/03; Kampala: UNHCR).

UNHCR and RLP (2012), *Working with Men and Boy Survivors of Sexual and Gender-Based Violence in Forced Displacement* (Geneva: UNHCR).

UNHCR and IDC (2016), *Vulnerability Screening Tool* (Geneva: UNHCR).

UNHCR ExCom (1985), 'Refugee Women and International Protection', *Executive Committee of the High Commissioner's Programme No. 39 (XXXVI)* (Geneva: UNHCR).

(1988), 'Refugee Women', *Executive Committee of the High Commissioner's Programme No. 54 (XXXIX)* (Geneva: UNHCR).

(1989), 'Refugee Women', *Executive Committee of the High Commissioner's Programme No. 60 (XL)* (Geneva: UNHCR).

(1990), 'Refugee Women and International Protection', *Executive Committee of the High Commissioner's Programme No. 64 (XLI)* (Geneva: UNHCR).

(2006), 'Conclusion on Women and Girls at Risk', *Executive Committee of the High Commissioner's Programme No. 105 (LVII)* (Geneva: UNHCR).

(2009), 'Conclusion on Protracted Refugee Situations', *Executive Committee of the High Commissioner's Programme No. 109 (LXI)* (Geneva: UNHCR).

Ussher, Jane M., Perz, Janette, Metusela, Christine, Hawkey, Alexandra J., Morrow, Marina, Narchal, Renu, and Estoesta, Jane (2017), 'Negotiating Discourses of Shame, Secrecy, and Silence: Migrant and Refugee Women's Experiences of Sexual Embodiment', *Archives of Sexual Behavior*, 46 (7), 1901–1921.

Vemuru, Varalakshmi, Araya, Yonatan Yehdego, Gossa, Endashaw Tadesse, Kalumiya, Charles Kalu, Nkunda, Dismas Rugason, Buyinza, Faisal, Okumu, Joseph, and Klose, Karoline Hild (2016), *An Assessment of Uganda's Progressive Approach to Refugee Management* (Washington, DC: World Bank Group; documents .worldbank.org/curated/en/259711469593058429/An-assessment-of-Ugandas-progressive-approach-to-refugee-management).

Villa, Paula-Irene (2019), 'Sex—Gender: Ko-Konstitution statt Entgegensetzung', in Beate Kortendiek, Birgit Riegraf, and Katja Sabisch (eds.), *Handbuch Interdisziplinäre Geschlechterforschung* (Wiesbaden: Springer), 23–33.

Vossoughi, Nadia, Jackson, Yo, Gusler, Stephanie, and Stone, Katie (2018), 'Mental Health Outcomes for Youth Living in Refugee Camps: A Review', *Trauma, Violence, & Abuse*, 19 (5), 528–542.

Voutira, Eftihia and Doná, Giorgia (2007), 'Refugee Research Methodologies: Consolidation and Transformation of a Field', *Journal of Refugee Studies*, 20 (2), 163–171.

Vu, Alexander, Adam, Atif, Wirtz, Andrea, Kiemanh, Pham, Rubenstein, Leonard, Glass, Nancy, Beyrer, Chris, and Singh, Sonal (2014), 'The Prevalence of Sexual Violence among Female Refugees in Complex

Humanitarian Emergencies: A Systematic Review and Meta-analysis', *PLOS Currents Disasters*, 1, doi: 10.1371/currents. dis.1835f10778fd10780ae10031aac10712d10773b10533ca10777.

Wachter, Karin, Horn, Rebecca, Friis, Elsa, Falb, Kathryn, Ward, Leora, Apio, Christine, Wanjiku, Sophia, and Puffer, Eve (2018), 'Drivers of Intimate Partner Violence against Women in Three Refugee Camps', *Violence Against Women*, 24 (3), 286–306.

Waldron, Sidney R. (1987), 'Blaming the Refugees', *Refugee Issues*, 3 (3), 1–19.

Walkup, Mark (1991), 'The Organisational Culture of UNHCR: The Myths of Humanitarianism and the Dysfunction of Benevolence' (Gainesville: Department of Political Science, University of Florida).

Weierstall, Roland, Schalinski, Inga, Crombach, Anselm, Hecker, Tobias, and Elbert, Thomas (2012), 'When Combat Prevents PTSD Symptoms —Results from a Survey with Former Child Soldiers in Northern Uganda', *BMC Psychiatry*, 12 (1), 1–8.

Welsh, Marc (2014), 'Resilience and Responsibility: Governing Uncertainty in a Complex World', *The Geographical Journal*, 180 (1), 15–26.

Werker, Eric (2007), 'Refugee Camp Economies', *Journal of Refugee Studies*, 20 (3), 461–480.

Wessells, Michael G. (2006), *Child Soldiers: From Violence to Protection* (Cambridge, London: Harvard University Press).

Wessels, Janna (2018), 'Feministische Herausforderungen an das Flüchtlingsrecht: von der zweiten zur dritten Welle', GENDER– Zeitschrift für Geschlecht, *Kultur und Gesellschaft*, 10 (2), 18–31.

West, Candace and Zimmerman, Don H. (1987), 'Doing Gender', *Gender & Society*, 1 (2), 125–151.

Williams, Timothy P., Chopra, Vidur, and Chikanya, Sharon R. (2018), '"It Isn't that We're Prostitutes": Child Protection and Sexual Exploitation of Adolescent Girls within and beyond Refugee Camps in Rwanda', *Child Abuse & Neglect*, 86, 158–166.

Winter, Yves (2012), 'Violence and Visibility', *New Political Science*, 34 (2), 195–202.

Wirtz, Andrea L., Glass, Nancy, Pham, Kiemanh, Aberra, Amsale, Rubenstein, Leonard S., Singh, Sonal, and Vu, Alexander (2013), 'Development of a Screening Tool to Identify Female Survivors of Gender-Based Violence in a Humanitarian Setting: Qualitative Evidence from Research among Refugees in Ethiopia', *Conflict and Health*, 7 (1), 13.

Wokorach, Mogi (2020), 'The Loud Silence: The Plight of Refugee Male Survivors of Conflict-Related Sexual Violence', Blog of the Refugee Law Project (refugeelawproject.org/index.php/blog-menu/g-s-blog/the-loud-silence-the-plight-of-refugee-male-survivors-of-conflict-related-sexual-violence).

Women's Refugee Commission (2018), *It's Happening to Our Men as Well. Sexual Violence Against Rohingya Men and Boys* (New York: Women's Refugee Commission).

Zimmermann, Lisbeth (2016), 'Same Same or Different? Norm Diffusion between Resistance, Compliance, and Localization in Post-conflict States', *International Studies Perspectives*, 17 (1), 98–115.

Zolberg, Aristide R., Suhrke, Astri, and Aguayo, Sergio (1986), 'International Factors in the Formation of Refugee Movements', *International Migration Review*, 20 (2), 151–169.

 (1989), *Escape from Violence. Conflict and the Refugee Crisis in the Developing World* (New York/ Oxford: Oxford University Press).

Zomorodi, Gitta (2016), 'Responding to LGBT Forced Migration in East Africa', *Forced Migration Review*, (52), 91–93.

Index

Page references for figures and images are given in *italics*.

Printed in the United States
by Baker & Taylor Publisher Services